COLLECTED WO

BERNARD LONEF

VOLUME 21

FOR A NEW POLITICAL ECONOMY

COLLECTED WORKS OF BERNARD

LONERGAN

FOR A NEW POLITICAL ECONOMY

edited by

Philip J. McShane

Published for Lonergan Research Institute
of Regis College, Toronto
by University of Toronto Press
Toronto Buffalo London

ISBN 0-8020-4385-2 (cloth)
ISBN 0-8020-8222-X (paper)

Reprinted 2005, 2011, 2013

Printed on acid-free paper

Canadian Cataloguing in Publication Data

Lonergan, Bernard J.F. (Bernard Joseph Francis), 1904–1984
Collected works of Bernard Lonergan

Partial contents: v. 21. For a new political economy / edited by Philip J. McShane.

Includes bibliographical references and index.
ISBN 0-8020-4385-2 (v. 21 : bound) ISBN 0-8020-8222-x (v. 21 : pbk.)

1. Theology – 20th century. 2. Catholic Church. I. McShane, Philip J. 1932– . II. Lonergan Research Institute. III. Title.

BX891L595 1998 230 C88-093328-3

The Lonergan Research Institute gratefully acknowledges the generous contribution of THE MALLINER CHARITABLE FOUNDATION, which has made possible the production of this entire series.

The Lonergan Research Institute gratefully acknowledges the financial assistance of the ERIC KIERANS toward the publication of this volume of the Collected Works of Bernard Lonergan.

University of Toronto Press acknowledges the financial support for its publishing activities of the Government of Canada through the Book Publishing Industry Development Program (BPIDP).

Contents

General Editors' Preface, FREDERICK E. CROWE and ROBERT M. DORAN / xi

Editor's Introduction, PHILIP J. MCSHANE / xv

PART ONE: FOR A NEW POLITICAL ECONOMY

1 **Why? What? How?** / 3
1 The Need of a New Political Economy / 3
2 The Nature of a New Political Economy / 5
3 A Note on Method / 8

2 **The Pure Process** / 11
4 The Basic Rhythmic Flow / 11
5 Introducing the Symbol *DA* / 12
6 The Dynamic Structure of the Basic Rhythm / 14
7 *DA*, *DA'*, *DA"* / 16
8 Functions of *DA'* and *DA"* in the Basic Rhythm / 17
9 Transformations of Dynamic Structure / 19
10 The Generalized Laws of Increasing and Decreasing Returns / 21
11 The Cyclic Phases of the Universal Rhythm / 23
12 The Pure Process / 26

3 Transition to Exchange Economy / 28
13 The Aim of This Chapter / 28
14 Property, Exchange, Value / 29
15 Markets / 32
16 Markets and the Exchange Economy / 33
17 Limitations of Exchange Economy / 35
18 Money / 37
19 Finance / 41

4 Outline of the Mechanical Structure of the Exchange Process / 42
20 The Exchange Process / 42
21 The Basic Equation / 43
21bis Transitional, Final, and Redistributional Markets / 43
22 Application of the Basic Equation / 45
23 The Crossover of the Primary and Secondary Circuits / 46
24 Provisional Theorem of Continuity / 47
25 Theorem of the Surplus / 49
26 Theorem of Costs / 50
27 Curvature of the Exchange Equations / 51
28 The Normative Proportion / 53
29 The Crossover Ratio / 54
30 Retrospect / 56

5 Equilibria of the Mechanical Structure / 57
31 Idea of the Equilibrium / 57
32 Reference System for the Exchange Equilibrium / 58
33 Monetary Phases / 59
34 General Formula of the Main Circuits / 62
35 The Distributor Multipliers / 66
36 The Trader Multipliers / 68
37 The Consumer Multipliers / 70
38 The General Theorem of Continuity / 73

6 Incidental Theorems / 76
39 The Aggregate Primary Price Spread / 76
40 Cyclic Variations in Prices / 81
41 The Mechanism of the Capitalist Phase / 83
42 Mechanism of the Materialist Phase / 87
43 Causes of Surplus Income / 89

44 Variations in Profits / 91
45 The Applied System of Reference / 93
46 Mechanism of the Favorable Balance of Trade / 94
47 Deficit Government Spending / 96
48 The Possibility of the Static Phase / 97
49 The Financial Problem / 100
53 Mechanism of the Cultural Expansion* / 106

PART TWO: FRAGMENTS, 1942–1944

7 **An Outline of Circulation Analysis** / 109
1 Viewpoint / 109
2 Method / 111

8 **A Method of Independent Circulation Analysis** / 113
1 Frame of Reference / 114
2 Normative Phases / 121
3 The Cycle of the Normative Phases / 128
4 The Effect of Net Transfers / 134
Appendix / 148

9 **Circulation Trends** / 152
9 Circulation Trends / 152
11 Trends / 155

10 **Circuit Velocities** / 163
9 Circuit Velocities / 163

11 **Prices, Costs, Profits** / 175
10 Price and Process Indices / 175
11 Systematic Costs and Profits / 179
10bis The Crossovers / 182

12 **Prices, Demand, Supply** / 184
7 The Exchange Economy / 184
a) *Prices* / 184

* This line was not included in Lonergan's original Table of Contents.

b) The Consistency of Prices / 185
c) Money / 186
d) Demand and Supply / 187
e) The Nature of Prices / 189
8 Prices / 192
f) The Dialectic of Prices / 194

13 **Superposed Circuits** / 196
14 Superposed Circuits / 196

14 **Random Pointers** / 203
1 The Fundamental Aspiration / 203
2 Some Transitional Searchings / 205
3 Economic Control / 211
4 Schumpeter, Keynes / 212
5 Some Scribbled Searchings / 214
Conclusion / 218

PART THREE: CIRCULATION ANALYSIS

15 **The Productive Process** / 231
Outline of the Argument / 231
4 The Productive Process / 232
5 Division of the Productive Process / 234
6 The Basic and Surplus Stages of the Productive Process / 238
7 Cycles of the Productive Process / 242
7bis Cycles in the Productive Process / 244

16 **Monetary Flows** / 246
7ter Classes of Payments / 246
8 Rates of Payment and Transfer / 252

17 **Accelerations, Cycles, Phases** / 259
9 Circuit Acceleration / 259
Appendix to Section 9 / 266
10 The Theoretical Possibility of Measurement of the Productive Process / 268
11 The Cycle of the Productive Process / 274
12 The Phases in Circuit Acceleration / 282

18 Cycles of Incomes and Prices / 285
13 The Cycle of Basic Income / 285
14 The Cycle of Pure Surplus Income / 292
15 The Cycle of the Aggregate Basic Price Spread / 301

19 Superposed Circuits / 308
16 Superposed Circuits / 308
17 The Balance of Foreign Trade / 310
18 Deficit Spending and Taxes (unfinished) / 317

Appendix: The Date of 'For a New Political Economy,'
FREDERICK E. CROWE / 319

Index / 325

General Editors' Preface

The general editors of the Collected Works of Bernard Lonergan wish to extend their deepest thanks to Philip McShane for the immense work he has done in bringing to publication this volume of Lonergan's writings and papers in the early 1940s on macroeconomics.

As Professor McShane's Introduction indicates, Parts 1 and 3 of the volume give us two of Lonergan's longer drafts from this early period: 'For a New Political Economy [FNPE],' dated around 1942, and 'An Essay in Circulation Analysis [ECA],' dated 1944. Part 2 of the volume collects a number of notes, fragments, and shorter essays that illuminate Parts 1 and 3, and are in turn illuminated by them. Together the three parts form a series of 'progress reports' that not only show a great mind at work but also provide background for Lonergan's ideas of nearly forty years later.

The original prospectus for the entire series of Lonergan's Collected Works envisioned a single volume, number 21, to be called 'Archival Material.' Since the archival material in the present volume is limited to papers on economics (and does not even cover all of them), it is clear now that there will eventually be several volumes of archival material, and so we have assigned the number 21 definitively to the present volume. Together with volume 15 it will give the reader ready access to what is available on Lonergan's thinking on macroeconomics: through the present volume to what seems to be his earliest work on the subject, and through volume 15 to what were in 1983 his final views.

Lonergan was regularly concerned with what we are doing when we do theology, or when we do economics, or when we 'do' any other subject.

And that immediately raises the question of what we are doing when we work on his thought, in particular which of his famous eight functional specialties we are engaged in. It is clear that the editor has done a laborious and extremely thorough work of research. It is clear too that his governing purpose was to do the research that would provide readers with the data needed for interpreting Lonergan. Still, neither here nor in volume 15 was it possible to separate research neatly from interpretation and history. The general editors are pleased, therefore, to have as subeditors for these two volumes researchers of Lonergan's macroeconomics whose interpretation too is especially worthy of our attention. We are convinced that their research will provide data for endless interpretation which will owe much to their own implicit exercise of that specialty.

Turning to matters of lesser importance, the general editors assume responsibility for the minutiae of style; here, as in all the volumes of the Collected Works, the *Oxford American Dictionary* and the *Chicago Manual of Style* are taken as guides; there is no attempt to make Lonergan's language inclusive; typos, punctuation, minor faults of grammar, and the like are corrected without notice; as a general rule, square brackets indicate editorial passages.

References to the Archives are of special importance in this volume. All the archival material on economics relevant here is contained in Batch II of the Archives, and specifically in Folders (or Files) 51, and 58 to 61, as numbered by Conn O'Donovan in a preliminary catalogue (1973). Later Robert Doran made a more detailed catalogue on a computer database, identifying sheaves or pages by A with a number; thus, the contents of the O'Donovan folders 1 to 63 are catalogued by Doran as A097 to A345, and the contents of the folders on economics as A314, and A330 to A337. In this volume references are given sometimes to the O'Donovan, sometimes to the Doran numbers. (Note also a reference [p. xxix, note 25] to Batch V, a set of files that, with several other 'batches,' was catalogued by McShane himself after this material was given to the Lonergan Center, Toronto, in 1972).

While our debt to Professor McShane can never be sufficiently acknowledged, we must not forget the others who contributed to the volume: Conn O'Donovan, for his work in cataloguing Batch II of the Lonergan papers; Eric Kierans, for preserving and then donating to our archives the precious manuscript of 'For a New Political Economy'; Marc Smith, for his research in the Burton S. Kierstead Archives at the University of New Brunswick, in the effort to find a lost Lonergan-Kierstead correspondence; Raymond Moloney, for similar research for lost documents in the Dublin Lonergan Centre; Nicholas Graham, for drawing up a detailed catalogue of the economics files in Batch II of the Lonergan Archives; James Clair, Eric Kierans, and Melbourne Mason, for funding that stage of the work; Thomas Daly who, with the help of Nicholas Graham and on the basis of the material the latter had collected and arranged, drew up a useful compendium of the economics papers; Michael Shute, for sharing his discoveries on economics in Batch I of the Lonergan papers; Robert Croken and Deborah Agnew of the Lonergan Research Institute in Toronto, for innumerable acts of cooperation in the work of bringing these volumes to print. Then, in discharge of a particular debt internal to the general editors, Fred Crowe must be allowed a word of thanks to Robert Doran, who not only moved the volume from manuscript to computer but almost alone did the work (very considerable it was, too) devolving upon the general editors. Finally, we are dependent on subsidies from generous sponsors: our debt to The Honourable Eric Kierans under this heading is acknowledged on another page.

FREDERICK E. CROWE

ROBERT M. DORAN

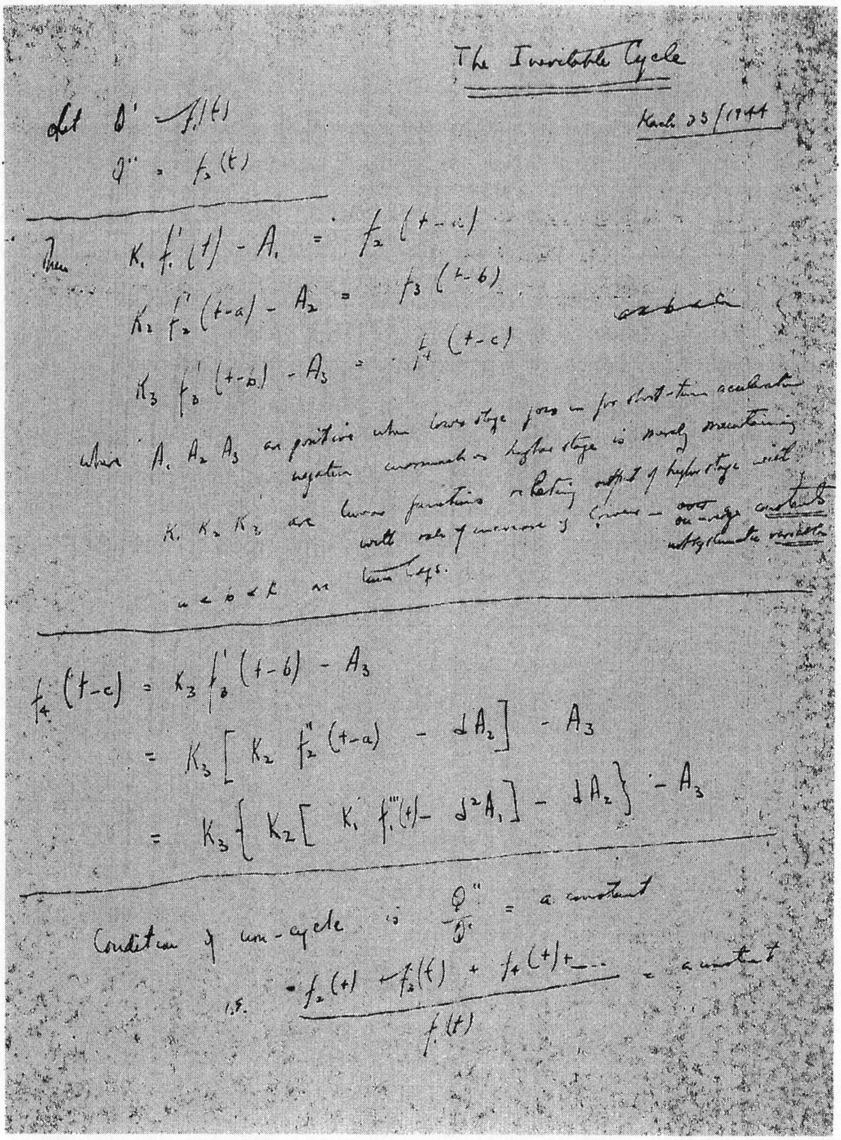

A fragment of Lonergan's scribbles from the early 1940s (see chapter 14, pp. 204–5, below) – the only dated page in all the archival material on economics from that period.

The Robert Mollot Collection

Editor's Introduction

This volume of Bernard Lonergan's economic writings contains almost the entirety of the fragments of typewritten work on economics prior to, and including, the 1944 version of the Essay in Circulation Analysis (below, ECA). The introduction to volume 15 of Lonergan's Collected Works gives the broad context of this achievement. The present introduction seeks to add certain precisions regarding the achievement. Most evidently there are to be noted the precisions that are forthcoming from the early texts; less evident are the precisions that emerge from reflection on the full significance of Lonergan's drive towards a restructuring of economic praxis. So, the introduction falls comfortably into two sections with titles 'Text' and 'Context.' Some readers may find the first section, dealing mainly with details of the presentation of the material in this volume, of lesser interest. But it should be perused, or returned to, in order to come to grips with peculiarities of the sectioning and numbering of the parts of this volume.

Before plunging into the details of the first section, it seems wise to give some general indications of the volume's contents.

Part One contains a text that treats macroeconomics more broadly then ECA. While most of the rest of the material in the volume has been in the Lonergan Archives, Toronto, since the early 1970s, this text became available only recently. It was in the possession of Eric Kierans since the late 1940s and was passed on by him to Frederick Crowe in the 1980s. It is probably to be dated (see Appendix) about two years before what has long been known as the 1944 version of ECA, the version that forms Part Three of the present volume. Between it and Part Three lie the transition efforts represented by Part Two. Part One contains a version of the analysis that is less developed and yet broader in its sweep than Part Three. The developments represented by the intervening efforts (Part Two) as well as the character of Part Three – topics to which we will return presently – confirm the view that Part One was written two or more years earlier than Part Three. The drive of all three parts bears witness to Lonergan's successful struggle both with theoretic and metatheoretic issues in economics, a struggle that would plausibly have occupied him for two years.

However, the dating is not a vital issue. One may take the content of this volume as coming from Lonergan's efforts during the Second World War, and leave it at that. What is of importance is the development of his thought on economics from the text of 'For a New Political Economy'[1] in Part One to the text of ECA in Part Three. One can detect a growing precision with regard to the scope of macroeconomics and in respect of the details of normative economic rhythms. An editorial introduction is not the place for such detecting, but I would note in passing that, while ECA stands out as focused normative economic analysis, the contents of the present volume as a whole invite the reader to a shift of context, an enrichment of perspective, a fuller concrete heuristic. The shift in context is evidenced by the title of Part One, 'For a New Political Economy': there is an explicit concern for a new world order of culture and economics, for a grounding of global and local economics in the enlightened self-interest not of the few but of the many. The enrichment of perspective bursts through, for instance, in the fuller indications of that same text regarding the nature of money, of short-term and long-term decreasing returns both of capitalism and of the business and busyness of financing. Finally, one is invited to a fuller concrete heuristic especially by the struggle of Part Two towards an integral analysis of such economic processes as turnover frequencies and turnover magnitudes. The significance of such incomplete struggling should not be overlooked. The second section of my introduction will seek to indicate Lonergan's fundamental functional specialist reorientation of real economic analysis. But it is as well to make the elementary point here that the focus of Lonergan's interest was, from the beginning, 'real analysis.'[2] In ECA he succeeds in expressing succinctly the

1 In the typescript title the word 'New' is encircled, and a note added above, initialed in Lonergan's handwriting, 'B.L.': 'Tone *that* down!' (italics his).

2 The fundamental character of real analysis is the topic of Lonergan's two main methodological works, *Insight* and *Method in Theology* (see below, notes 15 and 21). The elementary opposition involved is that between a luminous

heuristics of a normative component in that analysis, but paradoxically that normative reflection demands a massive mathematically complex refocusing of economic science on business as it actually occurs, locally and globally.[3] That focus, on the obsolescences and innovations of real businesses, will gradually and discomfortingly cut through the 'veil'[4] of financial and fiscal analyses and activities that pivot and parade on impoverished meanings of the word *credit.*

1 Text

Part One, 'For a New Political Economy,' requires very little comment: the text needed very little editing. I made no effort to bring the terminology into conformity with that of the later version. Such uniformization, at all events, would have obscured the changes of meaning. The original text contained no footnotes: all footnotes, therefore are editorial. The reader will note a peculiarity in the two concluding section numbers, both in the table of contents and in the text. There is a gap, which I retain from the original, between § 49 and § 53; it calls attention to the incompleteness of the work. The second last paragraph (§ 49) points to the need for a fuller treatment of finance; the final short paragraph (§ 53) is all there is of Lonergan's intended discussion of the static cultural phase.

At this stage it is appropriate to comment on the table of contents. I have noted the desire to present the original texts with a minimum of change. This has led me to a double numbering. Overall the volume has nineteen chapters which I numbered consecutively. These are editorial divisions, though in Part One they coincide with Lonergan's. But within the nineteen chapters there are subdivisions or paragraphs that retain the number Lonergan gave them in the original manuscript or draft or fragment, and they may or may not be numbered consecutively. In Part One, of course,

---

commitment to understanding the concrete and a truncated orientation to some shade of modeling. As the conclusion of the Introduction emphasizes, real economic analysis must aspire to a functional-specialist focus on the concrete. The need for such a collaborative analytic focus is best appreciated, of course, in its historical absence. See, for example, Michael Barratt Brown, *Africa's Choices: After Thirty Years of the World Bank* (New York: Penguin Press, 1995), the first two parts of which point painfully to the absence of real analysis, while the 'Framework for Cooperation' of its third part cries out for Lonergan's division of labor.

3 See notes 13, 14, and 15 below, and the text there.

4 Some pointers from Lonergan and Schumpeter on the history of 'the veil' are given below, pp. xxviii–xxix.

our numbers are again coincident with his, but in Part Three our first chapter (chapter 15) has sections 4, 5, 6, 7, and 7 bis – the numbers Lonergan used – and in Part Two the section numbers are even less orderly, and will at times seem almost random: for example, our chapter 9 has sections 9 and 11 because those are the numbers of Lonergan's original. The result is a lack of symmetry and uniformity in the table of contents, but the advantage is that the numbering keeps the reader closer to the original efforts of Lonergan. (I note here the one change I made in Lonergan's numbers: in the subdivisions of what is here chapter 11 he had two sections numbered 10; I changed the second to 10bis.)

I therefore chose this option over two others that were evident. In one of these other options the section numbers in each chapter could simply have been made uniform, starting from section 1 in chapter 1 in Part One, and returning to section 1 at the beginning of each chapter. Then this introduction would have had to contain a full list of correspondences. The advantage of this option would have been a clear uniformity, which seems a minor thing compared to the sense of Lonergan's own numbering with its suggestive ordering and gaps and omissions. The second of these other options I might have chosen was to have a double numbering for the sections; thus, our chapter 15 could have had for its sections the numbering 15.1 (4), 15.2 (5), etc., where the bracketed number is Lonergan's original. This would have the advantage of continually recalling Lonergan's divisions; the disadvantage would be the clumsiness of double reference in the long years of study of these sources that can be expected. So, the table of contents presents the reader with a more appropriate image of Lonergan's efforts, and later references will tend to make the original context present in ongoing research.

The difficulty of numbering is especially true of Part Two, which lacks the unity of the other two parts. I reordered material in a manner that identifies units of treatment, gathers into sections pieces that tackle the same topic at different stages of Lonergan's understanding, omits duplicate or partial and incomplete pages, relocates displaced pages, calls attention to significant marginal comments and jottings on the reverse side of pages or rejected typescript, and so on. The final ordering here, then, is not the order of the archival files nor does it convey a hypothesis on the order of Lonergan's writing. The ordering is dictated by a desire to facilitate the reader's understanding of the material and of Lonergan's drive towards the elements of a new macroeconomics. I have, obviously, some hypothesis on the order of composition, and it will raise its head occasionally.

It seems appropriate to describe the archival material as I found it and as it is referred to below. The material as I found it in 1973 was not paginated. It was contained in folders numbered 51 and 58 to 60, folder 60 containing also a large collection of loose pages of quotations from, and comments on books on economics. Later Nicholas Graham paginated a photocopy of the typed material, and I find it helpful to use that pagination for references, and I shall refer henceforth to page x of this ordering as Gx.[5]

A few comments on the Graham-paginated version are in order. The version, obviously, does not contain the reverse of any of the pages, on some of which are valuable handwritten sketches, a few of which are reproduced in facsimile in chapter 14. Page 81 of the version is out of place, and it is out of place in the original folder: it should be between G83 and G85. Page 74 does not belong in the sequence: in the original file it was folded and used to wrap G75–131. Page G67 is omitted because it is a single page, out of place, that gives what seems to be a piece of an earlier attempt at the topics of chapter 12, section 7: it corresponds to the ending of d) and the beginning of e).

Next, I note my reordering of the material into the chapters of Part Two.

Chapter	G
7	1–6
8	75–131
9	42–47, 56–66
10	26–41
11	48–55, 68–73
12	7–25
13	
14	Fragments, mainly from the reverse of originals of chapters 7–12. Also included here is the single page from folder 51.

The reader will notice immediately that chapter 13 has no corresponding pages in the paginated archival material. It is not, in fact, to be found in the folders mentioned. It is, very evidently, a version of the analysis of

5 Since there will be continual reference in this volume to the 'G' pages, I give here the folders of the O'Donovan catalogue in which they can be found (all are in Batch II): pages 1–47 are in Folder 58, pages 48 to 73 in Folder 59, and pages 74 to 131 in Folder 60.

superposed circuits that concludes ECA. It has been in my possession since around 1970, and I may have received it directly from Lonergan: he had sent ECA to me, as I recall, late in 1968.

I turn now to some details of the ordering of Part Two. The division into chapters and the chapter headings are, of course, mine.

Chapter 7 contains two short sections. Here, and throughout, I give the titles and the title numbers as Lonergan typed them. I surmise that the two sections represent an attempt at a fresh beginning after the sketchings of the wrapper page, G74. Indeed, I would place their composition after that of the text reproduced here in chapter 8. Were they a piece of a first version of ECA, whose sections are peculiarly numbered? Is there a missing version of the analysis? As I note below, regarding the content of chapter 9, there are certainly large sections of analysis that are not in the Archives. When I was assisting Lonergan, in the autumn of 1977, in his preparations for the spring presentation of *Circulation Analysis* at Boston College, I gave him a copy of these sections that I place here in chapter 7, suggesting that they would be a helpful beginning. He included them in the 1978 version of the analysis. I include them here as the beginning of Part Two because they do indeed provide a good orientation, to be read even before beginning Part One. I note immediately that the only noneditorial note of Part Two occurs in this chapter: a reference by Lonergan to Cassirer's work.

Chapter 8 is a very compact version, in four sections, of circulation analysis. Its four sections are a less developed version of ECA, corresponding roughly to sections 1–12. As noted already, this chapter was wrapped in the folder page G74: a facsimile of that page is included below in chapter 14. It seems to me of some significance, marking a methodological transition to a precise focus on circulation analysis. One can get the impression – I leave the reader to judge – that Lonergan interrupted his typing of 'Economic Activity' to reflect on his methods of analysis and presentation, the result being a shift from the broad sweep recognizable in Part One to the precision of the fragments of Part Two.

The first three sections contained in chapter 8 seem to have given Lonergan a satisfaction that led him to count the pages. At the top right-hand corner of what is now the first page of the chapter he wrote:

	Totals
1. pp. 11	
2. pp. 10	21
3. pp. 9	30

The fourth section, 'The Effect of Net Transfers,' is incomplete and has within it a few pages of a direction not followed (G115–117). These pages are omitted in this chapter but are included in chapter 14. As footnote 5 of the chapter indicates, the concluding page of this section is reconstructed from G131, and the basis of the reconstruction is included in chapter 14, section 2.

Chapter 9 contains two sections that are similarly titled. They can be seen to resemble both section 2 of chapter 8 and section 11 of ECA. All have a chart of phases in common, though the chart in ECA adds the sophistication of fractions, dQ/Q. However, the first section, '9. Circulation Trends,' has a first equation numbered (15) and so could be an early effort to follow on from section 8 of ECA, which ends with a set of equations numbered (14). The second section, '11. Trends,' is a more complex treatment of process and circulation trends. In it there is a quotation from the set of equations (14) just mentioned, but the equation numbers in it, as well as the title number, indicate that it belongs later in the text. Indeed, far from being a follow-up on section 8 of ECA, there are evidently substantial intervening sections that are missing. The equation numbers of this section run from (93) to (98), and at one stage there is a reference to 'equations (83) to (91) of the previous section.' Other equations quoted – (22), (32), (46), (53), (67), (68), (71), (72) – indicate a complexity of discussion that did not find its way into ECA.

Chapter 10 might seem to be another candidate as an earlier version of chapter 9 of ECA, inclusive of its appendix, but its first equation number is (20), which would leave a gap of five equation numbers, and earlier numbered equations referred to do not correspond to those of ECA. The direction it takes is towards an analysis of changes in monetary circulation in terms of changes in turnover magnitudes, turnover frequencies, and transitional payments. ECA, section 9, bypasses these difficulties. This chapter contains equations numbered (20) to (33). However, it does not appear to be a candidate for one of the missing sections prior to chapter 9, section 2: the equation (32) referred to in the latter does not match equation (32) of the present chapter.

Chapter 11 consists of three sections. The first two evidently belong together: this is clear from the continuity both of meaning and of equation numbers, which run from equation (19) at the beginning of section 10 to equation (33) in section 11. We have here yet another version of equation (32). Chapter 11, section 10, anticipates some of the discussion of ECA, section 10, and includes topics of section 13 of ECA, below. Chapter 11, section 11, anticipates ECA, section 14.

The third section of chapter 11 is section 10 again in Lonergan's version, but I have labelled it '10bis' to avoid confusion. It consists of two typewritten pages ending in mid-sentence. It does not belong with the other two sections. It is included here certainly because it happens to be in the same folder in the Archives, but also because it represents the same type of struggle to get from the broad analysis to details of the fluctuations intrinsic to successful economic process. In the present case, it reaches towards detail regarding the crossover that connects the two circuits by envisaging income groups and fluctuations of income. This topic is tackled from a different perspective in section 13 of ECA.

The fragments in chapter 12, some incomplete, center on the nature of price, demand, and supply. Their content relates more to parts of chapter 3 of 'For a New Political Economy' than to the content of ECA, so they may be seen as complementing the earlier work. A key to the omission of the topic in this form from ECA may be had from Lonergan's handwritten comments on the top of the first page, one of which draws attention to the problem of incidental definitions.[6] It might seem editorially correct to relocate the section marked 'f' after 'e' and before '8,' but in fact section 8 seems to have been produced prior to section f, and includes on its reverse side sketchings towards f. These sketchings are included in chapter 14, section 5. So section 8 may well have been rejected – it begins somewhat of a summary of section 7 – in favor of the addition of f. For these reasons I have listed this section as a separate section, *f.*

Chapter 13 is a single piece on superposed circuits which corresponds with sections 16, 17, and 18 of ECA. From its introduction it is evident that it has been preceded by sections similar to sections 13, 14, and 15 of ECA. It is close in meaning to the treatment in the corresponding sections of ECA, though fuller on deficit spending and taxes than the incomplete final section 17 of ECA. The rhythm of expression in it supports the view that it is an earlier version of the final sections of ECA, though it may possibly belong with earlier vanished versions of previous sections. To assist the reader, I have added at the conclusion of the chapter a diagram of the superposed circuits of the type that I found useful in attempting to present the analysis at the Boston Lonergan Workshop of 1977.

Chapter 14 draws attention to other pre-1944 archival material. It is peculiar in that it involves a much higher level of editorial selectiveness than is normal in presenting a section of the *opera omnia* of a thinker to the

6 See the note on the text there, p. 184.

public. Lonergan's paradigm shift in economics is so massive that every fragment of his efforts towards that shift is relevant to the challenge of reaching for his meaning. The pre-1944 fragments include, for example, more than one hundred pages of notes from various works on economics. Among these notes are comments on the authors as well as sketches, graphs, and notes representing his own developing view. Other fragments are stray typed pages set aside in various ways. Some are evidently put aside carefully: the 'folder 51' page included in this chapter is a clear instance of such care. Some pages are available to us because they were put aside in order that the reverse side might be used again. One amazing instance of this is the fragment on 'economic control' reproduced in this chapter under that title: it was found by Michael Shute on the reverse side of a typescript that deals with grace. The use of the word 'amazing' here brings us back to the claim of peculiar selectiveness. The rejected fragment on economic control is included here because of an editorial view of its central significance in reaching for the meaning of Lonergan's economics. Also reproduced in this chapter, in facsimile as well as in typescript, are handwritten sketchings from the reverse side of pages of the typescripts of Part Two of the present volume. Their significance is that they show Lonergan creatively scribbling in masterly control both of his own symbolism and of a mathematical economics that is relentlessly heuristic.

This chapter, then, is a sampling of fragments regarded as immediately relevant to the comprehension of Lonergan's economic analysis. Insofar as the selection involves oversights, corrections will occur through the publication of all the available fragments in a later volume of archival material.

Part Three aims at presenting as faithfully as possible the version of the analysis that Lonergan considered satisfactory when he left his work on economics aside sometime in 1944. The only date I have found relating to this is that given in section 1 of chapter 14 above: March 23, 1944. It was this 129–page typescript that Lonergan used in the first presentation of his economic theory in Boston College, Spring, 1978. It had been filed away since 1944, at which time he seemed to have failed to get the serious attention of any economist to whom he submitted his work.

It seemed best, in reproducing this 1944 version of Lonergan's economics, to allow the reader to have the exact text, including the manner in which the sections of the text were numbered. So, while I have divided the text into five chapters – the titles are mine – the numbers of the sections are given as they were in the original. Again, I have retained the exact text even to the extent of including some few mathematical errors. These errors were corrected in the text as it appears in volume 15, and I add notes with the corrections in this version. Notes are added giving modifications of the 1944 text that occur in that volume. The original contained no footnotes.

The sections in the text were labeled, after a one-page outline, sections 4–18, with a '7bis' and a '7ter.' Sections 1 and 2 of chapter 7 are obvious candidates for missing sections 1 and 2, but neither Lonergan nor I made this connection in the 1970s: they could well belong to other attempts. There is no candidate for a missing section 3 in the Archives: the only section labeled '3' is the third section of chapter 8 of Part Two, clearly not part of this version. Why, then, did Lonergan settle for starting the 1944 version with the topic of section 4? My analysis of the intellectual development of Part Two would suggest that he wished to cut out anything that did not pertain clearly to the analysis itself. So there is discernible an exclusion of larger contexts: not just the broad sweep of interest in Part One, but even the methodological comments represented by sections 1 and 2 of chapter 7.

2 Context

Towards the end of his life Lonergan expressed the desire to write a primer on economics.[7] One might claim that this was what he had been aiming at from the beginning of his work in the area in the 1930s, the result being a set of incomplete introductions to economics. Yet there was another dimension to those last years, and it is important to advert to that dimension at least sketchily here, since it is intrinsic to the restructuring of economic science.

First, however, we should pause over the character of the incomplete analyses represented by the two volumes of Lonergan's economics. The three versions in the present volume[8] can be viewed as in a more satisfactory state of completeness than the version in the other volume: they appear to have been rounded off by Lonergan to his own satisfaction before he put them aside. The version in volume 15 is another matter: putting it together was a difficult editorial challenge, since Lonergan was reaching, over those last years, for a presentation that would be more contemporarily adequate, while at the same time following up his larger interests.

7 Letter to Jane Collier of Cambridge, England, 12 June 1982.
8 Among the fragments in Part Two, chapter 8 stands out as a compact presentation of Lonergan's central thesis.

The analyses, however, rise uncomfortably above the present tradition of introductions to economics, and it is best to be alerted to the consequent difficulties from the start. The perspective towards which Lonergan leads is concretely heuristic, especially opposed to the abstract model-building, mathematical or not, that is currently fashionable. That perspective, in its fulness, involves cultural shifts that require some attention. However, it is best, first, to focus on Lonergan's work as it differs in its approach to elementary economcs. That difference may be broadly identified by appealing to Schumpeter's characterization of the fundamental need for economic theory to 'cross the Rubicon.' 'By "crossing the Rubicon," I mean this: however important those occasional excursions into sequence analysis may have been, they left the main body of economic theory on the "static" bank of the river; the thing to do is not to supplement static theory by the booty brought back from these excursions but to replace it by a system of general economic dynamics into which statics would enter as a special case.'[9]

No doubt some economists will say that macrodynamic economics is a present reality. That issue, I would claim, is to be settled not by random debate about the achievements of the disciples of Schumpeter, Keynes, Kalecki, whoever, but by a deep paradigm shift to a scientifically structured division of labor within economic analysis. But for the present we maintain our elementary focus by comparing Lonergan's analysis with that of Schumpeter.

Both in his *Theory of Economic Development* and in his two-volume *Business Cycles: A Theoretical, Historical, and Statistical Analysis of the Capitalist Process*, Schumpeter takes his start from the dynamics of a stable economy and moves to a consideration of the 'destabilizing' effect of entrepreneurial activity.[10] Lonergan, however, focuses immediately on such activity, particularly in its occurrence on the massive scale associated historically with economic cycles, revolutions, surges. He approaches that focus armed with precise analytic distinctions between basic and surplus activities, outlays,

9 Joseph Schumpeter, *History of Economic Analysis* (New York: Oxford University Press, 1954) 1160. To be referred to below as *HEA*.

10 Joseph Schumpeter's *The Theory of Economic Development* was first published in German in 1911. The English version appeared in 1934 (New York: Oxford University Press). His work on business cycles appeared in 1939 (New York: McGraw-Hill). Regarding the possible dependence of Lonergan on Schumpeter, I would recall the scribbled notes from which the quotation in section 4, chapter 14 is taken. From those notes it would seem that Lonergan was reading Schumpeter from the perspective of his own elaborated view.

incomes, etc., and it is extremely important to note that these distinctions are equally relevant to the understanding and control of an economy without major surges.[11]

Both the understanding and the control deserve passing comment. Lonergan insists on determinate understanding, whether the understanding is of the value of labor, the value of capital, or the propensities of consumers. There is no sidetracking into some labor theory of value,[12] no effort to build in measurement of capital,[13] and propensities are thrown not only into the strict analytic context already mentioned but into a normative context that transposes the meaning of rational expectations.[14] That analytic and normative context will eventually stimulate a massive reorientation of statistical analyses. Empirically determined historical distributions will be contextualized by contrafactual historical studies that generate schedules

11 Less precise forms of Lonergan's distinction are of course familiar. Kalecki stands out here: 'We shall subdivide the economy into two sectors producing investment goods and consumer goods, respectively. In each sector, we include the production of the respective commodity from the lowest stage. Thus the production of the materials and fuel will be allocated between the two sectors according to the uses that are made of them in the production.' *The Collected Works of Michal Kalecki*, ed. Jerzy Osiatynski (Oxford: Clarendon Press, 1993) 23 (in 'The Problem of Financing Economic Development'). He also writes of sectorizing taxation (pp. 34, 35, 40).

12 On value, see Part One, chapter 3.

13 The key point regarding determinacy is made on p. 237, and it is useful to relate this to Joan Robinson's claim, 'The student of economic theory is taught to write $O = f(L, C)$ where L is a quantity of labor, C a quantity of capital and O a rate of output of commodities. He is instructed to assume all workers alike, and to measure L in manhours of labor; he is told something about the index number problem involved in choosing a unit of output; and then he is hurried on to the next question, in the hope that he will forget to ask in what units C is measured. Before ever he does ask, he has become a professor, and so sloppy habits of thought are handed on from one generation to the next.' Joan Robinson, 'The Production Function in the Theory of Capital,' *Review of Economic Studies* 21 (1955) 81.

14 The contrast between Lonergan's expectations regarding expectations and the present tradition is neatly brought out by a comment on Robert Gordon's text on *Macroecomomics*: 'I now know how my analysis differs from Gordon's and presumably others. He gives as the empirically determined propensity to consume 75% and to save as 25%. For me these are variables with saving increasing in the surplus expansion and consumption increasing in the basic.' Letter of Lonergan to Philip McShane, 10 January 1979. Experts will recall further subtleties relating to the works of John Muth and Robert Lucas. See the work cited in note 16 below, the index under 'Rational expectations.'

of overarching possibilities, probabilities, actualities.[15] The normative context is no mystery: the double-circuited and credit-centered economy is as naturally demanding as any motor engine.[16] But the natural demand is multiply warped in our times by the vandalism of overreaching limited economic understanding and centralizing *Realpolitik*. The fully differentiated normative context will take subtle account of this in its cultivation of global control.

The control envisaged by Lonergan is, of course, democratic, something quite beyond present or past dreams, requiring a shocking educational reorientation.[17] And there is much else that is shocking: the democratic control has its parallel not in iron tracks but in ocean waves, a matter of coaching and coaxing the voyage of a global enterprise;[18] the focus is not on employment but on leisure and a quite different ethos of capital deepening;[19] center stage is occupied by the conception, affirmation, and implementation of *pure surplus income*,[20] the global dividend; but most especially

15 The context is Bernard Lonergan, *Insight: A Study of Human Understanding*, vol. 3 in Collected Works of Bernard Lonergan (Toronto: University of Toronto Press), chapter 4, section 2.2. Contrafactual historical studies, however, need the larger context of functional specialization to bring out their significance for dialectic and systematics.

16 The metaphor brings us to the heart of the matter. The central focus of advanced work at present may be taken as 'examining optimal behaviour' (Olivier Jean Blanchard and Stanley Fisher, *Lectures on Macroeconomics*, Cambridge, MA: M.I.T. Press,. 1993, p. 373). The metaphor would suggest that Lonergan's examination has the character of a driver's manual, where contemporary studies home in on organizing bad driving. The reader would do well, however, to venture into such a graduate text as the one cited, which seeks 'to present life at the frontier, showing the various directions in which researchers are currently working' (ibid. xi). I would note that such studies of actualities and probabilities, corrected by functional circuit distinctions, would be sublated by the larger analytic context mentioned in the previous footnote.

17 'Coming to grasp what serious education is and, nonetheless, coming to accept that challenge constitutes the greatest challenge to the modern economy' (CWL 15, § 24, conclusion). I would note that the economic core of this education is towards a democratic sensitivity to the demands of the two circuits. The issue of the quality of life is another matter. See C. Cobb, T. Halstead, and J. Rowe, 'If the GDP is up, Why is America Down?', *The Atlantic Monthly*, October 1995, pp. 59–78.

18 Relevant here is section 3 of chapter 14 below.

19 See below, chapter 2, section 9.

20 The Lonergan student will recognize the enormity of the challenge by linking 'pure surplus income' to topics of *Insight* such as 'pure formulations' and 'the pure desire to know practically.'

and initially there is the shocking yet evident need of a discontinuous leap to economics as an eightfold collaboration of global specialists.[21]

This last shock brings us to the topic of Lonergan's broader interest in those final years. The mood and drive of that interest can be intimated by two quotations which will complement Professor Lawrence's comment regarding Schumpeter's *History of Economic Analysis* as the *vade mecum* of those years.[22] The first is from a letter written as he neared the end of his 1981 course on circulation analysis:

> There remain four more Macro sessions, and I am finding helpful background for the Post-Keynesians in Schumpeter's HCE. Neoclassical 'neutral money' is not from Walras who sharply separates his *numéraire* from *monnaie* (1087). He finds the *Tableau économique* and the development of marginal analysis to move towards general equilibrium (918), and I would add that the equilibrium would not be both general and micro once macro is solidly established.[23]

The second quotation is an aside – I refrain from editing the spoken word – in an answer to a question regarding the relation of his analysis to liberal theories, midway through the same course in the following year:

> Schumpeter is important to me: his book is *History of Economic Analysis*. What he does is to go over the centuries and he picks out the significant people; and this fellow says this, and this fellow says this, and so on. And he builds up and he is able to skip people because he doesn't see anything significant coming into their work. Gradually, he puts together a picture for you. And you will be able to say ... like a thing I've been reading recently. There was a man at the end of the seventeenth century, Nicholas Barbon, who said interest is the stock, the rent; just as rent, the payment to the landlord, was rent for land. And by stock he meant working capital, it was real. And that led to what is called real analysis: identifying money with what money buys.

21 The eightfold structure is the central topic of Lonergan's *Method in Theology* (London: Darton, Longman & Todd, and New York: Herder and Herder, 1972; latest reprint, Toronto: University of Toronto Press, 1996). For its relation to economics see Philip McShane, *Economics for Everyone. Das Jus Kapital* (Halifax: Axial Press, 1998), chapter 5.

22 See CWL 15, Editors' Introduction.

23 Quoted from a letter of Lonergan to Philip McShane, 21 March 1981.

> That plagued a lot of nineteenth-century economics and to a great extent the economics of the first four decades of the twentieth century. Well, Barbon, he came out about 1693 with his discourse on grain and it didn't catch on at all. But somebody else came up with similar ideas, a little more fully presented, around 1750; his name was Joseph Massie. And he added on the ideas of Locke, Hume; and Turgot was added to the flock. However, Adam Smith came in on top of that and he more or less didn't learn anything from these later people after Barbon. After Adam Smith we are really in Barbon's theory.
>
> And that is the source of the problem of real analysis. If you want to treat money that doesn't make a difference, you can have a beautiful liberal monetary theory. But it doesn't say the way the thing works ...[24]

The Lonergan expert will recognize, perhaps, that Lonergan is pointing here towards the ongoing genesis of a genetic systematics that sublates historical studies. So, what Lonergan remarked of theology is true also of economics: '1) not a Platonic idea 2) but the many species [not individuals except as types, as dominating personalities] 3) in a genetically and dialectically differentiated genus.'[25] For the economist, however, this is strange territory. It can best be approached by raising the question, What was Schumpeter at in his *History of Economic Analysis*?

Even with only the clues of the two above quotations from Lonergan, one can surmise that Schumpeter was not doing ordinary history, reaching for von Ranke's *wie es eigentlich gewesen*. He was, in his own undifferentiated and incomplete way, struggling dialectically towards a genetic retrieval, ordering, and reordering of past struggles towards economic system. In Lonergan's view, that task is to be the task, not of any one economist, but a functionally ordered set of enterprises of different groups of specialists, with focus, for example, in a particular author such as Cantillon, or in the history of a system as it moves through Cantillon and Quesnay and onwards, or in the dialectical sniffing out of progress in the history of systems and applications, or in the later dependent task of reaching a genetic

24 I quote from a verbatim transcript of tape 9, by Nicholas Graham, of the lectures of Lonergan's Boston College course on Macroeconomics of Spring, 1982.

25 Quoted from unpublished notes of the early 1960s, available in the Lonergan Archives, Toronto, Batch v (McShane number v.6.h).

systematics that holds together, poised for selective application, the temporarily best within all of history's systems. That precise differentiation of tasks was certainly not envisaged by Schumpeter, but the forty years since his effort have provided ample evidence for the need that he implicitly faced.

The central issue is efficiency. I suspect some writer of a later time will look back at the undifferentiated muddling in economic theory of the turn of the millennium as Blaug views recent centuries of monetary theory: 'An almost indescribably analytic sloppiness characterized some 200 years of development in monetary theory.'[26] So I am led to recall Adam Smith's observation in the first chapter of *The Wealth of Nations*: 'The division of labour, so far as it can be introduced, occasions, in every art, a proportionable increase in the productive power of labour.' What has emerged in our time is a desperate need, and a pregnant possibility, of a division of labor on the level of mind and minding. The need in relation to the past has become increasingly manifest in the specialized searchings for textual integrities, for precise interpretations, for accurate histories, for discernments of progress. An equivalent fourfold need regarding the future lurks in the vague searchings for a basis of the three different goals of policy determination, economic planning, executive selectivity. Lonergan's fundamental achievement in economics is his discernment of the structure of the division of labor that would meet these needs with precision and so lift effete scholarship, disoriented science, and ineffective journalism, into a humanly efficient steering of the global enterprise.

A final methodological comment should bring us to our goal of contextualizing the analyses of these volumes.

Lonergan wrote in the early 1940s of Keynes's system as a basis of interpretation.[27] The same is more profoundly true of Lonergan's macrodynamics, for it is a precise explanatory foundational achievement. It meshes into his fuller methodology of economic collaboration to provide a cre-

26 Mark Blaug, 'Why is the quantity theory of money the oldest surviving theory in economics?' chapter 2 in Mark Blaug et al., *The Quantity Theory of Money from Locke to Keynes and Friedman* (Brookfield, VT: Edward Elgar Publishers, 1995) 43. I take the opportunity to note here that the most manifest gap in Lonergan's text is that which has numbers 51–53 in Part One of this volume. One might suspect that to be related to finance: some theoretic of credit, interest, etc., that would have paralleled and sublated Schumpeter's various efforts. Such a heuristic could have found a place in the other versions of the analysis.

27 See below, pp. 9–10.

ative and critical perspective for the differentiated reading of texts, of histories, of systematizations, of the content and marketing of policies.

Perhaps the reader is now in a position to move from these few pointers and the descriptive hints from Lonergan's comments quoted above to reach some suspicion of the nature and relevance of Lonergan's drive against contemporary methodological confusion, against the neglect of real analysis that is a prevalent ethos, and towards a more precise heuristic of what he omitted in his early efforts. We reach, then, I hope, some differentiating light on Lonergan's analyses. They are principally foundational works: grimly difficult reading, then, for someone seeking a beginner's view.[28] Certainly, the work of the last years of his life includes pointers towards an introductory primer. But the massively innovative primers that would meet millennial needs, 500-page texts of empirically rich, locally oriented, normatively focused non-truncated writing, are distant probabilities.[29]

28 I would suggest that the place to start work on Lonergan's economics is with chapter 1 of this volume, moving then to the text of 1944 as presented in either volume. See also 'The Value of Lonergan's Economics for Lonergan Students,' in Philip McShane, *The Redress of Poise* (Halifax: Axial Press, 1999). I have discussed the problem of reading economics, including texts by Gordon and Robinson, in chapters 1 and 3 of *Economics for Everyone.*

29 Relevant here is the heuristics of the transition from paradigm shift to the 'normal science' of texts and programs. See, for example, K.A. Pearce and K.D. Hoover, with a comment by A. Cottrell, 'After the Revolution: Paul Samuelson and the Textbook Keynesian Tradition,' pp. 183–222 of *New Perspectives on Keynes*, Annual Supplement to *History of Political Economy* (27), ed. A.F. Cottrell and M.S. Lawlor, Duke University Press, 1995. The book deals, in the main, with the diffusion of Keynes's view. One must hope for a like diffusion, however distorted, of Lonergan's view, in the new millennium.

PART ONE

For a New Political Economy

1

Why? What? How?

1 The Need of a New Political Economy

In the introduction to his *General Theory*[1] Mr Keynes considers the objection that only the more intelligent type of expert is able to understand the highly abstract theorems of modern economics. His answer is not altogether satisfactory. He says that if practical men such as politicians and bankers and industrialists do not succeed in grasping the issues, then inevitably they will be eliminated. Undoubtedly they will, but so shall we, for they are our leaders.

Nor is this difficulty remote and academic. It is the whole thesis of the totalitarian states that the democracies have missed the economic bus of the twentieth century. Last century, they say, democracy happened to be the successful political form. That is why England rose to world hegemony. But times have changed. Modern economy postulates the totalitarian state, and this time it is the Germans and Italians who are first in the field, and theirs is to be world leadership. Such is their view, and, as they like to believe, the present war is but an incident that happily will hasten the elimination of a way of life that definitely is out of date.

What is our answer? Certainly we do not propose to be eliminated. Certainly we intend, as Mr Churchill modestly remarked, to give a good account of ourselves. Certainly, too, we are right in our attitude, for we

1 John Maynard Keynes, *The General Theory of Employment, Interest and Money* (London: Macmillan, 1936).

fight for things more real, more profound, more certain, than the historical speculations of totalitarian economics. But when all this has been said, it remains that there does exist a very real problem, a problem that has to be solved if we are to use propaganda effectively against the enemy during the war, a problem that has to be solved if we are to face and democratically to surmount our economic difficulties after the war.

I think it will help a definition of this problem if briefly we contrast the old political economy of the early nineteenth century with its modern more nuanced, more complex, less colorful successor, the science of economics.

The old political economists were creative thinkers. They took into their hands the vast forces of nascent industrialism. They directed and molded the nineteenth-century development of commercial, industrial, financial, juridical, and even political structure. But what is more important, what differentiates the old political economists from many subsequent creators of a 'new order,' is that their mode of action was essentially and thoroughly democratic. Socialists, communists, totalitarians can put their theories into practice only if they obtain political power, only if they can set up a bureaucracy and regiment a people. Even then they find that their theories do not work too well; it is not enough to regiment the Russians by the Soviets, to regiment the Germans by the Nazis, to regiment the Italians by the Fascists. The whole world must be made to conform. Now the action of the old political economists was the very opposite of this. Their power was solely the power of argument. Their effectiveness was not through the state but through individual initiative. Their influence, in its basic tendency, was not to cripple but to release the spontaneity and the creativeness that reside not in red tape but in human beings, not in ideologies nor in parties nor in the advice of experts nor in five-year plans but in free men.

What, then, was the secret of the old political economists? How did they manage to create a new order through democracy? Obviously it was because they could speak to democracy. Because their whole doctrine could be synthesized in slogans. Because they could issue the imperatives of thrift, enterprise, *laissez faire*, intelligent self-interest. Because they could convince anyone who counted that their imperatives led to the best of all possible worlds.

I would not be thought to argue that modern economists were in error when by a gradual evolution they effectively discarded the old political economy and substituted their science. For the old economy, at least in the course of time, was found guilty of many errors, of errors demonstrated by fact and experience, of errors in method, of errors in principle. Certainly these had to be corrected. My sole contention is this, that they were corrected in the wrong way. For whatever the accuracy of economics, it certainly does not possess the old democratic spirit. So far from being able to address effectively the ordinary run of men, it cannot but doubt the ability of democracy's leaders to follow the labyrinthine course of its thought. The result is that the only solution it can ever offer to economic problems is by supplying a brain trust to an incipient bureaucracy, by supplying technicians for a totalitarian state.

The problem, I think, is clear. We cannot rely on the old political economy: it was democratic but has been found wrong. We cannot rely on the new economics: it is accurate but it can solve real problems only by eliminating democracy. What is needed is a new political economy that is free from the mistakes of the old, a democratic economics that can issue practical imperatives to plain men.

2 The Nature of a New Political Economy

In the previous section the need of a new political economy was expressed by its relations to the old political economy and to modern economics. A brief consideration of the general nature of science will enable us to define with greater accuracy just what is needed.

Dynamically a science is the interplay of two factors: there are data revealed by experience, observation, experiment, measurement; and on the other hand, there is the constructive activity of mind. By themselves the data are objective, but they are also disparate, without significance, without correlation, without coherence. Of itself, the mind is coherence; spontaneously it constructs correlations and attributes significance; but it must have materials to construct and correlate; and if its work is not to be fanciful, its materials must be the data. Thus thought and experience are two complementary functions; thought constructs what experience reveals; and science is an exact equilibrium of the two.

In working towards such an equilibrium the science stands successively on a series of levels each of greater generality than the preceding. Chemistry begins by classifying material objects, explains them by reducing them to molecules, explains the molecules by atoms and the atoms by subatoms, to sweep the whole into unity by the theory of motion or, if you prefer, energy. Similarly biology classifies living beings, distinguishes their parts by anatomy and the functions of the parts by physiology, proceeds to the more general level of cytology, and then to the subcellular order of chromosomes and genes, to sweep the whole into unity by some theory of evolution.

Now the movement from a less to a more general level of thought normally involves not only an enlargement but also a readaptation of the whole existing structure. A more profound viewpoint emerges, and this calls for a readjustment of the less general correlations. It will be well to consider a few examples.

Ptolemaic astronomy was a geocentric perspective that correlated movements in the sky by the circle, and spontaneous movements on earth by the rule that bodies fall according to their weight. The perspective was corrected by Copernicus; the correlation of planetary movements was shown by Kepler to be in terms of the ellipse; the law of falling bodies was shown by Galilei[2] to be a proportion between velocity and time squared. These advances are here corrections of mistaken theories; among them there is not the slightest movement towards a greater generality. Generalization comes with Newton, who attacked the general theory of motion, laid down its pure theory, identified Kepler's and Galilei's laws by inventing the calculus, and so found himself in a position to account for any corporeal motion known. Aristotle, Ptolemy, Copernicus, Galilei, and Kepler had all been busy with particular classes of moving bodies. Newton dealt in the same way with all. He did so by turning to a field of greater generality, the laws of motion, and by finding a deeper unity in the apparent disparateness of Kepler's ellipse and Galilei's time squared. In a sense he left Kepler's and Galilei's laws intact, for he in no way impugned their accuracy. But though he left them intact, he also reformulated them and gave them an entirely new interpretation; and integrated with this internal transformation there is the vast enlargement of the theoretical horizon.

Similarly the non-Euclidean geometers and Einstein went beyond Euclid and Newton. The latter were content with objects as they can be imagined: Euclid limited himself to three dimensions, and Newton thought of time as a parameter; they did so because we cannot imagine more than three dimensions and we cannot see time objectively the way we see distances. The non-Euclideans moved geometry back to premises more remote than Euclid's axioms, they developed methods of their own quite unlike

2 Lonergan refers thus, unconventionally, to Galileo Galilei (1564–1642), son of Vincenzo Galilei.

Euclid's, and though they did not impugn Euclid's theorems, neither were they very interested in them; casually and incidentally they turn them up as particular cases in an enlarged and radically different field. Finally, just as Newton went beyond Kepler and Galilei by introducing the calculus, so Einstein went beyond Newton by employing the new geometries to make time an independent variable; and as Newton transformed the formulation and interpretation of Kepler's laws, so Einstein transforms the Newtonian laws of motion.

To extract the significance from these examples, we observe that a scientific generalization makes a new beginning, in a more remote and abstract region of pure thought; and that in terms of this radically new viewpoint, it transforms, reformulates, reinterprets the correlations of earlier science without necessarily denying its truth.

It is, we believe, a scientific generalization of the old political economy and of modern economics that will yield the new political economy which we need. As was argued in the first section, economics corrected political economy in the wrong way. As now this paradox can be explained, economics corrected political economy not by moving to the more general field and so effecting the correction without losing the democratic spirit of the old movement, but by staying on the same level of generality and by making up for lost ground by going into the more particular fields of statistics, history, and a more refined analysis of psychological motivation and of the integration of decisions to exchange.

Plainly the way out is through the more general field. The more economics endeavors to be an exact science, the more incapable it becomes to speak to men, and the greater the necessity under which it lies to treat men the way the exact sciences treat atoms and guinea pigs: it has to put them under laboratory conditions with an Ogpu to keep them there and a group of commissars to plan the experiments; it is very, very, very scientific, but unless you mean by democracy not something like Finland but something like Russia, then it is not at all democratic. On the other hand, only those who beat the drums and blow the big horns on the bandwagon of science fancy science to be exclusively a matter of observation and experiment, measurement and statistics. Anyone with a grasp of the nature of science is fully aware that that is but one side of the picture, that thought is just as essential as fact and, indeed, the whole significance of fact. When, then, we ask for a fresh generalization, we are not moving a hair's breadth outside the orbit of science. On the other hand, we are asking for an instrument that democracy must have, for it is the broad generalization, the significant correlation, that effectively organizes free men without breaking down their freedom.[3]

3 A Note on Method

The method of a generalization cannot be judged by previous standards. On the contrary, unless there is a notable divergence, one can be certain that there is no generalization. This should be clear from what has been said already, but it will do no harm to reinforce the point, for the inertia coefficient of the human mind is normally rather high.

We are not going to discuss wealth or value, supply and demand, price levels and price patterns, capital and labor, interest and profits, production, distribution, and consumption. Because we are not, it certainly will be objected that our discussion has nothing to do with economic science, for economics is precisely the study of wealth and value, supply and demand, and so on. The answer is as follows. The discussion moves on a more general plane to terminate in a more general conclusion. Because the general includes the particular, a generalized economics cannot but include the particular economics with which my hypothetical opponent is familiar. His error lies in supposing that, because he knows only one particular economics, therefore he can never know more than one.

A related objection may be put as follows. Despite the fact that the argument is supposed to be a generalization, still at times it does descend to familiar things. There is no fault in that, for one cannot live in thin air. But there does appear to be this fault, that such descents to the concrete, insofar as they use familiar terms, do so in quite an unfamiliar fashion. Further, though the changes in connotation are reasonably clear, still there often is no attempt, and never an exhaustive attempt, to describe their denotation. The answer to this may be had, at least in part, from the nature of a gener-

3 At the end of the corresponding page of typescript there is a cancelled start to section 3, ending in mid-sentence at the conclusion of the page, thus: '§ 3. The Structure of a New Political Economy.
'A radical new beginning has to be found. We find it in the idea of economic activity. We shall not focus our attention on such particular things as wealth or value, supply and demand, price levels and price patterns, labor and capital, interest and profits, production, distribution, and consumption. I do not say we shall pay no attention to them, but that we shall attend only from a new viewpoint and we shall see them only in a new perspective. I do not say we shall deny any of the correlations that have been established with regard to this multiplicity of objects; but we shall find that these objects are objects of thought'

alization. Because it introduces a radically new perspective, it cannot but see things in a notably different way. This accounts for shifts in connotation of familiar terms, but it does not explain the systematic neglect of a study of denotations. The answer to that lies in the nature of a method: essentially method is adaptation of means to an end; if a single factor in an experiment cannot be measured with greater accuracy than a tenth, then one is wasting one's time bothering about the thousandths or millionths even though such accuracy can be had in measuring other factors. Now the conclusion of our inquiry will be a comparison of medieval, classical, and totalitarian attitudes to the economic field. The premises to this conclusion will consist in the patterns and phases of relations between certain more general rhythmic flows to be found in any slightly developed economy. In this movement from pure analysis to historical synthesis, any study of denotations inevitably would obscure the issue. On the other hand, it could not contribute any greater accuracy to the conclusion, for the conclusion stands on a level of generality quite indifferent to such matters of detail.

A third objection may take the form that we arrive at an historical synthesis without attempting any historical research. The answer is that no additional research is needed to justify such general conclusions as we present. To put the point differently, all historical study rapidly reaches the point where interpretation of the data can no longer be determined solely by the data. Thus it is that each nation tends to write its own history of the past and that each philosophy constructs its own theory of history. Similarly, in economic history, general conclusions depend much more on the validity of general principles of interpretation than on accuracy of factual detail. In an appendix to his *General Theory* Mr Keynes presents as a corollary a new interpretation of mercantilist thought: for the facts of the mercantilist period, he is content to go to a standard work of research; for the interpretation of those facts, he pays no attention to the laborious research workers who, as interpreters, merely reechoed classical views; on the contrary, he brings his own *General Theory* into play to show that, after all, the mercantilists might not have been the fools that classical theory makes them. The legitimacy of the procedure is evident, for, if research is necessary to determine in detail what the mercantilists thought and did, it cannot claim any competence in judging whether the mercantilists were wise or foolish. That question is answered only by economic theory, and each theory will give its own answer: the classicists have theirs, the Marxists no doubt offer another, and Mr Keynes has given us a third; nor is the cause of the divergence a difference in the factual data but a difference in the principles accepted by the judging mind. Accordingly, if we succeed in working out a generalization of economic science, we cannot fail to create simultaneously a new approach to economic history. Such an approach in itself is already a historical synthesis.

So much for objections that may trouble the reader in the method of this inquiry. It will be well to add a word of caution. If here we have insisted on the importance of generalization, that is only because generalization is our undertaking. We would not be thought to make little of the complementary element in science, the solid stimulus and the saving control of fact. On the contrary, it is only to give an account of enormous facts overlooked by political economy and by specialized economics that this generalization is undertaken; and it is only by a new study of facts, more fully grasped because more broadly seen, that our general conclusions can be made a source of practical applications.

2

The Pure Process

4 The Basic Rhythmic Flow

As Newton, according to the tale, forgot the distinction between planets swinging through the sky and apples falling in autumnal orchards, as he reached beyond Kepler's and Galilei's laws to the profounder unity of the theory of motion, so too must we forget distinctions between production, distribution, and consumption, and reach behind the psychology of property and the laws of exchange to form a more basic concept and develop a more general theory.

In any stage of human history from prehistoric caves to the utopias which our prophets describe with such vivid detail, among primitive fruit gatherers, among hunters and fishers, in the first dawn of agricultural civilization, along Egypt's Nile and Babylon's Euphrates, under India's mysticism, China's polish, Greek thought, Roman law, through the turmoil of the dark age and the ferment of the medieval period, in the European expansion and the modern world, everywhere one finds the pulsating flow, the rhythmic series, of the economic activities of man.

The world process, the physical, chemical, vegetal, animal, and human potentialities of universal nature, are ever stimulated, guided, aided by human effort to the goal of human survival and enjoyment, of human achievement, waste, and destruction. All such human activity occurs rhythmically in a series of impulses, and the aggregate rhythm is a compound of many minor rhythms of varying magnitudes and frequencies. But though the whole is rhythmic, not all is economic. Men strive in many fields: they organize human society by politics and war; they orientate their lives by philosophy and religion; they augment knowledge by science and perpetuate intuitions through art; they cool passion and regulate equity by law; they protect and hasten health by medicine; and generation succeeds generation in this heritage of culture through the testament of education. All of this is a rhythmic transformation of natural potentialities by human effort; none of it is, strictly, economic activity. Yet conditioning all culture and inextricably confused with it, there is the economic factor. Governments have budgets even when they do not balance them; religion and law must have their churches and courts, their books printed and housed, their ministers trained; art needs its materials and its galleries, science its laboratories, medicine its hospitals, education its far-flung hierarchy of schools, colleges, and universities. Thus the material fabric of culture's living home is economic, and underlying this superstructure there stands as foundation the purely economic field concerned with nourishment, shelter, clothing, utilities, services, and amusement.

Distinguish, then, in the universal rhythm of all human activity a pure superstructure of cultural activity, the material fabric of this superstructure, and the foundation of both together. The object of our investigation will be the general rhythm inasmuch as it is foundation and material fabric; or, inversely, we are to study the pulsating flow of human activity, except insofar as it is purely cultural. At a later stage of the argument, when we exclude primitive economies – south sea islanders, nomadic tribes of hunters, isolated feudal estates, Robinson Crusoes – it will be possible to give sharper contours, more clear-cut definitions, to the economic field. For then we shall take into account the juridical concepts of property and exchange. Meanwhile we must be content with the vaguer characterization given: juridical concepts, like all others, have to be developed; and there is no use attributing to the universal field a precision which in universal consciousness is slowly attained.

5 Introducing the Symbol *DA*

Henceforth we shall refer to the basic rhythm as *DA*, where *A* stands for 'economic Activity' and *D* recalls that the activity is a series of events, a flow of impulses, a compound rhythm composed of many minor rhythms of varying magnitude and frequency.

Since *DA* is but the first of about a dozen similar terms, it will be well to determine with some precision just what it means.

DA, then, refers not to an average but to an aggregate volume of flow: it refers to the emergence, the longer or shorter period of utility, and the disappearance, disintegration, or waste of an aggregate of meals, clothes, houses, farms, mines, roads, markets, ships, cities, factories, utilities, services, amusements, schools, courts, parliaments, hospitals, churches.

DA refers to this rhythmic flow as a quantitative rate. It means 'so much every so often.' Still, no attempt will be made to tell, How much every how often? We shall have to be content with distinguishing quantities qualitatively just as commonly we distinguish the quantitative differences of the several wavelengths of light by the qualitative differences of the spectrum. Thus we shall be able to speak of greater and less and approximately equal rhythms, to say that the economic rhythm of the United States in 1928 was notably greater than in 1932. But we shall not be able to say that the later rhythm was 49.302% of the earlier: for such a statement presupposes exact measurement, and we do not even consider devising a unit of measurement.

Though *DA* refers to an objective quantity, still it is not a mathematical symbol. For a mathematical symbol can refer only to what at least theoretically can be actually measured. But we offer no measuring rod, no delicate alloy containing in due proportions the different kinds of tons, barrels, miles, and hours of the universal rhythm. Accordingly, measurement is not possible, and *DA* cannot be a mathematical symbol. Not only is there no meaning to speaking of 49% of *DA*; there is not even a meaning in the application of ordinary algebra to *DA*, for instance, in applying the theory of quadratics or the rules of the integral calculus.

Finally, though ordinary algebra does not apply, it would be possible to devise a symbolic algebra. There is the symbolic algebra called logistic, that can be applied to any process of reasoning; still more precise an algebra could be applied to our process of reasoning because of its more numerous mathematical analogies. But that is by the way, for we have no intention to inflict a symbolic algebra on the reader. It will be far simpler and far clearer to point out mathematical analogies as they occur.

So much, then, for the precise meaning of *DA*. It is an aggregate rate or rhythm or volume of flow; it is a quantity, but quantitative differences are distinguished qualitatively as are colors; it is not a number nor an ordinary algebraic symbol, but it will be found to possess various mathematical analogies or parallels.

What has been said of *DA* will also be true of the similar terms to be introduced. The only difference is that, once money makes its appearance, it becomes possible to assign various units of measurement and so to approach still closer to the mathematical field.

6 The Dynamic Structure of the Basic Rhythm

The material structure of the basic rhythm is quite familiar. It consists in the series of production factors. Leather comes from the cattle farm to market. Dealers collect and redistribute the hides to tanners. The tanners pass them on to shoemakers, who transfer them, as shoes, through wholesalers and retailers to consumers. Each factor in this series is an economic rhythm, a set of routine performances, yielding so much every so often. But all the factors have to combine to give the ultimate product, so many pairs of shoes every so often.

Much more significant than this material structure of the basic rhythm is its dynamic structure. The latter consists in a number of different levels of production series: the series on the lowest level have a volume of flow that is proportionate to the volume of ultimate products; but the series on the next level have a volume that is proportionate to the acceleration of the lowest level; the series on the third level have a volume proportionate to the acceleration of the accelerator of the lowest; and so forth.

Thus, a ton of iron may be employed on any of three levels. Employed on the lowest level, one ton of iron yields one ton of automobile parts or farm implements. Employed on the second level, one ton of iron yields one ton of machinery for making automobiles or farm implements or what you please. Employed on the third level, one ton of iron yields one ton of machinery for making the machinery with which machines for making automobiles or other implements are made.

Here, plainly, each successive level accelerates the preceding. Another ton of iron on the lowest would give one or two or three more motorcars. But add a ton on the second level and one has, say, another machine for the making of motorcars; not for making one or two or three more, but for making an indefinite number more. Add a ton on the third level and the result is another machine tool, that is, a tool that makes the machines employed in factories; but the extra machine tool does not aim at merely one more factory, but at an indefinite number of factories; and each of the indefinite number of factories hopes to produce an indefinite number of motorcars.

In each case the ton contributes to a given flow: to the flow of motorcars; to the flow of factory equipment; to the flow of machine tools. But the three flows are related in an extraordinary fashion: equal increments in the different flows do not imply equal differences in the end result; an increment in the lowest level yields a proportionate increment on that level, a few more motorcars, for instance; an increment on the second level also yields a proportionate increment on that level, but its implication is an indefinite increment on the lowest level; similarly the third level stands in the same relation to the second as the second to the first.

This difference is the difference that exists between distance and velocity, velocity and acceleration. If you are traveling thirty miles per hour, how far are you going? The question admits no answer. You might be going three thousand miles or three hundred or thirty or three. Thirty miles per hour is indefinite with regard to distance; it simply tells how fast one intends to cover that distance. Again, if you press down the accelerator on your car one quarter of an inch, how fast are you going to go? The question has no answer. An acceleration does not mean, How fast? but, How much faster?

Now every form of economic activity is a set of routine performances. Each yields a 'so much every so often.' Thus every part of the basic rhythm is, in itself, of the nature of a velocity. But if we compare different rhythms to the ultimate product of goods or services, we find that some rhythms are proportionately related, others disproportionately. One may run a farm to produce so much foodstuffs per year, or one may clear land to produce so many farms per year. One may sail ships to transport so much trade per year, or one may build ships to supply so many more or so much bigger trading companies per year. One may operate an oil well to turn out so many barrels of oil per year, or one may drill oil wells to add each year so many more 'so many barrels per year.' Whether one runs a farm or clears land, whether one sails ships or builds them, whether one operates an oil well or drills new ones, in all cases the activity is a routine, a velocity, a 'so much every so often.' But though all are velocities, the function of all is not identical. The function of some is to be simply velocities; the function of others is to be velocities that accelerate other velocities. One set of rhythms constitute a series of production factors terminating in a flow of shoes; another set terminate in a flow of shoe factories. Each of the latter intends to produce a flow of shoes, so that a flow of shoe factories intends a flow of flows of shoes.

Of course, it is true that the higher the level, the lower the velocity of the rhythm. If one is going three hundred miles, one will not therefore travel at three hundred miles an hour. If one is traveling thirty miles an hour, one will not move the accelerator thirty miles but, rather, thirty millimeters. In fact, the whole point of a motorcar is that one can travel three hundred miles at thirty miles an hour merely by moving the accelerator thirty millimeters. Similarly, the whole point in clearing land is that one can have an annual produce indefinitely; the whole point in building ships is to carry trade not once but indefinitely; the whole point in having machines for making the machines with which ships are built is to equip an indefinite number of ship-building yards. Thus size is not the criterion of significance.

Further, it is important to observe not merely that dynamic structure is a matter of significance but also that the same material enterprise can have functionally different significances. It is all one to the manufacturer of motorcars whether he supplies private cars or lorries. But his activity in the former case is on the lowest level; his activity in the latter case is on the second or perhaps even the third level. Private cars are consumers' goods; lorries are producers' goods. Private cars add to the convenience and perhaps even the enjoyment of life; lorries speed up the processes of production and distribution. Each lorry is a flow of services; a flow of lorries from the factory is a flow of flows of services to consumers.

So much, then, for the structure of the basic rhythm. There is a material structure consisting in series of production factors. There is also a dynamic structure, a series of levels of production series, in which each successive level accelerates the preceding.

7 *DA, DA′, DA″*

The total aggregate of all rhythms at any instant has been represented by the symbol *DA*. We have now to consider two other aggregates, *DA′* and *DA″*, which together are equal to the total aggregate.

DA′ is the aggregate of *primary rhythms*, of the routines that are production factors on the lowest level. By definition, any increment in the primary rhythms tends to yield a proportionate increment in the field of ultimate products. If a family of Eskimos catch one more fish per week, they will tend to eat one more per week.

DA″ is the aggregate of *secondary rhythms*. Secondary rhythms include all that have an accelerating function with respect to the primary rhythms. In the abstract, it might be preferable to distinguish between the different levels of secondary rhythms, to give different names to simple accelerators, accelerators of accelerators, accelerators of accelerators of accelerators, and so on. It will be found, however, that the distinction has no significance beyond the first level: it is essential to distinguish between primary rhythms and their accelerators; but, in the main, there is no need to distinguish between different levels of acceleration. Accordingly, we lump them together to give an aggregate, *DA″*.

All that has been said on the nature of *DA* also applies to *DA′* and *DA″*. They are not averages but aggregates of particular rhythms. They are quantitative, so much every so often. They are not measured, but their magnitude is distinguished qualitatively the way wavelengths of light are distinguished. Nor as yet can they be measured, for as yet no unit of measurement has been assigned.

Clearly, there is some sense in which *DA equals DA′ plus DA″*. The latter two terms represent two parts of the first. But the equation is not arithmetic, for the terms are not numbers. It is not algebraic as yet, for the terms do not stand for numbers, though they will when a unit of measurement is assigned. At present the equation is true in the sense that the total quantity of steam in a cylinder is equal to the quantities on either side the piston when a method for measuring steam pressures has not been devised. For in both cases, the equality exists; but in neither is the equality strictly mathematical.

8 Functions of *DA′* and *DA″* in the Basic Rhythm

So far we have been laboring to make clear the distinction between *DA′* and *DA″*. We now have to consider what they do.

DA′, then, attends to final products, to goods and services that are wanted not for the sake of the economic process but for ulterior purposes. These are of two kinds: *ordinary* and *overhead*. Ordinary final products are the flows of food, clothing, shelter, amusement, ornaments, conveniences, utilities, and the like. Overhead final products pertain to the cultural superstructure of society: they are the flow of books, schools, hospitals, courts, prisons, armaments, public buildings, noncommercial roads and bridges, churches, and the like. Roughly, the two correspond to present ideas on 'public' and 'private' undertakings. However, it is well to avoid such a terminology as it begs the question on an important issue in political economy.

DA″ by definition attends to the acceleration of *DA′*. It does so in three ways.

First by *widening*, by increasing the number or size of the existing units of production.

Second by *deepening*, by increasing the efficiency of the existing units of production.

Widening increases ultimate production only by introducing a proportionate increase in the quantity of labor required. Deepening, on the contrary, makes an equal ultimate product the result of less labor.

Both widening and deepening may be subdivided. Widening may be on any of the accelerator levels: it may mean more factories producing shoes and motorcars; it may also mean more machine tools and construction firms producing and equipping more and more factories.

Similarly, deepening may accompany widening. In that case its effect is merely a shift in the distribution of labor. Men are employed less in existing undertakings, but new and bigger ones emerge to employ them. But there may be deepening without widening. In that case men are liberated from the field of economic activity: they may ascend to the field of cultural activities; or, in a poorly regulated society, they may descend to unemployment and the dole.

The two types of deepening may be distinguished as transitional and final. Transitional deepening is merely to make further widening possible. Final deepening gives man the benefit of leisure.

There is a third function of the secondary rhythms. Not only do they yield *effective* acceleration of the total rhythm by widening and deepening. They also yield the *theoretical* acceleration of maintaining *DA′* at any given rate of output. The accelerator in a motorcar is not at the zero position whenever the car is not going faster: it has to be pressed down some distance merely to maintain the acquired rate of speed. Similarly the secondary rhythms in *DA″* have to be kept at some 'so much every so often,' merely to keep the primary rhythms at their acquired rate. Accordingly, besides widening and deepening, there is also the work of maintenance, repair, and replacement; and this work constitutes a third function of *DA″*.

It will be convenient, subsequently, to refer to the *effective zero of DA″*. Theoretically, *DA″* is at zero when the secondary rhythms are zero, when they never produce anything. Effectively, *DA″* is at zero when, despite its very real 'so much every so often,' there is no increase in the rate either of *DA′* or of *DA″*.

As is plain, the greater the widening, the greater will be the subsequent rate at which maintenance, repair, and replacement will absorb the activities of *DA″*. This will be termed *a rise in the effective zero*. On the other hand, inasmuch as transitional or final deepening decreases the number of production units, reduces maintenance, and lengthens the life of instruments of production, to that extent it effects *a drop in the effective zero.*

9 Transformations of Dynamic Structure

Hitherto the dynamic structure of the basic rhythm has been studied in cross section. We have distinguished *DA′* and *DA″* and have enumerated their several functions. But there is nothing to prevent the several functions being simultaneous. Differences of time have now to be considered, and these consist in transformations of the dynamic structure.

There are two types of such transformation: transformations in the *content* of the economic rhythms; transformations in the *organization* of the rhythms. Differences in content may be illustrated by a comparison of primitive fruit gatherers, of hunters and fishers, of initial agriculture, of agriculture to which seaborne trade is added, and finally of the industrial transformation of crafts, trade, and even agriculture. On the other hand, differences in the human organization may be illustrated by developments in the idea of property, by the development from barter to money and from money to the supermoney of finance, by the development in economic theory determining different rules of conduct in medieval, in capitalist, in totalitarian society.

A study of these transformations will help integrate into a single view the ordinary and overhead functions of *DA′*, the widening, deepening, and maintenance effected by *DA″*.

In the first place, the process of transformation is a series of conditioned emergences. In making a coat of mail each new link has to be added to previous links, and similarly the successive stages of economic progress presuppose the previous stages and arise from them. Primitive hunting and fishing tribes add the small *DA″* of making weapons, nets, and boats to the still more primitive economy of fruit gatherers. Agriculture adds the ox and plough and the difficult idea of property to primitive gardening. To sustain agriculture a number of new crafts spring up; but the new crafts are themselves conditioned by the leisure which agriculture yields. An extension of the crafts will come only with large-scale commerce, nor can commerce at its centers, if not at the outposts, get along without the introduction of money. The new leisure created by the combination of agriculture, the mechanical arts, and commerce at once stimulates and makes possible the study of science; but science brings applied science, finance, and mass production to transform agriculture, trade, and the crafts and to unite men in an economic interdependence that stands at the opposite pole to the self-sufficiency of the primitive.

Each stage of the long process is ushered in by a new idea that has to overcome the interests vested in old ideas, that has to seek realization through the risks of enterprise, that can yield its full fruit only when adapted and modified by a thousand strokes of creative imagination. And every idea, once it has borne its fruit, has to reconcile itself to death. A new idea is new only when it first appears. It comes to man not as a possession forever but only as a transient servant; it has its day, glorious or foul; it lives for a period that is long or short according to its generality; but it may be succeeded by other alternatives, and in any case it will be transformed, perhaps beyond recognition, by higher generalizations. Thus the stagecoach disappeared before the train, the clipper ships gave way to steamers, domestic spinning wheels and looms were concentrated in power-driven factories, money changers yielded place to bill brokers, brokers to banks and financiers. Nor is it impossible that further developments in science should make small units self-sufficient on an ultramodern standard of living to eliminate commerce and industry, to transform agriculture into a superchemistry, to clear away finance and even money, to make economic solidarity a memory, and power over nature the only difference between high civilization and primitive gardening.

But we are not there yet. And for society to progress towards that or any other goal it must fulfil one condition. It cannot be a titanothore, a beast with a three-ton body and a ten-ounce brain. It must not direct its main effort to the ordinary final product of standard of living but to the overhead final product of cultural implements. It must not glory in its widening, in adding industry to industry, and feeding the soul of man with an abundant demand for labor. It must glory in its deepening, in the pure deepening that adds to aggregate leisure, to liberate many entirely and all increasingly to the field of cultural activities. It must not boast of science on the ground that science fills its belly. It must not glue its nose to the single track of this or that department. It must lift its eyes more and ever more to the more general and more difficult fields of speculation, for it is from them that it has to derive the delicate compound of unity and freedom in which alone progress can be born, struggle, and win through. Unity without freedom is easy: set up a dictator and give him a secret police. Freedom without unity is easy: let every weed glory in the sunshine of stupid adulation. But unity and freedom together, that is the problem. It demands discipline of mind and will: a keenness of apprehension that is not tied down to this or that provincial routine of familiar ideas nor yet has sunk to the jellyfish amorphism of scepticism; a vitality of response to situations that can acknowledge when the old game is done for, that can sacrifice the perquisites of past achievement, that can begin anew without bitterness, that can contribute without anticipating dividends to self-love and self-aggrandizement. The point is evident: a bureaucracy can imitate but it cannot create, for the spirit bloweth where it listeth, and all new ideas are ridiculous until the contrary is demonstrated by individual initiative, adapted by creative imagination, carried through by personal risk. Chaos can create, but it creates anything at all; it thinks of poison gas as well as anesthetics, and it uses both; it devises financial mechanisms that float brilliant booms and suffer incomprehensible slumps; it builds the wealth of cities and their slums; it inveighs against evil but it has to throw all civilization into the pot of experiment before it can discover whether another novelty will merit a blessing or a curse; it debauches the mind with a Babel of contradictions and leaves the will a prey to fantasy and fanaticism.

To conclude: all the functions of the primary and secondary rhythms are integral to the universal process. That consists not merely in widening, in deepening for more widening, and both for more cheap pleasures and amusements. The cultural overhead and the deepening that releases man to leisure and culture are also essential parts – parts too easily overlooked – in the world rhythm of economic transformations. Nor will it suffice to have some highest common factor of culture, to accept the physical sciences but not bother about their higher integration on the plea that that is too difficult, too obscure, too unsettled, too remote. That was titanothore's attitude to brain, and titanothore is extinct.

10 The Generalized Laws of Increasing and Decreasing Returns

The correlation of the different functions of *DA′* and *DA″* may be expressed again in terms of a generalization of two familiar economic laws: increasing returns and decreasing returns.

The simple statement of these laws regards particular enterprises at particular places and times. In England it was shown that additional blocks of land put under cultivation yielded a progressively smaller return. Later it was argued in America that the same procedure yielded progressively greater returns. Reconciliation of the antithesis was sought by saying that in an old country farming was subject to decreasing returns, but in a new country it enjoyed for a period the benefit of increasing returns. A generalization would give the proposition: the exploitation of any idea in any given field yields at first increasing and later decreasing returns.

Though perhaps this view can be defended, we are not concerned with it here but with a still more general issue. We redefine increasing and decreasing returns, taking as our point of reference the acceleration of the universal economic rhythm. Procedures that augment the possibility of further acceleration are said to yield increasing returns; on the other hand, procedures that reduce the possibility of further acceleration are said to yield decreasing returns.

In this sense all widening is subject to decreasing returns. For any widening increases the size and number of existing enterprises; accordingly it also increases the effort required for maintenance, repair, and replacement. This means that it raises the effective zero, and so transforms a greater proportion of *DA″* from the field of effective to the field of merely theoretical acceleration. Since under any given set of circumstances *DA″* is some finite magnitude, it follows that the higher the effective zero the less must be the possibility of further acceleration.

On the other hand, the progressive transformations of the dynamic structure yield increasing returns. An agricultural civilization is indefinitely better off than that of primitive gardeners or primitive hunters and fishers. Add commerce to agriculture and there follows a vast expansion of the mechanical arts. Transform commerce, the crafts, and agriculture by applied science and there emerges another vast expansion over the preceding situation.

The same point may be presented in a different way. Deepening, the increase in efficiency, reduces maintenance, repairs, and replacement; it lowers the effective zero, and so makes still further acceleration possible.

This possibility may be used by further widening. If so, there follow decreasing returns. However, if the widening terminates not in an ordinary but in an overhead expansion, that is, not in the improvement of material living conditions but in the improvement of the material fabric of culture, there should follow cultural development that prepares the way for another transformation of dynamic structure.

On the other hand, if the deepening is not used for further widening, then it must augment leisure. Such leisure may indeed be wasted, just as anything else can be wasted. But if it is properly employed, then it yields the cultural development that effects a new transformation.

In conclusion it is to be observed that, though transformation and deepening are the principles of increasing returns and widening the principle of decreasing returns, it does not follow that one is to be chosen and the other left. Man has to accept both. Transformation and deepening are the effective emergence of new ideas, but widening is their exploitation. If one merely exploits, then one stagnates. If one merely has new ideas without applying them in practice to the full, then the ideas are never tested properly and the possibility of further ideas that correct and develop their predecessors is eliminated. Essentially the universal rhythm of 'so much every so often' lies under the law of a higher rhythm. The higher rhythm is a succession of transformations followed by exploitations, or, if you prefer, a succession of exploitations that in the long run postulate a new transformation, a new beginning of greater potentialities.

11 The Cyclic Phases of the Universal Rhythm

We have now to express the higher rhythm in terms of the variables DA' and DA''. This expression consists in distinguishing four patterns in which the variables may combine and then in showing that the four patterns are apt to be the successive phases of a cycle.

First, both DA' and DA'' may be constant, with DA'' standing at the effective zero. This will be termed the *static phase.*

Second, DA'' may be increasing without increasing DA', which remains constant. This will be termed the *capitalist phase.*

Third, DA'' may be constant yet stand above the effective zero and devote its accelerating surplus to increasing ordinary DA'. This will be termed the *materialist phase.*

Fourth, DA'' may be constant yet stand above the effective zero and devote its accelerating surplus to increasing overhead DA'. This will be termed the *cultural phase.*

Before discussing the principle of the distinctions, it will be well to illustrate the various phases.

In the static phase, then, things tend to remain as they were. The economic process lies fallow: there is no increase in the means of production, or DA'' would not be constant at the effective zero; there is no increase in the ordinary DA' of standard of living or in the overhead DA' of cultural expansion. Though individuals may become richer by making other individuals poorer, there is no possibility of an aggregate increase of wealth, where wealth is understood dynamically.

On the other hand, the capitalist phase is the period of radical transformation. DA'' is increasing without increasing DA'. When Robinson Crusoe brought another field under cultivation, he augmented his work and his capital; but the task of clearing the field was greater than the subsequent task of cultivating it; and as long as he was engaged in the preliminary labor, he had more work but no more than the anticipation of a higher standard of living. Similarly, the industrial revolution of the nineteenth century transformed the means of production; the demand for labor was almost continuously strong; but only in the last quarter of the century did standard of living begin to rise generally. Again, in the Russian five-year plans a terrific impetus was given to industry, but the queues at the shops grew longer and more dismal. Essentially the capitalist phase is a period of enterprise and thrift: it exists, and its essential characters remain whether one is on a desert island, in the old England of Whigs and Tories, or in the brand new anticapitalist regime of the Soviets.

However, the capitalist phase is necessarily transitional. An increase in DA'' is meaningless unless it yields an increase in DA', for DA'' exists merely to accelerate DA'. Now DA' is ambiguous; it is either ordinary or overhead; either food, clothing, shelter, conveniences, utilities, amusements, and then it is ordinary; or else it is the material fabric of culture, the instruments of learning and the professions.

The materialist phase consists in DA'' turning its accelerating surplus from self-increase to the increase of ordinary DA'. Because there is a surplus, DA'' stands above the effective zero. Because this surplus is not directed to increasing DA'', it follows that DA'' remains constant. Because it is directed to increasing ordinary DA', it follows that the standard of living rises. The ideal of the period is 'a chicken in every pot.' Trade unions force wages upwards. Advertisements direct the masses to a new way of life. Intelligent executives favor both movements: they favor high wages to increase aggregate turnover; they employ advertisements to make their share of the aggregate as great as possible. For a portrait of the pure case of the materialist phase, it would be difficult to surpass our American scene. But the point to be grasped is that the movement is essentially simple: it is the same as Robinson's pleasure in eating or storing more corn after his second field had begun to produce; it is the same as the contemporary Russian phenomenon, at least according to the report that the queues at shops are not as long nor clothes so miserable as they were.

The cultural phase consists in DA'' turning its accelerating surplus to increasing overhead DA'. It is the medieval emergence of monasteries, churches, cathedrals, schools, universities, guild halls. It is the Renaissance patronage of the arts. It finds its modern exemplar, from the economic viewpoint, in the armament race and the economics of conducting a war. It is an age of new enterprise and of thrift without the anticipation of profits.

Certain more general remarks may now be made.

The capitalist, materialist, and cultural phases may very well be simultaneous. *DA″* may increase and at the same time increase both ordinary and overhead *DA′*. But, as is clear, this division of effort will yield less notable results in each of the three fields than would concentration on one alone. In any case, economic theory has to study the three separately, for their laws are distinct, and any real composition of the three is explained by a combination of the three sets of laws.

Because the phases are defined in terms of variations in *DA″* and *DA′*, it is widening that stands in the foreground of the descriptions. In point of fact, deepening will naturally accompany the three phases of expansion. In the capitalist and the materialist phases, deepening will redistribute labor to make more widening possible. In the cultural phase, it will liberate men from the economic to the cultural field, increasing the ministers of religion, the schools of the philosophers, the numbers of artists, scientists, professors, students, soldiers, sailors, airmen, and so forth according to the current conceptions and needs of the cultural field.

Though variations in population are connected intimately with economic phenomena, we prescind from them. There are two reasons for our procedure. First, economic structure and dynamism has a nature of its own no matter what the size of the population; our purpose is to study that general nature, for once it is known, the corrections to be introduced in view of increasing and decreasing population are easily made. Second, because this inquiry is concerned with general theory, it would only confuse issues to introduce incidental considerations of population movements; on the other hand, a satisfactory study of the general theory of population trends demands a separate work.

We have offered no contemporary illustration of the static phase, not because such illustration is not to hand, but because we do not care to anticipate our argument. The contemporary static phase is the slump, not because a static phase of itself is a slump, but because contemporary economic ideas work in practice only when there is an expansion. But proof of this position can be given only later.

Turning now to the definitions of the different phases, we note that they refer to pure cases, to first approximations. Just as the law of falling bodies asserts that the velocity is proportional to the time squared, so we assert the four phases. Both are true, but both demand special circumstances for exact verification to be possible. The law of falling bodies can be verified only in a vacuum. Similarly, as one moves from our abstract generality to concrete economic activity, new factors emerge, and the theory of their influence becomes a necessary complement to the general theory. We are content to affirm the necessity of such complementary theories without attempting to work them out. A scientific generalization is a big job, and there is no reason why one man should attempt to do it all by himself; on the other hand, there is no end of reasons why he should not make such an attempt. Not only can he not hope to succeed, but also the solution of democracy's problems cannot be anything but the creative effort of democracy itself, of widespread collaboration.

Finally, though the four phases ring the changes on *DA′* and *DA″* as constant or increasing, nothing is said of the possibility of either or both decreasing. The reason is not that such decrease is impossible. Economic decline is the continuous alternative to economic progress, to the three expansions or to the static phase when purely cultural activity expands without an increase of its material resources. But because decline is such a continuous alternative, it also is the result of blunders, and the number of possible blunders approaches infinity. For this reason we shall consider economic decline only incidentally to illustrate, without any pretense at complete enumeration, some of the possible blunders and their consequences.

12 The Pure Process

With the account of the cyclic phases our study of the pure economic process comes to an end. It will be well to summarize our conclusions.

There is, then, a universal economic rhythm, *DA*, a rate or volume of unmeasured, pulsating flow. This is composed of an indefinite number of particular rhythms, which materially combine in series of production factors, which dynamically constitute a set of levels with each successive level accelerating its immediate predecessor.

The aggregate of rhythms on the lowest level is termed *DA′*, the aggregate of primary rhythms. The aggregate of rhythms on higher levels is termed *DA″*, the aggregate of secondary rhythms. From the definitions it follows that *DA* equals *DA′* plus *DA″* at any given instant; also that *DA″* accelerates *DA′*; also that when *DA″* consists of many levels, one part of *DA″* accelerates the other.

DA″ effects either widening or deepening or mere maintenance. When it effects no more than maintenance, it is said to stand at the effective zero, to yield a merely theoretical acceleration.

DA′ effects either ordinary or overhead final products.

Deepening and overhead expansion combine to favor cultural development and produce the economic transformations which yield increasing returns. Widening and ordinary expansion combine to work out to the full the potentialities of any given stage of development; since such potentialities are limited, they yield decreasing returns. But there is no choice between increasing and decreasing returns; they constitute the essential ebb and flow of the universal rhythm.

Significantly different combinations of *DA′* and *DA″* as constant or increasing yield the four cyclic phases of this ebb and flow: a capitalist phase that transforms means of production; a materialist phase that exploits new ideas to raise the standard of living; a cultural phase that turns material well-being and power to equipping the development of cultural pursuits; a static phase in which the process lies fallow and noneconomic activity develops independently of material conditions.

This cycle never implies retrogression, a drop in the existing rates of the rhythms as a whole. It leaves them constant or it increases them. But this is not to deny economic decline, but merely to attribute it to blunders in universal management. As will be shown later, different economic theories are adapted to different phases of the cycle: medieval doctrine works well in the static or the cultural phase; classical doctrine suits the capitalist expansion, tolerates the materialist phase, but it needs illusory debts to run a war, and it cannot handle the static phase. However, a full consideration of this fact will be possible only when we have applied our general analysis of the pure process to the particular case of the exchange process. To that we now turn.

3

Transition to Exchange Economy

13 The Aim of This Chapter

In the preceding chapter certain points of perfect generality were isolated. The primary rhythms, *DA′*, began with the beginning of man, and they will last as long as economic activity. The secondary rhythms, *DA″*, began as soon as man began to fashion tools, and they will last as long as man has a body and a measure of intelligence. The succession of transformations and exploitations runs through the whole of economic history; not only are they evident in the past, but by the forces of progress and invention, by idealism and discontent, by the dialectic that makes every change a cause of further change, they will continue to be evident in the future.

It remains that this analysis of the pure process is, by itself, too general to be of any interest. There are other phenomena, almost as general, such as the use of markets and of money, on which nothing has been said. Obviously their place in the universal scheme has to be determined, for the economic process that sets us problems is not the pure process of primary and secondary rhythms but the exchange process in which the cyclic phases tend to become alternations of prosperity and misery.

However, because we aim at an economic generalization, it is impossible for us to differentiate the pure process by throwing in some particular exchange mechanism. It would be to desert our purpose if we at once proceeded to examine the influence of the basic rhythms in the medieval exchange process, or in the mercantilist exchange process, or in the nineteenth-century exchange process, or in that of the contemporary totalitarian states. Each of these is some special form of exchange economy, while an economic generalization must deal with the pure type.

But what is the pure type? That is a question that has not been answered, and so this chapter is devoted to answering it. We begin by defining the ideas of property, exchange, and value; we turn to the idea of the market and to the function of markets in the general process; we observe the limitations of this function and study the nature of money and finance. In this inquiry we are concerned, never with what happens to be or to have been, always with abstract generalities, with functional significance, with the pure laws and correlations that are the inevitable structure of an exchange process. The finance of London in 1830 or of New York in 1930 does not concern us, but only the pure purpose or function to be found in both those cases and, as well, in the activity of totalitarian technicians financing a five-year plan. Similarly we are concerned not with concrete details but with the abstract explanatory residue of significance that underlies property, exchange, value, markets, and money.

The result of the inquiry will be knowledge of the pure type of exchange economy. In the next chapter this pure type will be correlated with the pure process that has been studied already.

14 Property, Exchange, Value

The pure process does not move without every item standing in correlation with some particular person. There has to be someone to decide what is to be done, there has to be someone to do it, there has to be someone for whom it is done. The function of an exchange economy is to answer all these questions continuously, differences in exchange economies arise from different methods of determining these answers, and finally, different parts of exchange economies are concerned with different parts of the answers.

Property is a method of correlating particular persons with particular objects. The correlation is a right, that is, an autonomy vested in the person and exercised over the object. The object may be a person, as in slavery, a process, as in patents, or a thing. Again, the object may be considered in itself, as in the ownership of land, or in its use, as in the rental of land, or in its produce or fruits, as in dividends. In some form and to some extent property exists in every exchange process; but this fundamental idea varies from age to age, from country to country, as soon as one begins to inquire into its precise form and the limitations of its application. With such details we are not concerned.

Normally property rights are transferable, and the transfer is termed a contract. Of these transfers, the most important for us is the exchange. It is a bilateral contract, one entered upon by two parties. It is an onerous bilateral contract, for it imposes on both parties the obligation to surrender rights. Briefly, an exchange is a mutual transfer of property rights.

The exchange is effected by a coincidence of two decisions. If two parties decide to exchange, the exchange takes place. Otherwise it does not.

What causes the coincidence of decisions to exchange? Undoubtedly there are causes, but the causes are infinite. There is the whole realm of truth and the far larger realm of possible error. There is the stimulus of desire and of fear, of ambition and of passion, of temperament and of sentiment. At any given time or place any of these may be more prominent: desire plays a large role in free countries, and fear plays a large role in others; ambition presses forward the new citizens of new lands, and a sullen hopelessness presses further down the depressed classes of senile states; nationalist sentiment dominates with protection, and phlegmatic individualism with free trade. But neither the folklore of popular beliefs, the mythologies of antiquated science, nor the psychology of national and ethnic groups is of concern to any economic science, and least of all to an economic generalization. Accordingly, we dismiss the causes of decisions to exchange, with one exception.

That exception is obvious. Economic science itself has to exert an influence on decisions to exchange. Otherwise it cannot be an applied science in a democracy, but only the applied science of a national laboratory in which a dictator presides, commissars rule, and a secret police ensures laboratory conditions. However, the manner and mode of this influence will arise for consideration only after the content of economic science has been determined.

So much for the causes of decisions to exchange. The next point is the effect of an exchange, namely, the exchange value.

It is important to grasp that the exchange value is not an antecedent but a consequent of decisions to exchange. Accordingly, we elaborate this notion, treating in succession the general ideal of value and its different species: absolute value, relative value, economic value, and exchange value.

The general idea of value coincides with the idea of the good, of excellence.

This excellence may pertain to an object in itself, rise from it in isolation from all other things, and remain despite utter uselessness. Such is the *absolute value* of truth, of noble and heroic deeds, of the flower in the crannied wall.[1]

On the other hand, excellence may belong to an object in its relativity, its utility, its aptitude to excel in serving ulterior purposes. These *relative values* may be relative to any ulterior purpose, and so only some of them are relative to man.

Now among human relative values it is possible to distinguish varying degrees of abundance and scarcity; further, this abundance or scarcity may be understood in a general way, as when we say that air is abundant and radium scarce, or it may be referred to particular individuals, as when wheat is abundant in the grain elevators of Canada and scarce in war-torn Europe.

Complementary to this scale of scarcity relative to individuals there is another scale of economic activity endeavoring differently in different cases to reduce that scarcity and create abundance. When, then, an object is relatively scarce and men make an effort to reduce its scarcity, it becomes an *economic value.* Further, the economic value may be conceived as proportionate to the effort made: when there is no effort at all, the economic value is zero; when the effort is small, the value is small; when the effort is great, the value is great. Thus no effort is made to supply men with air, and so the economic value is zero; slight effort is made to improve the homes of the poor, and the economic value of such improvement is slight; vast efforts are made to supply armaments, and so their economic value is great.

Exchange value differs from economic value in two respects. First, an economic value relates an object to human effort, but an exchange value relates objects among themselves. Second, an economic value results from any decision to strive for the object, but an exchange value may be quite indifferent to the amount of striving, and in any case it emerges only from a coincidence of decisions to exchange.

For example, a horse or a team of oxen are economic values when men make the effort necessary to breed, raise, feed, and train them. But exchange value appears only when the owner of the horse and the owner

1 There is an obvious reference here to Tennyson's six-line poem of 1869, 'Flower in the Crannied Wall.' The poem is worth quoting here because of its intimation of the absolute value of which Lonergan writes: 'Flower in the crannied wall, / I pluck you out of the crannies, / I hold you here, root and all, in my hand, / Little flower – but if I could understand / What you are, root and all, and all in all, / I should know what God and man is.'

of the oxen decide to exchange. Further, this exchange value is not a matter of the efforts, desires, sentiments, ambitions, or hopes of the traders, though all of these may have entered into their decisions; the exchange value itself is simply the ratio in which the exchange is made; for instance, one horse is worth two oxen.

It may help to clarify the issue if one distinguishes between normative, probable, and actual exchange values. One may say, 'A horse is worth two oxen,' and mean that a buyer *ought* to give me two oxen for my horse, when in point of fact he will give me no more than one. Again, one may say, 'A horse is worth two oxen,' and mean that I am *likely* to get two oxen for my horse if I attempt that exchange. The first of these statements is with regard to a *normative* exchange value, and pertains to the science of ethics. The second of the statements is a *probable* exchange value, and it pertains to the art of forecasting. But the exchange value that concerns us is *actual* exchange value, and it emerges only subsequently to actual exchanges.

To conclude, an (actual) exchange value is the ratio or proportion in which different categories of property exchange.

15 Markets

A market is a place where traders meet in numbers, and this meeting *tends* to impose a twofold uniformity on exchange values. First, it tends to make uniform the ratios in which different categories exchange at any instant. Second, it tends to adjust these ratios to variations in supply and demand. The basis of these tendencies is as follows.

Both individual traders on any particular market and the different groups of traders that make up the several markets of the world are under the dire necessity of competing. They are all out to do business, and, *other things being equal,* no trader and no market will do much business unless its terms are as fair as the terms offered by the next trader or the next market. Now this does not merely mean that no trader and no market can succeed by consistently offering less than the others; it also means that if anyone succeeds in consistently offering more, then the others are as good as eliminated. But if there can be neither less nor more, there must be uniformity; not indeed the uniformity of suburban houses built from the same blueprint, but the uniformity of tendency arising from the pressure of competition; nor again a uniformity that disregards differences, but a uniformity that takes differences into account.

Thus a market tends to generalize the particular exchange values described in the preceding section. By setting up an interaction between large numbers of decisions to exchange, it tends to make all coincide in a common exchange ratio for each pair of categories of goods or services.

But not only is the set of exchange ratios the integration of a large number of decisions to exchange. It also integrates the still larger number of decisions not to exchange. For when people decide not to exchange, they do not necessarily mean they have no desire to exchange; they may mean that they do not wish to exchange at that ratio, yet would exchange were the ratio more favorable. The role played by these negative decisions appears as soon as one considers the other general tendency of a market, to settle on an exchange ratio at which supply and demand equate.

This tendency may be considered as the resultant of three factors. First (A), whenever any individual is determined to sell or buy a given category of goods, then he will be ready to offer more than competitors. Second (B), whenever supply fails to equate with demand, there will be a significant number ready to offer more or take less; if supply is excessive, sellers will be faced with the burden of unsold goods or services; if supply is deficient, buyers will be faced with privation. Third (C), a shift in the exchange ratio will tend to correct the excess or defect of supply; for that excess or defect is relative to the number of buyers, and a change in the ratio will effect a reconsideration of previous decisions; a change downwards will convert negative decisions into positive, to increase demand; a change upwards will convert positive decisions to negative, to decrease demand. From the second factor (B), it follows that disequilibrium of supply and demand tends to change the ratios of exchange values. From the third factor (C), it follows that change in the ratio tends to increase or decrease demand. Since the disequilibrium continues until demand equates with supply, it follows that the exchange ratios tend to vary till demand equates with supply.

16 Markets and the Exchange Economy

Markets have many other tendencies besides those described in the previous section. They tend to wholesale deception, to fraud, to sharp practice, to ruthlessness; they tend to exploit the snobbery of the rich, the ignorance of the masses, the impotence of the poor, the passions of human nature, the gullibility of the world's endless supply of fools. If we have said nothing of these tendencies, it has been only because we are concerned with the tendencies that stand in significant relationship with the mechanism of an exchange economy.

An exchange economy is an attempt to give a continuously satisfactory answer to the continuously shifting question, *Who,* among millions of persons, is to perform *which,* among millions of tasks, in return for *what,* among millions of possible rewards?

The answer it offers is as follows.

First, it distinguishes what people do or make for themselves, what they do for others expecting little or no return, and what they do for others expecting a proportionate remuneration. It decides that the first two can take care of themselves, and it concentrates its efforts on the third.

Second, it directs the aggregate of goods, services, and property that are for others, yet expect a proportionate return, to a pyramid of local, regional, national, and world markets of various kinds.

Third, it leaves it to the markets to control contributions and to apportion rewards.

The excellence of this solution is palpable. It leaves each one free to do as he pleases; but if what pleases him is not what others want, then demand will be zero and his reward zero. It encourages inventiveness and initiative in anticipating others' wants; for such anticipations are met with a strong demand and a high reward. It encourages each one to do his best, for excellence in performance creates favorable preferences or yields the efficiency which, when prices are uniform, produces a differential rent. It places the risks of production on producers, but it leaves control of production ultimately to the integration of consumers' decisions to exchange or not exchange. It apportions the measure of reward each is to receive by the integration of individual decisions, but it leaves the precise reward each receives to his individual choice.

The excellence of the exchange solution becomes even more evident when contrasted with the defects of a bureaucratic solution. The bureaucrat is under no pressure to anticipate precisely what people will want and to give it to them in the precise measure that they want it; he gives them what he thinks good for them, and he gives it in the measure he finds possible or convenient; nor can he do otherwise, for the brains of a bureaucracy are not equal to the task of thinking of everything; only the brains of all men together can even approximate to that. But further, even could the bureaucrat meet this issue, he could not do so continuously, for it is continuously changing; he has to work with plans, and every new demand as well as every new invention tends to upset the old plans and make a new beginning necessary; when a limited liability company has served its day, it goes to the bankruptcy court; but when bureaucrats take over power, they intend to stay. Finally, even if the bureaucrat could meet both these problems, he could not give them a human solution; men learn by experience; you can teach them to stay on one job by letting them roam about trying others; you can let them learn by experience that their abilities are not quite so great as they fancy; but when the pressure of terrorism is needed to oil the wheels of enterprise, then the immediate effect is hatred and the ultimate effect is either an explosion or else a servile degeneracy.

To conclude, the exchange solution is a dynamic equilibrium resting on the equilibria of the markets. Each producer produces not for himself but for others; he wants not his own products but a share in the products of others; and all others are in exactly the same boat. Thus every product of the exchange economy must mate through exchange with some other product, and the ratio in which the two mate is the exchange value. The generality of this equilibrium makes it indifferent to endless complexity and endless change; for it stands on a level above all particular products and all particular modes of production. While these multiply and vary indefinitely, the general equilibrium of the exchange process continues to answer with precision the complex question, *Who*, among millions of persons, does *what*, among millions of tasks, in return for *which*, among millions of rewards? Nor is the dynamic solution unaccompanied by a continuous stimulus to better efforts and more delicate ingenuity. For the uniformity of prices means that the least efficient of those actually producing will at least subsist, while every step above minimum efficiency yields a proportionately greater return.

17 Limitations of Exchange Economy

Progress cannot wear blinkers; so, if we have stressed the excellence of exchange economy, we must also be at pains to determine its defects.

A fundamental defect lies in the innocent first step of the solution, in which those who are willing to contribute for little or no return are brushed aside, to make the exchange system an exclusive club for businessmen.

With the psychological effects of this arbitrary procedure we are quite familiar. It produces the split personality of the businessman in his office and the respected citizen in his home. It turns out the pure types of the uplift worker who cannot get down to business, and of the common cynic who takes a business view of larger issues. But these psychological aberrations are but symptoms of a deeper malady.

Men are unequal in ability and in opportunity. Accordingly, if the productive processes are to yield their maximum of human satisfactions, then it is necessary that the less fortunate be able to demand more than they can supply, while the more fortunate supply more than they demand. Of itself, the productive process can give the fortunate more than they desire; moreover, it would like to treat all with a generous hand, for only by such generosity can it attain its maximum. But the delicate balancing of supply and demand necessarily limits each successive group of less fortunate men to the lower standard of living that their abilities and opportunities can command in the market.

Against this artificial nemesis humanitarian idealism revolts. A rigidly egalitarian system belongs to a perfectly egalitarian world; a world in which men are, in fact, unequal must find a different system. What system? If the idealism is sentiment without intelligence, it is as likely as not to mate with the underground cynicism of the revolutionaries to foist upon us a dictatorship of the proletariat in which the proletariat does not dictate, a dictatorship of the *Herrenvolk* in which the *Volk* obeys the *Führer.* But if that idealism can be brought to learn the discipline of logic and of scientific reflection, then it will impose a generalization of the exchange economy.

To determine the nature of such a generalization is the aim of this inquiry; but at once this at least is evident. The vast forces of human benevolence can no longer be left to tumble down the Niagara of fine sentiments and noble dreams. They have to be assigned a function and harnessed within the exchange system, for in no other way can that system shake off its fictitious fetters to move consistently towards its maximum.

There remains a further question, namely, Are there other limitations of exchange economy besides this inability to attain the maximum of satisfactions? Obviously there are, else the solution would not lie in generalization, in an integral transformation of the whole previous position. But I do not think there is any need to flog a whole row of dead horses; a flick at a particularly nauseating one is enough; indeed a wink is as good as a nod. Still, one point does deserve attention, and it is this. A generalization will postulate a transformation not only of the old guard and its abuses but also of the reformers and their reforms; it will move to a higher synthesis that eliminates at a stroke both the problem of wages and the complementary problem of trade unions; it will attack at once both the neglect of economic education and the blare of advertisements leading the economically uneducated by the nose; it will give new hope and vigor to local life, and it will undermine the opportunity for peculation corrupting central governments and party politics; it will retire the brain trust but it will make the practical economist as familiar a professional figure as the doctor, the lawyer, or the engineer; it will find a new basis both for finance and for foreign trade. The task will be vast, so vast that only the creative imagination of all individuals in all democracies will be able to construct at once the full conception and the full realization of the new order.

As I remarked in the opening chapter, the old political economists were the creative thinkers of the nineteenth century. Now I may add that a generalization of their thought involves a re-creation of all they dominated and a remodeling of all they influenced. My argument is the nineteenth century challenging the twentieth to surpass the old achievement by equaling the old inventiveness. It is a challenge that cannot be evaded, but no less is it a challenge that cannot be taken lightly. The nineteenth century did do something.

18 Money

If barter is replaced by the divided exchange, selling here and buying there, the economic process can attain a vastly greater magnitude and intricacy. But the divided exchange postulates a dummy that will bridge the intervals, short or long, between contributing to the process and sharing in its products. Further, if this dummy is to work satisfactorily, if it is to bridge the intervals fairly and adequately, then it must fulfil certain conditions.

The first of these is divisibility, so that any ratio of exchange decided by the market can be represented by a quantity of the dummy. Incidentally, the measure of such a quantity is termed a price.

The second condition is homogeneity, so that equal quantities will be equally acceptable; otherwise everyone will wish to sell for the better dummies and buy with the poorer ones; bad money drives out good. On the other hand, when homogeneity does not exist formally, it may be had virtually by discounting; thus a bill of exchange is not as good as ready cash, but the existence of discounting houses makes it the equivalent of cash. For this reason, the bill of exchange is part of the dummy; and the same holds for any systematic credit.

The third condition is that the dummy must be constant in exchange value, so that equal quantities continue to exchange, in the general case, for equal quantities of goods or services. The alternative to constant value in the dummy is the alternative of inflation and deflation. Of these famous twins, inflation swindles those with cash to enrich those with property or debts, while deflation swindles those with property or debts to enrich those with cash; in addition to the swindle each of the twins has his own way of torturing the dynamic flows; deflation gives producers a steady stream of losses; inflation yields a steady stream of gains to give production a drug-like stimulus.

The fourth condition is that the dummy be universally acceptable within a given area, so that anyone willing to exchange will be willing to surrender property, goods, or services for the dummy. Whether this fourth condition is distinct from the other three has been a matter of dispute. If one holds it to be distinct, then gold or some such commodity must always stand in some real correlation with the dummy; and if such real correlation is removed without affecting general acceptability, that is only because people have not enough brains to see that they are being fooled. On the other hand, if one holds the fourth condition not to be distinct from the other three, then any real correlation of the dummy with gold is superfluous, and the sole function of nominal correlations is to inspire confidence in those who have not enough brains to grasp that the other three conditions are sufficient.

The real issue is the value of the dummy, and especially the constancy of its exchange value.

The relative value of the dummy is its usefulness. It makes possible the vast expansion of the exchange process which barter could not effect.

The scarcity of the dummy is attended to by the technicians or the technical rules governing its issuance. Whether it issues from the printing press or from the credit structure makes no difference.

The economic value lies in human effort against this scarcity. When the economic process has not expanded beyond the barter stage, this economic value would be zero. On the other hand, once the process has expanded beyond the barter stage, it is only by liquidating civilization that one can return to barter; in consequence, the dummy becomes a necessity, and its economic value is the general form of all economic values; for, inasmuch as men strive for any economic end, they strive for the dummy which is the means to the end.

Finally, exchange value is the *ratio* or proportion in which are exchanged the different categories of objects for which men strive because they are useful and scarce. Thus, if a horse is worth a team of oxen, then a team of oxen is worth a horse; and similarly, if a pair of gloves is worth a dollar, then a dollar is worth a pair of gloves. However, if a horse comes to be worth three oxen or a pair of gloves a dollar and a half, the question arises, Has the value of horses risen or the value of oxen dropped? Has the value of gloves risen or the value of dollars dropped? To answer this question it is necessary to examine other exchange ratios. If it is found that, while the price of gloves rose, the price of everything else remained pretty much the same, then it is the gloves and not the dollars that have changed in value. On the other hand, if the rise in the price of gloves was accompanied by a proportionate rise in the price of everything else, then it was not everything else but only the dollars that changed in value.

So much for what is meant by the value of the dummy and the constancy of its value. It is now necessary to state the necessary and sufficient condition of constancy or variation in the exchange value of the dummy.

To this end we compare the two flows of the circulation: the real flow of property, goods, and services, and the dummy flow being given and taken in exchange for the real flow. At any instant the two flows must be equal in exchange value, otherwise the exchanges would not be taking place. The exchange value of the aggregate of the real flow is the aggregate of the dummy flow taken in exchange; the exchange value of the aggregate of the dummy flow is the aggregate of the real flow given in exchange. We merely state a truism.

But while it is true that the two flows must be equal in exchange value at any instant, it does not follow that the exchange value of one instant will be the exchange value of another. If the dummy flow increases or decreases without a proportionate increase or decrease in the real flow, then there is a shift in the ratio or proportion in which the dummy exchanges for property, goods, or services. On the other hand, if the dummy flow and the real flow vary in the same direction and to the same extent, then the ratio or proportion in which the exchanges occur remains the same. But this ratio or proportion is precisely what is meant by exchange value, when different instants or cases are compared. Accordingly, the necessary and sufficient condition of constant value in the dummy lies in its concomitant variation with the real flow.

More briefly, if there is concomitance between the two flows, then the proportion in which dummies and goods exchange remains the same. If there is a lack of concomitance, then this proportion changes. But exchange value is proportion. Therefore, the concomitance of the two flows is the condition of constant exchange value.

Certain points are to be observed. The condition of constant value says nothing about the quantity of dummies in existence; it speaks solely of their volume of flow; and equal volumes of flow can be had by a small quantity of dummies changing hands frequently, or a large quantity rarely. Next, the condition of constant value refers to any dummy whatever: it does not speak of gold to the exclusion of currency tokens, of currency tokens to the exclusion of bank credits, of bank credits to the exclusion of bills of exchange; no matter what is used to bridge the interval between selling and buying, it is a dummy; and it is with respect to the volume of flow of such dummies in the aggregate that the condition of constant value holds.

We may now briefly consider the question of gold, and we do so by considering a number of objections against the view that gold is objectively superfluous.

First, there is an argument from analogy. Gambling may proceed by laying down cash as in dicing, by using chips as in poker, by keeping score as in bridge. Similarly, the exchange process may use the cash of gold, the chips of currency tokens, or the scorecard of a banker's ledger. But the poker would not be poker if the chips were never cashed, and the bridge would be an unexciting pastime if the score were never paid. Similarly, an exchange process that had currency tokens and bank credits but no gold would be a fake.

The answer is that it would be a fake if gold were the sole objective of economic activity. But if one could buy anything with poker chips or on the credit of one's bridge score, then there would be no need to cash the chips or pay the score. Similarly, if one can buy anything with currency tokens or with bank credit, then the economic process that has no gold is not a fake; on the contrary, the fake has been removed and people are made to face the facts.

Second, it may be urged that money has two functions; it is not merely a medium of exchange but also a means of storing wealth. A monetary system without gold may be all right as a medium of exchange, but it is 'obviously unsound' as a means of storing wealth.

The answer is that either the hoarder proposes to use his wealth some day or else he proposes never to use it. In the latter case, it makes no difference what he stores. In the former, then any dummy of constant value will give him just as much for his store as will gold. Thus the first premise is nonsense: money as a means of storing wealth is simply money as a medium of exchange bridging a long interval between selling and buying.

If money retains a constant value over the long interval, then the bridging is done equitably and money has all the soundness that reason can demand.

Third, it will be urged that, unless gold is kept at the basis of the monetary system,. there is no ground to expect a succession of government officials and bankers to maintain constant value over any long interval.

The answer is that as long as the officials exercise discretionary powers, the objection is valid. The new political economy will have to find a generalization to replace the automatic method of old political economy by some new automatic method. What that generalization is cannot at present be discussed.

19 Finance

The necessity of finance is twofold. First there is the fact that the people with the money have not the brains to use it, while the people with the brains have not the money to use; thus finance transfers money from inoperative to dynamic positions in the exchange system. Second there is the fact that the economic process runs through a series of transformations and exploitations; the real flow varies, and the dummy flow has to vary concomitantly or else suffer inflation or deflation; moveover, the real flow attains volumes that greatly exceed previous maxima, and these peaks can be scaled only if the dummy has a notable elasticity.

By finance we understand the effort made to solve these problems. For the present, we may be content with that definition, for further discussion becomes possible only after we have analyzed the general exchange process.

4

Outline of the Mechanical Structure of the Exchange Process

20 The Exchange Process

If one directs the productive rhythms of chapter 2 to the markets defined in chapter 3, the result is an exchange process. Our immediate task is to work out the correlations that exist between the velocity and accelerator rhythms of production and the corresponding rhythms of income and expenditure. The set of such correlations constitutes a mechanical structure, a pattern of laws that stand to economic activity as the laws of mechanics to buildings and machines.

Two points are to be observed.

First, the combination of production and exchange limits the validity of our conclusions to instances in which production is governed by exchange. It is true, I believe, that the conclusions of the present chapter hold even when production is governed politically as under the Soviets; but this will become less and less true as the mechanical structure comes to be studied in greater detail.

Second, our inquiry differs radically from traditional economics, in which the ultimate premises are not production and exchange but rather exchange and self-interest, or later, exchange and a vaguely defined psychological situation. Our aim is to prescind from human psychology that, in the first place, we may define the objective situation with which man has to deal, and, in the second place, define the psychological attitude that has to be adopted if man is to deal successfully with economic problems. Thus something of a Copernican revolution is attempted: instead of taking man as he is or as he may be thought to be and from that deducing what economic phenomena are going to be, we take the exchange process in its greatest generality and attempt to deduce the human adaptations necessary for survival.

A discussion of this viewpoint leads so rapidly to philosophic considerations that here we must be content merely to state it.

21 The Basic Equation

Let *DA* be any rhythm of economic activity or any aggregate of such rhythms, a 'so much every so often' that is measured in exchange units, that is, in money.

Now *DA* will vary either because of variation in the rate at which goods or services are supplied or because of variation in the price level at which they sell. If *DQ* denotes the rate and *P* the price level, then

$$DA = P.DQ \tag{1}$$

Further, the sale will have, in every instance, two aspects: it will be expenditure to a buyer and income to a seller. Let, then, *DE* denote the corresponding rhythm of expenditures and *DI* the corresponding rhythm of incomes. Then

$$DA = P.DQ = DE = DI \tag{2}$$

where the terms refer to any rhythm or any aggregate of rhythms which are measured in any uniform manner with respect to each of the four terms.

This basic equation is no more than a truism. It states from four different viewpoints one and the same thing, for one and the same thing is at once (1) the value of production, (2) the multiplication of quantity by price, (3) an expenditure, and (4) an income, according as it is considered (1) in itself, (2) in its components, (3) relative to buyers, and (4) relative to sellers.

21bis Transitional, Final, and Redistributional Markets

The basic equation is a pure theorem. To give it a concrete meaning, it must be applied to some definite field or market or type of markets. Accordingly we distinguish transitional, final, and redistributional markets.

Now there exist series of markets in which the volume of activity in any one *varies in direct proportion* with the volume of activity of others in the same series. For instance, there is such variation in the sale of shoes by retailers, by wholesalers, by shoemakers, in the sale of leather by tanners and that of hides by cattle farmers. In any such series we term the last a *final market* and all the others *transitional markets.*

We shall not bother about the transitional markets, for their function is simply to distribute the aggregate receipts of the final market among the antecedent production factors. The consumer pays all the factors by paying the retailer in the final market.

However, two types of final market have to be distinguished. There is the final market for products of *DA′* and the final market for products of *DA″*. For clearly, secondary activity, *DA″*, is not transitional to primary activity, *DA′*: though there is a concomitant variation connecting the two, this concomitance is not a direct proportion but rather the concomitance of a velocity with its accelerator. Further, though the investor purchasing the products of *DA″* earnestly hopes that the consumer will pay in the long run, still, here and now, it is the investor and not the consumer who is paying. Further, even when the consumer will be paying, and it is not certain that he will, then *DA″* will go out of business unless there are further investors.

Thus there is a *primary final market* and a *secondary final market,* and these two include all the activity of the transitional markets of both *DA′* and *DA″*. However, neither is final in an absolute sense, for there are further sales even after the products have been sold on the final markets. Thus, the stock market redistributes investments, the secondhand trade redistributes liquidated undertakings and durable primary products, and the real estate business redistributes the ownership of land, which as the 'indestructible properties of the soil' was never even produced and much less sold on either the primary or the secondary final market.

Now these redistributional markets have no obvious concomitant variation with either primary or secondary activity. Redistributional activity is a function of the rapidity with which owners change their minds. On the other hand, the primary and the secondary aggregate rhythms are essentially productive rhythms and only incidentally a matter of change of ownership. *DA′* and *DA″* exist even when there are no exchanges, as on Robinson Crusoe's island, and even when the idea of property loses its economic significance, as in the U.S.S.R. But redistibutional activity, though it has its political equivalents in purges, deportations, confiscations, is in itself essentially an exchange phenomenon.

It follows, then, that redistributional activity is not included in the *DA′* and *DA″* of the productive rhythms. Accordingly, to denote its volume, its 'so much every so often,' a new symbol, *DA**, has to be introduced.

Thus the aggregate economic rhythm, already denoted by *DA*, comes to equal not merely the sum of *DA′* and *DA″*, but the sum of *DA**, *DA′*, and *DA″*. Further, *DA′* and *DA″* may be measured by the volume of activity at their final markets.

22 Application of the Basic Equation

The basic equation

$$DA = P.DQ = DE = DI \tag{2}$$

was worked out as true of any rhythm or any aggregate of rhythms. If, then, *DA** measures the aggregate of redistributional activity measured in exchange units over some interval, if *DA′* measures the aggregate of sales at the primary final market in a similar interval, and *DA″* measures the aggregate of sales at the secondary final market over the same time period, then from the basic equation we have it that

$$DA^* = P^*DQ^* = DE^* = DI^* \tag{3}$$

$$DA' = P'DQ' = DE' = DI' \tag{4}$$

$$DA'' = P''DQ'' = DE'' = DI'' \tag{5}$$

where each of the new terms is defined by the definitions of the different markets and by the meaning of the basic equation.

Thus the value in monetary units of aggregate redistributional activity over some interval, *DA**, is some quantity of property, *DQ**, sold at some price level, *P**, and constituting expenditure to some individuals to the amount *DE** and receipts to other individuals to the amount *DI**.

Similarly, the volume of primary products, *DQ′*, selling at the price level *P′*, is worth *DA′*. This rate of sale calls for a rate of expenditure, *DE′*, and generates a rate of income, *DI′*.

Similarly, the volume of secondary products, DQ'', selling at the price level P'', is worth DA''. This rate of sale calls for a rate of expenditure, DE'', and generates a rate of income, DI''.

Accordingly, we may speak of the values DA^*, DA', DA'', the quantitative rates DQ^*, DQ', DQ'', the price levels P^*, P', P'', the expenditure rates DE^*, DE', DE'', and the income rates DI^*, DI', DI'', of the redistributional market, the primary final market, and the secondary final market.

Similarly, we shall speak of the *redistributional field* to which pertains equation (3), of the *primary circuit* of equation (4), and of the *secondary circuit* of equation (5).

The rest of this chapter will be devoted to a study of the correlations of the primary and secondary circuits. Consideration of the redistributional field is held over to chapter 5.

23 The Crossover of the Primary and Secondary Circuits

DI' denotes the income derived from the sale of primary products, and DI'' the income derived from the sale of secondary products.

Now, in the main, it is these two flows of income that have to maintain the two rates of expenditure DE' and DE'', and, while it would be very simple if DI' maintained DE' and DI'' maintained DE'', it is quite easy to see that such is not the case.

In the first place, a notable proportion of DI'' is normally spent at the primary final market. Wage earners in the secondary field get their share of DI'' but they spend it as DE' to obtain food, clothing, shelter, amusement, etc. Owners spend part of their dividends in similar fashion. Taxes take their toll of DI'' and are disbursed for the overhead products of the primary final market.

On the other hand, some of DI' and of DI'' regularly goes to DE'', for every industrial undertaking has its costs of maintenance, repairs, and replacements, and these costs, according to the definitions of chapter 2, are purchases at the secondary final market. Further, there are at times net profits beyond what owners spend on themselves or in taxes or for depreciation, and normally these net profits derived from both DI' and DI'' move to DE'' to purchase the investments widening and deepening the industrial structure.

Thus there exists a crossover of the income rhythms. Not all of DI' is spent as DE' but part goes to DE''. Not all of DI'' is spent as DE'' but part goes to DE'.

24 Provisional Theorem of Continuity[1]

If the terms DA', DA'', P', P'', DQ', DQ'', DE', DE'', DI', DI'' refer to any given instant, and the same terms underlined refer to the next instant or turnover of the exchange process, the basic equations are duplicated with

$$DA' = P'DQ' = DE' = DI'$$

$$\underline{DA'} = \underline{P'DQ'} = \underline{DE'} = \underline{DI'}$$

and

$$DA'' = P''DQ'' = DE'' = DI''$$

$$\underline{DA''} = \underline{P''DQ''} = \underline{DE''} = \underline{DI''}$$

where $\underline{DA'}$ may be greater than, equal to, or less than DA', and $\underline{DA''}$ may be greater than, equal to, or less than DA''.

Now, if continuity is defined by equality of sales at the final markets in successive instants or turnovers, then the necessary and sufficient condition of continuity is that

$$DA' = \underline{DA'}$$

and

$$DA'' = \underline{DA''}$$

Leaving to the next chapter the full statement of this condition of continuity, we here examine it in its simplest if not its sole form.

Let primary income, DI', divide into two parts, so that $G'DI'$ moves to secondary expenditure, $\underline{DE''}$, and $(1 - G')DI'$ moves to primary expendi-

1 In Part One there is an explicit attention to lags that is absent in Part Three. Compare, for instance, the diagrams of pp. 64 and 65 with that of p. 258. Nor does lag analysis enter explicitly into any of the later diagrams. (My interpretation on this point differs from that presented in the appendix to CWL 15.) However, as the text on p. 273 makes evident, lags are still in the analysis. Detailed lag analyses will add complexities to Lonergan's elementary presentation, for example, in the treatment of the dynamics of price spreads; see the note to equation (19) of p. 77.

ture, $\underline{DE}'$. Similarly, let secondary income divide into two parts, so that $G''DI''$ goes to $\underline{DE}'$ and $(1 - G'')$ goes to $\underline{DE}''$. Then

$$\underline{DE}' = (1 - G')DI' + G''DI'' \tag{6}$$

and

$$\underline{DE}'' = (1 - G'')DI'' + G'DI' \tag{7}$$

On addition of these equations, G' and G'' disappear giving

$$\underline{DE}' + \underline{DE}'' = DI' + DI'' \tag{8}$$

which shows that the equations presuppose that the equivalent of total industrial income from one turnover is spent in its entirety on the next turnover.

Further, on condition that the income crossover is equivalent to a cancellation, so that

$$G'DI' = G''DI'' \tag{9}$$

then G' and G'' may be eliminated from both equation (6) and equation (7), giving

$$\underline{DE}' = DI'$$

and

$$\underline{DE}'' = DI''$$

which, in the equivalent form of an equation between $\underline{DA}'$ and DA' and of an equation between $\underline{DA}''$ and DA'', we have already seen to be the condition of continuity.

Since equations (8) and (9) are independent, it follows that continuity in its simplest form has a twofold condition. First, from equation (8), total primary and secondary income must be spent. Second, from equation (9), primary income moving to the secondary final market must equal secondary income moving to the primary final market.

25 Theorem of the Surplus

Because continuity presupposes the expenditure of income in its entirety, we have in equation (8) the truth of the view that in the general case there are no such thing as profits.

However, not all of *DE″* need be spent on maintenance, repairs, and replacements. A certain fraction, say S, may be being devoted to purchasing new capital goods and services for the widening and deepening of existing industry. Further, this rate of expenditure at the secondary market, *S.DE″*, will not appear initially in the accounts of any individual or any firm under the heading of costs in the ordinary sense of that term; on the contrary, it is part of the flow of investment; it is the outlay of fresh capital for capital goods and services.

Thus we are led to posit the theorem of the surplus. Let the activity of widening and deepening be termed surplus activity, and let its rate be *S.DA″*. Then necessarily to maintain this rate there will be a surplus expenditure, *S.DE″*. And necessarily this surplus expenditure will generate surplus incomes *S.DI″*, for what is expenditure to Jones is income to Smith.

Now this theorem explains the obvious fact that, theory to the contrary, profits may exist in the general case. Whenever there is surplus activity, *S.DA″*, there is poured into the secondary field a flow of investment expenditure, *S.DE″*, and this inflow makes it possible for traders to absorb from the circulation a surplus income, *S.DI″*. In other words, the condition of continuity expressed in equation (8), namely,

$$\underline{DE'} + \underline{DE''} = DI' + DI''$$

is satisfied not by the direct expenditure of total income but by the expenditure of a part of total income and by an inflow of investment compensating for an outflow of profits.

Let us recapitulate this point. Economists say that there cannot be any such thing as profits, for people cannot in the aggregate be earning more than is being spent. This is self-evident, for earning is only the receiving end of spending. However, our economic process has been running for a century on the anticipation of profits, so to say that profits are incidental accidents must be nonsense. That also is true, but it does not contradict the economists' assertion. For the people moved by the profit motive do not think of their investments as spending; they earn more than they spend by the simple device of calling part of their spending not spending but investment.

Observe that our definition of surplus income corresponds with 'excess profits' rather than 'profits.' Profits mean an excess of selling price over cost price, and normally traders do not include their private cost of living and taxes among their industrial or commercial costs. But $S.DI''$ is a flow of income beyond all cost of living, all taxes and charities, all maintenance and replacement: it is a net surplus, an excess profit that can be spent only by being invested.

Further observe that surplus income is distributed among primary traders as well as secondary. Some portion of secondary income, $G''DI''$, moves to the primary final market. This releases from primary income an equal amount, $G'DI'$, which may move to the secondary market and purchase not merely maintenance but also widening and deepening.

26 Theorem of Costs

The bookkeeping idea of costs cannot be of significance in a general industry, for the costs to one firm are the aggregate receipts to the next in the production series.

However, we may distinguish three kinds of costs that are pertinent to a general theory: initial costs, depreciation costs, and aggregate primary costs.

Initial costs are for capital equipment in the first instance. Such costs are $S.DE''$.

Depreciation costs are for the maintenance, repair, and replacement of existing capital equipment. Such costs are $(1 - S)DE''$.

Aggregate primary costs are relative to the community's standard of living, volume of taxes, and devotion to philanthropy. They come to DE', the aggregate sales of primary goods and services, both ordinary and overhead.

Now from the theorem on continuity, all these costs become the income that pays for their continuance.

DE'' becomes DI'' and divides into $G''DI''$ for the primary market and $(1 - G'')DI''$ for the secondary. DE' becomes DI' and divides into $G'DI'$ for the secondary market and $(1 - G')DI'$ for the primary.

Hence, aggregate primary costs are met partly by primary and partly by secondary income, by $(1 - G')\, DI' + G''DI''$.

Again, initial and depreciation costs are met partly by primary and partly by secondary income, by $(1 - G'')DI'' + G'DI'$.

Thus, when S is the surplus ratio, initial costs are met by $S[(1 - G'')DI'' + G'DI']$, and depreciation costs are met by $(1 - S)\ [(1 - G'')DI'' + G'DI']$.

Now the interest of these formulations lies in the light they throw on the common phrase 'The consumer pays.' As is clear, the primary consumers pay only for primary products: they pay *DE′*. They do not pay for the depreciation of either primary or secondary means of production: that depreciation cost is (1 – *S*)*DE″*. Nor do they pay the initial costs of capital equipment, which is *S.DE″*.

It is indeed true that the bookkeepers assign so much to production costs, so much to depreciation, so much towards a return of initial capital costs. It is also true that, when *DE″* is some positive quantity and when *S* is some proper fraction, then the crossover of secondary income to the primary market, namely, *G″DI″*, does release an equal surplus, *G′DI′*, from primary income; and this surplus enables primary traders to meet depreciation and besides have a net surplus for investment.

But what is not true is that bookkeeping practice defines a necessary and immutable law; and much less is it true that the reason why bookkeepers can assign so much to depreciation and so much to a return on capital is that primary consumers pay for depreciation and for the return on capital over and above aggregate primary costs.

There is no immutable law. *S* can become zero, when the investment market goes dead. *DE″* can become negligible, when all traders postpone repairs and replacements in equipment. In that case, aggregate income is solely *DI′* which equals *DE′*; and then it is impossible to collect depreciation costs and a return on capital, for that income does not exist to be collected.

Further, when it is collected, then it is collected not over and above aggregate primary costs but rather as a part of these costs, namely, the part contributed by secondary income crossing over to the primary field.

The proof of the objective validity of this theorem of costs lies in the familiar booms and slumps. In a boom profits are large because there is large expenditure for widening and deepening. In a slump aggregate large profits disappear because this surplus expenditure has disappeared.

To conclude, the consumer pays: he pays for what he becomes owner of. But the investor also pays: and the possibility of the investor's capital outlay being returned at some rate *S.DI″* is simply the enterprise of other investors making capital outlays at some rate *S.DE″*.

27 Curvature of the Exchange Equations

M. Léon Walras developed the conception of the markets as exchange equilibria. Concentrate all markets into a single hall. Place entrepreneurs behind a central counter. Let all agents of supply offer their services, and the same individuals, as purchasers, state their demands. Then the function of the entrepreneur is to find the equilibrium between these demands and potential supply.

The conception is exact, but it is not complete. It follows from the idea of exchange, but it does not take into account the phases of the productive rhythms. As has been shown, economic activity moves through a series of transformations and exploitations; and this series generates the succession of capitalist, materialist, cultural, and static phases. Now each phase in an exchange economy will have its exchange equilibrium, but the equilibria of the different phases differ radically from one another.

By this cyclic variation within the exchange equilibria there is effected the 'curvature of the exchange equations.'

In the capitalist phase, the secondary rhythms are widening and deepening themselves. The wider and deeper they are, the more widening and deepening they can effect. Hence in the capitalist phase, the surplus ratio *S* is increasing. Surplus activity, surplus expenditure, and net surplus income are becoming greater and greater. To make a large profit is, in the general case, not a matter of brilliant enterprise. It is inevitable. It would occur even if all the attempted new enterprises were blunders. For if there is surplus expenditure, there cannot but be net surplus income.

In the materialist phase, the secondary rhythms are widening and deepening the primary rhythms. But the wider these rhythms are, the greater the maintenance that the secondary rhythms have to effect, and, since they are not increasing themselves, there is no increase in the widening and deepening they can effect in the primary. *S* is some proper fraction, but it is decreasing. No matter how intelligent and efficient traders may be, *S* cannot but be decreasing; for with surplus expenditure decreasing, net surplus income cannot but follow suit.

The cultural phase is more complicated, but for the present we may assimilate it to the materialist phase.

In the static phase, *S* is zero. There is no widening and no deepening. This does not mean that primary rhythms may not continue at their acquired level, no matter how great that may be. It does not mean that all depreciation costs are not met. It merely means that the industrial structure is not becoming bigger and bigger. And it also means that, in the aggregate, there is no surplus income.

Thus the equilibria of the exchange equations may be attained with surplus income increasing, decreasing, or zero. When the whole motive force of economic activity is based on the anticipation of profits, this variation in net surplus income will be projected resonantly throughout the whole economic field. The increasing surplus ratio *S* of the capitalist phase heralds the bright dawn of a boom. The decreasing surplus ratio of the materialist phase overclouds the heavens and foretells a hurricane. The zero surplus ratio of the static phase is the most incomprehensible of mysteries, for what can be done when there is no net surplus income?

28 The Normative Proportion

If the equation of the primary market is divided through, term for term, by the equation of the secondary market, then we obtain a third equation which we shall term the normative proportion. Hence from

$$DA' = P'DQ' = DE' = DI'$$

and

$$DA'' = P''DQ'' = DE'' = DI''$$

we get

$$DA'/DA'' = P'DQ'/P''DQ'' = DE'/DE'' = DI'/DI'' \qquad (10)$$

Now *in the long run* the normative proportion must be an increasing quantity.

For DQ'/DQ'' must in the long run be an increasing quantity, since any increase in DQ'' involves a flow of increases in DQ'. Secondary rhythms, DQ'', accelerate primary rhythms, DQ'.

On the other hand, there is no reason to suppose that P'/P'' varies inversely with DQ'/DQ''. On the contrary, the primary and the secondary selling-price levels, P' and P'', should seem to be interlocked; they may vary independently to some extent; but there is no reason to suppose that the price of labor or the price of materials or the rates of profit are due to become greater and greater in the secondary field and less and less in the primary.

Hence, because DQ'/DQ'' is an increasing quantity in the long run, it follows that $P'DQ'/P''DQ''$ will also be an increasing quantity. And from this it follows that all the terms equal to $P'DQ'/P''DQ''$ will also be increasing quantities.

The statement regards the 'long run.' Indeed, as we have seen, in the short term the capitalist phase increases DQ'' without immediately increasing DQ'; but every capitalist phase implies a subsequent materialist or cultural phase, and then DQ' increases out of all proportion to the increase in DQ''.

Now, if the normative proportion is an increasing quantity, it follows that secondary income, DI'', must ever be a smaller and smaller fraction of total income, $DI' + DI''$. And if DI'' is ever a smaller and smaller fraction of total income, then $S.DI''$, net surplus income, must ever be a smaller and smaller fraction of total income.

It follows that the profit motive is subject to decreasing returns.

It also follows that in a highly developed state of industry and commerce, only the vast enterprise reaching from raw materials to primary consumers will be able to net a notable surplus. For with surplus a small fraction of aggregate turnover, only a vast turnover will succeed, on the average, in realizing a more than microscopic surplus. Thus the gradual elimination of small enterprises, which we are witnessing, does not prove that small enterprises are inefficient producers or unsatisfactory dealers; it only proves that they are not big enough to grab what surplus may exist.

Finally, it follows that dividends and interest, inasmuch as they are not distributed to a rentier middle class but concentrated in the coffers of selfish multimillionaires, must become ever smaller and smaller. The basis of the qualification is that dividends and interest are not necessarily classified as net surplus income; they may be income for standard of living or for philanthropy, and then they are not part of $S.DI''$ but part of DI'.

29 The Crossover Ratio

It has been shown that a condition of continuity is defined by the cancellation of the income crossover. By equation (9)

$$G'DI' = G''DI''$$

where, by transposing the terms, we find

$$DI'/DI'' = G''/G' \tag{11}$$

so that on the assumption of continuity, G''/G' equals the normative proportion. This enables us to state the normative proportion in terms of the fraction of primary outlay that moves to the secondary market G' and of the fraction of secondary outlay that moves to the primary market G''.

Hence, writing the values of G' horizontally and the values of G'' vertically, we place in columns the corresponding values of DI'/DI'', that is, of the normative proportion.

G'	50%	20%	10%	5%	1%	0.1%
G''						
50%	1	2.5	5	10	50	500
80%	1.6	4	8	16	80	800
90%	1.8	4.5	9	18	90	900
95%	1.0	4.75	9.5	19	95	950
99%	1.98	4.95	9.9	19.8	99	990
100%	2	5	10	20	100	1000

As the table makes clear, a variation in G' is much more significant than a variation in G''. If G' were 10% and G'' were 90%, then G' moving to 5% would advance the proportion from 9 to 18, but G'' moving to 95% would advance the proportion from 9 to only 9.5. Inversely, when G'' is 90% and G' is really 10% but estimated to be 20% by over-zealous depreciation charges and by depressed wages, then a normative proportion of 9 is given a monetary distribution corresponding to a proportion of 4.5. The result is an overproduction or an insufficient purchasing power or a maldistribution (or whatever it is safe to call it, for superficial economists fancy the thing cannot exist) that generously slices off about half of existing economic activity. We say 'about half' for the proportion 4.5 is a relative term: secondary activity may increase, and then the proportion is four-and-a-half times something greater than what it was nine times greater; on the other hand, as eventually will be the case, secondary activity may decrease, and then the proportion becomes 4.5 times something smaller than before.[2]

2 The odd English of the text is expressive of a creative typing satisfied with accurate awkward compactness. Its revised expression cannot be brief. Let us consider an economy in which basic activity is nine times that of surplus activity. Now add a sharp eccentric shift, from 10% to 20% of total basic income, in basic 'investment money' (prescind from planning, lags, etc.). This will effect an initial lift in surplus activity, but a drastic cutback in basic flow. That flow is 'now' 4½ times greater than the increased surplus flow: it had been nine times greater than the unincreased surplus flow. However, there is a surplus contraction on the horizon: then the basic becomes 4½ times greater than the decreased surplus.

30 Retrospect

We set out in this chapter to indicate the existence of an objective mechanical structure of economic activity, of something independent of human psychology, of something to which human psychology must adapt itself if economic activity is not to become a matter of standing in a tub and trying to lift it.

As was to be expected, we found it. The chapter would not have been begun unless we knew how it was to end. But I do not think something has been found that does not exist. On the contrary, it should seem that we have succeeded merely in formulating certain phenomena which have become rather painfully obvious. The profit motive works very well in a capitalist phase when the surplus ratio is increasing; it works less and less well in the materialist phase when the surplus ratio is decreasing; it has no leverage at all in the static phase when the surplus ratio is zero; and it works less well in each successive stage or cycle of economic development.

However, this chapter has merely outlined our line of thought. The fundamental theorem of continuity has not been considered fully but only in its simplest solution. Accordingly, we proceed to a more detailed examination of the general mechanical structure of the exchange process.

5

Equilibria of the Mechanical Structure

31 Idea of the Equilibrium

The basic equations of the previous chapter do not represent equilibria of different things but only different aspects of the same thing. They connect expenditure at a given market (*DE*), value of goods sold (*DA*), the same value in terms of quantity of and price (*P.DQ*), and the income or aggregate receipts derived from the sales (*DI*). Since all four terms refer to the same thing or flow of things, necessarily they are equal.

However, there is some function connecting present expenditure at any given market with previous receipts from that market. For if the real flows of goods and services move, as it were, in straight lines from the potentialities of universal nature to the enjoyment or achievement, the waste or destruction, of human activity, on the other hand the dummy flows of money and monetary substitutes, of cash and credit, move in circles. The same currency is used over and over; the same accumulation sustains indefinitely a given volume of credit.

One must not be misled by the name 'circulation' into thinking of dummies as moving with an angular velocity. They lie very quietly in the reserves of individuals, firms, banks. Only at the instant of exchange or loan do they move, and then their movement is instantaneous. The meaning of the term 'circulation' is that these instantaneous movements in various directions have to balance with opposite movements. There has to be an equilibrium.

This exchange equilibrium has not, indeed, the rigidity characteristic of physical mechanics. For a time any fund or reserve may take in more than it gives out, or give out more than it takes in. But essentially these are short-term phenomena. No fund can receive more than it gives without some other fund giving more than it receives; and no fund can permanently give more than it receives, for funds, like rivers, can be permanent principles of flow only on condition that they permanently are fed by tributary streams.

32 Reference System for the Exchange Equilibrium

To study the exchange equilibrium it is necessary to introduce a system of reference, a method of listing the different funds or accumulations that are standing in equilibrium.

Such a system may be of any degree of generality. The absolute minimum of generality would be to list all the individual persons, firms, banking institutions, etc., that possessed funds. Such a procedure would be very thorough, but it would not be science, for science is of the general and it is guided not by quantitative considerations but by the selection of significant differences.

Now from the outline of the preceding chapter, three sets of differences appear to be significant. First, there is the difference between the redistributional field and the main circuits: in the redistributional field there is merely the change of ownership; in the main circuits exchange is not merely change of ownership but also the moving forward of the primary and secondary rhythms of goods and services. Second, within the main circuits (the primary and secondary rhythms), there exist two distinct final markets with distinct series of transitional markets resting on each. Third, while the transitional markets are solidary with their respective final markets, it remains that both final markets call for a distinction between supply and demand, between producers and dealers on the one hand and, on the other, consumers and investors. This gives five subdivisions: the universal process divides into the redistributional field and the main circuits; the main circuits divide into the primary and the secondary; both of these divide into traders (producers and dealers) and consumers (including investors).

Let us define a *balance* as a sum of money or credit held in view of some definite purpose or indefinite eventuality. Then, from the viewpoint of our analysis, there exist five types, and so five aggregates, of balances.

First, there are the *redistributional balances*, that is, dummies held for redistributional purposes and eventualities. Such are the reserves assuring the liquidity of banks, insurance companies, underwriters, dealers in stocks and bonds; such also are accumulations for the purchase of land, used capital equipment, and secondhand primary products such as houses, used motorcars, and the like.

Second and third, there are the *trader balances.* Every trader (producer or dealer) has to face a financial gap between the initiation of his turnover and its completion: he has to purchase materials, unfinished or finished goods; he has to pay wages and salaries; and it is only when he has sold his product that the monetary return of his outlay begins. To bridge this gap he must have circulating capital, and the amount of circulating capital on hand in the aggregate of instances gives the amount of money in the trader balances. These, according to our analysis, divide into *primary trader balances and secondary trader balances.*

Fourth and fifth, there are primary and secondary consumer balances. The outlay of traders generates income to firms and individuals, but not all income is immediately spent. Some goes out in driblets; more goes out in chunks; and there is a remainder that stands on guard against eventualities or migrates to the redistributional field. Hence the money individuals hold or the credit they acquire with a view to purchases at the primary final market are termed *primary consumer balances.* Similarly, the money individuals or firms hold for the maintenance, the widening, or the deepening of the existing industrial and commercial structure are termed the *secondary consumer balances.*

So much, then, for our reference system. On the principle of equilibrium, defined in the preceding section, there must be in the general case an equilibrium between movements into each of these and movements out to all the others. See at once the diagram, p. 64.

33 Monetary Phases

While the principle of equilibrium holds in the general case, it remains that there is an exception. There is such a thing as the creation of money and the creation of credit, and to the extent of such creation there can exist an excess of outward over inward movements.

Let us suppose that the power of creation resides in the redistributional field, that the *excess* of movements from the redistributional field to the primary trader balances is DT', where DT' measures so much every so often, and may be positive, zero, or negative according as the excess is in favor of the traders, of no one, or of the redistributional field.

Similarly, let the excess movement from the redistributional field to the secondary trader balances be DT''; the excess to primary consumer balances be DC'; and the excess to secondary consumer balances be DC''.

It follows that, when the redistributional balances are in equilibrium with the other four balances (primary and secondary trader, primary and secondary consumer), then

$$DT' + DT'' + DC' + DC'' = 0 \tag{12}$$

for, under such circumstances, though any one balance may be gaining from the redistributional balance or losing to it, still such gain or loss will be compensated by the losses or gains of other balances.

However, there is such a thing as the expansion and contraction of credit, and, presumably, it has a ground in economic structure and a relation to trader and consumer balances. Accordingly, let us write, more generally

$$DT' + DT'' + DC' + DC'' = DM \tag{13}$$

so that as DM is positive, zero, or negative, the trader and consumer balances will be gaining from the redistributional balances or in equilibrium with them or losing to them.

This gives three *monetary phases*: *monetary expansion* when DM is positive; *monetary continuity* when DM is zero; and *monetary contraction* when DM is negative.

There immediately rises the question, What is the correspondence between the three financial phases and the phases of the real flows? Does a real expansion, such as the capitalist and materialist phases, postulate a monetary expansion? Does the real static phase, when goods and services are produced and sold at constant rates, postulate monetary continuity? Does economic decline, when production and sales are dropping, postulate monetary contraction?

In general the answer would seem to be affirmative. Neither monetary expansion nor monetary contraction seems normal to the static phase, for then we should have to suppose that the same rates of production and sales would normally involve an ever-increasing or an ever-decreasing quantity of money. On the other hand, unless the real expansion postulated a monetary expansion, there would be no possibility of explaining the development of financial technique. For if the real process can expand without monetary expansion, then why the long and sustained outcry against idle accumulations of wealth, why the complaint that rose against laws condemning interest, why the mercantilist doctrine that sought to obtain for each state a maximum share in the world's gold, why the growth of the discounting houses, of banks, of the pyramid of gold reserves, currency, and bank credit? All these things point to a single cause, that real expansion postulates monetary expansion. Finally, there is the concomitance of a volume of credit that increases with increasing production and sales [and] decreases with decreasing production and sales; even though this by itself is not conclusive, still in conjunction with the points already mentioned, we are led to infer that expansion, continuity, and contraction in the real and in the dummy flows are concomitant.

The same conclusion may be reached by another way. In general, prices rise in a real expansion and fall in a real contraction. Hence, if the velocity of money remains the same, then in the real expansion both rising prices and rising production would demand a positive *DM*, while in a real contraction both falling prices and falling production would permit a negative *DM*. On the other hand, if *DM* were to remain at zero in both the real expansion and the real contraction, then the velocity of money in the circuits would have to increase in an expansion not only with the increase of production but also with the increase of prices; similarly, in a contraction, the velocity would have to decrease not only with decreasing production but also with decreasing prices.

Now it should seem that the velocity of the dummies in the main circuits is tied to the velocity of production and sales. In the redistributional area, it is true, the velocity of money is simply a function of the velocity with which owners change their minds: it can become enormous when a number of men trade back and forth the same things with the same money, and this arises when the stock market becomes a gambling casino; on the other hand, it can drop almost to zero when everyone becomes convinced that little or nothing is to be gained by exchanging actual possessions for new acquisitions. But in the main circuits, things are radically different.

Here the monetary velocity is connected with a real velocity. There is a 'so much every so often' of money handled; but there is also a 'so much every so often' of goods and services supplied. It is not the mere number of times that money is transferred that counts, but the rapidity with which money transference can effect real transference. Thus, speculation on the commodity markets may involve a very high velocity of money, but this increased velocity is accompanied by an equally increased velocity of movement of goods; further – and this is the point – even were this velocity of goods and money infinite, the rest of the process would require just as much money as ever. For, plainly, the work for money to do is to move, say, wheat from the western plains to the householder's table, and increasing the number of owners that intervene in the process gives no more than a phenomenal increase in the velocity of money. Similarly, motorcar producers may sell to middlemen on order or by the month or by the year; but whatever the arrangement, it is clear that either producers or middlemen will have circulating capital tied up during the whole period from the initiation of production to the moment of final sale; if producers sell on order, then their circulating capital sustains most of the burden; if they sell only by the year, then the burden falls on the middlemen.

On this showing, the velocity of money in the main circuits is tied to the velocity with which goods are produced and sold. The same conclusion is arrived at if we look at the obverse picture, the rate at which incomes are spent. On incomes there are daily demands, weekly demands, monthly demands, yearly demands, and lifetime demands. Common to all of these is that each represents a sale; also common to all of these is that the income meeting the demands is derived, in the general case, from the outlay of producers and dealers. Again we see that the velocity of money in the main circuits coincides with the velocity, the time interval, between the initiation of production and the moment of final sale.

But if the velocity of money in the main circuits is tied to the velocity with which goods and services are produced and delivered, then since this velocity varies only with the efficiency of industrial and commercial enterprises, it follows that there is a strict correspondence between the static phase and monetary continuity, between the real expansion and the monetary expansion, between the drop of a slump and monetary contraction. When the main circuits expand to supply more and more goods at higher prices, velocity may increase somewhat because efficiency increases; but this increase falls short, it should seem, of dispensing with the need of more money to handle the greater volume of trade. Similarly, in the contraction of industry and commerce, there is a smaller volume of goods at lower prices, and also there is a decrease in monetary velocity because of lost efficiency in production and sale; but it does not appear that the decrease in velocity is at all equal to the decrease in monetary volume.

34 General Formula of the Main Circuits

The equilibrium between the redistributional balances on the one hand and, on the other, the trader and consumer balances has been argued to lie in a correspondence between financial phases and real phases. In a real expansion, such as the capitalist or the materialist phase, the redistributional balances must constantly be losing to the other four; there is needed a positive *DM*, and this positive *DM* in turn calls forth the arts of financial technique. On the other hand, in a static phase *DM* is zero, while in a real decline there is financial contraction and financiers make *DM* negative by cutting down the size of their creation.

It is now necessary to consider the equilibrium between the trader and the consumer balances.

Traders, then, receive aggregate receipts from the final markets at the rates *DI′* and *DI″*. They distribute these sums among themselves by means of the transitional markets, that is, by purchasing materials, unfinished and finished goods. Next they lay aside a portion of receipts in depreciation funds, and these, from our definition, are secondary consumer balances. Further, they pay out wages and salaries for the continuance of their enterprises; they pay dividends and long-term interest to stockholders and bondholders; they contract or pay off short-term loans; they mourn the decease of liquidated enterprises and welcome new arrivals.

Now of these transactions, additions, and subtractions, part regard the redistributional area, and are covered by *DT′* and *DT″*, which may be positive, zero, or negative. But in the main they regard the consumer balances: in particular, such is the destination of wages and salaries, of long-term interest and dividends, and of depreciation charges. Let us say, then, that primary traders disburse to the consumer balances some fraction, *T′*, of *DI′*; and that secondary traders disburse to the consumer balances some fraction, *T″*, of *DI″*.

Thus, primary traders receive from primary consumers *DI′*, and they return to primary and secondary consumers combined *T′DI′*. Similarly, secondary traders receive from secondary consumers at the rate *DI″*, and they return to primary and secondary consumers combined at the rate *T″DI″*.

Henceforth, *T′* and *T″* will be termed the trader multipliers. Obviously, they have some connection with *DT′* and *DT″*. For when primary trader outlay is consistently in excess of primary trader receipts, it follows that *DT′* will have to be positive to make up the difference. Similarly, when *T″* is greater than unity, *DT″* will have to be positive to make up the difference. Inversely, *T′* and *T″* at unity permit *DT′* and *DT″* to be zero; and *T′* or *T″* below unity permits *DT′* or *DT″* to be negative.

It remains that some determination has to be made of the proportion in which *T′DI′* and *T″DI″* divide between primary and secondary consumer balances. Practically, this tends to take place according to the distribution of income: were all income distributed equally, then most probably the whole of it would be spent at the primary final market; on the other hand, because a number of individuals receive more than they care to spend or can spend at the primary final market, there is left over a surplus for secondary consumer balances.

But, however the division takes place, let us say that some fraction G' of $T'DI'$ moves to secondary consumer balances and the remainder $(1 - G')\,T'DI'$ to primary consumer balances. Similarly, let some fraction G'' of $T''DI''$ move to primary consumer balances and the remainder, $(1 - G'')\,T''DI''$, to the secondary consumer balances.

Then primary consumers will receive the sum of the rates $(1 - G')\,T'DI'$ and $G''T''DI''$, while secondary consumers will receive the sum of the rates $(1 - G'')\,T''DI''$ and $G'T'DI'$.

These rates express the levels of potential effective demand. Actually, consumers will be spending some fraction, proper or improper, of their incomes. If these fractions are C' and C'', then their expenditures, $\underline{DE}'$ and $\underline{DE}''$, are defined by the equations

$$\underline{DE}' = C'\,[(1 - G')\,T'DI' + G''T''DI''] \tag{14}$$

and

$$\underline{DE}'' = C''\,[(G'T'DI' + (1 - G'')\,T''DI''] \tag{15}$$

where $\underline{DE}'$ and $\underline{DE}''$ may be equal to, greater than, or less than DI' and DI'' since they refer to different economic instants or turnovers.

A diagram will summarize all that has been said.

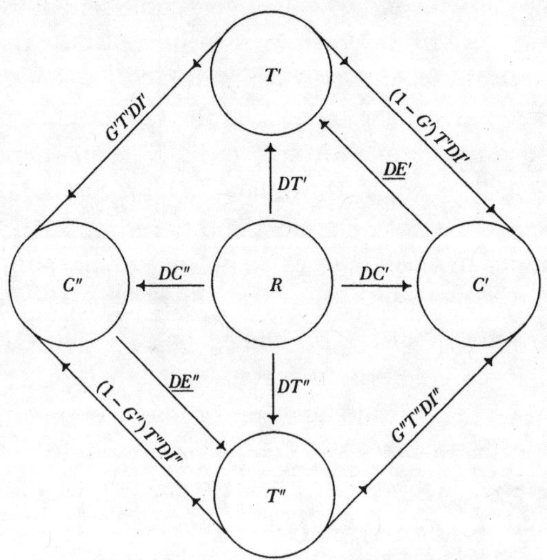

Accumulations are denoted by circles, movements by arrowheaded lines. R is redistributional, T' primary trader, T'' secondary trader, C' primary consumer, C'' secondary consumer balances. Movements are as explained in the text.

Another diagram represents main circuits alone.[1]

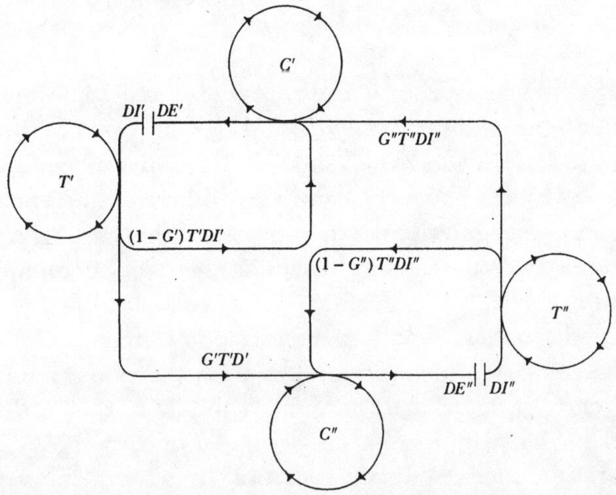

T' and T'' represent the lag between return and outlay of circulating capital.

C' and C'' represent the lag between the receipt and the expenditure of consumer income and investment income.

The breaks in the circuit (upper left and lower right corners of rectangle) are the final markets.

Trader gross receipts are multiplied by T' and T'', respectively, to give $T'DI'$ and $T''DI''$.

These are divided by G' and G'', respectively.

Primary consumers receive $(1 - G')\,T'DI' + G''T''DI''$, and are spending $C'[(1 - G')\,T'DI' + G''T''DI'']$.

Secondary consumers receive $(1 - G'')\,T''DI'' + G'T'DI'$, and are spending $C''[(1 - G'')\,T''DI'' + G'T'DI']$.

1 This sentence begins a new page, p. 82 bis, of the original typescript. There the sentence reads, 'Another diagram representing main circuit alone.' It would seem to have been added by Lonergan from another effort at handling the topic, because on this page 'G' and '$1 - G$' are interchanged both in the text and in the diagram. I have revised the page to bring it into conformity with the previous diagram and text.

35 The Distributor Multipliers

The formulae of the main circuits, namely,

$$\underline{DE'} = C'[(1 - G')T'DI' + G''T''DI'']$$

$$\underline{DE''} = C''[(1 - G'')T''DI'' + G'T'DI']$$

connect aggregate receipts of one turnover, DI' and DI'', with aggregate expenditure on the next turnover, $\underline{DE'}$ and $\underline{DE''}$, by means of three pairs of unknowns: the *trader multipliers* T' and T'', the *distributor multipliers* G' and G'', and the *consumer multipliers* C' and C''. We have now to examine these unknowns, and we begin with the distributor multipliers G' and G'', which have already been considered in the initial theorem of continuity in the simple case in which T', T'', C', and C'' is each equal to unity (§ 24).

Primary trader outlay, including depreciation charges and dividends, is $T'DI'$. Since primary trader receipts are from the primary final market, then, as a general rule, primary consumers should receive $T'DI'$ to spend at that market. Similarly, since secondary trader outlay is $T''DI''$, secondary consumers should receive income at that rate to have the money to spend at the secondary final market.

However, because of the crossover of the income rhythms, primary consumers receive $(1 - G')T'DI' + T''G''DI''$. The condition of this equaling $T'DI'$ is

$$T'DI' = (1 - G')T'DI' + G''T''DI''$$

or

$$DI'/DI'' = G''T''/G'T' \tag{16}$$

Similarly, if the $(1 - G'')T''DI'' + G'T'DI'$ received by secondary consumers is to be enough for them to return $T''DI''$ to secondary traders through the secondary final market, then

$$T''DI'' = (1 - G'')T''DI'' + G'T'DI'$$

or

$$DI'/DI'' = G''T''/G'T' \tag{16}$$

which is the same condition.

The significance of this condition is fairly obvious. The Industrial Revolution brought forth the precepts of thrift and enterprise: thrift so that money would not be spent at the primary final market but accumulated for the secondary final market; enterprise so that it would not merely be accumulated but also spent by investment. The ground of this precept was the Industrial Revolution itself: T'' was large because the structure of industry was being rebuilt; T' was small because the change in structure had not yet begun to bring forth the fruits of a higher standard of living. Because T'' was large, G'' had to be so much smaller, where G'' measures the proportion of secondary outlay going to primary consumers. Because T' was small, G' had to be that much greater, where G' measures the proportion of primary outlay going to secondary consumers.

On the other hand, the subsequent materialist phase inverted these precepts. The new industrial structure began to yield a higher standard of living: T' became large, and T'' no bigger than it had been; hence G' had to decrease and G'' to increase; more secondary outlay had to move to primary consumers and less primary outlay to secondary consumers. Wages rose; the former perquisites of wealth came within reach of workers; and installment buying enabled primary consumers to purchase expensive objects out of their incomes in the same manner as they purchased food and shelter.

Thus the distributor multipliers are intimately connected with the objective composition of industry and commerce, with what we have termed the normative proportion DI'/DI''. This proportion defines the objective situation, T' and T'' define the modifications effected in that situation by trader outlay, while the equation (with T' and T'' transferred)

$$DI'T'/DI''T'' = G''/G' \tag{16}$$

states that the distribution has to be in conformity with the situation as modified, with DI'/DI'' multiplied by T'/T''.

There is, of course, no absolute necessity that the distribution be effected in this manner. But there is a conditioned necessity. For unless the distribution follows the equation, then the objective composition of industry cannot attain the goal it is setting itself. If in the Industrial Revolution the recipients of income were not guided by the precepts of thrift and enterprise, then the Industrial Revolution would have been a failure. Every new enterprise would have been deserted before it was completed because all available income was being spent at the primary market. Again, unless the materialist phase is guided by the precepts of higher and higher wages and is aided by the consumer credits of installment buying, then the materialist phase remains a mere pipe dream: instead of income going to those who will buy more primary products, it goes to old Moneybags, who already has all the primary products that he can think of desiring, who can succeed in spending his income only by finding opportunities for investment; and these opportunities for investment do not exist for the excellent reason that the primary rhythms are not able to sell what they are producing now and so are still less able to sell more.

Thus nemesis awaits any violation of the ratio

$$T'DI'/T''DI'' = G'/G''$$

for to violate it is to give one set of consumers less money than goods to be bought, and to give the other set less goods than money to buy them with. Moreover, not only is G''/G' a two-edged sword at one time defending capital and at another defending labor, but as well it is an extremely sharp sword. As appears from the table already given (§ 29), small variations in G' can give disproportionately large variations in the distribution of income.

36 The Trader Multipliers

To examine the meaning and function of the trader multipliers T' and T'', we may take the general formulae

$$\underline{DE'} = C' \, [(1 - G')\, T'DI' + G''T''DI'']$$

$$\underline{DE''} = C'' \, [(1 - G'')\, T''DI'' + G'T'DI']$$

and make two suppositions. First, we shall suppose that G' and G'' are observing the normative proportion DI'/DI'', as modified by the ratio of the trader multipliers T'/T'', so that primary consumers receive income at the rate $T'DI'$, and secondary consumers receive income at the rate $T''DI''$. Second, we suppose that both primary and secondary consumers are spending their entire income, either in itself or in its equivalent, so that C' and C'' are unity. It follows that

$$\underline{DE'} = T'DI'$$

and

$$\underline{DE''} = T''DI''$$

so that the aggregate receipts of primary traders will equal their total outlay, and similarly the aggregate receipts of secondary traders will equal their total outlay.

Under these conditions it follows that the primary circuit is remaining at the same level, increasing, or decreasing according as T' is unity, greater than unity, or less than unity. Similarly, it follows that the secondary circuit is remaining at the same level, increasing, or decreasing, according as T'' is unity, greater than unity, or less than unity.

Further, with the added assumption of constant price levels, one may define the static, capitalist, materialist, and cultural phases in terms of T' and T''.

In the static phase DQ'' is constant at the effective zero and DQ' is constant. It follows under our assumptions that T' and T'' will both be equal to unity.

In the capitalist phase, DQ'' is increasing and DQ' is constant. It follows that T' will be unity and T'' will be above unity to a degree proportionate to the rate of increase of DQ''.

In the materialist and the similar cultural phase, DQ'' is constant but stands at some level above the effective zero, and DQ' is increasing. It follows that T'' will be unity and that T' will be above unity to a degree proportionate to the rate of increase of DQ'.

Finally, in an economic decline – the slumping part of the slump – T' and T'' will be below unity according as DQ' and DQ'' decrease.

Next, if one removes the assumption of constant price levels, then it should seem that in the static phase T' and T'' will still be unity. For there is no apparent reason why price levels should vary when real supply and real demand are constant in the aggregate. On the other hand, for reasons that will be made clearer later, there is a general tendency for prices to rise in an expansion and to drop in a decline. Hence in the capitalist phase both T' and T'' will be above unity, but T'' higher than T'; in the materialist phase, on the other hand, both T' and T'' will again be above unity but T' higher than T''.

This connection of T' and T'' with the phases throws light on the desirable variation of G''/G' with $T'DI'/T''DI''$. DI'/DI'' defines the general situation in terms of the composition of industry and commerce, in terms of the ratio of primary to secondary rhythms. T'/T'' represents the actual variation in the general situation, and indicates the new situation towards which the process is moving.

The ultimate reason for this meaning and significance of T' and T'' is that they denote variations in supply. The trader multipliers above unity mean immediately that traders are hiring more labor and purchasing more materials than in the previous turnover; at unity they mean that traders are supplying at the same rates as previously; below unity they mean that traders are decreasing the rates of supply.

The whole analysis of the trader multipliers may be summarized by saying that these multipliers are accelerators of the main circuits: above unity they accelerate the circuits positively; at unity they effect a zero acceleration; below unity they accelerate in the generalized mathematical sense of deceleration.

Analogously, one may speak of the distributor multipliers G' and G'' as accelerators. Their zero acceleration is defined by

$$T'DI'/T''DI'' = G''/G'$$

when the crossover of income rhythms is equivalent to a cancellation. Above this zero, G''/G' accelerates the secondary circuit and decelerates the primary; below it, the ratio accelerates the primary and decelerates the secondary. Just as one might make a locomotive leap off the tracks to the right or to the left by blocking the steam conduits to the pistons on this side or on that, so the economic process can be wrecked by the stupidity of capital or by the stupidity of labor, by the demand of high profits or high wages out of due season.

37 The Consumer Multipliers

The nature of the consumer multipliers has been determined in part by the foregoing argument. For when C' and C'' are unity and G''/G' is observing the modified normative proportion, then according to T' and T'' the economic phase will be static, capitalist, materialist, cultural, or a decline. It follows that C' and C'' at unity represent a state of consumer satisfaction. The trader and distributor multipliers are setting the pace, and whatever it is, consumers are nodding approval.

However, it will be worth while examining more closely the meaning of C' and C'' at unity.

Primary consumers receive income at the rate $(1 - G')T'DI' + G''T''DI''$. Secondary consumers receive income at the rate $(1 - G'')T''DI'' + G'T'DI'$. Let us give names to these cumbrous formulae and speak of the potential level of primary or secondary effective demand. For plainly consumers can demand effectively and can do so indefinitely up to the level of their incomes.

Further, primary consumers spend at the primary final market at the rate $C'[(1 - G')T'DI' + G''T''DI'']$, and secondary consumers spend at the secondary final market at the similar rate $C''[(1 - G'')T''DI'' + G'T'DI']$. These formulae may be denoted as the actual levels of effective demand.

Then C' or C'' at unity means that consumers are spending to the full extent of their incomes.

More exactly, C' at unity does not imply that there exist no savings for whatever purpose, whether for old age, or the education of children, or the purchase of a home, or the payment of a debt, or the security of insurance. It simply means that the aggregate of all such savings is counterbalanced by the present expenditure of past savings and the present contraction of debts to be paid by future savings. Thus there is no particular difficulty in C' standing at unity. The world's proportion of misers and spendthrifts, of optimists and pessimists, has only to find an equilibrium.

Again, C'' at unity does not forbid traders accumulating depreciation charges in funds against future needs or gradually concentrating dividends that a masterly sum of monetary capital may be at their disposal. It simply requires that present depreciation charges and dividend distributions be balanced by present depreciation expenditure plus present purchase of new capital equipment.

So much for C' and C'' at unity. They mean that consumers in the aggregate are nodding approval to whatever phase the traders are giving them; and this approval consists in translating potential effective demand entirely into actual effective demand.

It follows that, when C' and C'' differ from unity, then consumers are disapproving the action of traders: above unity they are asking for more than traders are giving them; below unity they are asking for less. Just as T' and T'' signify variations in supply, so C' and C'' signify variations in demand.

Now it is to be observed that in *limiting cases* these variations in demand effect variations in economic phase. Thus in the capitalist phase T'' is above unity: if C'' is also above unity then secondary production will be increasing its rate of self-increase; if C'' is below unity, then secondary production will be decreasing this rate of self-increase, and such decrease will eventually move T'' from above unity to unity and then below unity. Similarly with regard to C' and T', for there cannot be any sustained rate of production without a corresponding rate of sales.

Further, it is to be observed that the action of the consumer multipliers is cumulative. Suppose the potential level of secondary demand to be 100 and C'' to stand at 90%. Then 90 will be spent at the secondary final market to give traders 90 as their aggregate receipts. Now there will be no encouragement for traders to make T'', say, 110%, to offset the action of C'' and bring the potential level of effective demand back to 100. At most T'' will be 100% to give secondary consumers the 90 they spent. If now C'' remains at 90%, then secondary expenditure drops down to 81, and another turnover under the same conditions will bring it down to 72.9. The same holds for C' and T'.

This cumulative action of C' and C'' reveals an iron law regarding consumer expenditure, namely, unless both primary and secondary consumers in the aggregate spend all their income, then they are decreasing their income by the amounts they are failing to spend. In other words, in the aggregate neither primary nor secondary consumers should save; if they do, they exchange a rate for a mere quantity, an income for an equal lump sum, a dollar a day for a dollar; moreover, they change a real expansion into a static phase, and a static phase into economic deline. The slogan is, then, Spend what you get or you won't get it to spend.

Consider now the opposite hypothesis, that C' or C'' stands above unity.

With regard to C'' this is quite possible. Even though every turnover with C'' above unity denudes the secondary consumer balances, still these balances can attract a positive DC'' that will replenish them from the redistributional field. The dividends of net surplus encourage investment. And so, there has developed the intricate mechanism of floating companies, underwriters, brokers, stock markets, and a gambling public to canalize accumulations towards the secondary consumer balances.

Nonetheless, one must note that a positive DC'' is needed not to conduct an expansion at any acquired rate but only to increase the rate of expansion. With C'' at unity there can be any phase, even the self-increasing capitalist phase. When C'' is above unity, there is not merely an expansion but the expansion of an expansion, the booming of a boom. And C'' has to remain above unity only a relatively short time for the economic process to be careening along after the fashion of a drunken youth on a motor highway.

On the other hand, C' has not the same facilities for attracting a positive DC'. In general, primary consumer balances are hand-to-mouth affairs which would be wiped out even by a single concerted effort to make the actual level of effective demand higher than the potential level. Further, this concerted effort would not result in primary consumers receiving a greater flow of goods and services unless traders had been warned to anticipate it and had organized to satisfy it; for without such warning and organization, the only effect of C' above unity would be to raise the primary final market selling-price level P', which will always obligingly step up whenever DQ', its slow-moving partner in

$$DE' = P'DQ' = DA' = DI'$$

is not ready to smile an increase.

This leads us to conclude that C' is a rather passive factor in the economic process. It is disastrous for primary consumers to spend less than they earn, and, on the whole, it is impossible for them to spend more. C' remains at unity through rain and shine, nodding approval in the aggregate (though, of course, it can select this rather than that as it pleases) to whatever traders supply. On the other hand, C'' is the big strong man with the loud gruff voice, though with not too much between the ears. In optimistic mood he rises above unity and things do hum. Net surplus pours in at an increasing rate, and minor tycoons attribute this flow of wealth to the brilliance of their enterprise and the efficiency of their execution. Then, like the peripateia in classic drama, the heavens change their color. The rate of net surplus begins to fall as capitalist turns to materialist phase. The children of this world sell their holdings to the children of light. New investment stops, and this drop of C'' below unity wipes out aggregate net surplus. Sooner or later the secret will leak out, and then the stock market crashes.

38 The General Theorem of Continuity

An initial and provisional theorem of continuity was enounced in a preceding chapter (§ 24). Now it may be indicated in its full generality.

The analysis has revealed that the economic system is a pattern of aggregate dynamic relationships arranged in different kinds of velocity and accelerator rhythms. In the real order there are the primary and the secondary rhythms, with the former accelerated by the latter. In the monetary order there are the rhythms of excess release from the redistributional area to the primary and secondary rhythms; and again, the former accelerate the latter.

Now the general theorem of continuity is that this complex machine has a nature that must be respected. Absolutely, there is no necessarily right value for the monetary accelerators DT', DT'', DC', DC''; again, absolutely, there is no necessarily right value for the six multipliers C', C'', T', T'', G', G''. But what is true is this: as soon as a few of these are determined, the rest become determined within ever narrower limits, for all form part of an organic whole; to violate this organic interconnection is simply to smash the organism, to create the paradoxical situations of starvation in the midst of plenty, of workers eager for work and capable of finding none, of investors looking for opportunities to invest and being given no outlet, and of everyone's inability to do what he wishes to do being the cause of everyone's inability to remedy the situation. Such is disorganization. Continuity, on the other hand, is the maintenance of organization, the stability of the sets and patterns of dynamic relationships that constitute economic well-being in a society.

While the provisional theorem of continuity (§ 24) did regard the static phase, it is important to observe that the general theorem regards any phase. There is a general historical movement of ideas, opportunities, and decisions integrating into that major rhythm in which transformations are followed by exploitations only to bring forth new and deeper transformations. Within this broad historical scheme of things, the role of any age, and still more of any country, is but a small thing: the past was settled by our forebears, and the future will be in the hands of posterity; only the present is ours, and it is only within limits that we may make of the present what we wish. Our starting point is already determinate: we have to face things as they are; we may never lose sight of them or attempt to reckon without them. But not only is there ever the broad and unalterable datum of things as they are; there are also the limitations which this datum imposes on things as we are going to make them.

The theorem of continuity is the abstract and formal aspect of such limitations in the economic order. At the moment the exchange process is static or expanding or contracting. We may like it so or we may wish it different. But in any case there is some determinate range of values of the multipliers and of the monetary accelerators – of C', C'', T', T'', G', G'', of

DC', *DC"*, *DT'*, *DT"* – that corresponds with such a decision. Moreover, there has to be an internal coherence between these values, and to violate this coherence is to rout economic organization. Just as the movements of the controls of an airplane must be coordinated and all coordinations are not possible at all instants, so also the economic machine has its controls, which can be moved only in concert and only in a limited number of ways at any given time.

Such is the general theorem of continuity. In the abstract and in a general way, it affirms that the economic process can proceed only within the limits of equilibrium of the various phases. To step outside them is to bring about a general breakdown.

6

Incidental Theorems

A few applications of the foregoing analysis will serve a double purpose: it will give our abstractions something of a local habitation and a name by linking them with the concrete problems of our time; in particular, it will drive home the point that the possible equilibria of the exchange process are limited, and that this limitation imposes on man an obligation of adaptation and conformity under the threat and penalty of economic frustration.

39 The Aggregate Primary Price Spread

The formula for the primary circuit was shown to be

$$\underline{DE'} = \underline{P'}\,\underline{DQ'} = C'[(1 - G')DI'T' + G''T''DI''] \tag{14}$$

where, on the right-hand side, $(1 - G')T'DI'$ is primary consumer income from the primary circuit and $G''T''DI''$ is primary consumer income from the secondary circuit. In a special sense already defined (§ 26), primary consumer income may be considered as equal to costs. Hence, when the rate of primary production is Dq' at a cost price level p', and the rate of secondary production is Dq'' at a cost price level p'', then

$$p'Dq' = (1 - G')\,T'DI' \tag{17}$$

and

$$p''Dq'' = G''T''DI'' \tag{18}$$

so that by substitution in the formula for the primary circuit we have

$$P'DQ' = C'(p'Dq' + p''Dq'') \tag{19}$$[1]

and if we suppose that

$$Dq' = u{\cdot}DQ' \tag{20}$$

then

$$P'DQ' = C'(p'uDQ' + p''Dq'')$$

or

$$C'p''Dq'' = (P' - C'up')DQ' \tag{21}$$

Now a preliminary understanding of this formula may be had by introducing two suppositions: first, that primary consumers are translating potential effective demand into actual effective demand so that C' equals unity; second, that the rate at which primary goods and services are being supplied happens to be equal to the rate at which they are being sold, so that u equals unity. Then equation (21) becomes

$$p''Dq'' = (P' - p')DQ' \tag{22}$$

which expresses in terms of price levels and production rates the provisional condition of continuity that primary surplus equals secondary costs. May it be recalled that surplus includes depreciation costs and that the costs of which we speak do not include depreciation but do include taxes, ownership standard of living, and any type of philanthropy.

The interesting item in equation (22) is the $(P' - p')$, which is the spread between selling price and cost price. This price spread may be applied immediately to cases in which ownership extends from the field of raw materials to the final market. When, however, there is a series of pro-

1 Note the lack of correspondence with equation (14) above. Precise inclusion of lags would complexify the analysis here, as it would also the treatment of the same topic in section 15 of Part Three.

duction factors linked by transitional markets, we may distinguish a corresponding series of cost price levels, $p_1, p_2, p_3, \ldots$ and, as well, of selling-price levels, $P_1, P_2, P_3, \ldots$ so that

$$(P' - p') = (P_1 - p_1) + (P_2 - p_2) + (P_3 - p_3) + \ldots \tag{23}$$

since the aggregate primary price spread is equal to the sum of price spreads enjoyed at the relevant transitional markets.

To return to equation (22), it affirms that the aggregate primary price spread is a function of two purely objective factors, of the rate of secondary costs, $p''Dq''$, and of the rate of primary production, DQ'. The greater $p''Dq''$ and the lower DQ', then the greater the price spread; on the other hand, the smaller $p''Dq''$ and the greater DQ', then the smaller the price spread. Obviously, there is no necessary correspondence between this law and either the classical view that profits are due to intelligence, enterprise, and risk, or the Marxian view that profits are due to reckless exploitation of labor. Given an increase in secondary costs, $p''DQ''$, without any immediate increase in primary production, DQ', then the primary price spread will increase no matter how benevolent and stupid the entrepreneurs may be: indeed, it will increase even in Bolshevist Russia, where to avoid constant inflation the state must take the surplus which it denounces capitalists for taking. On the other hand, given a decrease in secondary costs with no corresponding decrease in primary sales, the primary price spread is bound to contract, no matter how wicked and clever and enterprising the entrepreneurs may be; it contracts even in the lands of most rugged individualism.

Intimately connected with the objectively varying price spread is the phenomenon of price spirals. When the primary price spread is increasing, primary consumer income is inflating or, if you prefer, the purchasing power of money is decreasing. This leads to a demand for higher wages, and this demand will be met, for entrepreneurs are enjoying higher profits because of the increasing price spread. But the higher wages can effect only a rise in the primary selling-price level; they do not modify the price spread except perhaps to increase it by increasing secondary costs; in consequence, primary consumer income will be at least as inflated as before, and further demands for higher wages will not solve the problem but only raise selling-price levels still higher. Left to itself, this price spiral mounts up and up until a saturation of the investment market reduces secondary costs by cutting down Dq'', and the expansion of the primary markets increases DQ'.

Inversely, when the price spread is contracting, then consumer income is deflating. Wage earners will be in a position to accept a reduction of wages, for things are cheaper. On the other hand, the entrepreneurs who fancy profits due to their intelligence, and who are convinced that they are as intelligent now as they ever were, will be able to produce convincing evidence that their profits are disappearing. Thus, a contracting price spread may lead to a reduction of wages. But this reduction will not restore the volume of secondary costs: its immediate effect will be to reduce these costs and further contract the price spread; and it is only the few investors who know their business that will find the low costs of new enterprise more alluring than the falling primary price level is deterring. Thus, consumer income will continue to deflate; profits will continue to vanish; and demands for further wage reductions will arise. The nonsense is self-perpetuating till a change in investment outlook creates a new situation.

However, we are dealing with a simplified equation. Let the factor u be reintroduced, leaving C' at unity, so that

$$p''Dq'' = (P' - up')DQ' \qquad (24)$$

where

$$Dq' = u \cdot DQ' \qquad (20)$$

Thus, when primary production is greater than primary sales, u is greater than unity; inversely, when primary sales are greater than primary production, u is less than unity. The former arises when the anticipated market is greater than the actual market, as in a boom; the latter when the anticipated market is less than the actual market, as in a slump. But in a boom the price spread is expanding because of an increasing $p''Dq''$; and if u is above unity, then it will have to expand still more. On the other hand, in a slump the price spread is contracting, and with u below unity it has to contract still more. For the effect of u above unity is to make a large price spread $(P' - p')$ fill the role of a small one; and its effect when below unity is to make a small price spread fill the role of a large one. Hence divergence between the actual market and the anticipated market tends to reinforce objective movements expanding or contracting the aggregate primary price spread.

If now C' is introduced, we have

$$C'p''DQ'' = (P' - C'up')DQ' \qquad (21)$$

and it is easy to show that proper action on the part of consumers can rectify all variations in the price spread. If the spread is becoming too great, let C' be less than unity. Then as coefficient of $p''Dq''$ it will change the exigence for a large price spread into an exigence for a small one, and as coefficient of p' it will enable a small price spread to meet an exigence for a large one; the result is a scissors action lopping off the price spread. Similarly, when the spread is too small, then with C' above unity the scissors action is reversed: a small $p''Dq''$ becomes equivalent to a large one, and a large $(P' - p')$ is given the effect of a small one.

However, one must not be too optimistic. C' below unity is possible; it is achieved by a doctrine of thrift for the rich and wise and a practice of paying subsistence wages to the poor and stupid. But C' above unity could be possible only with the aid of Major Douglas and his Consumer Dividends, for C' above unity means that people spend more on primary goods and services than they have income to spend.[2]

Still, one may not infer that Major Douglas is therefore right. For the Consumer Dividends either are inflationary or else they are recovered by taxation, when they become a program of public works with no work done, or else they are recovered by selling bonds, and then we have deficit government spending, which will be considered later. What is quite certain is that a flow of money cannot be injected into the exchange process without the alternatives of inflation, taxation, or bonds being imposed.

The only sound solution to the problem of price spirals is the difficult solution. When the price spread is contracting, entrepreneurs have to accept the fact that it is contracting; more generally, it has to be recognized that profits and the profit motive suffer from decreasing returns, as the normative proportion demonstrates; the attempt to pass on the effect of a decreasing price spread by lowering wages is futile, and with this futility known and accepted then the downward spiral is eliminated. It is indeed true that the contracting price spread, when there is a series of production factors, hits first and most the final factors: they have paid earlier factors under the anticipation of a rate of profit which they cannot realize;

2 Major Clifford Douglas (1879–1952) attracted public attention in the 1920s with his idea of social credit: the issuance of extra money to consumers, or of subsidies to producers, to stimulate production. His views were aired in A.R. Orage's socialist publication in 1919 and in Douglas's first book, *Economic Democracy* (1920). Douglas's view became better known through the poet Ezra Pound in Italy and through the Social Credit Party founded in Alberta, Canada, in 1935. Douglas's principles were virtually abandoned by the end of the 1930s, although the Social Credit Party survived.

some method for mitigating this burden is, perhaps, needed, for it may well be that the expanding spread did not benefit first and most the final factors. But whatever the precise solution or mitigation to be discovered and worked out, the general principle is quite clear.

Similarly, when the price spread is expanding and consumer income is inflating, then the remedy is not an increase of wage rates. The remedy lies in the hands of consumers themselves, for what causes the inflation of income is not merely the increase of primary income from the secondary circuit together with the constancy of primary production, but also the fact that primary consumers are attempting to spend their more money for the same quantity of goods. You say your income is inflating; but the cause of this is that you are spending on consumer goods too great a proportion of it; spend less and the inflation will stop; spend still less and the inflation will turn to deflation.

This is a harsh doctrine bidding producers to be content with decreasing profits and consumers to offset a rising market by curtailing consumption. But any other doctrine is illusory: an expansion of the secondary circuit does not increase, here and now, the primary circuit; it means more work but not more real wages in the aggregate and so lower real wages on the average. Now this decrease in average real wages can be spread about by the inflation of consumer income, and the only alternative to the inflation is for the consumers who can do so to curtail their consumption and so save their money instead of raising price levels and passing their money on to create a price spread and greater profits for producers. Inversely, the contraction of the secondary circuit necessarily involves the contraction of surplus income, and the only function of Major Douglas's injection of Consumer Dividends is to create by inflation a pseudo surplus so that producers may enjoy a profit to which they are not entitled.

40 Cyclic Variations in Prices

The broad historical tendency of transformations leading to exploitations to be followed by further transformations defines a long-term economic cycle. The means of production are rebuilt on a new and better model in a capitalist phase; the new industrial structure yields an increasing standard of living in a materialist phase; and, theoretically, it should be possible to swing into a static phase at the peak of the materialist expansion, so that a maximum aggregate standard of living is enjoyed while a further industrial transformation is awaited. This theoretical sequence will be termed the *pure cycle* to distinguish it from its familiar truncation, the *trade cycle*, in which the materialist expansion never reaches its maximum and is followed not by a static phase but by the economic decline of a slump.

Concomitant with these cycles there is apt to be a rise and fall of prices. The capitalist phase will exert pressure on sections of the labor and commodity markets to raise the secondary cost price level p''; the increased volume of traffic in the secondary circuit means an increased Dq''; the product of these, $p''Dq''$, unless C' drops below unity, calls for a proportionate increase in the aggregate primary price spread $(P' - p')$; and if there is any yielding to complaints about inflated consumer income, then P', p', and p'' begin to spiral upwards.

The materialist phase will begin to supervene. This imposes a great and general pressure on the whole labor and commodity markets, so that both p' and p'' rise. On the other hand, secondary production, Dq'', will slacken sooner or later, while primary sales are on the increase, so that DQ' mounts. This contracts the aggregate primary price spread. Surplus income is becoming a smaller and smaller fraction of aggregate income. Profits fall, and any attempt to stabilize them by reducing costs sends the primary selling-price level P' spiraling downwards; and if a society accepts the classical assumption that profits are the measure of soundness, then this absence of profits will put an end to enterprise. Thus the materialist expansion is truncated in a welter of falling prices.[3]

In the pure cycle of the ideal society things would not be so. The upward and downward price spirals would be eliminated, for there is no reason why consumers should be given an increase of income to buy products that do not, as yet, exist, and similarly there is no reason why producers should attempt to obtain profits that are not to be had. Again, labor is not going to

3 In the original typescript here there is a canceled paragraph (ending in midsentence) which is a prior attempt at what follows in the text. The paragraph reads: 'It may not be entirely useless to indicate what would occur in the well-ordered economy of an ideal society. First, there would be neither the upward nor the downward price spirals: producers would not attempt to obtain profits that do not exist, and consumers would not attempt to purchase goods and services that are not being produced. Second, labor leaders would see to it that fluctuations in employment were either eliminated or compensated, and this would eliminate or reduce the alternate competition of industries for labor and of labor for work to stabilize monetary wages. Third, the financial fraternity would be responsible for the constancy of the value of money, and so it would hold in check by direct and indirect means all aggregate fluctuation of commodity prices; for it is both wise and inevitable that one commodity become dearer and another cheaper as'

be content with fluctuating employment, and the elimination of such variation will stabilize the labor market and wage rates. Finally, commodity prices will not be allowed to run wild: aggregate fluctuations result in a variation of the value of money; particular fluctuations result in the undue depression or expansion of particular branches of industry. The one element of truth in the classical doctrine of freely moving prices is that in a transformation of economic structure, such as was the commercial and later the industrial revolution, there cannot remain the old price pattern. It is not true that the new price pattern can be anything at all, or that a desirable price pattern will be arrived at automatically; the automatic results are upward and downward spirals, alternations of overtime and of unemployment, the undue expansion or depression of various industries, and the trade cycle instead of some approximation to the ideal pure cycle which, if it curbs booms, also seeks immunity from slumps.

41 The Mechanism of the Capitalist Phase

The question is, Just how does the capitalist expansion work? The answer envisages the pure case, the first approximation.

By definition the capitalist phase consists in the self-increase of secondary enterprise, DQ'', while primary enterprise, DQ', remains constant. Connecting these real phenomena with monetary phenomena are the price levels, P' and P'', for

$$P'DQ' = DA' = DE' = DI' \tag{4}$$

and

$$P''DQ'' = DA'' = DE'' = DI'' \tag{5}$$

Probably there will be an upward movement of the price levels P' and P'': expansion is initiated financially, and the resistance of the real order to transformation (the latter's inertia or the inefficiency percentage of finance) appears directly in a rise of P'' and indirectly in a rise of P'. However, this phenomenon is not the kernel of the capitalist phase but incidental to it, so on a first approximation we may suppose price levels to be constant; the procedure is parallel to that of elementary mechanics, which begins by prescinding from friction.

Thus we have DA' constant and DA'' increasing. It follows that T' will be unity and DT' will be zero, while T'' will be above unity and DT'' positive. Internal stability is to be assumed in a first approximation, so that we have

$$G''/G' = T'DI'/T''DI'' \tag{16}$$

which will be a decreasing ratio, that is, the secondary circuit is becoming an ever greater fraction of total activity. Finally, since any phase is compatible with the consumer multipliers at unity, we may assume them to have that value; it follows that DC' and DC'' may be assumed to be zero.

On this schematic analysis the significant element appears to be the positive value of DT'': there has to be a positive flow from the redistributional balances to the secondary trader balances, and this is not offset by any other flow to the redistributional area; DT', DC', and DC'' may all be zero. Accordingly, if we suppose investment to originate in the redistributional area, and to divide into three parts – a first part spent within the redistributional area for land, good will, and secondhand equipment, a second part spent at the secondary final market for new capital equipment such as buildings and machinery, and a third part added to the trader balances as new circulating capital – then we are led to disagree with the common view that savings equal investment. In the strict sense, savings are part of primary and secondary consumer income: hence, since DC' and DC'' equal zero, we have it that savings equal the part of investment that purchases new capital equipment; in other words, net surplus results from widening and deepening, and generates the possibility of paying for another equal block of widening and deepening. In a larger sense, savings might be made to include the receipts from the sale of land, secondhand capital equipment, good will, and the like: in this way it would be possible to suppose that savings covered two out of the three parts of investment, namely, the part spent at the secondary final market and the part spent in the redistributional area. But the third element remains unaccounted for on the assumption of savings equaling investment; DT'' is a positive flow from the redistributional area to the secondary trader balances, and it is offset by no equal and opposite flow; it effects the net increase in circulating capital in the main circuits, and there cannot be an equal and opposite flow from the main circuits unless we suppose that the main circuits can handle an ever-increasing quantity of goods with prices stable and no increase in the quantity of money; that supposition we have already argued to be, in general, false (§ 33). It remains, then, that investment equals savings, in the broadest sense, plus the net increment in circulating capital.

Where this net increment comes from will be considered later. The immediate question is, What does it do? First of all, it enables traders to make $T''DI''$ continuously greater than DI'', so that on each turnover, aggregate outlay is greater than aggregate receipts. Next, when C' is unity and $G''/G' = T'DI'/T''DI''$ as we have assumed, then the total increment in secondary trader outlay goes to increase secondary consumer income. Finally, with C'' at unity, as we have assumed, total secondary income is spent, so that on each turnover secondary consumers are spending more than on the previous turnover and secondary traders are receiving back their ever-increasing outlay in its entirety.

Such is the internal mechanism of the capitalist phase in the pure case. It is an increase in the volume of the secondary circuit that is initiated by DT'' being positive, that is effected by T'' standing above unity, that is carried out effectively when $G''/G' = T'DI'/T''DI''$ and when both C' and C'' are at unity. The element of functional significance is that DT'', which is a velocity, so much money every so often, effects an acceleration, $D.DI''$, so much more money every so often every so often. Thus, if DT'' is \$10,000 a day, then secondary circulating capital will increase \$10,000 a day; next, if this circulating capital is employed in industries whose period of turnover is three months, then every day the volume of the secondary circuit, DI'', will be increased by \$10,000 per three months. It is as though one were inflating an automobile tire while the wheel was turning: there would be two velocities of air, the velocity from the pump to the tire and the velocity of the rotating tire; and every new block of air from the pump would mean that that much more air moved with the velocity of the wheel. The reverse process of a blowout would represent the negative value of DT'' or DT' or DC'' or DC'.

It is now necessary to go back over our assumptions, for ordinarily either P' and DA' will be increasing or C' will be less than unity with C'' correspondingly greater. The capitalist phase is an expansion of the secondary circuit, of surplus expenditure, surplus activity, and surplus income. Usually, however, the lower income brackets, which devote nothing to investment, receive some of this surplus income. Either they save it or else they spend it at the primary final market. If they save it, then C' drops below unity; a negative DC' becomes possible, such as bank deposits or insurance premiums; and then an equal and opposite DC'' will enable secondary consumers to continue increasing their rate of expenditure so that secondary traders continuously recover their ever-increasing aggregate outlay. On the other hand, this element of surplus may not be saved but spent at the primary final market, and then either P' increases or DQ' increases. If P' increases and simultaneously $G''/G' = T'DI'/T''DI''$, then primary traders will be simply increasing the price spread and sending back to the secondary circuit whatever the secondary has sent to the primary. Again, the secondary expansión continues unperturbed: it has both a real and a monetary increase, but the monetary increase circulates through both the primary and the secondary circuits; DA' increases though both DT' and DC' are unity, because the more and more money going round the secondary circuit also goes round the primary circuit. This is the case of inflation of consumer income, and ordinarily it leads to the upward price spiral which we have already considered. On the other hand, if the increased expenditure at the primary market is met by a rise in DQ' as well as in P', then the materialist phase superposes on the capitalist phase; this mechanism will be considered in the next section.

Another significant departure from the assumptions we made is that C'' may be greater or less than unity. If, then, C'' is below unity, secondary traders are not receiving back their increasing outlay: the result will be that they desist from increasing it, next that they begin to contract it, making T'' less than unity, and finally that they lower P'', the secondary selling-price level. Clearly, this puts an end to the capitalist phase. There would be the same result if C'' did not rise above unity when C' drops below unity, as described above. Otherwise, when C'' is above unity, then secondary consumers are attempting to increase the rate of the expansion; this attempt may be met simply by a rising P'', when secondary traders increase their price spread; or it may be met by an increase in DQ'' answering the double accelerator pressure of both DT'' and DC''.

So much, then, for a first approximation to the mechanism of the capitalist phase. The essence of the phase is that DT'' is positive, T'' above unity, and that this action of T'' is cumulative. Thus secondary traders at the end of each turnover must get back their total outlay and then increase it. They may get it back in any of three ways: either the total increment goes directly to secondary consumers and C'' is at unity; or part goes to primary consumers who do not spend it and then C'' must be above unity; or part goes to primary consumers who spend it, but primary traders merely increase price levels and price spreads to hand the resultant surplus to secondary consumers for investment. Concomitant phenomena are an increase in redistributional activity effecting the reinvestment of profits, providing the increment in circulating capital, redistributing titles to land and secondhand equipment, and speculating on the rise in the capitalized values of the stock market. The first three are intrinsic to the investment flow; the last results from the increasing proportion of surplus income in total income, the rise of dividends. Extremely probable is the inflation of primary consumer income, and under classical ideas this inevitably results in price spirals. Independently of this price movement there will also be rises in the sections of the commodity and labor markets that pertain to the secondary field of industry.

42 Mechanism of the Materialist Phase

As the pure case of the capitalist phase is the expansion of the secondary circuit, so the pure case of the materialist phase is the expansion of the primary. Essentially this phase consists in DQ' increasing and DQ'' constant. To work out the monetary phenomena in the simplest case, we may begin again by assuming P' and P'' to be constant, C' and C'' to be unity, DC' and DC'' to be zero, G''/G' to be equal to $T'DI'/T''DI''$.

On the analogy of the preceding analysis, DT' will now be a positive flow, effecting the increment of primary circulating capital, enabling primary producers to keep T' greater than unity and so make the outlay of each aggregate turnover greater than the gross receipts of the preceding; further, because G''/G' equals $T'DI'/T''DI''$, the total primary outlay, $T'DI'$, will go to primary consumers, and because C' is unity, this ever-increasing primary income will be entirely spent either in itself or in its equivalent.

On the other hand, DT'' may be zero and C'' unity, so that both DQ'' and DA'' are constant. Because, however, DQ'' will be above the effective zero or replacement level (§8), the secondary circuit will not merely maintain but also expand the primary; initially this expansion will be at some constant rate, which, as the demand for repairs and replacements increases with the increasing primary structure, will gradually decline. Thus this phase is entropic unless C'' occasionally rises above unity.

As before, investment equals savings in the widest sense plus the net increment in circulating capital. The same argument holds *mutatis mutandis.*

The essential difference between the capitalist and the materialist phases is that, while in the former, aggregate net surplus increases with the widening of the secondary circuit and, simultaneously, primary consumer income is likely to be inflated, now aggregate net surplus becomes a smaller and smaller proportion of total income, according to the long-term rule of the normative proportion, and primary consumer income deflates (increases in purchasing power). The reason for this is clear: the capitalist expansion increases surplus activity, surplus expenditure, and surplus income; the materialist expansion increases primary activity, primary income, and primary expenditure. Or, to put the same point differently, the aggregate primary price spread varies directly with secondary costs, $p''Dq''$, and inversely with primary final sales, DQ'. Thus the materialist expansion is uphill work for the profit motive: the greater the primary volume of production, the greater must be the volume of primary income, the smaller the proportion of net surplus in total income, the smaller the percentage return on capital investment, the less the attraction of investment, and the weaker the will of the financial fraternity to supply the more and more money needed to maintain the excess release, DT', to primary trader balances. However, this entropy of the profit motive is not absolute, for profits are not identical with net surplus: profits include ownership standard of living, taxes, contributions to philanthropic ends; net surplus does not. Thus the profit motive becomes weaker and weaker in the materialist phase only in the measure in which a society's entrepreneurs are not small investors or businessmen out to raise their standard of living but financial tycoons interested in making more money merely to have more to invest.

It is difficult to generalize about price movements in this phase. Because the secondary circuit is constant and primary consumer income is deflating, there will be a tendency to cut wages and commodity prices. On the other hand, there will be an increasing demand for labor and for commodities, and this will tend to raise prices. Finally, the steadiness of stockmarket quotations will depend on the distribution and use of income: if the distribution is wide and what is distributed spent in the primary field, then stocks should be steady; if, however, the increment in income tends to go to Moneybags, who cannot increase his primary expenditure, the materialist expansion collapses; for C' is being forced below unity and primary producers cannot keep increasing their outlay when sales are falling.

Another inherent difficulty in the materialist expansion is to get primary consumers to spend the whole of their increasing income. Evidently, unless they spend it, it cannot keep circulating, and much less can it keep increasing. Nonetheless, there is a difficulty about spending it. In part this arises from the preceding capitalist phase, in which thrift is the rule of wisdom and, to that extent, the common good coincides with individual prudence. But as well it is reasonable for a man to save more when he earns more, for a higher standard of living postulates a higher reserve of savings.

Now it is plain that the primary circuit cannot generate these increments in primary consumer balances: traders have to get back their outlay or go into bankruptcy; they are doing all they can do to give consumers the increased income to purchase the increased flow of goods and services; they cannot do more. Thus, another source has to be found. This might be had if surplus were widely distributed, especially in the capitalist phase; for then all inclined to save would come to the materialist expansion with their saving already done. Alternative to this would be the institution of consumer credit by creating a positive *DC′* for purpose of savings; but this would presuppose a high level of economic education and restraint, for if, in the aggregate, the savings tended to be spent, the effect would be inflationary. If anyone wishes to know where, on this last suggestion, the positive *DC′* would come from, the only answer possible at present is that the source would be the same as that of the positive *DT′*. In any case, the problem of spending is a real one: salesmanship, advertising, and installment buying prove that.

43 Causes of Surplus Income

Before going on to the analysis of the mechanism in the cultural and in the static phase, it will be well to treat a number of other points. Of these the first is the causes of surplus income.

Aggregate income necessarily equals aggregate expenditure. However, there may exist a type of expenditure that is not regarded as expenditure because it is apt to yield a return; this is termed investment, and, obviously, a continuous flow of investment will yield a continuous flow of income that has no other function except being invested. This we have termed net surplus income: it is equal to expenditure for the widening and deepening of the primary and secondary flows. We have now to enumerate the causes or conditions of this surplus activity, expenditure, and income.

The first condition is that without this flow there would exist a measure of underemployment and underproduction. Thus the first cause of the surplus flow is that labor, industry, and commerce do more work than otherwise. They work not merely for the present but, as Joseph Stalin remarked of his great capitalist enterprise, the five-year plans, they work also for the future.

An effect of this surplus flow is the inflation of primary consumer income. There is more work but this surplus work does not yield here and now a greater product for primary consumers. Thus, on the average though not in the aggregate, primary consumer income as real income decreases, as monetary income inflates. This inflation has to be accepted, for if it is not accepted, then prices will begin spiraling, money lenders will take fright, and the whole effort at expansion will collapse. A second cause, then, of the flow of surplus is the general acceptance of an inflation of primary consumer income.

Alternative to this inflation there is the practice of thrift, not merely by the rich but also by those in the lower income brackets. Or, if the latter cannot grasp the utilitarian calculus of advantages, then the payment of subsistence wages will do as a substitute for thrift on the part of the poor. But one of the three – inflated income, thrift, or subsistence wages – has to be practiced in the capitalist phase; they have to be practiced to some extent even in the materialist phrase, but as there the need for them is ever decreasing, this change for the better is in itself a solution.

A third cause of surplus income is savings. These are of two kinds, those of the poor young man who later becomes a millionaire, and those of the millionaire's son who does not spend his secondary income at the primary market. The first type of savings is the thrift that is an alternative to the inflation of consumer income; the second type is the investment of money generated by the flow of investment for the purpose of being invested. The first type lowers C' below unity and raises C'' above unity; the second type merely keeps C'' at unity.

A fourth cause is financial technique. Beyond savings there is needed the liquidity of the redistributional area to facilitate the exchange of titles to land and to securities; there also has to be provided the source of the excess releases DT' and DT'' from the redistributional area to the trader balances.

A final and fifth cause is the emergence of ideas, the taking of risks, and the enterprising conduct of affairs. Of its nature an expansion has to be a voyage into the unknown: even in backward countries in which the expansions of the more advanced are merely imitated, as in the Russian five-year plans, there are some new ideas, some risks, and some enterprise. Further, it would be desirable, of course, that the ideas be sound, the risks prudent, the enterprise intelligent; but as far as the existence of the surplus flow is concerned, this is definitely a minor matter. Anything new will do. A group of cultural morons, ballyhoo artists, and pompous tycoons can effect the surplus flow and grow rich on it. Nor is this possibility a matter of pure theory alone.

The surplus flow, then, has five causes: an increase in the rates of work and of production; an average decrease in primary real income, to select the most common of the alternatives; a habit of saving and investment among those who receive more income than they can decently spend on their standard of living; a developed financial technique; and a flow of new opportunities, new ideas, and new enterprises.

44 Variations in Profits

Gross profit is the difference between selling price and cost price multiplied by the volume of turnover during a given period. Net profit subtracts various items from this – depreciation, interest, amortization – but as these are fairly constant, it may be said that variations in profit are due to variations in price spread and in turnover.

The price spread we have to consider is not the aggregate primary price spread of § 39, which is in direct correlation with aggregate net surplus, but the particular price spread of any given enterprise; it includes not merely surplus but also primary income, such as income for ownership standard of living, taxes, philanthropy. Similarly the turnover to be considered is not the aggregate turnover but that of some particular undertaking. Thus our symbols DI', DI'', $P' - p'$, etc., refer to aggregate flows and levels; they tell us what is to be had at any given instant; but the particular price spread and the particular turnover tell us who gets it.

Thus aggregate turnover may vary greatly, but it is not likely that the turnover of any particular enterprise will vary in exact concomitance. Where an inelastic demand is being met, there will be very little variation. Where an elastic demand is being met, the variation will be far greater in the particular case than in the aggregate.

Again, the objective process may move through the trade cycle: in the capitalist phase net surplus will be increasing, in the materialist it will decrease relatively, and in the slump it will disappear. But the price spread of particular industries need show no concomitance. Where there are the sheltered rents of monopoly, the price spread need not vary at all. Where rents are unsheltered, the variation will have to be great enough to compensate for the lack of variation in other instances.

The point in both cases is clear. If X plus Y successively equals 30, 20, and 10, and if X successively equals 25, 20, and 15, then necessarily Y will equal successively 5, 0, and –5.

No less clear is the inevitable result of this situation. Enterprises will divide into two classes, the sound and the unsound. The 'sound' will establish either an outright monopoly or its practical equivalent of interlocking directorates: they will produce for as much of the aggregate demand as is inelastic; they will learn and practice the technique of killing competition; and they will charge monopoly prices. The 'unsound' enterprises will stand on the fringe of this happy hunting ground to reap a profit in times of boom and to lose their investment in times of depression. But note why they are unsound. It is not because they lack enterprise, nor because they do not meet a real demand, nor because they lack intelligence. It is because they are not members of the gentlemanly ring that conspires against the public and forces upon it an economy of scarcity. It is because there is such a thing as the trade cycle. And the cause of both the trade cycle and the ring is the gullibility of society in accepting profit as a criterion of satisfactory enterprise.

Profit is not such a criterion. Profit merely demonstrates the profit-maker's ability to get a lion's share out of aggregate income. Tell men to seek profit and tell them that profit is the result of intelligence, enterprise, and risk. Things will go well for a while. But sooner or later even the stupidest will realize that the maximum return for their money is through monopoly prices and inelastic demand. This maximum return coincides with the minimum welfare of the community. It tends to yield a perpetual and artificial scarcity.

But there is more than this. The differences between variations in profits in different enterprises constitute the greatest problem with regard to the elimination of slumps. When there exists the net surplus of an expansion, then the 'sound' enterprises, even though they take the whole of this surplus, will leave at least primary income for the standard of living in nonmonopolistic or unsheltered undertakings. But when the net surplus of the expansion ends with the expansion, then the 'sound' enterprises do not cease earning their large profits. Where do these profits come from? Not from net surplus, for there is none. Therefore, from the primary and the depreciation income of other undertakings. These either struggle along barely making ends meet or else they go to the wall. As some go to the wall, the pressure on others increases. And if things are really bad, this process continues till the 'sound' have undermined even their own position. A lion's share is only a pittance when only lions share.

Accordingly, if the exchange process is to move through the cycle without undergoing the periodic and sickening nosedives when marginal firms are eliminated and strong ones threatened, when unemployment swells incredibly and the delicate fabric of trade channels is torn to shreds, then the principle of the *level floor* will have to be accepted, developed, and put into effect. One can conceive the various industries as limited areas in the floor of a river: some are out in the center, others near the bank; and in each case profit varies with the volume of water flowing perpendicularly above. Now, as the economic process moves through the cycle, this volume of water varies; some always flows over the central part of the riverbed; but there are droughts when the area near the shoreline is left high and dry. The principle of the *level floor* would change the river into a canal: it can hardly aim at equalizing the depth of the flow throughout the whole industrial structure; but it can endeavor to deepen the shallows and fill in the depths. Just how this is to be done is another question; to it we revert later.[4]

45 The Applied System of Reference

Hitherto the generality of our inquiry has enabled us to deal with an extremely abstract and schematic system of reference; we have been studying the interdependence and interaction of monetary flows to and from redistributional, primary, and secondary trader, and primary and secondary consumer balances; and we have been doing so, because this very limited reference system enables us to see and grasp the essential mechanical structure of velocity and accelerator flows in the exchange process.

We have now to indicate the method of applying this essential structure to more concrete and complicated problems, and this method is simply the expansion of the system of reference.

The expansion may be achieved first by division. Thus, redistributional balances may be divided into different kinds of redistributional balances: for instance, the balances of bankers, of insurance companies, of underwriters, of speculators and brokers in stocks and real estate. The trader balances may be divided according to the different kinds of industry and commerce. Similarly, one may distinguish different types of consumption. But one thing is to be noted: such divisions do not alter the essential mechanical structure; one may put several smaller circles in place of the larger circles representing the aggregate balances; but it still will remain true that in the real order the primary circuit is accelerated by the secondary, and in the financial order both primary and secondary are accelerated by the redistributional excess releases.

4 Lonergan did not return to the problem of the level floor. A fitting place for its discussion would have been after § 49 on the financial problem, where there are three missing sections.

The expansion may also be achieved by multiplication. The argument hitherto has dealt with any theoretic closed system. But in the concrete we have the several exchange processes of the several nations, each with its own redistributional, trader, and consumer balances. Nor is any of these a closed system. Capital may migrate from the redistributional area of one nation to that of another; traders in one produce for consumers in another. It follows that instead of a single mechanical structure we have several interacting mechanical structures.

Whether from mental fatigue or from objective impossibility, I do not see that a general study of the interactions of several mechanical structures is possible. The problems are far too complex. However, what is possible is the solution of particular issues. Then a definite and limited objective is assigned the inquirer, and as these issues arise he can prescind from an infinity of irrelevances to track down the precise point in hand.

46 Mechanism of the Favorable Balance of Trade

Suppose two countries *A* and *B* each with its mechanical structure. Let *A* have some rate of excess exports of value *DX*, so much every so often. Let *B* pay for this in a first period by exporting gold of equal value *DY*, so much every so often; and in a second period let the payment be by floating loans in *A*, again at the rate *DY*, so much every so often.

The first point is that *DY* constitutes an additional flow of net surplus income in country *A*. In any closed system aggregate expenditure and income must be equal; but in the open system *A*, there is a part of aggregate income, *DY*, of which the corresponding expenditure takes place from outside. To put the point differently, the citizens of *A* buy all their production, minus *DX*, continuously; but they receive all their income, including *DY*, continuously. Thus *DY* is an additional flow of net surplus income.

The second point is that this additional flow of net surplus enables the profit motive to function continuously. It has been argued that the profit motive is a matter of decreasing returns, that net surplus rises in a capitalist phase, falls in a materialist phase, vanishes in a static phase. But now there is introduced a new principle of net surplus, the favorable balance of foreign trade; and this principle, whatever its variations, is independent of the phases of internal mechanical structure.

But is this favorable balance a possibility? Suppose that *B* is paying *A* in gold. Then on classical theory prices in *A* will rise and prices in *B* will fall, and inevitably this will cut down *A*'s foreign market and increase *B*'s; the favorable balance will be eliminated.

This general argument is valid as far as it goes. However, *A* may not put this gold into circulation, and then its prices will not rise; or it may put it into circulation only to meet the monetary requirements of an expansion, to supply the *DT′* and *DT″* that enable traders continuously to increase their outlay; and it may be able to conduct this expansion without suffering from a rise in prices; for instance, it may hold to the doctrine of thrift and subsistence wages for rich and poor respectively, and it may obtain its raw materials by developing the untouched resources of colonies. On the other hand, *B* may not suffer any depletion of the gold it has actually in circulation; the gold it exports may be from idle accumulations or from mines; further, *B* may not be any one country but several that are in turn drained of their surplus gold.

Thus the favorable balance can be regular for a while, even though conducted against the import of gold; and once that game is played out, then *A* can continue exporting a surplus of goods against an internal rate of foreign loans. Suppose that the citizens of *A* subscribe to foreign loans at the rate *DZ*, which is equal to *DX* and *DY*; superficially this process can be perpetual. A exports goods at the rate *DX*; *B* pays at the rate *DY*, which it secures through the loans *DZ*; and since *DY* is net surplus to *A*, *A* can always buy the loans *DZ*. On this showing *A* always enjoys a rate of net surplus independently of its phase; and since this net surplus is always invested, there is no danger of the inflation implicit in the import of gold.

However, there is a fly in the ointment: principal and interest. Either *B* pays these each year, so much for interest and so much for the amortization of capital, or else it increases its debt by that much more each year. In the latter case, its credit will crash sooner or later. In the former case, there will be an ultimate saturation of the foreign loan market, but this may be a long, long way off. Meanwhile, interesting things take place. *B* pays interest and amortization of principal on a mounting foreign debt; it pays by export; it pays by mounting exports, and these directly or indirectly are to *A*. Thus *A* is confronted with an alternative: either it allows its own industry gradually to decline to be able to absorb this import from its debtors, and then it becomes a mere rentier nation; or else it defends its industry by tariffs, refuses the import from the debtors, and thereby forces the debtors to repudiate their debts. Neither solution is acceptable. The rentier nation is torn by internal strife: for declining industry drives its proletariat against the wall of unemployment, while the spectacle of the wealthy living on their foreign investments incites the unemployed to the fury of revolution. On the other hand, the repudiation of debts puts an end to foreign lending as the mechanism for a favorable balance of trade.

47 Deficit Government Spending

When the game of the favorable balance is played out, a very similar substitute can be found in deficit government spending. Let the government spend each year some sum, *DX*, beyond its income; since all expenditure generates income, this *DX* will generate an equal net surplus income, *DY*, which resembles in most respects the net surplus from the favorable balance; finally, to prevent inflation let the government sell annually bonds, *DZ*, equal to *DX* and *DY*. Superficially the process may be perpetual, if those who receive the surplus *DY* purchase the equal bonds *DZ*.

The benefit of deficit government spending is that it enables an economy regulated by the idea of profit to continue functioning when there is an insufficient proportion of surplus income resulting from real expansion. Profits are a matter of decreasing returns. When the returns tend to vanish they can be restored artificially by a favorable balance of trade or by deficit government spending.

Another advantage of deficit spending is that it simplifies taxation. A perfect taxing mechanism would convert the surplus *DY* into government income without any recourse to bonds. But perfect taxing mechanisms are hard to devise, and the issuance of bonds has the favor of the rich, while taxes have the disfavor of all. Like everyone else, politicians know on which side their bread is buttered.

It remains that there are limits to deficit spending.

First, there is no use selling the bonds against bank credit. To prevent inflation, they have to recover the *DX* that has been spent and has become surplus income *DY*.

Second, *DX* cannot involve a greater proportion of total production than people are willing to contribute to the state. The labor and commodities purchased with *DX* are the labor and the property of a section of the community; up to a point the community does not mind giving these to the government when there is a pleasant flow of cash and bonds; but beyond that point the community wants this labor and these commodities for the individual satisfaction of its members, and then the hocus-pocus is no use.

Third, there is the little matter of principal and interest. This has to be attended to, or it will become impossible to sell the bonds. But it can be attended to only by an ever-increasing burden of taxation. And the taxes can be paid only to the extent that the recipients of the interest and the amortization are a rentier class spending their income for the products of the rest of the community's work and property. Thus it is important that the ownership of the bonds be distributed very widely; otherwise the only method of payment open to the government would be the slightly equivocal method of confiscation.

A fourth limitation is the willingness of the community to have an ever greater and ever richer rentier class living off the income of government bonds; and a fifth limitation is the declining gullibility of those who buy the bonds, for ultimately this game will be as played out as the favorable balance of foreign trade; no nation can increase its rentier class indefinitely, just as no nation can afford to become a rentier nation living off the industry of other nations.

48 The Possibility of the Static Phase

The static phase is a limiting position between expansion and decline. Its chief characteristic is the absence of net surplus. The incomes of all individuals may be as high as you please, but they all must be spent; and practically none of the spending is investment. Again, one individual can become richer, but only because another becomes poorer; there is no question of all individuals becoming richer, because in the aggregate, income and ownership remain as they were.

But is the static phase possible? The importance of the question is evident. Perpetual acceleration is an impossibility: no speed king would even dream of it; he might dream of setting ever higher records of velocity, but to attain the highest and then keep on going faster and faster with never a letup, that is evidently fatuous. Similarly, the economic machine cannot accelerate indefinitely: you can double or quadruple or decuple world production; but you cannot keep on decupling indefinitely. But if the economic machine cannot enjoy perpetual expansion, must it, the moment expansion ceases, go into the nosedive of decline and crash? It must if the static phase is not possible.

The conditions of the static phase are that C' is unity so that present savings equate with present primary consumer borrowing and present expenditure of past savings, that C'' equals unity so that present depreciation charges equal present expenditure for repairs and replacements, that the rate of investments is equaled by the rate of liquidations, that T' and T''

are unity so that trader outlay equals trader receipts, that G''/G' equals DI'/DI'' so that profits suffice to give owners and moneylenders their standard of living and to enable industries to keep in repair.

The first difficulty is psychological. The static phase is a somber world for men brought up on the strong drink of expansion. They have to be cured of their appetite for making more and more money that they may have more money to invest and so make more money and have more money to invest. They have to be fitted out with a mentality that will aim at and be content with a going concern and a standard of living. It is not an easy task to effect this change, for, as the Wise Man saith, the number of fools is infinite.[5]

The second difficulty is that the curve of expansion has to flatten out gradually into the static phase. The capitalist expansion increases DQ'' to some level that exceeds, say by dQ'', the effective zero or replacement level. The materialist phase uses this excess production of the secondary field to expand the primary; and as this expansion takes place, less and less of the excess dQ'' goes to producing new industries and more and more to replacing and repairing existing ones; the effective zero rises. However, unless the effective zero rises up to DQ'' to eliminate dQ'', then the static phase will be initiated by a sudden contraction of the secondary field; this creates unemployment as well as underproduction, and so the static phase would begin with the messy problem of redistributing labor and writing down capital.

A third difficulty concerns the financial structure. In the static phase finance has no function, for there is no problem of supplying more and more money, DT' and DT'', to enable the main circuits to expand; and there are not enough new companies being formed to keep promoters, underwriters, brokers, etc., busy.

5 The wise man is the author of Ecclesiastes; the statement is quoted several times from the Vulgate by Thomas Aquinas. This reference is to the first line of p. 124 of the typescript. On p. 124 verso there is the same first line followed by what no doubt was a rejected effort at p. 124, which reads: 'The second difficulty is that the curve of expansion has to flatten out gradually into the static phase. One cannot jerk into it. The capitalist phase raises secondary production higher and higher above the replacement level. The materialist phase increases primary production and by this increase gradually diverts secondary activity from producing new industries to replacing old. But if the materialist phase is truncated, then the static phase will not begin properly; for the cutting short of primary expansion means that secondary activity is condemned to a sudden contraction; and this sudden contraction means that men will be out of work and secondary industry will be operating under capacity.'

But the major difficulty is the fourth, that of the price pattern. The price pattern is the mechanism that divides aggregate income among the various branches of industry and commerce. Now, when there exists a flow of net surplus, whether this is due to real expansion or to a radically favorable balance of foreign trade or to deficit government spending, then the price pattern is not a matter of grave concern. Even though a number of enterprises are getting much more than their fair share of aggregate income, still the existence of surplus makes it possible for the rest to have at least enough primary income to maintain a decent standard of living. When, however, the flow of net surplus disappears – and it is bound to disappear at times, for none of its causes can be permanent – then the price pattern becomes a matter with the most serious implications. For if any enterprise takes to itself more than a fair share of aggregate income, then other enterprises are bound to have less than a fair share; they will suffer, not in the sense that they get none of the surplus, for there is no surplus; they will suffer in the sense that they have not enough to maintain the standard of living of owners, creditors, and employees. Hence the emergence of the slump: vast industries such as agriculture or mining or what you please may be hopelessly depressed; endless concerns meeting a real demand and necessary to the national economy find themselves faced with liquidation. To meet this crisis the state has to step in subsidizing necessary undertakings, taking over frozen assets, and softening the blows of destiny generally lest the whole economy collapse.

At the root of this lies a radical flaw in the classical theory of prices. The classicists argue that if any undertaking is supplying what people really want, then people will pay enough for its product to keep the business going; it follows that subsidies are merely devices for making the taxpayer shoulder the burden of individual inefficiency or inadaptation. The facts about subsidies show that this conclusion is false, and, in fact, the premise is false as well. What individuals will pay for is what is to their individual interest as individuals. But individuals have other interests, no less real and no less imperious. They are members of a whole hierarchy of groups, and they share other interests in common with each of these successively wider circles: there are the interests of their firm, the interests of their locality, the interests of their region, the interests of their country, their stake in the continuity of world economy; in addition there are class interests, social interests, cultural interests, religious interests. All of these interests are real, but the classical price mechanism ignores them; it isolates the individual in the narrowest and lowest of his interests, and then leaves it to labor organizations and strikes, to interlocking directorates and monopolies and lockouts, to state intervention and lobbying and tariffs and subsidies, to nationalism and armaments and economic imperialism and wars, to fight out unjustly and stupidly and even brutally the issues which should be settled by a competent theory of prices and properly developed price system.

To conclude, there is no intrinsic impossibility to the static phase, but we shall have to do a lot of thinking and a lot of educating before we can hope that our exchange processes will swing easily and gracefully from an expansion into a static phase instead of falling clumsily and painfully into a slump.

49 The Financial Problem

Let us suppose a flow of investment in excess of liquidations and of magnitude, *DJ*, so much every so often. Let *DJ* originate in the redistributional area and divide into three parts, DJ^*, DJ', DJ'', where DJ^* is spent in the redistributional area, DJ' goes to the primary circuit, and DJ'' to the secondary circuit.

The implication of the investment flow is that the real flows of goods and services are expanding, and, on a first approximation, DJ^* will equal the cost of land and capital equipment, DJ' will equal DT', DJ'' will equal DT'', DC' and DC'' will be zero. Thus, as long as the expansion lasts there is an excess release from the redistributional area to the main circuits: this is of magnitude DJ' plus DJ'' and is equal, over the period, to the net increment of circulating capital in use. As was shown in the analysis of the mechanism of the capitalist and the materialist phases, this rate of increase of circulating capital is the motive force of the expansion.

Essentially the financial problem consists in finding a stable and permanent solution for the monetary requirements of a long-term expansion. We may begin by enumerating what certainly are unsatisfactory solutions.

The problem is not solved by bringing into use hitherto unused accumulations of money. For unused accumulations are quite limited, and once they have all been brought into use then the problem returns.

The problem is not solved by a rate of gold production. There is no ground for the anticipation that the rate of increase of circulating capital will be exactly the rate of gold production. There is no sufficient reason for confining the former rate to the latter.

The problem is not solved by mercantilism, by a favorable balance of trade that increases the exporting country's gold stock. For obviously this decreases the gold stock of other countries and so merely robs Peter to pay Paul.

The problem is not solved by systematic deflation, by making the same quantity of money do more work through falling prices. Falling prices kill enterprise; they cut off the margin of profit.

The problem is not solved by merely greater efficiency in the use of money. For we cannot be sure that greater efficiency will be forthcoming whenever it is needed. New devices that make the same quantity of money do more work are always a possibility. But they are always an uncertain possibility.

Underlying these arguments there is usually this postulate: money is an instrument invented to fulfil a definite task; it is not the ultimate master of the situation. One has to place first human society which is served by the economic process, and second the economic process which is to be served by money. Accordingly, money has to conform to the objective exigences of the economic process, and not vice versa.

We have now to go deeper. It was shown (§ 18) that money may be conceived either as a commodity, say gold, or as an account. Now the foregoing rejection of greater efficiency, of systematic deflation, of mercantilism, of bringing into use unused accumulations, all goes to show that money of account has to enter into the solution. But the question is this: Is money to be essentially a commodity such as gold and then supplementarily an account, or is it to be purely and simply an account?

The classical view makes money essentially gold and supplementarily an account. Gold is at the basis of finance, and the rest is superstructure with a validity conditioned by the ability to meet demands for gold. To study this position, let us say that the quantity of gold is Q, that its value is U, that the use of money of account multiplies the quantity by some factor K, and that the velocity with which money moves is V (an average 'every so often' for the total quantity KQ). Then if Q^*, U^*, K^*, V^* refer to these four in the redistributional area, Q', U', K', V' in the primary circuit, Q'', U'', V'', K'' in the secondary circuit, since

$$DA = DA^* + DA' + DA''$$

it follows that

$$QUKV = Q^*U^*K^*V^* + Q'U'K'V' + Q''U''K''V'' \qquad (28)$$

which simply means that the aggregate volume of economic activity is equal to the sum of the aggregates in the three defined areas.[6]

Now, if money of account is limited by the ability to meet demands for gold, then *K* will be perhaps 30: the treasury issues currency to three times its gold reserve, and the banks keep deposits to cash in the ratio of ten to one. There results a vast possibility of expansion over what would have existed were money strictly a commodity, and at least for the moment this is deemed sufficient. However, this use of a gold standard has three difficulties.

The first arises from international movements of capital. Possible demands for gold are 30 times the gold there is, so that if 4% of the possible claims were made with a view to the export of capital (suppose that foreign investors decide to liquidate their holdings), then the country either loses its gold, and besides declares itself insolvent, or else it goes off the gold standard. Apart from instances of such general crisis or conspiracy, minor removals of gold from one country to another mean disproportionately large variations in the volume of their activity. *Q* is but one factor in *QUKV*, yet this tail wags the whole dog. It is in this wagging that Mr Hawtrey finds the cause of the nineteenth-century trade cycle.[7]

6 In the original typescript, there is a next paragraph of six deleted lines at the end of p. 128, ending the page in midsentence. It is a prior attempt at what follows in the text, and reads: 'Now this financial method makes it possible to conduct a long-term expansion. *DT′* and *DT″* can continue as excess releases from the redistributional area as long as the factor *K* can keep increasing. And really there is no limit to the size of the factor *K*: money of account is simply a system of public bookkeeping, and there is no law of bookkeeping that limits the totals in the ledger; the only law of bookkeeping'

7 'Hawtrey's first systematic exposition of his theory of the cycle, *Good and Bad Trade*, was published in 1913, but according to the author, the book was begun in 1909 ... *Good and Bad Trade* is much more than an unoriginal compendium ... it is rather a *locus classicus* of monetary explanations of the business cycle' (David Laidler, *The Golden Age of the Quantity Theory* [Princeton: Princeton University Press, 1991] 101). Lonergan refers to the view expressed in R.G. Hawtrey's *Monetary Reconstruction* (2nd ed., London, 1926) in handwritten notes (Archives, Batch II, folder 60) on F. Hayek, *Monetary Theory and the Trade Cycle* (London: Jonathan Cape, 1933). Lonergan quotes p. 135 of Hawtrey's work: 'so long as credit is regulated with reference to reserve proportions, the trade cycle is bound to recur.' Schumpeter notes (*HEA* 1121), 'Hawtrey's analysis makes business cycles, as he himself put it, a purely monetary phenomenon ... Throughout the twenties, Hawtrey's theory enjoyed considerable vogue. In the United States, especially, it was the outstanding rationalization of the uncritical belief in the unlimited efficacy of the open-market operations of the Federal Reserve System that prevailed then.'

A second difficulty is the financial crisis and the financial crash. The magnitude of *K* at any instant is conditioned by confidence: people have to have confidence that the banks will meet demands; and the banks have to have confidence that their debtors will meet their obligations. Obviously, the moment that *K* begins to contract no one can have confidence, for the effective quantity of money, *QK*, is decreasing while a sudden universal suspiciousness starts the demands for cash payments increasing. Panic follows, and the whole volume of economic activity is cut down to a fraction of its former self as liquidations multiply and smash the delicately woven fabric of the channels of trade.

This second difficulty usually comes in like a second crushing wave to make a slump certain and secure. The objective process is moving through the materialist phase towards a static phase on the level of the peak of the expansion. Net surplus is decreasing. Firms whose rents are unsheltered find their profits disappearing. Moneylenders look askance at requests for renewal of short-term loans, a renewal that is necessary if the DT' and DT'' already released to the main circuits is not to be recalled and a deceleration of the process to replace the former acceleration. Things waver, then slip, then slide, and after the crash strong men wring their hands and wonder how best they can pick up the pieces.

And incidentally these crashes are a perfect instrument for the concentration of wealth. There is nothing really wrong with the firms that go under. Their former owners are ruined, but the wise men who neither risk nor labor but take mortgages and interest are now rich in the lost wealth of others.

A third difficulty of the gold standard is that it effectively places money before men. If money were simply an account and banking frankly a system of public bookkeeping, then other causes of surplus and not merely financial technique could reap a reward. An expansion or a favorable balance of foreign trade or the benefits of deficit government spending are not merely matters of financial arrangement. There is more work to be done. There is the inflation of primary consumer income. There is the expenditure of natural resources. These should receive consideration. But when money of account is conditioned by the possibility of meeting demands for gold, then that condition has to be satisfied or else all is ruined; and to satisfy that condition it is necessary for the objective exigences of the real process to be subordinated to the putative laws of money.

It is because money is conceived as essentially gold and only supplementarily an account that the flow of new circulating capital to the main circuits DT' and DT'' tends to be more and more only a volume of short-term credit. Clearly this does not meet the exigence of the objective process. The idea of an expansion is not a future contraction. The idea is that the volumes of flow will increase and then will stay increased. Short-term loans enable them to increase, but they prevent them from staying increased. It is true that the volume of short-term industrial and commercial credit may remain at some high level over a notable period. But it is also true that suddenly or on brief notice the whole volume may shrink to a mere fraction of itself. Such shrinkage is the reverse process to the expansion: men plan and labor to accelerate the real flows, and then the bankers decide that the real flows have to be decelerated; and the devil of it is that, on the assumption that money is essentially gold and only supplementarily an account, the bankers are perfectly right; their job is to maintain their liquidity and to keep monetary expansion within some assigned ratio to gold; their job is not to meet the objective needs of the exchange process, and it cannot be that until all real and putative relations of money to gold have been eliminated, expunged, destroyed.

However, I would not be thought to be merely drawing conclusions from the facts of present experience. Today the gold standard is dead, and its future revival most unlikely. In its place we have credit control and managed money, and the present difficulty is that these tend to be merely a gold standard without gold. In a thousand ways the old mentality persists and rules. What is needed is a frank avowal that money is simply a system of public bookkeeping, and then a coherent and thorough transformation of all monetary practice in accordance with the fundamental fact. Thus we define the financial problem as the problem of working out and applying the view that money is public bookkeeping. The grounds for this position may be summarized as follows.

Money is an instrument invented by man to make possible a large and intricate exchange process. While there is no simple and even perhaps no ascertainable correlation between the quantity of money and the volume of exchange activity, it remains true that variations in the volume, if not to result in inflation or deflation, postulate some variations in the quantity. Now in the long run these variations in quantity can be had only by the introduction of a money of account, but if the money of account – its title to be called money was indicated in § 18 – stands side by side with a commodity money, then not only are there the undue perturbances of the exchange process from international movements of capital and from financial crises and crashes, but the whole economy comes to be regulated not by the social good, not by the objective exigences of the economy itself, but by the money invented to serve the objective process and the social good. For when the money of account is conditioned by a relation or law connecting it with the stock of commodity money, then the money of account has to obey this law; on the other hand, the exchange process has its own objective laws, and these laws have to be subordinated to the law of money, for without money (which will be present or absent according to the law of money) exchanges cannot take place no matter how useful, how desirable, how necessary. To put the matter more vividly: the objective process has an exigence for a pure cycle, but the law of money can be satisfied only in a capitalist phase and the earlier part of a materialist phase; in consequence we have not the pure cycle but the trade cycle; as net surplus drops, the volume of credit contracts; as credit contracts, the volume of economic activity contracts; the expansion ends by reverting to a pre-expansion position or something worse.

On the other hand, when we say that the idea of money as a system of public bookkeeping has to be worked out and applied, we mean above all the necessity of a money whose laws coincide with the laws of the objective economic process, so that instead of conflict between real possibility and financial possibility we shall have harmony, and instead of bookkeepers exercising a dominating role they will fill a duly subordinate position. Thus, schematically, in the capitalist phase there will be a release of more money both to give the DT'' to the secondary circuit and to obtain for the redistributional area its necessary measure of liquidity; in the materialist phase there will be similar operations, and as well the need of a positive DC' to keep C' at unity will be explored; in the static phase the liquidity of the redistributional area will be reduced but the funds released along DC', DT', and DT'' will not be recalled as though the idea of an expansion were a subsequent crash. Now to work out in detail the conditions under which this must be done, and to prescribe the rules that must be observed in doing it, is a vast task. It means thinking out afresh our ideas of markets, prices, international trade, investment, return on capital. Above all it means thinking out afresh our ideas on economic directives and controls. And if we are to do this, not on the facile model of the totalitarian or socialist regimes which simply seek to abolish the problems and with them human liberty, then there will be need not merely for sober and balanced speculation but also for all the concrete inventiveness, all the capacity for discovery and for adaptation, that we can command.[8]

53 Mechanism of the Cultural Expansion

By a cultural expansion is meant a rate of increase in the production of overhead primary products, of the things by which civilization is defended, developed, maintained.

8 The short section 53, to follow, fills the remainder of this last page, p. 133, of the original typescript. There is, then, no discussion of the dynamics of the cultural expansion which Lonergan had introduced in section 11. Further, there are three section numbers unused. Note 2 above suggests one topic that might have been treated at this stage. There is no evidence in the Archives – sketches, notes, whatever – of further elements for these concluding sections. The state of the typescript and its table of contents suggest that, for some reason, Lonergan closed off this work neatly here. Perhaps he had a sense of what became clear later (see the Introduction, pp. xx, xxiv), that a strict circulation analysis would not deal with this topic.

PART TWO

Fragments, 1942–1944

7

An Outline of Circulation Analysis

1 Viewpoint

It is the viewpoint of the present inquiry that, besides the pricing system, there exists another economic mechanism, that relative to this system man is not an internal factor but an external agent, and that present economic problems are peculiarly baffling because man as external agent has not the systematic guidance he needs to operate successfully the machine he controls.

On classical analysis economic mechanism is the pricing system. It coordinates spontaneously a vast and ever shifting manifold of otherwise independent choices of demand and decisions of supply. But man does not stand outside this machine; he is part of it; his choices and decisions are themselves the variables in the system. It follows that there is no possibility of setting down methodically,[1] on the one hand, the exigences of the machine and, on the other, the consequent performance of man. A study of the mechanics of motorcars yields premises for a criticism of drivers, precisely because the motorcars, as distinct from the drivers, have laws of their own which drivers must respect. But if the mechanics of motors included, in a single piece, the anthropology of drivers, criticism could be no more than haphazard.

There is at present an abundance of economic criticism. It is haphazard

1 The word 'methodically' is written in by Lonergan over the deleted typed word 'systematically.'

criticism. It does not proceed systematically from solid premises. It is the intuition of socialists who find a radical incoherence in individual choices and decisions and leap with a gay profusion of rhetoric to the *simpliste* solution of subordinating preferences and expectations to the benevolence of a tyranny. In contrast the criticism of traditional economists is the soul of sobriety. It is acute, informed, exact, subtle. But perhaps one may doubt that it is inspired, that it suffers from the imperious pressure of really significant ideas. Too often does one learn that problems are very complex indeed, that this or that element in the complexity may be singled out as especially troublesome, that such and such a makeshift perhaps meets the issue more satisfactorily than others which have been advocated. For as makeshift follows makeshift, it becomes increasingly difficult to distinguish between a democratic and a totalitarian economy.

But economists can be champions of democracy as well as advisers to dictators or planning boards. The proof of the possibility is a historical fact: the old political economists were champions of democracy; and if the content of their thought has been found inadequate, its democratic form is as valid today as ever. That form consisted in the discovery of an economic mechanism and in the deduction of rules to guide men in the use of the economic machine, a rule of *laissez faire* for governments and a rule of thrift and enterprise for individuals. It is now fully apparent that these rules serve their purpose only in particular cases, but it is still insufficiently grasped that new and more satisfactory rules have to be devised. Without them human liberty will perish. For either men learn rules to guide them individually in the use of the economic machine, or else they surrender their liberty to be ruled along with the machine by a central planning board.

The reality of that dilemma measures the significance of an effort, however tenuous and incomplete, to formulate the laws of an economic mechanism more remote and, in a sense, more fundamental than the pricing system. Now there is little dispute that the dilemma is real, for the liberal dream of an automatic economy has, like all dreams, at long last broken. The necessity of rational control has ceased to be a question, and the one issue is the locus of that control. Is it to be absolutist from above downwards? Is it to be democratic from below upwards? Plainly it can be democratic only in the measure in which economic science succeeds in uttering not counsel to rulers but precepts to mankind, not specific remedies and plans to increase the power of bureaucracies, but universal laws which men themselves administrate in the personal conduct of their lives. Thus the breaking of the liberal dream of automatic progress provokes a revision of judgment on the old political economists. Their greatness lay not in fostering an amoral devotion to automatism but in developing an economic science and from it issuing universal precepts of proper economic conduct. The automatism is a husk that has withered and fallen, and to cling to it is to fall into the totalitarian abyss. The old science and the old precepts have gone the way of Ptolemy and Newton. But to deny the possibility of a new science and new precepts is, I am convinced, to deny the possibility of the survival of democracy.

2 Method

The method of circulation analysis resembles more the method of arithmetic than the method of botany. It involves a minimum of description and classification, a maximum of interconnections and functional relations. Perforce, some description and classification are necessary; but they are highly selective, and they contain the apparent arbitrariness inherent in all analysis. For analytic thinking uses classes based on similarity only as a springboard to reach terms defined by the correlations in which they stand. To take the arithmetic illustration, only a few of the integral numbers in the indefinite number series are classes derived from descriptive similarity; by definition, the whole series is a progression in which each successive term is a function of its predecessor. It is this procedure that gives arithmetic its endless possibilities of accurate deduction; and, as has been well argued,[2] it is an essentially analogous procedure that underlies all effective theory.

On such a methodological model circulation analysis raises a large superstructure of terms and theorems upon a summary classification and a few brief analyses of typical phenomena. Classes of payments quickly become rates of payment standing in the mutual conditioning of a circulation; to this mutual and, so to speak, internal conditioning there is immediately added the external conditioning that arises out of transfers of money from one circulation to another; in turn this twofold conditioning in the monetary order is correlated with the conditioning constituted by productive rhythms of goods and services; and from the foregoing dynamic configuration of conditions during a limited interval of time, there is

2 A note here by Lonergan: 'See, for instance, Ernst Cassirer, *Substanzbegriff und Funktionsbegriff*, Berlin, 1910.'

deduced a catalogue of possible types of change in the configuration over a series of intervals. There results a closely knit frame of reference that can envisage any total movement of an economy as a function of variations in rates of payment, and that can define the conditions of desirable movements as well as deduce the causes of breakdowns. Through such a frame of reference one can see and express the mechanism to which classical precepts are only partially adapted; and through it again one can infer the fuller adaptation that has to be attained.

However, to set up such a systematic unit of terms and theorems is a logical procedure with norms and criteria of its own. The nature of this task leads the descriptive economist to use, as much as possible, the language of ordinary speech, to be content with resemblances that strike the eye, to move through easy stages of generalization to a nuanced picture of what, in the main, takes place. Again, the statistical economist has his own criteria. He will take advantage of a specialized terminology but, as far as he is concerned, the only justification for a terminology is a proximate possibility of measurements; further, he has no objection to recondite generalizations, but his generalizations resemble not the generalizations of mathematics but those of positive science. Now as the statistical approach differs from the descriptive, the analytic differs from both. Out of endless classificatory possibilities it selects not the one sanctioned by ordinary speech nor again the one sanctioned by facility of measurement but the one that most rapidly yields terms which can be defined by the functional interrelations in which they stand. To discover such terms is a lengthy and painful process of trial and error. *Experto crede.* To justify them, one cannot reproduce the tedious blind efforts that led to them; one can appeal only to the success, be it great or small, with which they serve to account systematically for the phenomena under investigation. Hence it is only fair to issue at once a warning that the reader will have to work through pages in which parts gradually are assembled, before he will be able to see a whole and pass an equitable judgement upon it.

8

A Method of Independent Circulation Analysis[1]

Circulation analysis is a set of definitions, postulates, and deductions relevant to monetary circulation. Such a systematic construction of terms and theorems might be worked out within a wider theoretical context. Thus, its concepts might be derived from the concepts of value theory; its postulates might be modifications of postulates regarding value; its deductions might be special cases of the more general deductions concerning scarce objects with alternative uses. Such a procedure offers the obvious advantages of theoretical unity; analytic apparatus is all in one large, nicely articulated, and agreeably complicated piece. However, like the armor of Saul, it is apt to be too cumbrous for David. Just as one can study Euclidean geometry without the slightest suspicion that it is a particular case of a more general geometry, so also one can attempt an independent circulation analysis in which the formation of concepts, the choice of postulates, and the seriation of deductions are dictated not by the higher exigences of value theory but by the more immediate and more germane considerations of the monetary circulation itself. In that fashion one would obtain an independent analytic tool which, from its general compactness and simplicity, would perhaps prove more efficient in the solution of certain types of problem. No doubt, once such an independent tool were constructed and found successful, theorists would be troubled by profound questions regarding the developments that might result from the mutual interaction of equilibrium and circulation analysis. But such thoughts cannot occupy us here. It

1 Attention was already drawn, in the Introduction (p. xx) to Lonergan's note at the top right of the corresponding page in the typescript.

is enough that we attempt to indicate by concrete example a method of independent circulation analysis in the belief that it offers special advantages in handling some economic issues.

1 Frame of Reference

The productive process of an exchange economy operating in a closed area offers the most favorable starting point for a study of a monetary circulation. For a circulation is not so much a rotational movement as an aggregate of instantaneous events, namely payments, which stand in circular series of relationships; and while a productive process is rectilinear rather than circular, it does provide, by the technical dependence of each successive stage of production upon previous stages, a correlative and almost palpable ground for series of relationships between payments. Thus, each element or stage of the material process has its proper outlay, payments of immediate factors of production in wages and salaries, rents and royalties, interest and dividends, depreciation charges and undistributed profits. Next there is the building up of prices as these elements are united materially into a growing product and simultaneously the outlays upon the single elements are added into a growing volume of transitional payments from subsequent to previous units of activity. At the end of these lines of production are the finished products, the aggregate receipts of industry and commerce, and the aggregate expenditure of final buyers.

All such payments form a class by themselves. They stand in a network that is congruent with the technical network of the productive process. They recur with the recurrence of its routines. In the main they vary with variations in the volume of these routines. But above all, their connection with production is immediate: they emerge not though repercussions or as responses to external stimulus but are, so to speak, the immanent manifestation of the productive process as a process of value. For in an exchange economy production is not a merely technical affair of designing, assembly, processing, and distribution; intrinsically it is an economic affair, an expression of preference and choices, and so not merely production, as some technical experts seem to fancy, but production for sale, production in view of and at every instant adapted to payments.

Payments, then, forming a network congruent with the network of the productive process, shall be termed operative, and from among them two boundary classes are selected: the aggregate receipts that are also the expenditure of final buyers; and the aggregate outlays that are also the income of factors of production. Let *DR* and *DE* be the aggregate sums of money that in a given interval are receipts and expenditure; let *DO* and *DI* be the aggregate sums of money that in the same interval are outlay and income; so that by definition *DR* = *DE* and *DO* = *DI*. Further, let us say that money held in reserve for expenditure is in the demand function of the economy; and that money held in reserve for outlay, or on its way to outlay through transitional payments, is in the supply function. Note, however, that it is not assumed that *DO* is identical with *DR*, or that *DE* is identical with *DI*. Such an assumption, in general, would be contrary to fact. Not only are there other exits and entrances to the supply and demand functions besides outlay and expenditure, receipts and income; but even if these other lines of communication did not exist, it would not be clear that all the receipts of an interval become outlay in the same interval, or that all the income of an interval becomes expenditure in the same interval.

Besides the operative payments described above there are in any economy other, redistributive payments. Such payments we define negatively; they form a remainder class of all payments that are not operative, that do not stand in the network congruent with the network of the productive process. The existence of this remainder class follows from the fact that property is a broader category than the current supply of goods and services. There are things never produced, such as an economy's endowment of natural resources. There are other things that, though produced, already have become the property of final buyers. Most of these may be sold, and the payments for them will be termed redistributive; for on the one hand such payments change titles to ownership, redistribute property, but on the other they are not operative, not intrinsic to the forward movement of industry and commerce. It is to be observed that such payments remain redistributive even when they mark the reentry of property into the productive process; to reenter the process is one thing; to be in the process is another; the former gives no more than one single payment; the latter is a source of income; the junk dealer receives an income but people selling junk to junk dealers receive single redistributive payments.

The demand and supply functions were defined above as sums of money held in reserve for expenditure and outlay; the redistribution function will be defined by all other sums of money. Thus, this function is not only the seat, so to speak, of money held in reserve for redistributive payments; it is also the seat of all idle money, and also of all money mobilized for general purposes. This general mobilization is the most important feature in the redistribution function inasmuch as finance may be defined as the art of procuring money for any purpose. However, with regard to financial operations it is necessary to distinguish between the service rendered and the commodity procured: payments for the services of financiers are final operative payments that appear in aggregate expenditure; on the other hand, transfers of the commodity in which the financier deals are redistributive payments. While this distinction may be applied readily enough to the transactions of bankers, brokers, underwriters, a more complex instance appears in insurance; here payments of premiums have to be divided into a final operative payment of services, proportionate to the outlay of the insurance company in wages, salaries, rents, dividends, and a redistributive payment, proportionate to the company's redistributive payments of awards; and, of course, this application of the distinction is only a first approximation that attends simply to the essential business of insurance of collecting premiums and paying awards; but it suffices for present purposes.

The next step is to introduce two more rates, *DD* and *DS*, similar to *DE*, *DR*, *DO*, *DI*. In the given interval *DD* is the net transfer of sums of money from the redistributional function to the demand function, while *DS* is the net transfer from the redistributional function to the supply function. Since *DD* and *DS* are net transfers they may be positive, zero, or negative; an excess in favor of the demand or supply functions is counted positive; an excess in favor of the redistributional function is counted negative. *DS* consists in movements to and from circulating capital; thus when entrepreneurs increase their volume of business by selling securities or contracting short-term loans, *DS* is positive; when on the other hand they decrease their volume of business, to purchase securities or pay off loans, *DS* is negative. As *DS* is the balance of monetary movements from redistribution to supply, so *DD* is the balance from redistribution to demand. In the given interval some income will be diverted from expenditure to the redistribution function; it goes to savings, the redistributive part in insurance, the liquidation of debts, the purchase of securities or of other redistributional property such as secondhand motorcars, private homes, farms, factories. In the same interval there is also an opposite movement: savings of earlier intervals are now spent; property is sold to meet current demands; payments of debts or awards of insurance companies go to education, medical fees, and so forth. The excess of the latter movement over the former in the given interval is the quantity *DD*.

A three-point circulatory system has now been defined. At any instant sums of money are either in the supply function, the demand function, or the remainder redistribution function. If at the beginning of an interval there is a sum S in supply, D in demand, and R in redistribution, then at the end of that interval one finds in supply the sum $(S + DR + DS - DO)$, in demand the sum $(D + DI + DD - DE)$, and in redistribution the sum $(R - DS - DD)$. Adding these three, one obtains $(S + D + R)$ since DR and DE, DI and DO, are identical pairs. It follows that the circulation exists by definition.

However, this three-point system has now to be enlarged into a five-point system by a subdivision of the supply function into basic supply and surplus supply and by a subdivision of the demand function into basic demand and surplus demand. The transformation turns upon a distinction between final buyers who are consumers and final buyers who are producers. It will be recalled that a final buyer is one who makes a final operative payment, and, indeed, it is easy enough to think of consumers as final buyers. However, one must not do so for the wrong reasons. A consumer is not a final buyer because he consumes the object bought and so precludes any subsequent sale; a consumer is a final buyer because he is not a middleman buying only to sell again. Thus, durable consumer goods just as much as food or fuel enter into final sales; the fact that motorcars, private homes, and so forth may be sold again, and often are sold again, is a fact of redistributive and not of operative exchange; the consumer is the final buyer because his payment was the last in the series of operative payments. Still greater difficulty seems to attend the conception of producers as final buyers. Here three distinct confusions seem to arise, coalesce, and so cover over one another's insufficiency. Let us attack them in detail. First, most of a producer's payments are transitional or initial: payments of wages are initial; payments for raw materials that are processed are transitional; but payments for the factory and the machinery with which the processing is done are final, the last of the series of operative payments made upon factory and machinery. Second, it is true that factory and machinery may later be sold, but such a sale is not operative but redistributive; one does not expect producers to sell their factories just as one expects them to sell what they make in their factories; only construction companies make a business of selling factories, and their final buyers are the producers who pay for them. Third, it is again true that producers in purchasing and maintaining capital equipment hope to get their money back; but this hope is not a hope of reselling capital equipment but a hope of profits from continued ownership; you may have traveled enough on a railway to have paid for a mile of track; but no question arises of the railway company ceding you the ownership of a mile of track, because there was no question of your buying that; what you bought was transportation.

Final buyers, then, fall into two classes, consumers and producers. It follows that we can distinguish between the basic expenditure of consumers and the surplus expenditure of producers. Similarly, we can distinguish between the basic receipts from the sale of consumer goods and services and the surplus receipts from the sale of producer goods and services. Further, we can distinguish between basic outlay, the reward of factors in the supply of consumer goods and services, and surplus outlay, the reward of factors in the supply of producer goods and services. Let *DE′* be the rate of basic expenditure, *DE″* the rate of surplus expenditure, *DR′* (= *DE′*) the rate of basic receipts, *DR″* (= *DE″*) the rate of surplus receipts, *DO′* the rate of basic outlay, *DO″* the rate of surplus outlay, all in any given interval. Next, it follows that the basic demand function is set up by sums of money in reserve for basic expenditure, the surplus demand function is set up by sums of money in reserve for surplus expenditure, the basic supply function is set up by sums of money in reserve for basic outlay, and the surplus supply function is set up by sums of money in reserve for surplus outlay. The five-point frame of reference has been defined. Finally, as *DS* and *DD* were defined as net transfers from redistribution to supply and demand, we may now define *DS′* as the net transfer to basic supply from the redistribution function, *DS″* as the net transfer to surplus supply, *DD′* as the net transfer to basic demand, and *DD″* as the net transfer to surplus demand, all in the given interval. At this point it will be well to collect results by drawing a diagram, say a baseball diamond, with the redistribution function in the pitcher's box, basic demand at home base, basic supply at first, surplus demand at second, and surplus supply at third.[2] *DD′*, *DS′*, *DD″*, *DS″* may be denoted by arrows pointing from the pitcher's box to the bases; *DE′* by an arrow from home base to first, and *DE″* by an arrow from second base to third. But before *DO′* and *DO″* can be represented on the diagram, one has to settle their relations to *DI′* and *DI″*.

DI′ is defined as the quantity of income entering basic demand in the given interval, and *DI″* as the quantity of income entering surplus demand in the same interval. It will be convenient to maintain the identity of aggregate outlay and income so that

2 See the diagram in section 34 of Part One, or in chapter 16, section 8, of Part Three; also relevant are the comments in note 2 of chapter 13.

$$DO' + DO'' = DI' + DI'' \qquad (1)$$

and hence all income will be supposed to enter the demand functions at least for an instant; if its real destination is the redistribution function, that fact can be represented by negative values of DD' and DD''. Next, it cannot be supposed that all basic outlay becomes basic income and all surplus outlay becomes surplus income. At least some basic outlay becomes surplus income, namely, the depreciation charges that purchase maintenance of capital equipment from surplus supply. Again, at least some surplus outlay becomes basic income, namely, wages paid to labor which are spent for consumer goods and services. Thus, there is a crossover at which part of the basic circuit of expenditure, receipts, outlay pours into surplus income and simultaneously part of the surplus circuit of expenditure, receipts, outlay pours into basic income. Let G' be the fraction of basic outlay that becomes surplus income in the given interval, and G'' be the fraction of surplus outlay that becomes basic income in the same interval. Then,

$$DI' = (1 - G')DO' + G''DO'' \qquad (2)$$

$$DI'' = (1 - G'')DO'' + G'DO' \qquad (3)$$

The diagram may now be completed: $(1 - G')DO'$ marking an arrow from first base to home; $G'DO'$ marking an arrow from first base to second; $(1 - G'')DO''$ marking an arrow from third base to second; and $G''DO''$ marking an arrow from third base to home. At times, it will be convenient to deal simply with the difference between the two crossover rates, $G'DO'$ and $G''DO''$; let the difference between them in the given interval be the quantity DG so that

$$DG = G''DO'' - G'DO' \qquad (4)$$

When this difference is zero, the crossovers will be said to be in equilibrium; hence one has

$$DG = O \qquad (5)$$

or alternatively in terms of G' and G''

$$G'/G'' = DO''/DO' \qquad (6)$$

either of which may be taken as the condition of crossover equilibrium. It is to be noticed that equation (4) makes it possible to write equations (2) and (3) more simply, viz.,

$$DI' = DO' + DG \tag{7}$$

$$DI'' = DO'' - DG \tag{8}$$

Finally, let us compare the aggregate sums of money in the five functions at the beginning and at the end of any given interval. If at the beginning these sums are respectively R, D', S', D'', S'', then at the end of the interval the sums will be respectively

$$R - DD' - DS' - DD'' - DS''$$

$$D' + DI' + DD' - DE'$$

$$S' + DR' + DS' - DO'$$

$$D'' + DI'' + DD'' - DE''$$

$$S'' + DR'' + DS'' - DO''$$

On adding these one obtains the initial sums R, D', S', D'', S'', since DE'' and DR', DE'' and DR'', $(DO' + DO'')$ and $(DI' + DI'')$ are all equal by definition. Since the redistribution function is the home of finance, it is to be noted that unlike the initial sums D', S', D'', S'', the sum R is a variable: it increases with the production (or import) of gold, with increases in the fiduciary issue, with increases in bank credit.

Before advancing further with the analysis, it will be well to review and consolidate. A circulation is an aggregate of instantaneous events, namely payments, which stand in circular series of relationships. Payments have been arranged in five classes: redistributive, basic expenditure, basic outlay, surplus expenditure, surplus outlay. Corresponding to each class of payments there has been posited a monetary function of money held in reserve for payments of the class; thus there is a redistribution function, a basic demand function, a basic supply function, a surplus demand function, and a surplus supply function. These five functions supply the points of reference of the frame. Transfers of money from one function to another take place at given rates, so much money per interval; nine symbols have been selected and defined to represent these rates of transfer, namely, *DD′*, *DS′*, *DD″*, *DS″*, *DE′*, *DE″*, *DO′*, *DO″*, and *DG*; another six symbols are also used, namely, *DR′*, *DR″*, *DI′*, *DI″*, *G′*, and *G″*, but all of these are determinate when the first nine are determinate, with the sole exception that *G′* and *G″* cannot be separated.

This frame of reference pays no attention to monetary operations within the given five functions. Thus in the supply functions money moves in complex fashion from receipts to outlay with increases or decreases of monetary circulating capital effected by *DS′* and *DS″*; similarly, within the redistribution function there are the manifold transfers of financial operations. Now the frame of reference neither denies the existence nor refuses to acknowledge any importance in all such movements within functions. It simply prescinds from them. It expresses a viewpoint that sees the monetary circulation as fundamentally a matter of a basic circuit of expenditure, receipts, outlay, and income concerned with consumer goods and services, of a similar surplus circuit of expenditure, receipts, outlay, and income, with a crossover in which these two circuits mingle, and with a central area of redistribution which not only is a remainder function gathering together the odds and ends that do not fit into the definition of operative payments but also a function of general monetary mobilization that conditions and so controls accelerations in the basic and surplus circuits. A justification of the value of this viewpoint can be had, of course, only from the interpretations and definitions of economic phenomena to which it leads.

2 Normative Phases

The frame of reference that has been devised views the circulation in the cross section of a single interval and not in the process over several intervals. To attain the latter, much more important viewpoint, the notion of normative phases is introduced. A phase is defined as a series of intervals in which the difference between the first interval and the second is also found between the second and the third, between the third and the fourth, and so on throughout the series. Thus, a phase is a period of uniform and cumulative change. Phases are said to be normative when, first, the systematic variation from interval to interval is defined in terms of variation of basic and surplus outlay and, second, certain simplifying conditions are posited with regard to crossover equilibrium, movements from the redistribution function to basic and to surplus demand, and lags between income and expenditure. Thus, normative phases are types of moving frames of reference from which more complicated movements of the circulation can be studied.

Let the suffixes 1, 2 be added to the terms of the frame of reference, namely, DO', DO'', G', G'', DI', DI'', etc., when these terms are used with reference to any two successive intervals; for example, DI''_1 and DI''_2 are the values of DI'', the rate of surplus income, in any two successive intervals.

Next, let D^2O' and D^2O'' be the increments of basic and surplus outlay determined by the comparison of two successive intervals, so that

$$D^2O' = DO'_2 - DO'_1 \tag{9}$$

$$D^2O'' = DO''_2 - DO''_1 \tag{10}$$

Similarly, one may define D^2I', D^2I'', D^2E', D^2E'', etc. However, with regard to G' and G'', the fractions of outlay that cross over to the opposite type of income, it will be most convenient to write

$$DH = G''_2/G'_2 - G''_1/G'_1 \tag{11}$$

so that DH is the relative change in the crossover fractions.

Now the first element in the definition of the normative phases is a systematic variation of basic and surplus outlay. But D^2O' and D^2O'', the increments of outlay, may be positive, or zero, or negative. On this simple head one obtains nine types of phase; their names and definitions are given in the following table; to these is added a third column under the rubric DH, which is not immediately relevant.

Phase:	D^2O'	D^2O''	DH
Static Phase:	0	0	0
Basic Expansion:	+	0	+
Surplus Expansion:	0	+	–
Compound Expansion:	+	+	
Basic Contraction:	–	0	–
Surplus Contraction:	0	–	+
Compound Contraction:	–	–	
Basic Disequilibrium:	–	+	–
Surplus Disequilibrium:	+	–	+

The principle of the nomenclature is simple: six of the nine phases are expansions or contractions; expansions when outlay is increasing, and contractions when outlay is decreasing; these expansions and contractions are divided into basic, surplus, and compound according as basic outlay, surplus outlay, or both are increasing (expansion) or decreasing (contraction). When one type of outlay is increasing and the other decreasing, there is said to be a disequilibrium; a disequilibrium is named basic when basic outlay is the weak sister, surplus when surplus outlay is. There remains only the static phase in which both basic and surplus outlay are constant.

The second element in the definition of normative phases is a set of simplifying conditions. Their effect will be to make the other variables of the basic circuit, DI', DD', DE', DS' dependent on DO', and similarly the other variables of the surplus circuit, DI'', DD'', DE'', DS'' dependent on DO''. Thus, the definitions of the phases in terms of the variation of DO' and DO'' become definitions in terms of a systematic variation of all the variables.

The first of these simplifying conditions is a postulate of crossover equilibrium. It will be recalled that the rate of crossover difference, DG, is defined by

$$DG = G''DO'' - G'DO' \tag{4}$$

so that when crossover equilibrium makes this difference zero

$$DO'/DO'' = G''/G' \tag{6}$$

Hence, in the static phase, when DO' and DO'' are both constant, crossover equilibrium is satisfied by a constant ratio of the crossover fractions; G''/G' is the same ratio, interval after interval, and so DH is zero. On the other hand, when one of the pair DO' and DO'' is varying while the other is constant, the ratio G''/G' has to be constantly undergoing adaptation if crossover equilibrium is to be maintained; thus, in the basic expansion, the surplus contraction, and the surplus disequilibrium, DH has to be increasing, while in the surplus expansion, the basic contraction, and the basic disequilibrium, DH has to be decreasing. Finally, in the compound expansion and the compound contraction, when both rates of outlay are varying in the same direction, one cannot conclude immediately whether DH has to be positive or zero or negative to give crossover equilibrium; in these two cases a blank was left in the third column, DH, of the table of names and definitions of the phases.

The postulate of crossover equilibrium may be stated more concretely as follows. G'' is the fraction of surplus outlay going to basic demand: thus, $G''DO''$ includes nearly all the wages in surplus outlay and a notable proportion of salaries, rents, royalties, dividends; everyone has to live, to purchase consumer goods and services. Similarly, $(1 - G')$ is the fraction of basic outlay going to basic demand; it is similar in character to G'', and indeed, since people do not regulate their spending according as their income is from basic or from surplus production, one may expect that

$$G'' = 1 - G' \qquad (12)$$

Hence one may eliminate either G' or G'' from the condition of crossover equilibrium, writing

$$DO'/DO'' = (1 - G')/G' = G''/(1 - G'') \qquad (13)$$

The meaning of the condition now becomes clear. While people do not regulate their spending according to the origin of their income, they do have to regulate it according to the proportion of consumer goods and services in total production. If the production of consumer goods and services involves an outlay that is four times as great as that involved in the production of producer goods and services, then four-fifths of total income have to move to the consumer market; otherwise crossover equilibrium fails. On the assumption expressed in equation (12) above, four-fifths of total income move to the consumer market when G'' is 80% and G' is 20%. In the static phase these percentages would remain unchanged. But in the expansions and the contractions these percentages have to be changing constantly. If a basic expansion makes DO'/DO'' equal to 5, then G'' has to advance from 80% to 83.3% while G' has to recede from 20% to 16.6%. On the other hand, if a surplus expansion makes DO'/DO'' equal to 3, then G'' has to recede from 80% to 75% while G' advances from 20% to 25%. Of course, when we say that G' or G'' have to undergo certain modifications, we speak of no objective and necessary cause; we merely enunciate the consequent of the hypothesis of crossover equilibrium. With regard to the verifiability of that hypothesis in actual economic history, we are inclined to be very sceptical. Under the profit criterion there is a marked bias in favor of a large G' and a small G'', so that surplus expansions are prolonged and basic expansions short-lived.

The second of the simplifying conditions defining normative phases is an equilibrium between the thrifty and the spendthrifts, between the melancholy who put their earnings aside in anticipation of future rainy days and, on the other hand, the sanguine who cannot fancy the future being as bad as the present and so spend what they have, and what they can borrow, with an open hand. In precise form this second postulate is that

$$0 = DD' = DD'' \tag{14}$$

Movements from the redistribution function to basic demand are canceling, interval by interval, with movements from basic demand to the redistribution function. Similarly, movements between surplus demand and the redistribution function result in a cancellation. Such movements may be as great or as small as you please; they may vary enormously or not at all; the postulate is satisfied as long as the aggregate result is, in each case, a cancellation. Obviously, this is very much a simplifying condition. At a single stroke it brushes aside all the complications of the equation between savings and investment until such time as these questions can be discussed profitably.

The third of the simplifying conditions is that basic expenditure keeps pace with basic outlay, and that surplus expenditure keeps pace with surplus outlay. The possibility of this 'keeping pace' has been secured by the two previous postulates. Crossover equilibrium makes basic income exactly equal to basic outlay, and surplus income exactly equal to surplus outlay. For

$$DI' = DO' + DG \tag{7}$$

$$DI'' = DO'' - DG \tag{8}$$

and crossover equilibrium means that DG is zero. Next, the equilibrium between the sanguine and the melancholy prevents this income from running off to the redistribution function to the depletion of the demand functions as also it prevents the demand functions from becoming clamorous because of excess releases from the redistribution function. Thus, the possibility of expenditure keeping pace with outlay has been provided for. The postulate is that expenditure not merely can but actually does keep pace. And, as is clear enough, this postulate is implicit in the idea of types of phase initiated by outlay. For suppose that outlay increased and expenditure did not follow; plainly enough, entrepreneurs would take the hint and desist from their expansion; and if they did desist, the phase would change, for the phase in question would be defined by increasing outlay. Thus, this third simplifying condition is not so much an additional postulate as an implication of our method of procedure. It remains, however, that some attempt be made to declare more precisely what is meant by expenditure 'keeping pace.' In the first place, it does not mean that in each interval

$$DE' = DO'$$

$$DE'' = DO''$$

Such a postulate would disregard entirely the fact of a production period, that, for example, in an expansion outlay begins to increase, and keeps increasing, considerably in advance of the arrival of the increment of goods and services on the final markets. Equality of expenditure and outlay interval by interval would mean a rise of price levels to enable the increased income to be spent when the increment of goods and services was not yet on sale; similarly, it would mean a drop of price levels to enable decreased income to clear the market before the market began to suffer a curtailment of supply. Thus, the postulate of continuity, of 'keeping pace,' has to be put in the form of such equations as

$$DE'_j = DO'_i \qquad (15)$$

$$DE''_j = DO''_i \qquad (16)$$

where the suffixes i and j refer to two different intervals, and the time between these intervals is equal to the weighted average production period of the goods and services undergoing increase or diminution. In this precise form, the postulate of continuity is not particularly realistic; but it may not be out of place to observe that there is no necessity of realism at this point of the inquiry. The function of theory is to construct ideal lines from which one can approximate systematically towards the real lines; our present concern is to obtain clear and definite ideal lines.

The fourth and last of the simplifying conditions has to do with the velocity of money in the basic and surplus circuits. The postulate is framed as a conditioned correlation, namely, that D^2O' and DS', and similarly D^2O'' and DS'', are simultaneously positive, zero, or negative, except insofar as this is prevented by the already posited postulate of continuity which also regards monetary velocities in the circuits. The correlation itself amounts to saying that when DS' or DS'', the net transfers from redistribution to the demand functions, are positive, then the decrease in velocity will not be so great as to cause D^2O' or D^2O'' to be negative; again, when DS' or DS'' is negative, the increase in velocity will not be so great as to enable D^2O' or D^2O'' to be positive. In the main these suppositions are plausible enough: industry and commerce generally are not brisker when there is a contraction of short-term loans, nor are they slackening when short-term loans are expanding. What is not plausible is the exact correlation of a zero D^2O' with a zero DS', and a zero D^2O'' with a zero DS''. But while this is not plausible, it remains a convenient assumption for the moment. So much for the correlation of the net transfers to the supply functions with the increments in the rates of outlay. It has been said that this correlation is supposed only insofar as it does not conflict with the postulate of continuity, with the postulate that there is a lag, proportionate to production periods, between changes in the rates of income and of expenditure. The possible conflict becomes apparent as soon as one attempts to envisage the process of an expansion or contraction. Let us say that DS' is some positive quantity k, over a series of intervals. The immediate effect is an increment of basic outlay of, say, k' per interval, where k' is a function of k and of the velocity in the basic circuit. Thus, in the first interval DO' becomes, say, $(m' + k')$. In the second interval, DS' again transfers k, and this makes possible, we may suppose, another addition of k' to the rate of basic outlay. But the question arises whether this k' is to be added to m' or to $(m' + k')$. If increases in the rate of expenditure do not lag behind increases in the rate of income, one would be inclined to say that in the second interval DO' is $(m' + 2k')$. But when one has postulated lags proportionate to production periods, one has to choose the other alternative. Thus, the effect of a net transfer of k per interval will raise DO' from m to $(m' + k')$ in a first interval, and so give a positive D^2O', then for a series of intervals equal to the lag between increments of income and increments of expenditure, it will maintain DO' at $(m' + k')$, and so give a zero D^2O' when DS' is positive; finally, only at the end of this lag will DO' set forth on its full expansion with increasing receipts combining with the net transfers from redistribution to basic supply to give the series $m' + k'$, $m' + 2k'$, $m' + 3k'$, $m' + 4k'$, and so make D^2O' equal to k' interval by interval. Thus, there is a real conflict between the present velocity postulate and the previous postulate of continuity; accordingly, we have made the velocity postulate conditioned, so that the postulate of continuity prevails. Except for lags in D^2E' and D^2E'', a positive or negative value of DS' or DS'' gives a corresponding positive or negative value of D^2O' or D^2O''.

So much for the idea, the names, the definitions, and the simplifying conditions of the normative phases. Under the defined conditions any phase can be had by controlling DS' and DS''. According as these are positive, zero, or negative, D^2O' and D^2O'' will be positive, zero, or negative in virtue of the conditioned velocity postulate. According as D^2O' and D^2O'' are positive, zero, or negative, it follows by definition that DO' and DO'' are increasing, constant, or decreasing. By the postulate of crossover equilibrium, DI' is always equal to DO' and DI'' is always equal to DO''. By the postulated equilibrium between the thrifty and the spendthrifts initiative is removed from the demand functions, and by the postulate of continuity the rates of expenditure DE' and DE'' keep pace in due time with the rates of outlay DO' and DO''. Thus increased outlay in due time returns to the supply functions to join with present increments and give the cumulative effect of the expansions; similarly, decreased outlay in due time is manifested in decreased receipts, and this negative joined with the negative action of a minus DS' or minus DS'' gives the cumulative effect of the contractions. A positive DS' maintained over a series of intervals will make the basic circuit bigger and bigger; a negative DS' will make it smaller and smaller; a zero DS' will leave it constant. Similarly, DS'' controls the surplus circuit. Thus, the idea of normative phases has enabled us to take our static frame of reference and transform it into nine types of dynamic frames of reference.

3 The Cycle of the Normative Phases

We must now revert to our point of departure. The division of payments into redistributive and operative, expenditure-receipts and outlay-income, basic and surplus, was based upon relations between the payments and the productive process. Then the process was forgotten: two circuits of expenditure, receipts, outlay, income were set up, and conditions were defined under which the acceleration of the circuits was made dependent upon movements of money between the redistribution function and the basic and the surplus supply functions. This gave the nine normative phases, but we have now to inquire into the relation between such phases and the productive process. The result of this inquiry will be twofold: it will reveal an analogy of productive phases parallel to the monetary phases already defined; and it will arrange all such phases into a series, into the unity of a cycle.

Let us suppose a complete list made of all types and qualities of goods and services sold at the basic final market in either or both of two successive intervals. Let the prices and quantities of the first of these intervals be

$$p_1, p_2, p_3, \ldots p_n$$
$$q_1, q_2, q_3, \ldots q_n$$

and let the increments of these prices and quantities emerging in the second interval be

$$dp_1, dp_2, dp_3, \ldots dp_n$$

$$dq_1, dq_2, dq_3, \ldots dq_n$$

so that one can write with complete accuracy

$$DE'_j = \Sigma\, p_i q_i \tag{17}$$

$$DE'_k = \Sigma\, (p_i + dp_i)(q_i + dq_i) \tag{18}$$

$$D^2E' = \Sigma\, (q_i dp_i + p_i dq_i + dp_i dq_i) \tag{19}$$

where the third equation results from the subtraction of the first from the second, the suffixes j and k refer to any two successive intervals, and the summations are taken by giving i successively all values from 1 to n.

On inspection of the third equation (19), it is apparent that the increment of basic expenditure, D^2E', consists of three elements: the first depends entirely upon price increments; the second depends entirely upon quantity increments; and the third is a mixture of both, a product of price increments and quantity increments. Immediately there arises the problem of determining to what extent D^2E' results from price change and to what extent it arises from quantity change. To meet it we define terms and distinguish cases. Let DP' be the average increment of prices and DQ' be the average increment of quantities; and let us suppose that these increments are added to a price index P' and a quantity index Q'. However, before these definitions can be made more precise, two cases have to be distinguished: market continuity, when the product of price increments by quantity increments, $dp_i dq_i$, is relatively small and so may be neglected in an approximate estimate; and market discontinuity, when this product is not relatively small and so may not be neglected.

In the case of market continuity the relations between P', DP', Q', DQ' are defined by the equations

$$P'Q' = \Sigma\, p_i q_i \tag{20}$$

$$P'DQ' = \Sigma\, p_i dq_i \tag{21}$$

$$Q'DP' = \Sigma\, q_i dp_i \tag{22}$$

By assigning any numerical value for P', the price index, one can at once determine numerical values for Q', DQ', and DP'. Further, with regard to a series of intervals, one can choose price and quantity indices

$$P'_1, P'_2, P'_3 \ldots P'_n$$

$$Q'_1, Q'_2, Q'_3 \ldots Q'_n$$

that satisfy the exact series of equations

$$P'_j Q'_j = DE'_j \tag{23}$$

and fall within the limits determined by the approximate equations

$$P'_k = P'_j + DP'_j \tag{24}$$

$$Q'_k = Q'_j + DQ'_j \tag{25}$$

In this manner, there will be only one purely arbitrary number in the double series of indices, say P'_1, the price index of the first interval of the series.

In the case of market discontinuity, DP' and DQ' will cease to be algebraic symbols and become mere symbolic abbreviations, that is, one gives up the problem of assigning numerical values to DP' and DQ' and becomes content with determining on the whole whether or not there is upward or downward price or quantity change, whether DP' and DQ' are positive, zero, or negative. In general such determination offers little difficulty. For if there is market discontinuity, then $\sum dp_i dq_i$ is large; and from an inspection of the terms in the summation one can tell whether this is the result of increasing or decreasing prices, of increasing or decreasing quantities. In any such instance one may conclude that DP' and DQ' are positive or negative, though one cannot say what numerical increments are to be added to the price index P' and the quantity index Q'.

There remains an ambiguity, namely, the case of the emergence of new types or new qualities of goods and services. If we suppose that in the previous interval, when their quantities were zero, their prices were also zero, then the total receipts from these goods and services appear in the summation $\sum dp_i dq_i$. If, on the other hand, we project their prices backwards from the second interval to the first, then the same total receipts appear in the summation $\sum p_i dq_i$, for then the price increments dp_i are zero instead of the initial prices p_i being zero. A balance of considerations seems to favor the latter procedure. Accordingly, it is here assumed, though one must bear in mind its implication, namely, that there is a case when DQ' is zero yet a qualitative acceleration is going forward because new types and qualities of goods and services are displacing older types and qualities.

So much for the definitions of DP' and DQ' and, in the case of market continuity, of the indices P' and Q'. In like manner we suppose defined P'', Q'', DP'', DQ'', which have the same meaning with regard to final sales of surplus goods and services as P', Q', DP', DQ' have with regard to final sales of basic goods and services.

So far attention has been directed to the analysis of the increments per interval of final expenditure, D^2E' and D^2E''. We have now to turn to the factors in these increments, and first to the indices of quantity change, DQ' and DQ''. It has been argued that, in general, it is possible to tell whether these indices are positive, zero, or negative. Hence it follows that one may define nine quantity phases in parallel fashion to the nine circulation phases already examined. Thus, a quantity static phase is a series of intervals in which both DQ' and DQ'' remain zero; a quantity basic expansion is a series of intervals in which DQ' is positive and DQ'' zero; a quantity surplus expansion is a series of intervals in which DQ' is zero and DQ'' positive; and similarly there is a quantity compound expansion (+, +), a quantity basic contraction (–, 0), a quantity surplus contraction (0, –), a quantity basic disequilibrium (–, +), and a quantity surplus disequilibrium (+, –).

In the short run such quantity phases may result from mere variations in the use of existing capital capacity; thus, the present war has witnessed a great increase in the use of railroads with very slight addition to railway capital equipment. In a still shorter run quantity phases may result from the mere depletion or piling up of inventories or stocks of goods, from the lengthening or shortening of hours of labor, and so on. In such instances there is no correlation between basic and surplus quantity variations. But in the long run, and especially in the very long run, such a correlation exists. It is that surplus production is the accelerator of basic production. In other words the correspondence between the two is not a point-to-point but a point-to-line correspondence; a new ship is not needed for every trip across the seas, nor a new shoe factory for every new pair of shoes; one ship yields a flow of voyages, one factory yields a flow of shoes, and so a series or flow or stream of surplus goods and services corresponds to a series of series, a flow of flows, a stream of streams of basic goods and services. Now such a correspondence, if it is to be expressed not in terms of expectations of the future but in terms of present fact, is a correspondence of accelerator to accelerated. Thus, with regard to any given pattern of combinations of production factors, there is some long-term average quantity of surplus production necessary for the maintenance and the renewal of both surplus and basic means of production. When Q'' stands at that average, then the accelerator of the system is merely overcoming what may be termed the system's friction. There results a quantity static phase: both DQ' and DQ'' are zero. If the system is to move into a long-term expansion, this movement has to begin with a surplus quantity acceleration: surplus production has not merely to maintain or renew existing capital equipment but has to reach a level at which it turns out new units of production and maintains or renews a greater number of existing units; this gives the quantity surplus expansion; DQ'' is positive but DQ' as yet remains zero. The quantity surplus expansion has its most conspicuous instances in industrial revolutions and five-year plans, in which standards of living do not improve while a national industrial equipment is wholly transformed; indeed, in such a movement it may happen that standards of living may deteriorate, and then one has the closely allied basic disequilibrium in which DQ'' is positive and DQ' negative. Eventually, however, this increasing the means of producing the means of production reaches its goal and turns to increasing basic products. The new units now emerging are not surplus but basic; thus DQ'' stands at zero while DQ' is positive; there is the quantity basic expansion, the general rise in standard of living that is the normal objective of the previous surplus expansion. It may very well happen that the standard of living begins to rise before the increase of the surplus process comes to a halt: the phase then is the quantity compound expansion with both DQ'' and DQ' positive. Again, it may happen that the increase of the surplus process was overestimated, and so the basic expansion will be interrupted momentarily by a surplus disequilibrium in which DQ'' is negative, with Q'' moving down to a lower average level, while DQ' remains positive. Finally, unless this transforming process is immediately followed by another, the basic expansion eventually reaches its term, and a new static phase on a notably higher level than the initial static phase results.

Thus, the quantity phases have an inner logic of their own. They are not merely a list of possible dynamic configurations but they naturally fall into a series, into a cyclic process, that moves from a static phase through surplus expansion, basic disequilibrium, compound expansion, surplus disequilibrium, and basic expansion, towards a new static phase in which a higher standard of living is attained permanently. Now this cycle has two features. In the first place, it is grounded in the nature of things. A higher standard of living in an economic community is, generally, both a qualitative and a quantitative improvement of the flow of basic goods and services. To attain that improvement, the community has to set about transforming its pattern of combinations of production factors. Such a transformation postulates at the outset an increase of surplus production and so a surplus expansion with perhaps a basic disequilibrium. However, once this condition is fulfilled, there follows the increase of the standard of living in a compound and then a basic expansion with perhaps a period of surplus disequilibrium. Finally, the higher standard of living reaches its peak, the maximum possible within the transformed economy, and once it is attained there is no more to be done than maintain it. The second feature is that this cyclic process, grounded in the nature of things, does not coincide in all respects with the familiar trade cycles. The latter are marked by basic and surplus and compound contractions, while no mention of contractions was made in the logical scheme by which an economic community moves systematically from a lower to a higher standard of living. Thus it is necessary to distinguish between pure cycles, which omit contractions, and perturbed cycles, in which the upward movement of the pure cycle is cut short by a general contraction. Generally there is no objection to the pure cycle, which yields an improvement of living standards; equally generally there is vehement objection to the trade cycle, which begins with the movements of the pure cycle but ends up with something very different. However, the pure cycle is for the moment the mere suggestion of a possible theoretic construction; later we shall return to it, but the present point is simply the observation that quantity phases are phases of a process.

The analysis of D^2E' and D^2E'' revealed not only quantity factors of acceleration, DQ' and DQ'', but also price factors, DP' and DP''. The significance of the latter is that they mark a divergence between the circulation phases, defined in terms of D^2O' and D^2O'', and the quantity phases, defined in terms of DQ' and DQ''. Accordingly, it is not worth while to set up a further group of nine price-level phases, since DP' and DP'' simply indicate what might be described metaphorically as the inertia of the quantity process of goods and services in its response to accelerations initiated in the circulatory process of payments. Rapid increases or decreases in the circulatory process have not a proportionate effect in the quantity process but are in part absorbed by positive or negative price increments. Thus booms are notoriously inflationary and slumps deflationary. Hence DP' and DP'' are best taken as indices of divergence between circulatory and quantity phases.

The main analytic apparatus is now complete. The two acceleration systems have been defined: a circulatory system consisting of two connected circuits that are accelerated by an external redistribution function; a quantity system of two parts in which one part is the long-term accelerator of the other. In each of these acceleration systems nine phases of a cyclic process have been defined in parallel fashion, with postulates determining the normative phases of the circulatory system, and an inner logic or ground in the nature of things indicated as the normative or pure cycle of the quantity process. Finally, indices of price increments serve as markers of the divergence between the two systems.

4 The Effect of Net Transfers

The basic circuit is connected with the redistributional function by two routes: net transfers to supply, DS', and net transfers to demand, DD'. Similarly, the surplus circuit is connected by two routes: net transfers to supply, DS'', and net transfers to demand, DD''. In defining the normative phases, the correlation of these net transfers with the rates of the circuits was evaded by the introduction of postulates. It is now necessary to determine, in so far as possible, what the correlation is.

The existence of the problem is apparent. For instance, DO' is a rate, so much money going to basic outlay every so often. The increase of this rate may result from an increase in the quantity or from an increase in the velocity of money, so that one might write

$$D^2O' = (m.dv) + (v.dm) + (dv.dm) \qquad (26)$$

where m is a quantity of money and dm its finite increment, and v is a velocity of money and dv its finite increment. Evidently, unless one knows the conditions under which money changes its velocity in the circuits, one cannot tell when a net transfer, DS', is needed to effect an increase of DO'. Further, unless one knows some correlation between DS', which is an increment of circulating capital, and dm, which is an increment in the quantity of money in outlay, one is still in the dark about the relations between DS' and D^2O'.

A general solution of the problem is not as difficult as might appear. We have to deal not with the quantity and velocity of money in all and any payments but only with the quantity and velocity in operative payments. But operative payments have been defined as standing in a network congruent with the network of the productive process; it follows that we have to deal with quantities of money congruent with the values emerging in the productive process, and with velocities of money congruent with the velocities of the productive process. In fact we shall be able to deal with the more precise ideas of turnover size and turnover frequency instead of the ill-defined ideas of quantity of money and velocity of money.

Perhaps the first step will best be an illustration of this correlation. Suppose that two shipbuilders, *A* and *B*, each launch a new ship every 15 days, that *A* has 5 ships under construction at once while *B* has 10, and so that *A* completes another ship every 75 days while *B* requires 150 days. To avoid irrelevant differences, we may suppose that all ships are similar in all respects, that they are sold as soon as they are launched for the same selling price, and so that total receipts and the aggregates of costs and profits are the same in both instances. There are then two equal volumes of business: each receives the selling price of one ship every 15 days; and each proceeds to make aggregates of initial and transitional payments at the same rate. However, this identity of volumes of business does not involve an identity of quantities and velocities of money. *A*'s turnover is an aggregate of receipts and payments on 5 ships, while *B*'s turnover is an aggregate of receipts and payments on 10 ships. When *A* sells a ship, he has been making payments on it for 75 days, on a second ship for 60 days, on a third for 45 days, on a fourth for 30 days, on a fifth for 15 days. But when *B* sells a ship, he has been making payments on it for 150 days, on a second for 135 days, and on a third to a tenth ship for periods of 120, 105, 90, 75, 60, 45, 30, and 15 days respectively. Thus, *A*'s volume of business is a matter of 5 ships every 75 days, while *B*'s is a matter of 10 ships every 150 days. The two volumes are equal, but *A* moves money twice as rapidly as *B*, yet moves only half as much as *B*.

The difference between turnover size and turnover frequency has been put with exaggerated clarity. It remains that the same distinction can be made with regard to every entrepreneur in basic or in surplus supply. Each one is performing a certain number of services or contributing to the supply of a certain number of products at once. Such performance or contribution takes a certain amount of time. But once this time has elapsed, the entrepreneur proceeds to a new batch of services or products. Thus entrepreneurial activities fall into a series of repeated routines. Further, each of these routines form financial unities: receipts come in for the goods or services supplied; transitional payments are made to other entrepreneurs for their contribution to the supply; initial payments are made to the immediate factors; and the aggregate of transactions regarding that batch of goods or services is closed. Thus, the production period has its correlative in the monetary order, namely, the turnover period; and similarly the value of the goods processed or the services rendered in the production period has its monetary correlative in turnover size.

Certain clarifications are in order. The turnover period is not necessarily identical with the production period, for the turnover period is the period of both production and sale. If the first shipbuilder, *A*, could sell a ship no oftener than once every 16 days, his production period might remain 75 days but his turnover period would lengthen to 80 days. The production period sets a lower limit to the turnover period, but turnover periods lengthen when sales do not keep pace; and in the limit decreasing sales lead to a reduction of turnover size. Thus, if *A* could sell one ship only once every 19 days, he might deliberate between having 5 ships in construction at once with a turnover period of 95 days, or reducing his construction to 4 ships at once with a turnover period of 75 days.

Turnover size will be measured by the transitional and initial payments arising from the turnover. When the entrepreneur's operations are constant, turnover size will also be equal to the receipts from the turnover. When, however, the entrepreneur is increasing or decreasing the scale of his operations, receipts differ from turnover size, and this difference involves a net transfer from or to the redistribution function. Thus if decreasing sales led the first shipbuilder to have only 4 ships under construction at once, his active circulating capital would decrease by one-fifth; the receipts for 5 ships are not needed to meet the initial and transitional payments on 4. Later, if increasing sales encourage a return to a turnover of 5 ships at once, then circulating capital that had gone off to the redistribution function has to return; receipts from 4 ships do not suffice to meet the transitional and initial payments on 5. It may be noted, finally, that we make provisions further on for the complication caused by increasing or decreasing inventories, that is, stocks of goods kept on hand to meet sudden increases in demand.

Let us now systematize the results obtained. With regard to all the entrepreneurs in basic supply during a given interval, let r_{ij} be the initial payments of the *i*th entrepreneur in his *j*th turnover or fractional turnover during that interval, and let s_{ij} be the corresponding transitional payments. Then the aggregate initial payments of basic supply during the interval, which is the definition of DO', may also be expressed as a double summation of r_{ij}, so that

$$DO' = \Sigma\Sigma\, r_{ij} \tag{27}$$

and similarly the volume of transitional payments, which may be termed DT', is another double summation, namely,

$$DT' = \Sigma\Sigma\, s_{ij} \tag{28}$$

Next, if we define turnover frequency as the number of turnovers of a given entrepreneur in a given interval, and observe that this number may be a fraction, proper or improper, it will be possible to find average values for the initial payments and other average values for the transitional payments in the successive turnovers of each entrepreneur during any given interval. This makes it possible to replace the double summations by single summations so that

$$DO' = \Sigma\, r_i n_i \tag{29}$$

$$DT' = \Sigma\, s_i n_i \tag{30}$$

where n_i is the turnover frequency of the *i*th entrepreneur in the given interval and the summations are taken with respect to all entrepreneurs in basic supply.

If now two successive intervals are compared, and it is found that the *i*th entrepreneur increases his initial payments by dr_i, his transitional payments by ds_i, and his turnover frequency by dn_i, then the increments in DO' and DT' will be

$$D^2O' = \Sigma\, (r_i dn_i + n_i dr_i + dn_i dr_i) \tag{31}$$

$$D^2T' = \Sigma(s_i dn_i + n_i ds_i + dn_i ds_i) \tag{32}$$

where again the summations are taken with regard to all entrepreneurs in basic supply. Equation (31) gives a correlation between changes in velocity of money and changes in the rate of basic outlay. Basic outlay can increase, through the increase of monetary velocity, to the extent that turnover frequencies can increase; and turnover frequencies increase in two ways: first, by the elimination of lagging sales so that turnover periods are reduced to the size of production periods; second, by the introduction of more rapid methods of production, provided that these more rapid methods are accompanied by an increased efficiency in sales. This correlation is far from being a model of precision, but at least it takes variations in DO' from changing monetary velocity out of an obscure region of pure indetermination. Changing production periods are observable phenomena; so also are brisker and slower sales; without either of these we cannot suppose that DO' varies from changes in monetary velocity; and with these one can suppose no more than a limited and proportionate change of monetary velocity. Other changes in DO' have to be attributed to net transfers, DS'.

There remains the question, To what extent does DS' effect an increase or decrease in DO'? For evidently DS' does not effect solely the quantity increments dr_i, but also the quantity increments ds_i. Consider the equation

$$\Sigma\, s_i n_i = \Sigma\, v_i r_i n_i \tag{33}$$

in which the left-hand side gives the volume of transitional payments in the interval while the right-hand side multiplies by a v_i the volume of initial payments. What is the multiplier v_i? At a first approximation it is the number of times the product per interval of the *i*th entrepreneur is sold transitionally during the interval. Thus, when the *i*th entrepreneur deals immediately with consumers, v_i is zero. When his product per interval is sold once transitionally during the interval and once finally, then v_i is one. When three-quarters of his product is sold four times and one-quarter is sold five times, exclusive of final sales, then v_i is (4 × ¾ + 5 × ¼) or four and one quarter. But this gives only the first approximation to v_i. At a second approximation one has to take into account that, particularly in the more distant transitional sales, it is not the product of the present interval but the product of previous intervals that is being sold transitionally. These products may differ in quantity and in price from the present interval's $r_i n_i$, but it remains that there is some numerical proportion between the payments they involve. Thus a further correction can be introduced into the calculation of the transitional velocities v_i, and it must be introduced to satisfy equation (33). It will be convenient to term the latter type of variation of v_i its conventional variation, while variation in the number of transitional sales will be called its independent variation.

So much for the general functional relation between initial and transitional payments, equation (33). If we suppose that turnover frequencies are constant, then the relation between increments dr_i, ds_i, dv_i is given by

$$\sum (r_i dv_i + v_i dr_i + dr_i dv_i) = \sum ds_i \tag{34}$$

The immediate effect of increments in outlay per turnover, dr_i, is offset by the opposite increments in transitional velocities, dv_i, according to the convention of the preceding paragraph; hence increments in transitional payments per turnover, ds_i, do not appear at once, for the transitional buyers do not increase their payments when the *i*th entrepreneur increases his outlays but when they purchase his increased products. On the other hand, as soon as these purchases begin, the convention works in the opposite direction, for the increments dv_i now have the opposite sign, and though dr_i may have returned to zero, r_i is standing on its new level. Next, if one turns from these short-term effects, one may suppose that v_i remains constant so that dv_i is zero; this gives the long-term correlation

$$\sum v_i dr_i = \sum ds_i \tag{35}$$

which holds in a successful acceleration of the whole process. Now the net transfer from or to the redistributional function, DS', is the proximate source of increments in circulating capital needed for both transitional and initial payments. Hence, when turnover frequencies are constant and accelerations are successful, that is, the increased product is sold all along the line, then

$$DS' = \sum (dr_i + ds_i) \tag{36}$$

which with equation (35) gives

$$DS' = \sum (1 + v_i)\, dr_i \tag{37}$$

Thus, the net transfer DS' is equal to the increments in active monetary circulating capital; and these increments are equal to the increments in outlay per turnover, plus multiples of the latter depending on the number of transitional sales.

One must be content merely to mention the possibility of independent variations of v_i. These emerge in changes in the structure of transitional payments when, for example, a merger eliminates, or the breakup of a large corporation into smaller units creates, a proprietary barrier that involves transitional payments. If the aggregate of outlays remains the same, one may expect the second term of the left-hand side of equation (34) to summate to zero, positive instances of dr_i canceling against negative instances. The same holds for the third term. Hence one would get

$$\sum ds_i = \sum r_i dv_i \tag{38}$$

so that the merger, in which dv_i is negative, would give negative increments in active monetary circulating capital devoted to transitional payments. The breakup of a corporation would have the opposite effect. However, such structural changes affect not only transitional payments but also turnover frequencies; the length of the turnover periods determines the quantity of money required for payments in each turnover and so the new pattern of instances of dr_i and ds_i. Thus while circulating capital needed for transitional payments decreases in one respect, this may be offset by other requirements.[3]

The argument now moves forward to a fresh topic. Monetary velocities in basic supply have been shown to be a function of turnover frequencies, and turnover frequencies a function of the efficiency of sales and the length of production periods. The division of net transfers DS' between monetary circulating capital for initial payments and for transitional payments has been made a function of transitional velocities, v_i, which depend on the number of times the product of a given entrepreneur is sold transitionally in the standard interval. It remains that we complete the circuit with a consideration of income velocities and of additions to income by net transfers DD'.

As a matter of convenience let us divide entrepreneurs into three classes:

3 This concludes G114. The text immediately following begins at G119. The intervening pages G115–G117 are an earlier attempt to continue. They are reproduced in an appendix to this chapter. G118 is also included there, although it does not belong to the sequence. It begins with the word 'expansion' as does G127, but it is not a prior version of that page. Its topic is broader and more elementary.

an initial group, E_i, which makes no transitional payments; a group of middlemen, E_j, whose transitional payments form the total receipts of the initial group; and a final group, E_k, whose total receipts are basic expenditure DE', and whose transitional payments are the total receipts of the middlemen. There are two conventional elements in this structure of basic supply. The first conventional element lies in the manner of the description: we speak of groups of entrepreneurs when really we have no interest in entrepreneurs; we are studying not entrepreneurs but payments in their circular relationships, and in fact, the entrepreneurs in the three groups are mere figureheads; what they stand for are sets of payments and receipts, and really what is under discussion are such sets. The second conventional element lies not in the nomenclature but in the structure itself. No real structure of basic supply admits the elegant simplicity of the above description; there are endless complications, and these complications are not constant but shifting. But whatever the complications and their changes, there is one constant feature, namely, the balancing of ledgers, the equality of receipts and payments. The complexities of interdependence represented by the balancing of ledgers are not the object of our study, but that balancing itself. Hence we are content to study such balancing under the simple conditions of three groups of entrepreneurial figureheads.

Let us say that the volume of payments per interval of the initial group, E_i, is $\sum r_i n_i$, of the group of middlemen, E_j, is $\sum (r_j n_j + s_j n_j)$, and of the final group, E_k, is $\sum (r_k n_k + s_k n_k)$, where r denotes initial payments, s transitional payments, n turnover frequencies, and the three summations are taken with respect to all instances of i, j, and k respectively. Then, since initial payments are identical with outlay we have

$$DO' = \sum (r_i n_i + r_j n_j + r_k n_k) \qquad (39)$$

On the further assumption that in each case payments of the interval equal receipts of the interval, we have

$$DE' = \sum (r_k n_k + s_k n_k) \qquad (40)$$

$$\sum s_k n_k = \sum (r_j n_j + s_j n_j) \qquad (41)$$

$$\sum s_j n_j = \sum r_i n_i \qquad (42)$$

Equation (40) states that the receipts of the final group are equal to their initial and transitional payments. Equation (41) states that the receipts of the group of middlemen are equal to their initial and transitional payments. Equation (42) states that the receipts of the initial group are equal to their initial payments, which *ex hypothesi* are their sole payments. But the transitional payments of the final group are identical with the receipts of the middlemen, and the transitional payments of the middlemen are identical with the receipts of the initial group. Hence the summation of $s_k n_k$ appears in both (40) and (41), and the summation of $s_j n_j$ appears in both (41) and (42). On the elimination of these summations, it appears that DO' and DE' are equal, for both equal the summation of the rates of initial payments per interval. Let us further suppose crossover equilibrium, so that DG equals zero, and DO' equals DI'. It then appears that the condition and, inversely, the consequent of entrepreneurial receipts equaling entrepreneurial payments is that the expenditure of basic demand, DE', equals the income of basic demand, DI'.

Now it is important to distinguish two different aspects of equations (39) to (42). Under a certain aspect these equations express a truism: if entrepreneurial receipts and payments equate, then they equate not only among entrepreneurs but also between entrepreneurs and the third party, demand. But under another aspect the same equations, so far from expressing a necessary truth, express an almost unattainable ideal, namely, a dynamic equilibrium to which any actual process continually attempts to approximate by varying prices and changing quantities of supply. To study the truism is to study bookkeeping, to study the art of double entry, and to learn the magic of the variable items, profit and loss, which perforce make the books balance. To study the ideal is to study equilibrium analysis. The bookkeepers are wise after the event. But if the entrepreneurs are to be wise, they have to be wise before the event, for their payments precede their receipts, and the receipts may equal the payments but they may also be greater or less, to give the entrepreneur a windfall profit or loss. Such justification or condemnation of payments by receipts the bookkeeper records but the entrepreneur has to anticipate, and the grounds of his anticipations, their effects upon his decisions, and the interaction of all decisions form the staple topic of equilibrium analysis. Now the viewpoint of the present discussion is neither that of the bookkeeper nor that of the equilibrium analyst. Equations (39) to (42) are regarded not as a set of facts recorded by bookkeepers, nor as an ideal which entrepreneurs strive yet ever fail to attain, but as a first approximation to the law of the circulation in the basic circuit. The first approximation to the law of projectiles is the parabola: one might, if one chose, consider projectiles as aiming at or tending towards the ideal of the parabola yet ever being frustrated by wind resistance; one might elaborately describe the trajectory of the projectile as an indefinite series of parabolas, each one in succession the goal of its tendency only to be deserted because adverse circumstance set it on another track. In such a description of trajectories there is to be found at least a superficial resemblance with the statement that an economy is tending towards equilibrium at every instant, though towards a different equilibrium at every successive instant. But whatever the resemblance, and however deep and significant the difference, we here propose to take a circuit in equilibrium as a first approximation to the law of the circuit and examine first the implications of this law and then the second approximations that are relevant to our inquiry.

If we suppose that equations (39) to (42) represent any first interval and that in a second interval, in which crossover equilibrium is assumed, the increments in the terms are D^2O', D^2I', D^2E', D^2R', dr_i, dr_j, dr_k, dn_i, dn_j, dn_k, ds_j, ds_k, then the conditions that the acceleration is a success, that is, that the acceleration has extended round the circuit in accordance with the first approximation to the law of the circuit, are to found in the following equations.

$$D^2O' = D^2I' = \Sigma\ (dr_in_i + dr_jn_j + dr_kn_k + r_idn_i + r_jdn_j + r_kdn_k) \qquad (43)$$

$$D^2E' = D^2R' = \Sigma\ (dr_kn_k + r_kdn_k + ds_kn_k + s_kdn_k) \qquad (44)$$

$$\Sigma\ (ds_kn_k + s_kdn_k) = \Sigma\ (dr_jn_j + r_jdn_j + ds_jn_j + s_jdn_j) \qquad (45)$$

$$\Sigma\ (ds_jn_j + s_jdn_j) = \Sigma\ (dr_in_i + r_idn_i) \qquad (46)$$

These equations are derived by substituting in equations (39) to (42) a $(r_i + dr_i)$ for an r_i, etc., etc., multiplying out the expressions, neglecting the products of two increments, such as dr_idn_i, and eliminating through (39) to (42) the products containing no increments, such as r_in_i. The initial substitution implies that the increments are such as to satisfy the conditions defined by the initial equations. The final elimination separates the conditions of an equilibrium circulation from the conditions of a successful acceleration of a circulation. The neglect of the products of two increments makes equations (43) to (46) approximate except when one is considering pure frequency accelerations (when all instances of *dr* and *ds* are zero) or pure quantity accelerations (when all instances of *dn* are zero).

The significance of equations (43) to (46) is conceptual. They provide a definition of a successful acceleration of the basic circuit, a meaning for the already indicated distinction between a pure quantity acceleration and a pure frequency acceleration, a basis of discussion for abortive accelerations, and finally a means of contrasting such circulatory success or failure with the success or failure of acceleration of the productive rhythms.

Our first task is to complete our inspection of the circuit. There remains the question of quantities of money and velocities of money in basic demand. Now if we define DD' by the equation

$$DD' = DE' - DI' \tag{47}$$

there seems no lack of plausibility. The equation means that savings are in the redistribution function, so that when people in basic demand are spending more than they earn, they are transferring savings to basic demand to make up the difference; again when they are spending less than they earn, they are creating savings and so transferring money from basic demand to the redistribution function. However, this equation has a further implication, namely, that income velocities, in the aggregate, cease to be an added variable in the system. By giving DD' the above precise meaning, one eliminates such suppositions as that DD' adds to the quantity of money in basic demand merely to decrease the velocity of money there or, inversely, that it subtracts from the quantity of money there merely to increase its velocity. DD' has been tied down to an exclusive role of quantity acceleration, and income velocities in the aggregate are determinate when DI' and DE' are determinate. To put the same point differently, the concept of income velocities has been eliminated; there is a rate of income, DI'; there is a rate of expenditure, DE'; but between the two there is no rate, but only a quantity of money, which DD' has the function of increasing or decreasing. This last statement assimilates the analysis of the basic demand function to that of the basic supply function; for in supply we consider only rates of payment, turnover sizes, and frequencies, and between such rates we do not posit virtual monetary velocities but only quantities of money in reserve, quantities which DS' augments or diminishes.

If now we revert to equations (43) to (46), we observe that the successful acceleration of the circuit involves two types of increments: quantity increments, dr_i, dr_j, dr_k, ds_j, ds_k; and frequency increments, dn_i, dn_j, dn_k; reference to D^2O', D^2I', D^2E', D^2R' is omitted since they are but other names for the same realities. Now with respect to the quantity increments, the question arises, To what extent are they due to DS', and to what extent are they due to DD'? In other words, the quantity increments show that there is more money in circulation, say DM', where DM' is defined by the equation

$$DM' = \sum (dr_i + dr_j + dr_k + ds_j + ds_k) \qquad (48)^4$$

or on the suppositions of equation (37)

$$DM' = \sum [(1 + v_i)\, dr_i + (1 + v_j)\, dr_j + dr_k] \qquad (49)$$

the summations being taken with respect to all instances of *i, j,* and *k,* that is, with respect to all members of the three groups of entrepreneurs. Now when we were engaged in the study of basic supply, it was natural to consider this total quantity increment as the work of the net transfer DS'; but evidently such a total increment in the whole circuit may to some extent be the work of DD', so that

$$DM' = DS' + DD' \qquad (50)$$

Which, then, of the two net transfers has the preponderant role in increasing or decreasing the quantity of money in the circuit?

First, with regard to increases, it should seem that the role of DD' can be little more than initial stimulation. People may spend more than they earn by drawing on savings, but they cannot do so to any great extent. To give DD' a preponderant role would make quantity accelerations of the basic circuit both small and short-lived. On the other hand, our society has developed vast mechanisms to provide entrepreneurs with the means of making large and sustained additions to the quantity of money in the circuit. It practiced mercantilism to obtain more gold when money was gold. It developed banking and bills of exchange. It replaced a gold currency, first with a gold standard fiduciary issue, and later with what is to all practical purposes a new kind of money, money-of-account. These developments did not take place to enable consumers to spend more than they earn, but

4 In equations (48) and (49) Lonergan did not place a summation sign to the right of the equal sign, but rather parallel horizontal lines; but from the context and from the mention of 'summations' immediately after equation (49) one may conclude that the parallels are to be read as Sigma. The noncompletion of the symbol would seem to indicate that he did not work towards finalizing this attempt. The problem recurs at note 1 of chapter 19.

to enable entrepreneurs to increase the size of their turnovers. Consumers cannot pay interest on their consumption or even on the increments in their consumption. But entrepreneurs can pay interest on the size of their turnovers. There is a second argument. It is that in an economy in which supply is responsive to demand, any positive action of DD' would immediately stimulate entrepreneurial expansion. The middlemen and the initial group would begin increased turnovers before they began to receive increased receipts. The increased initial payments in the turnovers would mean an increased rate of income, so that to maintain a positive DD' a further immediate increase in the rate of expenditure would be necessary. There is a third argument which follows out of the second, namely, that at the beginning of an expansion outlays are increasing more rapidly than goods at the final market, so that the increase in income is larger than the immediately available increase of objects on which income may be spent; hence unless DD' is negative and people are spending less than they are earning, prices will rise to give a positive DP' and make excessive expenditure equal to insufficient goods. But as soon as a negative DD' is needed to prevent price inflation, a positive DD' would only accentuate the price inflation; and while this positive action on the part of DD' would reduce to some extent the need of positive action on the part of DS', it also would increase that need especially if the acceleration of the supply of goods and services continues; for the rising price level would be communicated back from the final market through all the transitional markets, and at the same time a demand for increased wages would arise, so that the whole basis of calculation of initial and transitional payments is raised.

The three arguments tend to show that quantity acceleration of the circuit through the action of DD' is impossible, inasmuch as people cannot to any great extent spend more than they earn; unnecessary, inasmuch as entrepreneurs will effect the quantity acceleration in response to any real stimulus; inadvisable, inasmuch as such[5] activity is apt to raise price levels

5 This concludes G127. The remainder of the section has been reproduced from G131, a facsimile of which is given in chapter 14, p. 220. G128–130 are rejected pages. G128 and G130 are rejected attempts at continuing from G123, which begins with the paragraph 'The significance ...' (p. 144 above). Each page has substantially the same beginning paragraph, then G128 continues:

> The first step is a consideration of the general conditions of such an acceleration. Insofar as there are increments in the quantity of initial or transitional payments per turnover, the net transfers DS' and DD' have been active. For variations in income velocities can be eliminated from the discussion by defining DD' by the equation

and so to multiply the need for more money throughout industry and commerce. No one of the three arguments is peremptory, but the three combined tend to limit positive action by DD' to a stimulation of the quantity acceleration and to leave DS' the main part of the work of providing the increased quantities of money for the increased turnovers.

Mutatis mutandis, the same arguments that hold at the beginning of the acceleration hold throughout its duration. For any rate of acceleration of goods and services, DQ', goods in production are in advance of goods on the final market, and increasing income is in advance of the possible basic expenditure at initial prices. This lag is a function of DQ', increasing with

---

$$DD' = DE' - DI' \tag{47}$$

This is not arbitrary

G130 has another version of this paragraph:

> The first step is a consideration of the general conditions of the successful acceleration, and, to begin, there is the question whether income velocities are a further variable or whether they are determinate when the already assigned variables are determinate. Two considerations favor the second alternative. The first is that income velocities are periods of time between initial payments and final sales; but the assigned variables determine the quantity of initial payments per turnover and the number of turnovers per interval; they also define the quantities of money involved and the rapidity of turnovers of final sales. It follows that the aggregate of income velocities have some determinate index. Again, if a circular flow is successful, then the elements of the flow are not piling up at one point to leave a vacuum at another

Both these attempts end abruptly with the page incomplete. G129 centers on the same topic, but it is not immediately connectable with the other pages. It is a half page of typescript which reads as follows:

> in terms of known, i.e. already assigned variables.
>
> This procedure is not arbitrary even though the argument used involves an arbitrary control over the precise meaning to be attributed to 'money in the demand function' and 'net transfers during an interval.' The absence of pure arbitrariness may be shown by establishing the same result in another way. The assigned variables determine the quantities and rates of initial payments; per turnover; they also determine the quantities and rates of final sales; per turnover; but the initial payments are income and the final sales are expenditure. The quantities and velocities in basic demand begin from income and end at expenditure; changes in the quantities are determinate when DD' is determinate; but if we know the rate of flow at either end and the quantity in between, we also know the velocity in between.

its increase, and decreasing with its decrease; and corresponding to the size of this lag there is some single advance in prices, DP', that clears the basic market with DD' at zero. When the lag changes another change in prices is necessary if DD' is still zero. But then when the acceleration DQ' eventually becomes zero, a positive DD' is for the first time desirable, namely, to prevent the negative DP' implied in the disappearing lag.

Appendix[6]

Equations (36) and (37) tacitly assume that the increased quantities of money involved in increasing turnovers are derived exclusively from the net transfer to basic supply, DS'. This tacit assumption has now to be corrected. The quantity of money in the basic circuit may increase or decrease in three ways: by a net transfer to basic supply, by a net transfer to basic demand, and by a crossover disequilibrium. Let DM' be this increase in quantity of money in a given interval, so that

$$DM' = DS' + DD' + DG \tag{39}$$

where the parallel equation for the surplus circuit would be

$$DM'' = DS'' + DD'' - DG \tag{40}$$

since a positive DG empties the surplus circuit in favor of the basic while a negative DG empties the basic circuit in favor of the surplus (see equation 4 above).

The next question is whether DM' may replace DS' in equations (36) and (37). The answer involves some determination of the concept of income velocities. Let us write

$$DD' = DE' - DI' \tag{41}$$

so that savings are in the redistribution function: when people spend less than they earn, the difference gives a negative DD'; and when they spend more than they are earning, they are drawing on savings in the redistribution function and effecting a positive DD'. The effect of this equation (41) is to eliminate the concept of income velocities. There is a rate of income,

6 See above, p. 140, note 3.

DO'; there is a rate of expenditure, DE'; but between these two there is no rate but only a quantity of money which DD' increases or diminishes in a manner that equilibrates the two terminal rates DO' and DE'. This device assimilates the analysis of velocity in basic demand to the analysis already given for basic supply: for in supply there were posited no velocities of money between payments, but simply rates of payment with quantities of money between them and DS' as the proximate source of variations in these quantities.

A further effect of equation (41), more relevant to the present issue, appears on recalling that

$$DI' = DO' + DG \tag{7}$$

so that

$$DE' = DO' + DG + DD' \tag{42}$$

so that basic expenditure equals basic outlay plus the crossover difference plus the net transfer to basic demand. But basic expenditure is also basic receipts, that is, the receipts of the entrepreneurs who deal immediately with consumers. Now such receipts over an interval may be equal to or greater than or less than the payments, initial and transitional, of these entrepreneurs over the interval. Let us assume that at the end of each interval these entrepreneurs make up their books, transfer a positive difference to the redistribution function to give a negative element in DS', or make good a negative difference by effecting a positive transfer from the redistribution function. Then

$$DM' = \Sigma\ (ds_i + dr_i) \tag{43}$$

and on the suppositions of equation (37)

$$DM' = \Sigma\ (1 + v_i)\ dr_i \tag{44}$$

The foregoing results may be put more precisely. It will be recalled that $r_i n_i$ and $s_i n_i$ are approximate average figures over the interval and that dr_i, ds_i, dn_i are increments found by comparing the averages of two intervals. However, there is another notation, already mentioned, that makes r_{ij} the exact initial payments and s_{ij} the exact transitional payments of the *i*th entrepreneur in his jth turnover or fractional turnover during the interval. Let us define dr_{ij} and ds_{ij} as the increments emerging from the comparison of two successive turnovers, figures being taken from complete and not from fractional turnovers. Further, let DM' be the quantitative increment of money in the circuit during the same interval and not, as hitherto, the increment in the second of two intervals under comparison. Then, on the suppositions of equations (42) and (43)

$$DM' = \Sigma\Sigma\ (dr_{ij} + ds_{ij}) \tag{45}$$

and since it is always possible to find numbers, u_{ij}, such that

$$\Sigma\Sigma\ ds_{ij} = \Sigma\Sigma\ u_{ij} dr_{ij} \tag{46}$$

one can also write

$$DM' = \Sigma\Sigma\ (1 + u_{ij})\ dr_{ij} \tag{47}$$

where all summations are taken first with respect to turnovers j and then with respect to entrepreneurs i. In this notation varying velocities, that is, turnover frequencies, appear in the number of terms in the summations with respect to j.

[G118][7] expansion. Finally, the cycle initiated by the movement of the process from an initial static phase through a surplus expansion, a basic disequilibrium, a compound expansion, a surplus disequilibrium, and a basic expansion, may be said to have a normative goal in the attainment of a new static phase on a higher level. But to advance steadily towards that goal, to avoid the interruptions of basic, surplus, compound contractions, the agents of the economy have to adapt their preference schedules and correct their expectations to each of the successive phases. For the cycle has an objective logic of its own, and its successive phases postulate different preferences and different expectations. On the other hand, to believe and act up to the belief that the preferences and expectations proper to, say, a surplus expansion are equally legitimate and satisfactory pragmatically in a basic expansion or a static phase, that is to invite a type of disaster which by its frequent recurrence has become familiar.

7 See above, p. 140, note 3.

This brings us to the second difference between a Robinson Crusoe and a large-scale exchange economy. The latter is a monetary economy, and the use of the medium of exchange can act as a screen that hides from view the objective necessity of changing preferences and expectations in accordance with change in productive phases. When Robinson is clearing a new field, he is incapable of the illusion that that activity enables him to have more to eat here and now. When Robinson is reaping greater harvest from more numerous fields, he is incapable of the illusion that the corn he will not care to eat can be transmogrified into the capital equipment of, say, a power plant or another cleared field. But the multitudinous Robinsons of the exchange economy are rewarded with money whether they clear fields of [The page ends here.]

9

Circulation Trends

9 Circulation Trends

Trends are determinate relations between successive intervals. Circulation trends are determinate relations between the rates of payment and of transfer in successive intervals. With respect to any two successive intervals, *i* and *j*, let a suffix, *i*, added to a rate of payment or transfer denote the rate during the earlier of the two intervals, and a suffix, *j*, denote the rate during the later interval. Further, let the symbol D^2 denote the change of rate from one interval to another so that, for example,

$$D^2O' = DO'_j - DO'_i \qquad (15)$$

and similarly in the case of all other rates.

Nine classes of circulation trend are distinguished according as D^2O' and D^2O'' are positive, zero, or negative. The names of the classes are given most simply in a table, as follows.

	D^2O'	D^2O''
Level:	0	0
Basic Expansion:	+	0
Surplus Expansion:	0	+
Compound Expansion:	+	+
Basic Contraction:	–	0
Surplus Contraction:	0	–

Compound Contraction:	–	–
Basic Disequilibrium:	–	+
Surplus Disequilibrium:	+	–

Thus, a circulation level is a series of intervals in which the rates of basic and of surplus outlay remain constant from one interval to the next. In the circulation expansions one or both rates of outlay is increasing but neither is decreasing. In the circulation contractions, one or both rates is decreasing but neither is increasing. In the disequilibria one rate is increasing and the other decreasing.

The discussion of circulation trends presupposes some correlation of the variables DO', DO'', DG, DE', DE'', DS', DS'', DD', DD'', all of which, as far as definitions go, are independent. Hence the notion of a normative trend is introduced, and the procedure will be to examine, first, normative trends and, secondly, the various possible departures from the normative.

Normative trends are defined as series of intervals in which D^2O' and D^2O'' are as defined in any one of the nine classes and, as well, the following equations are satisfied.

$$0 = DG = DD' = DD'' \quad (16)$$

$$D^2E' = D^2O' = V'D^2S' \quad (17)$$

$$D^2E'' = D^2O'' = V''D^2S'' \quad (18)$$

and there is supposed some initial interval in which

$$0 = DS' = DS'' = DO' - DE' = DO'' - DE'' \quad (19)$$

so that

$$DS'_n = D^2S'_2 + D^2S'_3 + \ldots + D^2S'_n \quad (20)$$

$$DS''_n = D^2S''_2 + D^2S''_3 + \ldots + D^2S''_n \quad (21)$$

Equations (16), (17), (18) hold in each interval of the series of intervals constituting the trend. Equations (19) need be no more than a hypothetical initial interval providing a definite frame of reference for subsequent changes. Equations (20) and (21) refer to any nth interval. Finally, V' and

V'' in equations (17) and (18) are velocity coefficients relating changes in DS', DS'', which are pure rates of transfer, to changes in DO', DO'', DE', DE'', which are rates of payment.

Two main questions arise: first, are the normative trends possible, and what are their conditions? secondly, what departures from the normative trends are possible, and what are their conditions? The significance of these questions is that they provide a systematic method of investigating the possible functional relations of the independent variables over a series of intervals.

The possibility of the normative trends seems to follow from an examination of their definition. Their fundamental feature is that in each interval the rate of basic outlay equals the rate of basic expenditure, and the rate of surplus outlay equals the rate of surplus expenditure. This follows for the first interval from equations (19) and for subsequent intervals from equations (17) and (18). Such equality of, respectively, basic and surplus outlay and expenditure is no more than the affirmation of continuity in two circuits interval by interval: it is unreal insofar as it disregards the possibility of lags; but to disregard lags is to remain within the limits of theoretical possibility. On the other hand, equalities of outlays and of expenditure affirm a necessary tendency of the circulation: the general condition of a circulation is that entrepreneurs receive back the equivalent of their outlays, so as to be able to repeat them, and similarly that demand receives back in income the equivalent of its expenditure, so as to be able to repeat it.

It is to be noted that the equality of outlay and of expenditure does not exclude profits. Profits are the part of initial payments which entrepreneurs pay to themselves; as far as the equality of outlay and expenditure goes, that part may be as large or as small as you please. Further, it is not necessary that profits be spent in themselves for expenditure to keep pace with outlay; any expenditure of an equivalent sum not derived from current income will enable expenditure to keep pace with outlay even if profits are not spent; finally, the equality of expenditure and outlay does not disappear simply because expenditure is not keeping pace with outlay, for then outlay may keep pace with expenditure, and in fact that is what happens, since against falling sales entrepreneurs reduce the scale of their operations.

The second feature of the normative trends is that crossover equilibrium is maintained. The surplus circuit does not gain from the basic nor the basic from the surplus. Though there is a crossover, still each circuit carries on as though there were none. This is a theoretical possibility and, obviously, a simplifying condition to be introduced as long as one wishes to examine not the interactions of the circuits but the process within each circuit.

The third feature of the normative trends is the neutrality of the demand functions. *DD′* is zero, and *DD″* is zero. This does not mean that there are no savings. It does mean that present earnings, which are not spent, are balanced by the present spending of past earnings. With respect to the basic demand function, this involves an equilibrium between the sanguine people who borrow to meet current expenses and the melancholy who put by for rainy days more than they are ever going to spend. With respect[1]

[a] to the surplus demand function, *DD″* at zero means that expenditure of funds for surplus goods and services, whether derived from current surplus income or from mobilizations of money in the redistributive function

[b] to the surplus demand function, *DD″* at zero involves an equilibrium between current surplus income that is not spent and, on the other hand, the movement by investment from the redistributive function to the surplus demand function.

Finally, the increase or decrease per interval of rates of outlay and of expenditure are attributed in each circuit to either of two factors

11 Trends

Trends are determinate relations between successive intervals. Two types of trend are considered: process trends and circulation trends. Both have the same general form, namely, on certain suppositions with regard to intervals 1, 2, 3, ... *i*, *j*, ... *n*, the quantitative process of goods and services or the circulatory process of payments and transfers behaves in such and such a fashion. Nine classes are distinguished in each type of trend; names of the classes and their definitions are to be had in the following table.

1 There follow, in the archival copy, two versions of the next page of the manuscript, both incomplete. Both are included here in what seems the order of their composition. It is plausible to assume that, after the second attempt at continuing, Lonergan abandoned this particular line of development.

Process Trend:	DQ'	DQ''
Circulation Trend:	DM'	DM''
Level:	0	0
Basic Expansion:	+	0
Surplus Expansion:	0	+
Compound Expansion:	+	+
Basic Contraction:	–	0
Surplus Contraction:	0	–
Compound Contraction:	–	–
Basic Disequilibrium:	–	+
Surplus Disequilibrium:	+	–

Thus the nine process trends are defined according as process indices DQ' and DQ'' are zero, positive, or negative. Similarly, the nine circulation trends are defined according as circuit increments in the quantity of money, DM' and DM'', are zero, positive, or negative. In each case the nine classes are complete enumerations with respect to all possible values of two variables. If over a series of intervals, DQ' is zero and DQ'' is positive, the process trend is a surplus expansion. If over a series of intervals, DM' is negative and DM'' is positive, the circulation trend is a basic disequilibrium.

To complete the definitions of the process trends, it is necessary to specify the meaning of DQ' and DQ''. Let, then, DQ' be defined by the rates of basic expenditure, DE'_i and DE'_j, in any two successive intervals, i and j. Let DQ'' be defined by the rates of surplus expenditure, DE''_i and DE''_j, in the same two successive intervals. With DE'_i, DE''_i, DE'_j, DE''_j determinate with respect to process and quantities, calculation of DQ' and DQ'' proceeds as outlined in equations (83) to (91) in the preceding section.

It is to be observed that process trends are merely functions of aggregate weighted quantities sold at the basic and the surplus final markets. Differences that do not appear in the process indices do not affect the trend. Hence, if one quantity increases and another decreases proportionately to the respective weights, indices which regard aggregates are unaffected. Accordingly, any amount of qualitative change may be going on without any change of trend. It follows that the process level differs enormously from the neoclassical stationary state. The latter is a pattern of unchanging routines. But the process level, at least in theory, is compatible with an industrial revolution moving along in a straightjacket.

The circulation trends are functions of changes in the quantity of money available in the basic and the surplus circuits. Their general character may be deduced from the circuit equations. However, it will facilitate the course of such a deduction to set down at once a few general theorems: (a) there is a concomitance of variations in initial, transitional, and final payments of uniformly specified types; (b) the rates of absorption, DA' and DA'', are no more than incidental adjustments; (c) with D^2S' at zero over a series of intervals, DS' may be positive, zero, or negative over the same series of intervals; and the same holds for D^2S'' and DS''; (d) the difference between turnover differences of transitional payments made and turnover differences of transitional payments received is an adjustment factor; (e) turnover frequencies are resultant, and not initiating, factors of acceleration.

First, there is a concomitance of variations in initial, transitional, and final payments of uniformly specified types. The ground of the concomitance lies in the definitions of the terms: transitional payments are initial payments in a process of double summation; final payments are initial payments at the end of the double summation. Any one of the three may begin to move out of step, but unless the others follow, then it has to revert to its original level. There will be lags proportionate to the production-and-sales period between different rates. Transitional movements may change their route so as to involve more or fewer transitional payments, and so give greater or less aggregates of transitional payments. But apart from incidental differences of such a nature, variations are concomitant. There can be no systematic divergence over a series of intervals with one rate increasing and another zero, constant, or decreasing.

Secondly, the rates of absorption, DA' and DA'', represent no more than incidental adjustments. They were defined by the equations

$$DA' = DI' + DD' - DE' \tag{67}$$

$$DA'' = DI'' + DD'' - DE'' \tag{68}$$

Now DI' and DI'' represent money earned per interval; DE' and DE'' represent money spent per interval; if DD' and DD'' were defined as the excess of money spent and not earned over money earned and not spent per interval, then DA' and DA'' would always be zero. It is desirable, however, to define DD' and DD'' in terms of savings, and not to count as savings the money earned at the end of one interval and spent at the beginning of the next. Thus DA' and DA'' represent the excess of the carry-over from this interval to the next over the carry-over from the previous to the present interval. As such, they are not systematic factors in a trend but incidental adjustments.

The third theorem follows immediately from definitions. DS' is a turnover sum, D^2S' is a turnover difference. As long as DS' is the same interval after interval, D^2S' will be zero. The same holds for DS'' and D^2S''.

The fourth theorem regards the significance of T' and T'', which are defined by the equations

$$T' = D^2t' - D^2T' \qquad (93)$$

$$T'' = D^2t'' - D^2T'' \qquad (94)$$[2]

Now D^2T and D^2t do not refer to the same turnovers. This may be seen by inspecting the following equations and checking by equations (24) and (36).

$$D^2T = \Sigma\Sigma\ dT_{ij} = \Sigma\Sigma\ (T_{ij} - T_{ij}') \qquad (53\ \&\ 22)$$

$$= \Sigma\ (T_{in} - T_{i0}) \qquad (95)$$

where the constant K has been omitted and the limits result from the fact that

$$dT_{i1} = T_{i1} - T_{i0} \qquad (22)$$

On the other hand, since

$$dt_{i1} = t_{i2} - t_{i1} \qquad (32)$$

it follows that

2 The five last lines of G59 were canceled by Lonergan. They are reproduced in this note, since they represent not a mistaken direction but a hurry forward to his fourth theorem. The theorem emerges in a fuller form after the next few paragraphs of analysis. The canceled text reads: 'Evidently, on the supposition of synchronized turnovers, T' and T'' are always zero: transitional payments made are then identical with transitional payments received. Without synchronized turnovers, T' and T'' tend to zero as to a statistical average. Hence within intervals they represent factors of adjustment.'

$$D^2t = \Sigma\ (t_{in'} - t_{i1}) \tag{96}$$

where n' is written for $(n + 1)$ and K again is omitted. Hence with respect to three successive intervals, D^2R and D^2T refer to the last turnovers of the first and second, while D^2t, D^2O, and D^2S refer to the first turnovers of the second and third. For turnovers O and n are the last turnovers of the first and second intervals, while turnovers 1 and $(n + 1)$ are the first turnovers of the second and third intervals.

With regard to T' and T'', then, on the supposition of synchronized turnovers and a constant acceleration, the difference between turnover difference of transitional payments, D^2T and D^2t, will be always zero. Without synchronized turnovers but with constant acceleration, T' and T'' tend to zero as a statistical average. Finally, insofar as the acceleration is changing, T' and T'' tend to some positive or negative quantity as statistical averages. However, changes of acceleration are incidental adjustments; they are not trends but intensifications or reversals of trends.

The fifth theorem is that changes in turnover frequency are resultant rather than initiating factors of acceleration. Granted an acceleration is in progress, one may expect a greater efficiency of production and sales to supervene and intensify the acceleration. For with the acceleration in progress, opportunities to introduce improvements multiply and selling is strong. On the other hand, without an acceleration in progress, opportunities to introduce improvements are restricted while the weakness of sales prevents the greater efficiency in selling necessary to convert shorter production periods into shorter turnover periods. Finally, in a deceleration of the process one may expect turnover frequencies to diminish; sales are falling; and reduced rates of production prevent the most efficient use of means of production.

To turn now to the circulation trends. It has been shown already that

$$DM' - DA' = D^2R' + D^2T' \tag{71}$$

$$DM'' - DA'' = D^2R'' + D^2T'' \tag{72}$$

Since the two equations are similar, one may discuss their implications without distinguishing between basic (′) and surplus (″) rates. On the supposition that DM is positive over a series of intervals, then, since DA is an incidental factor and since D^2R and D^2T keep pace, it follows that both D^2R and D^2T will be positive over the series of intervals; again, if DM is negative, then D^2R and D^2T will be both negative; and if DM is zero, then D^2R and D^2T will average zero.

The conclusions hold no matter what the reason for DM being positive, zero, or negative. It may be any solution of the equations defining DM' and DM'', namely,

$$DM' = DS' + DD' + DG$$

$$DM'' = DS'' + DD'' - DG \qquad (14)$$

and so an acceleration of the circulation may be due to excess transfers to supply, DS, to excess transfers to demand, DD, or to a crossover difference, DG. The relative importance of the three in effecting accelerations of the circuit may be estimated as follows. With DD', DD'', DG each at zero, entrepreneurs are receiving back their aggregate outlays (including the payment of profits to themselves). In such a situation, demand is neutral and prices may be termed normal. On the other hand, with DD', DD'', DG above or below zero, there is a strengthening or weakening of aggregate demand independently of supply; demand is not neutral but asks for more or for less; and since this asking is independent of supply, it can effect nothing but an upward or downward movement of prices (unless it is very slight and met out of inventories). Now the upward or downward movement of prices will stimulate at once the whole series of speculative producers to increased or decreased scales of operation, and, in the main, such changes in the scale of operations involve excess transfers from or to the redistributive function. In current practice changes in the quantity of money in the circuits are changes in the volume of short-term loans; and short-term loans are made not to purchasers but to producers; they affect not DD' and DD'' but DS' and DS''. It would seem that in general DM' and DM'' depend on DS' and DS'', while the role of DD', DD'', DG is to act as stimulants to the scale of operations of agents of supply.

By combining equations (65) and (93), (66) and (94), one obtains the correlations of turnover differences in the form

$$D^2R' + D^2S' = D^2O' + T' \qquad (97)$$

$$D^2R'' + D^2S'' = D^2O'' + T'' \qquad (98)$$

where T' and T'' are adjustment factors discussed above. Since the equations are similar, the argument may disregard the distinction between basic (′) and surplus (″). With D^2S at zero over a series of intervals, D^2R and D^2O tend to be equal. But with D^2S at zero, DS is constant interval by interval; however, this constant may be positive, zero, or negative; so that D^2R and D^2O tend to be equal whether increasing, averaging zero, or decreasing. Hence with D^2S at zero, according as DS is positive, zero, or negative, one has D^2R, D^2T, D^2t, and D^2O similarly positive, averaging zero, or negative. The circulation is expanding, level, or contracting interval after interval. Entrepreneurs are receiving back in final payments (and transitional payments) all that they are spending in initial payments (and transitional payments); no matter how great the aggregate income they are paying to themselves, it keeps coming back. To intensify or reverse any such trend, DD', DD'', DG may provide stimulation, but, in the main, the work will be done by a positive or negative D^2S which effects a change in DS.

So far the argument has dealt with turnover differences. One now has to ask how do DO', DR', DO'', DR'' behave when with DM positive, zero, or negative interval by interval over a series of intervals, D^2R, D^2T, D^2t, D^2O are similarly positive, averaging zero, or negative. Immediately one notes that DO and DR are turnover sums and so vary either from variation in turnover magnitude or from variation in turnover frequency; thus because

$$DO' = \Sigma_i \sum_1^n i'_{ij} \qquad (46)$$

DO' may be greater either because instances of i'_{ij} are greater or because there are more instances; and there may be more instances of j from increasing turnover frequency, or more instances of i because additional new units of enterprise exceed liquidated units; and in the latter case the turnover frequency of the additional units may raise or lower the existing average frequency per unit of turnover magnitude.

Now with respect to change of turnover magnitudes, which include the excess, positive or negative, of new units of enterprise over liquidated units, the turnover differences D^2R, D^2O, etc., give information only on the first and last turnovers of each interval. However, we have a source of information with regard to intermediate turnovers in the conclusion that, in the main, DM' resulted from DS' and DM'' from DS''. For DS' and DS'' are also turnover sums, double summations of m_{ij}, which is the difference between payments made in the later turnover and payments received in the earlier turnover with respect to all turnovers. For DS to be positive, zero, or negative, interval by interval over a series of intervals, means that the aggregate of turnover magnitudes during an interval are above, or at, or below the average of the previous interval. Hence DO' and DR', DO'' and DR'', as far as turnover magnitudes are concerned, have their trend determined as increasing, averaging zero, or decreasing according as DM' and DM'' respectively are positive, zero, or negative.

As to the change in turnover frequencies, the change in the general average from the replacement of old firms by new firms and the emergence of additional new firms cannot be determined generally. On the other hand, as argued previously, there should seem to be a tendency for turnover frequency to increase during an expansion but be hampered and decrease during a contraction. However, the expansions have to be both process and circulation expansions, and, similarly, the contractions have to hold in both orders; for turnover frequency is a matter of the efficiency of both production and sales. In situations that are neither double expansions nor double contractions the probabilities of change in turnover frequency are less determinate: a circulation level is less incompatible with change[3]

3 The text ends in mid-sentence. As in the previous section, one gets the impression of a line of inquiry being abandoned.

10

Circuit Velocities

9 Circuit Velocities

In the preceding section there were defined two monetary circuits, each involving two independently varying rates of payment and an independently varying quantity of money. The basic circuit involved the rate of basic expenditure, DE', and the rate of basic outlay, DO', and during the interval its quantity of money increased by DM'. The surplus circuit involved the rate of surplus expenditure, DE'', the rate of surplus outlay, DO'', and during the interval its quantity of money increased by DM''. Further, the whole system of movements became determinate by the addition of another variable, the crossover difference DG. For with DE', DO', DM', DE'', DO'', DM'', and DG, there are equations which determine by identity DR', DI', DD', DS', DR'', DI'', DD'', and DS''. To increase the implicational compactness of the analysis, this section investigates relations between rates of payment and quantities of money, between DO' and DE' and, on the other hand, DM', between DO'' and DE'' and, on the other hand, DM''.

Now the relation between a rate of payment and a quantity of money is the velocity of money. By definition rate of payment is equal to quantity multiplied by velocity; and it is to be noted that velocity of money is not an additional entity but only a conclusion derived from the fact that rates and quantities may vary independently. Even if there were only one dollar in existence, it would be possible for a number of people to spend a hundred dollars a day; to achieve this, everyone would have to spend the dollar as soon as he received it; and however fantastic, the illustration makes obvious that an aggregate rate of payment of several hundred dollars a day is possible with one dollar.

However, a circuit velocity is not any velocity of money. Its measure lies not in the number of times a given quantity of money changes hands but in the number of times it makes a determined circuit. A basic circuit velocity is a movement of money from basic expenditure, through basic receipts, to basic outlay, through basic income, back to basic expenditure. A surplus circuit velocity means traversing the similar surplus circuit. How many times money changes hands on the way is a matter of indifference. The one question is how rapidly it gets back to its starting point. Evidently, circuit velocities are much more definite than monetary velocities in general, for they involve not merely any exchanges but definite circular series of exchanges.

It is the purpose of this section to show that in the basic and surplus circuits respectively the quantity of money varies with the magnitude of turnovers and the velocity of money with the frequency of turnovers. The consequence of this theorem will be a correlation of the added quantities of money, *DM′* and *DM″*, with increases in the rates of outlay, *DO′* and *DO″*, through the mediation of another variable, namely, the production period.

The theorem will be established by generalizing the analysis of an illustration. Suppose two shipbuilders, *A* and *B*, who each launch a new ship every 15 days. Suppose further that *A* has 5 ships under construction at once and so completes a ship every 75 days, while *B* has 10 ships under construction at once and so completes a ship every 150 days. To eliminate irrelevant differences we may suppose also that each ship is sold as soon as it is launched, that all are sold for the same price, and so that payments to *A* are at the same rate as payments to *B*, and again that payments by *A* (including initial payments of profits to himself) are at the same rate as payments by *B*. There are, then, two equal volumes of business: the selling price of one ship every 15 days. On the other hand, the magnitude of *A*'s turnover is half the magnitude of *B*'s; and the frequency of *A*'s turnover is twice the frequency of *B*'s. The magnitude of *A*'s is only half of *B*'s, because when *A* is paid for a ship, he has been making payments for its construction over a period of 75 days, payments on a second ship for 60 days, on a third for 45 days, on a fourth for 30 days, and on a fifth for 15 days; on the other hand, when *B* is paid for a ship, he has been making payments on it for 150 days, on a second, third, fourth, fifth, sixth, seventh, eighth, ninth, and tenth for respective periods of 135, 120, 105, 90, 75, 60, 45, 30, and 15 days. Thus, *B*'s need of circulating capital to bridge the gap between payments to him for his ships and payments made by him transitionally and initially is twice as great as *A*'s need; yet *A* carries on the same volume of business, because he moves money twice as rapidly.

It will emphasize a few points to change the illustration slightly. Let us suppose that *A* could sell a ship no oftener than once every 16 days. It still remains possible for him to keep his production period at 75 days per ship, but inevitably his turnover period lengthens to 80 days per ship. He can produce as rapidly as ever, but he cannot sell as rapidly; and in an exchange economy production is production for sale. Further, in the limit decreasing sales effect a reduction of turnover magnitude; as sales dropped from one ship every 15 days to one ship every 16, 17, 18 days, the first shipbuilder, *A*, might lengthen his turnover period in each case; but when sales dropped to one ship every 19 days, then most probably he would revert to a shorter turnover period of 76 days but with 4 instead of 5 ships under construction at once. Thus, at a first approximation only do turnover periods coincide with production periods. Decreasing efficiency of sales makes the turnover period longer than the production period. But in the limit decreasing efficiency of sales restores what is approximately the minimum turnover period with, however, a decreased turnover magnitude. In the opposite case of increasing sales, the inverse theorem holds. As sales advanced to one ship every 14, 13, 12 days, the first shipbuilder would have to put 6 ships under construction at once and then 7 under construction; when supplying one ship every 14 days, the turnover period of 6 ships would be 84 days; with one every 13 days, the period would be 78 days; with one every 12 days, there would have to be 7 ships under construction at once and the turnover period would increase to 84 days.

This analysis now has to be generalized. Every entrepreneur carries on at any given time a certain volume of business. In this volume of business there are two components: a quantity of monetary circulating capital, and a frequency of use of the quantity of monetary circulating capital. The quantity of monetary circulating capital varies with variations in the magnitude of his turnovers; and the magnitude of the turnovers varies with two factors: first, the number of items in production at once, and second, the monetary value of each item. The frequency of use of monetary circulating capital also varies with two factors: first, with the period of time taken to effect the required physical change that is the entrepreneur's contribution to the productive process, and second, with the additional time that may be needed for the entrepreneur to sell his contribution. Obviously, if the entrepreneur effects no physical change, then the additional time for selling is the whole time of his turnover period.

The next step is to proceed from each entrepreneur to all entrepreneurs. To make this advance it is well to use symbols. With respect, then, to the *j*th turnover or fractional turnover of the *i*th entrepreneur in the standard interval of time, let r_{ij} be the aggregate of initial basic payments,[1] r''_{ij} be the aggregate of initial surplus payments, s_{ij} be the aggregate of transitional basic payments, s''_{ij} be the aggregate of transitional surplus payments. It follows that in the *j*th turnover or fractional turnover of the interval the *i*th entrepreneur moves a total quantity of money represented by the sum

$$r_{ij} + r''_{ij} + s_{ij} + s''_{ij} \tag{20}$$

If he is engaged exclusively in supplying basic goods or services, the second and fourth elements of the sum are zero. If he is engaged exclusively in supplying surplus goods and services, the first and third elements of the sum are zero. In any case the third and fourth elements of the sum are paid transitionally to other entrepreneurs, while the first and second elements are paid initially, that is, to the entrepreneur's own factors of production. The total sum represents the *i*th entrepreneur's monetary circulating capital in the *j*th turnover of the interval. It represents monetary circulating capital both in the sense in which monetary circulating capital exists when an entrepreneur begins business, but then it does not include profits and similar elements in initial payments, and also in the sense in which monetary circulating capital exists in any turnover subsequent to the first, though then it does include profits and similar elements. Again, it represents monetary circulating capital, not as received from other entrepreneurs or from final buyers in payments to the *i*th entrepreneur, but as paid by the *i*th enterpreneur either initially or transitionally; thus the sum represented by expression (20) may be greater or less than the sum paid to the *i*th entrepreneur in the *j*th turnover, for the given entrepreneur in that turnover may be enlarging or decreasing the scale of his operations, and in doing so he will be drawing upon a positive excess transfer from the redistributive function or contributing to a negative excess transfer.

Further, expression (20) as a sum gives the monetary circulating capital

1 In this section Lonergan does not use primes for basic variables; hence r_{ij}. On the general principle of not modifying the terminology in this volume, the text has not been changed.

of the ith entrepreneur in the jth turnover of the interval. But the suffix j varies from one entrepreneur to another. One entrepreneur may have fifty-two turnovers in the interval, another twelve, another four, another one, another merely the fraction of a turnover, or the last part of one turnover and the beginning of another. Still, in any case each entrepreneur has a definite number (which may include fractions) of turnovers during the interval; and the suffix j, considered in all its instances, supplies an initial indication of what this turnover frequency is. Thus, expression (20) as a sum gives a turnover magnitude; turnover frequencies vary not with this sum of money but with the suffixes j.

Let us now consider the following summations.

$$o_i n_i = \sum_j r_{ij} \tag{21}$$

$$o''_i n''_i = \sum_j r''_{ij} \tag{22}$$

$$DO' = \sum_i o_i n_i = \sum_i \sum_j r_{ij} \tag{23}$$

$$DO'' = \sum_i o''_i n''_i = \sum_i \sum_j r''_{ij} \tag{24}$$

Here, r_{ij} are the initial basic payments of the ith entrepreneur in his jth turnover of the standard interval. The first equation (21) adds up the initial basic payments made by the ith entrepreneur during the whole interval: it is the sum of initial basic payments, $r_{i1}, r_{i2}, r_{i3}, \ldots$ to j terms where j is the number of turnovers or fractional turnovers. This sum is identical with the product $o_i n_i$, where n_i is the number of turnovers in the interval of the ith entrepreneur and o_i is the average per turnover of his initial basic payments. Note that o_i differs from r_{ij} as an average differs from a series of exact figures: o_i is the average of $r_{i1}, r_{i2}, r_{i3}, \ldots$ which, multiplied by an exact n_i, gives $\sum_j r_{ij}$.

Next, with respect to equation (23), DO' has already been defined as the aggregate of initial basic payments of the interval. Consequently it is equal to the sum of all instances of $o_i n_i$, and so to the double summation of all instances of r_{ij}. Similarly, one may obtain equations (22) and (24) with respect to initial surplus payments during the interval.

So much for initial payments, r_{ij} and r''_{ij}, per turnover. But there are also transitional payments, s_{ij} and s''_{ij}, per turnover, and the immediate task is to grasp their relation to the initial payments. The question is, Are the transitional payments the same sums of money as the initial payments or are they additional sums of money? In both cases the answer is affirmative. They are the same sums of money in the sense that eventually every transitional payment becomes an initial payment: one entrepreneur pays another, who may pay a third, and so on, but eventually that payment is used to be divided up among the factors of some entrepreneur in initial payments. But it is also true that transitional payments are additional sums of money in the sense that the quantity of money required to carry on the business of basic supply is

$$\sum_i (r_{ij} + s_{ij}) \tag{25}$$

and the quantity of money required to carry on the business of surplus supply is

$$\sum_i (r''_{ij} + s''_{ij}) \tag{26}$$

the summations being taken with respect to all instances of i in any one set of contemporaneous instances of j. For the quantity of money required is the aggregate of monetary circulating capital. Monetary circulating capital includes not merely money to pay immediate factors of production but also money to pay for the contributions of other entrepreneurial units. Granted that in the proximate future the money for transitional payments will become money for initial payments, it remains that now it is for transitional payments and at the proximate future date it will have to be replaced by other money for transitional payments. There would be a relevance to a consideration of future dates if at future dates transitional payments and the requirements of circulating capital to meet them would vanish. But there is no vanishing, and so no relevance.

The same conclusion may be reached by another route. The function of transitional payments is to shorten turnover periods. Were s_{ij} smaller, r_{ij} in other instances of i would have to be greater. Suppose a manufacturer produces 1000 products per month each month of the year; suppose he enjoys monopolist advantages and can force dealers to buy the 1000 products each month; suppose the product can be sold only seasonally, so that in May, June, and July 9000 products can be sold but in the rest of the year only 3000, say 1000 in August and 250 in each of the remaining months. Let the manufacturer sell at $100.00 a product, so that his turnover is $100,000.00 a month. Now the aggregate of dealers accumulate the products at the rate of 750 a month from September to April, and at the end of April they have on their hands 6000 products for which they have paid $600,000.00; at the end of May they have in stock 4000, at the end of June 2000, at the end of July and at the end of August zero. Thus, their aggregate circulating capital has to reach $600,000.00 at a minimum during April. But if the manufacturer lost his monopoly advantage so that dealers could buy as they pleased, then he could not run his business of a monthly turnover of $100,000.00; he would have to build the warehouse and increase his monetary circulating capital, provided he kept to the same production rates, for the dealers would refuse to foot the interest bill and other carrying costs. Thus, in calculating aggregate monetary circulating capital, one is calculating the amount of money required to bridge the gap between the aggregate of final sales and the aggregate of initial payments to all factors from sources of raw materials up to sales to final buyers. The burden of these monetary carrying costs will fall entirely on one entrepreneur if there is only one; and in that case there will be no transitional payments. But if there are several entrepreneurs, and so also transitional payments, then the longer periods of monetary carrying costs are divided, and it is this division that transforms what would be circulating capital for initial payments into circulating capital for transitional payments.

Now to put the matter analytically, consider the following equation:

$$\sum s_{ij} = \sum v_i r_{ij} \tag{27}$$

This states that with respect to any contemporaneous set of turnovers, j, the aggregate of quantities of money, s_{ij}, required for transitional basic payments is equal to the aggregate of quantities required for initial basic payments, r_{ij}, multiplied by some factor v_i. This factor v_i will vary in the case of each entrepreneur according to the number of times his contribution to the productive process during one of his turnovers, namely r_{ij}, is found to be the property of some other entrepreneur on its way to final sales. Thus, if the ith entrepreneur is a retailer conducting final sales, v_i is zero. If the ith entrepreneur is a wholesaler with the same turnover as the retailers to whom he sells, v_i is unity. If the wholesaler's turnover period is twice that of the retailers to whom he sells, v_i is one-half. Universally, entrepreneurs at any instant are carrying some multiple of each r_{ij}; they are carrying that multiple because they have made transitional payments for it and have not yet recovered their payments; and the aggregate of quantities of money required for transitional payments at any time is equal to the aggregate of quantities required for initial payments multiplied by that elusive multiple v_i.

It is to be noted that v_i varies in two ways: relatively and absolutely. It varies relatively inasmuch as the present r_{ij} is greater or less than the earlier instances now on their way to final sales. It varies absolutely inasmuch as greater efficiency of production and of selling, or again less efficiency, means that there are fewer or more instances or fractional instances of r_{ij} between the *i*th entrepreneur and final sales of his contribution.

The next step is to turn to increments of circulating capital. Let us define the increments dr_i, ds_i, dr''_i, ds''_i by the difference between the respective types of initial and transitional payments at the beginning and at the end of the standard interval of time. Thus, if initial basic payments of the *i*th entrepreneur at the beginning of the interval are r_{ij} and at the end of the interval are r_{ij}', then

$$dr_i = r_{ij}' - r_{ij} \tag{28}$$

with parallel definitions for the other three terms. Hence the aggregate increase of basic circulating capital during the interval is

$$\sum_i (dr_i + ds_i) \tag{29}$$

and if one defines a multiplier u_i, somewhat similar to v_i, by the equation

$$\sum_i ds_i = \sum u_i dr_i \tag{30}$$

one may write as well for the increment of basic monetary circulating capital during the interval

$$\sum_i (1 + u_i)\, dr_i \tag{31}$$

and similarly for the increment in surplus monetary circulating capital during the interval

$$\sum_i (dr''_i + ds''_i) = (1 + u''_i)\, dr''_i \qquad (32)$$

where all summations are taken with respect to each i or each entrepreneur.

Let us now return to DM' and DM'', which were defined as the increments during the interval of the quantities of money available within the basic and the surplus circuits respectively [equations (13) and (14)] and were shown to be equal to the increments in basic and surplus supply respectively at the end of the interval [equations (18) and (19)]. Consider, then, whether one may write

$$DM' = \sum_i (1 + u_i)\, dr_i \qquad (33)$$

$$DM'' = \sum_i (1 + u''_i)\, dr''_i \qquad (34)$$

so that the increment in the quantity of money in the basic or surplus circuit during the interval is equal to the increment in basic or surplus monetary circulating capital during the same interval. The condition of the truth of these equations (33) and (34) is that either the entrepreneurs have not yet paid out this increment in initial payments at the moment the interval ends or else, if they have paid it out, the basic increment has already returned from basic demand to basic supply and the surplus increment has already returned from surplus demand to surplus supply. On the other hand, if the increment has been paid out and has not yet returned to the same supply function, then either it has gone to the opposite supply function or else to the redistributive function. For by the definitions of DD' and DD'', equations (11) and (12), the quantity of money in either demand function is the same at the end of each interval as it was at the beginning, and consequently the increments in the demand function are zero. Thus, the truth of equations (33) and (34) is a matter of timing the end of the interval or, alternatively, of correcting the right-hand sides of the equations by subtracting any initial payments made towards the end of the interval but, at least for the moment, lost to the circuit by migration to the other circuit or to the redistributive function. In pure theory it is simpler to suppose timing; in practice corrections would have to be the procedure.

Now it may be noticed that nothing has been said about the velocities of money in the demand functions. The reason is that the analysis pins these velocities down to functions of velocities in the supply functions. Velocities in the supply functions are a matter of turnover frequencies; but the turnover on one side generates income by initial payments and on the other side takes in the expenditure of final payments; if the demand functions spend their income in expenditure more rapidly or more slowly, this automatically shortens or lengthens turnover periods; on the other hand, because DD' and DD'' merely make good the difference between DE' and DI', between DE'' and DI'', quantity variation is shifted from the demand to the redistributive function. This shift of quantity variation to the redistributive function makes income velocities entirely dependent upon turnover frequencies and so eliminates the need of introducing a further pair of variables.

To collect results, the monetary circulation of the basic and surplus circuits per interval is determined by the rates of payment DE', DO', DE'', DO'' and the crossover difference DG, and it is further determined by changes in quantity of money per interval, DM' and DM''. In terms of these rates the other terms of the system may be defined as follows.

$$\begin{aligned} DE' &= DR' \\ DE'' &= DR'' \\ DI' &= DO' + DG \\ DI'' &= DO'' - DG \\ DD' &= DE' - DI' \\ DD'' &= DE'' - DI'' \\ DS' &= DM' - DD' - DG \\ DS'' &= DM'' - DD'' + DG \end{aligned} \qquad (35)$$

though another determination is necessary to distinguish between G' and G'' since

$$DG = G''DO'' - G'DO' \qquad (5)$$

The question raised in this section was whether it was possible to correlate changes in quantity, DM' and DM'', with rates of payment, DE', DE'', DO', DO''. The answer is had by comparing equations (23), (24), (33), (34). To write them out together, we have

$$DO' = \sum_i o_i n_i = \sum_i \sum_j r_{ij} \tag{23}$$

$$DO'' = \sum_i o''_i n''_i = \sum_i \sum_j r''_{ij} \tag{24}$$

$$DM' = \sum_i (1 + u_i)\, dr_i \tag{33}$$

$$DM'' = \sum_i (1 + u''_i)\, dr''_i \tag{34}$$

The first two equations state that rates of outlay per interval are a single summation of average outlays o_i and o''_i per turnover multiplied by turnover frequencies or, again, are a double summation of exact outlays per turnover. The last two equations state that the circuit increments in quantities of money are equal to single summations of increments in outlays per turnover over the interval, dr_i and dr''_i, plus the multiple of these increments, u_i and u''_i, that are increments in transitional payments. Further, the last two equations are subject to a supposition of timing or else to correction for losses to the circuit in question.

Thus the relation of DO' and DM', or again of DO'' and DM'', under the supposition or correction required, is as follows. DM' and DM'' increase both transitional and initial payments with the part going to the increase of initial payments (outlays) depending on multiples u_i and u''_i. The quantitative increments of outlays appear in the terms of the series r_{i1}, r_{i2}, r_{i3}, ..., and again in r''_{i1}, r''_{i2}, r''_{i3}, ... which are summated to give DO' and DO''. On the other hand, DO' and DO'' vary independently of these increments, for the number of terms in the series are increased or decreased by changes in turnover frequency, which give the velocity components of DO' and DO''. Further, changes in turnover frequency not only affect the number of terms in the series of outlays, r_{ij} and r''_{ij}, but also affect the multipliers u_i and u''_i. A more rapid turnover frequency decreases these multipliers while a slower turnover frequency increases them: suppose an entrepreneur with a monthly turnover producing an object that (a) three months and (b) two months later is sold to final buyers; on the first supposition u_i is 3, on the second u_i is 2.

Thus, turnover frequency has a double effect: a higher frequency both increases rates of outlay, DO' and DO'', without any increment in circulating capital for initial payments and, at the same time, effects a decrease in circulating capital for transitional payments; inversely a lower turnover frequency decreases rates of outlay and increases requirements for circulating capital. Similarly, DM' and DM'' have a double effect: they increase monetary circulating capital both for initial and for transitional payments, the division between the two types of payment depending on the pattern of turnover frequencies.

11

Prices, Costs, Profits

10 Price and Process Indices

To indicate correlations between accelerations of the monetary circuits and accelerations of the productive process, it is necessary to introduce price and process indices. The present section is a summary presentation of some fundamental definitions.

When any quantity q_i of any object i is exchanged for any quantity q_j of any object j, then it is always possible to determine a ratio p_{ij}, such that

$$q_i = q_j p_{ij} \tag{19}$$

In any such case, p_{ij} is the price per unit of the object j, and this price is measured in units of the object i.

Transformations from prices measured in one unit to prices measured in another unit are ruled by the equations

$$p_{ij} p_{ji} = 1 \tag{20}$$

$$p_{ij} p_{jk} = p_{ik} \tag{21}$$

as may be shown readily by writing down the definitions of p_{ji}, p_{ji}, p_{ik}, on the analogy of equation (19), and then eliminating in two ways the terms q_i, q_j, q_k.

Money is a medium of exchange and a common measure of prices. A medium of exchange is any object, from Homeric hides through pieces of eight to digits in a banker's ledger, which under given historical conditions regularly appears as at least one term of the vast majority of exchanges. A common measure of prices is had when all prices are expressed in units of the same object.

With respect to equations (20) and (21), if the object *i* is money and if the objects *j* and *k* are different and not money, then by equation (20) the price of the object *j* in monetary units is the reciprocal of the price of money in units of the object *j*; further, by equation (21) the price of the object *k* in units of the object *j* is equal to the monetary price of the object *k*, divided by the monetary price of the object *j*.

Prices measured in nonmonetary units will be termed real prices; they are to be understood whenever a price is denoted by using a double suffix. On the other hand, it is superfluous to have a suffix to denote money in monetary prices, which henceforth will be defined by the equation

$$m_i = p_i q_i \tag{22}$$

where q_i units of any object *i* are exchanged for m_i units of money, so that the monetary price of the object *i* is p_i. Then the price of money in units of the object *i* is the reciprocal $1/p_i$; and the price of the unit of the object *j* in units of the object *i* is the quotient of the two monetary prices p_j/p_i, so that equation (21) becomes

$$p_i p_{ij} = p_j \tag{23}$$

where p_{ij} is a real price and both p_i and p_j are monetary prices.

As appears from equation (23), the real price p_{ij} determines no more than a ratio between the monetary prices p_i and p_j. Hence monetary prices may all change while real prices remain unchanged; further, a change of monetary prices may have two components, a change of real prices and a further change of monetary prices. In this case the second component, and in the former case the total change, is a change in the price of money. Inflation is a fall, deflation is a rise in the price of money.

The consistency of prices is the consistency of equations representing simultaneous exchanges in the same economy. If prices are consistent, it is impossible to obtain directly or indirectly from simultaneous exchange equations two different prices, say p_i and p'_i, for the same object, *i*. Now the consistency of prices may be postulated by taking it as a definition of the object *i*, so that any apparent inconsistency is attributed to the presence in the exchange of some further object, *j*. Then in reality p'_i becomes a mistaken expression for two prices, namely, $(p_i \pm p_j)$. The price p_j of the latent object *j* may be the price of special services, of more agreeable circumstances, of pride of purse; it may be the price of information, of the use of agents, of transportation; it may be the price of exceptional initiative, of foresight, of knowledge, of great acumen; or negatively it may be the price of lack of foresight, of lack of initiative, of ignorance, of gullibility. Generically one may say that p_j is the price of a lack of consistency, but it is always possible in any particular case to give a specific content to this generic interpretation; otherwise, it would be impossible to account for the difference in prices, and it would be meaningless to assert that prices tend to be consistent.

The latter view, that prices tend to be uniform throughout the economy though actually they never attain uniformity, is the more common one. It offers the advantage that the analysis of exchange is not loaded with latent objects, and so in practical discussions it is a preferable mode of statement. The foregoing statement, however, has the theoretical advantage of greater generality and simplicity; and it is presupposed by the affirmation of a tendency to uniformity which is no more than a tendency to reduce latent prices to a minimum.

If prices are consistent, the price of money is consistent. It follows that there is one price of money for the whole economy, and that inflation and deflation are variations in this one price and so affect all monetary prices in like manner.

To define price and process indices, let *DZ* be any definite rate of payment, which in a first interval is DZ_i and in a second interval is DZ_j, where D^2Z_j is the excess of the latter over the former. Let *z* be any object sold in either of these two intervals and paid for in the rate *DZ*. Let p_z be the price, q_z the quantity sold in the first interval; and let $(p_z + dp_z)$ be the price and $(q_z + dq_z)$ be the quantity sold in the second interval. Thus, summing with respect to all instances of *z*, one has

$$DZ_i = \Sigma\, p_z q_z \qquad (24)$$

$$DZ_j = \Sigma\, (p_z + dp_z)\ (q_z + dq_z) \qquad (25)$$

$$D^2Z_j = DZ_j - DZ_i = \Sigma\, (p_z dq_z + q_z dp_z + dp_z dq_z) \qquad (26)$$

Let the price indices and process indices of the two intervals be P_i, P_j, DQ_i, DQ_j, and let the definitions of these indices be the solution of the equations

$$P_iDQ_i = DZ_i \tag{27}$$

$$P_jDQ_j = DZ_j \tag{28}$$

$$P_j = P_i + DP_j \tag{29}$$

$$DQ_j = DQ_i + D^2Q_j \tag{30}$$

$$DQ_iDP_j = \Sigma\, q_zdp_z \tag{31}$$

$$P_iD^2Q_j = \Sigma\, p_zdq_z \tag{32}$$

where, in general, the last two equations must be mere approximations.

It follows that the definitions of the indices are in themselves no more than approximations. The reason is not difficulty of obtaining information about p_z, dp_z, q_z, dq_z, nor the fact that the prices may have to be averaged, though both those difficulties also exist. Nonetheless, even with perfect information and no averaging, the definitions of the indices remain approximate, unless the four sums of p_zq_z, p_zdq_z, q_zdp_z, dp_zdq_z happen to be a fourfold proportion; for in fact these four sums are by the defining equations made equal to P_iDQ_i, $P_iD^2Q_j$, DQ_iDP_j, $DP_jD^2Q_j$, which are a fourfold proportion; but there is no ground to expect that the four summations will also be in proportion. Hence equations (31) and (32) are only approximate, and so the definitions are approximate.

Though for six unknowns there are the six equations (27) to (32), still the fourfold proportion introduces a condition of consistency and so leaves an infinity of solutions possible. Hence the solution is by introducing any arbitrary base, say 100, as the value of P_i. This determines DQ_i by (27); thence follow approximate determinations of DP_j and D^2Q_j by (31) and (32), and of P_j and DQ_j by (29) and (30); a check and adjustment of P_j and DQ_j follows by (28).

The significance of the indices is that they provide a differentiation between increments in prices and increments in quantities sold as the rate of payment moves from DZ_i in one interval to DZ_j in the next. The corrected value of DP_j indicates the price increment, and that of D^2Q_j indicates the quantity increment.

Thus, the condition that an increment in the rate of payment is accompanied by a proportionate increment in quantities sold is that *DP* is zero; on the other hand, the greater is *DP*, the greater is the inertia of the process of goods and services against circuit accelerations.

The process indices disregard all process change that has no aggregate quantitative manifestation. Increments in one quantity may cancel against increments in other quantities when the two sets are of opposite sign. Similarly, changes in quality do not appear in the indices when the emergence of the new is balanced by disappearance of the old. Hence D^2Q is an increment per interval in the aggregate of price-weighted quantities.

11 Systematic Costs and Profits

Price and process indices provide a method of denoting the concomitance or divergence of the productive process and the monetary circulation. It is now necessary to consider the interaction of the two, and, to begin, it will be well to consider certain general phenomena of particular importance in a 'capitalist' economy.

Systematic costs and profits are costs and profits in much the same sense as forced savings are savings, that is, they bear an important relation to costs and profits in individual units of enterprise but they are variables not of any individual unit but of the total situation in any exchange economy. Thus by systematic costs and profits are meant neither the costs and profits of the accountant nor again the windfall profits and losses of the equilibrium analyst. For the accountant, costs and profits are a division of payments made with a relation to payments received. For the equilibrium analyst, windfall profits and losses are accidental variations in the distribution of the receipts of industry and commerce. On the other hand, systematic costs and profits are a division of aggregate initial payments to factors of production, and the division is based upon the tendency of the products to effect an acceleration of the total economy. The significance of this division is that the resultant acceleration tends to reduce, and in the limit to reduce to zero, whatever systematic profits may have existed.

The aggregate of initial payments in any interval is the sum $(DO' + DO'')$, which is identical with total income $(DI' + DI'')$. Systematic profits are defined as $K.DO''$ where K has any value in the range of 0 to 1 inclusively, and is defined as the fraction of surplus initial payments made with respect to surplus products which are supplied not to replace or maintain worn-out or obsolescent equipment but are increasing the capacity and efficiency of old units of enterprise or fitting out new units.

Now systematic profits have a twofold significance. First, with regard to the monetary circuits it is plain that to maintain rates of payment at their acquired levels total income has to be spent either in itself or in its equivalent: were $DE' + DE''$ to drop permanently behind $DO' + DO''$, there would result a continuous contraction of the circulatory process until it was reduced to zero. However, it makes a notable difference whether total income is being spent for basic products and the maintenance and replacement of capital equipment or, on the other hand, there is over and above that expenditure an element, $K.DO''$, which purchases additional capital equipment. To begin, there is the psychological difference: in the former case people are merely making a living; no matter how high their standard of living may be already and no matter how much they are adding to it, still they are adding only to their enjoyment and not to their ownership of industrial and commercial sources of wealth; this runs counter to current ideas on the 'successful man' who can emerge only when there is in income an element, $K.DO''$, which ministers to the increase not only of living standards but as well, over and above all increase of living standards, to the increase of ownership of means of production. Besides this psychological difference, there is a monetary difference: $K.DO''$ yields an equal $K.DI''$; now there is no necessity that the recipients of $K.DI''$ should also be the spenders of $K.DI''$; the continuity of the circuits at their acquired levels is assured as long as DD'' remains zero, so that the recipients of $K.DI''$ may devote this part of their income to the purchase of redistributive goods, to real estate or stocks and securities, to augment their prestige or to increase their financial power, as long as this subtraction from the circuits is balanced by an equal and opposite movement from the investment market to the purchase of surplus goods and services.

Besides the psychological and the monetary significance of systematic profits, there is also a real significance. The products generating systematic profits fit out new firms and expand old firms. Insofar as this constitutes a net increment of capital equipment, by overbalancing the effects of the current rate of liquidation of units of enterprise, the productive process tends to accelerate in long-term style. Insofar as the net increment occurs in surplus units, the surplus stage is due for acceleration immediately and the basic stage is due for a still greater acceleration ultimately. Insofar as the net increment occurs in basic units, the basic stage is due immediately for an acceleration.

However, these real effects of systematic profits have a repercussion on systematic profits themselves. In the long run, as has been shown, the acceleration of the productive process involves a decrease of K as the portion of surplus activity devoted to maintenance and replacement increases with increasing capital equipment. However, the movement towards this ultimate position is full of interest. Let H be the ratio of systematic profits to total income, so that

$$H = K.DO''/(DO' + DO'')$$

or

$$H/K = DO''/(DO' + DO'') \tag{33}$$

If now we follow through the emergence and development of a long-term acceleration, we find a first period in which H is increasing, a second period in which H is decreasing, and a third period in which H is zero. As the long-term acceleration begins, DO' is constant but both K and DO'' are increasing; H increases as does the product of K and DO'' in the numerator with a slight drag because of the presence of DO'' in the denominator. Further, this first period lasts as long as DO'' is increasing more rapidly than DO', that is, as long as the efforts of the surplus stage are more on equipping the surplus than the basic stage of the process; for then H is still increasing though less and less rapidly as DO'' approaches the rate of acceleration of DO''. However, every increment in the surplus stage stands at least point-to-line to increments in the basic stage, and unless the expansion of the surplus stage is mere blundering, sooner or later DO' will begin to increase more rapidly than DO'' while at best K is constant. Then H begins to decrease, and the more successful the expansion of the basic stage, the more rapid the rate of decrease. Finally, K begins to decrease, as the surplus stage has to devote more of its efforts to mere maintenance and replacement; and if the long-term acceleration works itself out K returns to zero and H has to reach zero ahead of K.

The single condition to this movement (if we abstract from the favorable balance of foreign trade and from deficit government spending, which will be discussed later) is that there does not supervene a rate of liquidation of old or new firms to eliminate from systematic profits their tendency to accelerate the productive process. Thus there is possible a dynamic situation in which the surplus stage of the process is yielding capital equipment that generates systematic profits, but not yielding an aggregate increment of consumer goods that reduces the ratio of systematic profits to total income. This situation is most easily verified in an industrial revolution that is the work of 'new' men: because an industrial revolution is in process, the new capital equipment is simply displacing old equipment; because the industrial revolution is the work of 'new' men, the displacement of old equipment occurs not as a cost of obsolescence on existing firms but as fresh investment constituting the emergence of new firms. On the other hand, the more industrial and commercial enterprise is in the hands of vast corporations which by their command of talent and resources stand in a virtually impregnable position, the less would seem the possibility of evading the effects of variations in systematic profits by a concomitant rate of liquidations.

Further, it may be noted that it would be absurd for the great corporations to attempt to plan an elimination in the variations of the ratio of systematic profits. For while the planning itself would be possible, perhaps, the objective of the planning would be manifest stupidity: what would be planned would be a steady flow of surplus products that did not yield their increment in basic products; it would be a matter of devising better machinery and more efficient organization, of effecting both, and then of using them as though they were not better than what already existed. It would be a planned economy in which the idea of the plan was to effect a maximum change in the surplus stage while keeping the basic stage in a relative status quo.

10bis The Crossovers

The distinction between the two circuits involves a crossover from basic outlay to surplus income and from surplus outlay to basic income. It has been argued that unless these two cancel ($DG = 0$) the process is apt to be submitted to an expansion of one circuit and a contraction of the other. We have now to investigate the conditions of their canceling.

Let all recipients of income, whether basic or surplus, be divided into groups of n_i members each. Let each member of the same group receive approximately the same income per interval, o_i, and devote the same proportion of income, g_i, to expenditure at the basic final market. In any later interval let the situation have changed to the extent that in group i numbers have increased by dn_i, income per interval by do_i, and the proportion of income devoted to basic expenditure by dg_i. Then basic income per interval, DI', and the increment of basic income per interval, D^2I', may be expressed as summations with respect to all instances of the groups i.

$$DI' = \sum g_i o_i dn_i \qquad (16)$$

$$D^2I' = \Sigma\ (g_io_idn_i + o_in_idg_i + n_ig_ido_i + g_ido_idn_i + o_idn_idg_i + n_idg_ido_i + dg_ido_idn_i) \tag{17}$$

If DI' is visualized as a rectangular solid, then D^2I' may be visualized as the elements added to expand the rectangular solid, three plates added to three faces, three bars added along three edges, and a little cube added to the corner.

To estimate the relative importance of the various components of D^2I' one may note the following. As one passes from group to group one finds that as o_i increases, n_i decreases and also g_i decreases: the greater the income, the fewer that receive it and the smaller the proportion of it spent on consumer goods and services. With regard to the increments, dg_i is always quite small since it is a change in a proper fraction, dn_i may be quite large as employment increases or decreases, and do_i may be extremely large amounting in the aggregate to billions of dollars as an economy moves from the peak of a boom to a slump or from a slump to an all-out war effort. Further, dg_i is usually opposite in sign to do_i: savings increase somewhat more rapidly than aggregate income; however, in the highest income brackets changes in income are apt to be canceled by the opposite changes in dg_i, while as income decreases this tendency is more and more reduced until in the lowest brackets the effect of increased rates of savings may be small. Hence, for notable changes in basic income, one has to look to the factors $g_io_idn_i$ and $n_ig_ido_i$ and, with respect to these two, one may discount positive increments to income in groups which already are spending all they intend or can manage to spend on consumer goods and services.

Now the condition of crossover equilibrium ($DG = 0$) may be written from equation (11) in the form

$$DO'/DO'' = (1 - G')/G' \tag{16}$$

where

$$DI' = (1 - G')\,(DO' + DO'') \tag{9}$$

Hence when the ratio DO'/DO'' is decreasing, G' has to increase, and when DO'/DO'' is increasing, G' has to decrease to satisfy the[1]

1 The text ends here, at the bottom of G55. The effort might have been continued on lost pages, or it may have been abandoned in expectation of the different approach of Part Three, chapter 18, section 13.

12

Prices, Demand, Supply

7 The Exchange Economy[1]

In any economy with a degree of development beyond that of primitive fruit-gathering it is possible to verify the existence of a productive process with basic and surplus stages. The restrictive supposition of an exchange economy is now introduced. It involves property, exchange, prices, money; it postulates a correlation between quantities produced and quantities sold; also it postulates systematic modifications of prices when the productive process accelerates. The latter postulate will be outlined in the next section; this section is devoted to setting down a series of definitions; and as the matter is familiar, treatment will be summary.

a) Prices. If a quantity q_i of objects in a class i is exchanged for a quantity q_j of objects in a class j, then it is always possible to assign a ratio, p_{ij}, such that

$$q_i = q_j p_{ij} \tag{2}$$

The ratio so defined is named a price; and the price p_{ij} is said to be the price of a unit of j measured in units of i. From the definition it also follows that

1 Above this title are Lonergan scribbles: The 'Problem, 1°, Incidental Definitions 2°, The Source of the Problem'.

$$q_j = q_i p_{ji} \tag{3}$$

$$q_j = q_k p_{jk} \tag{4}$$

and the solution of the three equations gives

$$p_{ij} p_{ji} = 1 \tag{5}$$

$$p_{ij} p_{jk} = p_{ik} \tag{6}$$

More generally, with respect to n classes of objects, there are possible $n(n-1)$ different ratios, but of these only $(n-1)$ are independent ratios; the remaining $(n^2 - 2n + 1)$ are deducible from the independent $(n-1)$ by the formulae (5) and (6).

b) The Consistency of Prices. By the consistency of prices is meant, first, that at any one time in a given economy there is to be found but a single price, p_{ij}, or its reciprocal, p_{ji}, in all exchanges of classes i and j and, secondly, that any of the $n(n-1)$ ratios between quantities in n classes is deducible from any $(n-1)$ independent ratios.

This consistency of prices may be postulated by making it a definition of the objects in the n classes. Suppose two exchanges or two sets of exchanges represented by

$$q_i = q_j p_{ij} \tag{7}$$

$$q'_i = q'_j p'_{ij} \tag{8}$$

where

$$p_{ij} < p'_{ij} \tag{9}$$

then one may always write

$$p'_{ij} = p_{ij} + p_{ik} \tag{10}$$

where p_{ik} is the price of some other object or objects. This other object usually may be described as special services, more agreeable circumstances, pride of purse; as the employment of agents, information, transportation;

as the neglect of introducing these three; as lack of foresight, lack of initiative, ignorance, gullibility. As a last resort one can always say that p_{ik} is the price of a lack of consistency.

If equations (7) and (8) do not represent exchanges directly but are deduced from equations representing exchanges between classes *i* and *h*, *j* and *h*, it is equally possible to introduce a further object, whose price is p_{ik}, and so explain the apparent lack of consistency as before.

In a word it is postulated that the classification of objects exchanged carry analysis far enough that prices be consistent.

c) Money. When in the vast majority of exchanges one of the objects exchanged always belongs to some given class, that class of objects is named the medium of exchange. If, further, all prices are measured in units of the medium of exchange, that medium is also the common measure of prices. Money is defined as the medium of exchange and the common measure of prices.

When m_i units of money are exchanged for q_i units of the object *i*, then it is always possible to assign a ratio, p_i, such that

$$m_i = q_i p_i \tag{11}$$

where p_i is defined as the monetary price of the object *i*. If in an exchange of the object *j* one has

$$m_j = q_j p_j \tag{12}$$

then on condition that

$$m_i = m_j \tag{13}$$

it follows that

$$q_i = q_j p_j / p_i \tag{14}$$

From a comparison of equations (14) and (2) one has

$$p_{ij} = p_j / p_i \tag{15}$$

which relates the monetary prices of *i* and *j* with the real price, p_{ij}.

d) Demand and Supply. The equation defining real prices involves three variables: q_i, q_j, p_{ij}. Similarly the equation defining monetary prices involves the three variables m_i, q_i, p_i. We have now to consider equations involving only two variables, namely, p_i and q_i. They are of the form

$$q_i = f_d(p_i) \tag{16}$$

$$q_i = f_s(p_i) \tag{17}$$

where equation (16) is called the demand function of the class of objects, *i*, and equation (17) is called the supply function of the class of objects, *i*. The subscripts *d* and *s* denote demand and supply respectively.

A demand function may be defined as resulting from the summation of demand schedules. A demand schedule may be constructed by asking an individual what is the most he is prepared to pay for 1, 2, 3, ... units of the class of objects, *i*. To answer the question the individual concerned has to consider the equation

$$M = p_i q_i + k \tag{18}$$

where M is the quantity of money at his disposal, $p_i q_i$ the sum of money he would have to pay for q_i units costing p_i apiece, and the remainder for other purposes would be the sum k. If he prefers to pay p_1 for one unit rather than do without the object, then he has a demand schedule with respect to the object. Again, if p_2 is small enough, he may prefer to pay $(p_1 + p_2)$ for two units rather than devote his money to other purposes. Similarly, with regard to a third, fourth, fifth, etc., until the point is reached at which any lowering of price fails to elicit a preference for a further unit. Now by questioning all individuals one may discover how many demand schedules for the class of objects, *i*, exist and what they are. Further, though the demand schedules make prices a function of quantities, the summation of demand schedules is effected by asking what quantity is sold at given prices. Hence a complete survey yields a function

$$q_i = f_d(p_i) \tag{19}$$

such that for any price within a given range there is a determinate quantity of the class *i* sold and, as follows from the definition of demand schedules, with quantities increasing as prices decrease. There is not, however, any correspondence of infinitesimal increments.

As the demand schedules make clear, the demand function varies with variations in the circumstances of individuals. A demand schedule for the class of objects, i, becomes stronger as the quantity of money, M, increases; it becomes weaker as the individual prefers to have a greater remainder, k, to devote to other purposes than the purchase of the object i. There is not then some one demand function but a category of demand functions; at any time some one demand function exists; but it is subject to change as changes emerge in M and k.

Supply schedules yield a supply function as demand schedules yield a demand function. There are, however, differences. The question to be put is not what is the most you are prepared to pay but what is the least you are ready to accept for 1, 2, 3, ... units of the class i. The ground of this difference is that for the seller the relevant equation is

$$k = p_i q_i + M \tag{20}$$

for the greater the quantity he sells and the higher the price, the greater the remainder k. Further, with respect to goods and services produced, there are distinct categories of supply schedules and supply functions. Supply schedules and functions may be constructed with respect to immediate sales, with respect to present production for future sales and so with respect to a series of future dates, and finally with respect to the initiation of new enterprises. Again, when any function is determined with respect to some one of these categories, it is capable of variation in view of unexpected changes of circumstance. However, with respect to immediate sales there always exists some one supply function

$$q_i = f_s(p_i) \tag{20}$$

and other existent supply functions may be regarded as potential modifications, more or less proximate, of the immediate function. Within a given range, there is a determinate value of q_i for every value of p_i, and, in general, as q_i increases, p_i will first decrease and then increase. The latter assertion is true when the quantity supplied is in the vicinity of the production optimum: there is not so little demanded that the use of the best methods is unprofitable, nor again so much that the best methods available are unequal to handling so great a quantity.

Granted the existence of both demand and supply functions valid with respect to concrete conditions, there remains the question of solutions.

Now, if a solution exists, it occurs where the least eager buyer and the least eager seller come to terms. For the postulate of consistency of prices admits only one price; and, while more eager buyers would pay more and more eager sellers take less, still a higher or lower price, emergent in particular cases, could not be generalized. On the supposition of a higher price, less eager buyers could find sellers ready to sell at a lower price. On the supposition of a lower price, less eager sellers could find buyers ready to buy at a higher price. But at the price at which the least eager buyer and seller come to terms, all more eager buyers and sellers exchange at an advantage, and leave on the markets only buyers who will pay less than this price and only sellers who require more than this price.

When, then, there is a solution to a demand and supply function, it determines a price at which the least eager buyer and the least eager seller come to terms, and at this price there is sold the maximum quantity that could be sold on the supposition of consistent prices and the given demand and supply functions.

e) The Nature of Prices. Prices are the marginal comparative valuations of the community. By a *valuation* is meant any judgment of appreciation on any grounds with respect to any object. By a *comparative valuation* is meant a decision with respect to alternatives: of two events, say *A* and *B*, either alone is possible; the comparative valuation decides in favor of one and against the other; it prefers *A* to *B* or *B* to *A*. By a *marginal comparative valuation* is meant a decision with respect to alternative quantities. The issue is not, Either *A* or else *B* but not both. One may decide in favor of some of *A* and some of *B*, but the more one takes of *A*, the less one can have of *B*, and vice versa. Thus the marginal comparative valuation has to decide in favor of some pattern, say *x* of *A* and *y* of *B*, against an indefinite number of other equally possible patterns.

Now any productive process sets a continuous problem of marginal comparative valuation. From a given stock of materials and with a given quantity of labor and management, a variety of goods and services in a greater variety of quantitative patterns may be supplied. But the more there is supplied of any one, the less there can be of one or more others. Hence on the supposition of definite stocks of materials and a definite quantity of labor and management, goods and services are a matter of alternative quantities. But the supposition may be removed. Count labor and management as negative leisure of various kinds: then the greater the supply of goods and services, the less the leisure and vice versa. Again, the greater the present use of materials, the less is either or both present leisure or future available materials. Thus, the whole productive process is a problem of alternative quantities, and the problem is reborn every instant.

The solution of such a problem necessarily is a set of marginal comparative valuations. These decisions have to be made. In a Robinson Crusoe economy, Robinson makes them. In an exchange economy, everyone, according to the measure of his influence on prices, contributes to making them. In a socialist economy, the long-term decisions regarding surplus goods and services are made by a planning authority, while the short-term decisions regarding basic goods and services are left to a price mechanism insofar as this is compatible with the decisions of the planning board and with the necessity of maintaining that board's reputation as an excellent institution with a superb personnel. But no matter what the political organization of the economy, the pattern of the productive process has to be determined; and the determination of that pattern is a set of marginal comparative valuations, of decisions with respect to alternative quantities.

Now it is the characteristic of the exchange economy to make not one but two sets of marginal comparative valuations. A first set occurs in supply, in decisions to produce. A second set occurs in demand, in decisions to buy what is produced. Producers are faced with the problem, With how much of materials, labor, management, capital equipment, are how much of objects in classes *i, j, k,* ... to be produced? In the matter explained above, the problem is one of alternative quantities. There is needed the solution of a differential equation of the type

$$0 = A_i\, dx_i + A_k dx_k + A_j\, dx_j \ldots \tag{22}$$

where x_i, x_j, x_k, ... are the quantities to be determined, and the coefficients A_i, A_j, A_k, ... are all positive, so that more of any one quantity means less of some other quantity or quantities. Now a solution of this equation may be written in the form

$$x_i = x_z r_{iz} \tag{23}$$

$$x_j = x_z r_{jz} \tag{24}$$

$$x_k = x_z r_{kz} \tag{25}$$

and so on, where x_z is some known quantity and r_{iz}, r_{jz}, r_{kz}, ... are known ratios. Such ratios resemble prices in one respect and differ from prices in another. Like prices they are ratios between quantities. Unlike prices, they are not ratios emergent pragmatically in exchanges, but ratios emergent pragmatically in decisions to produce. Both prices and what may be termed production ratios are matters of fact; but the matter of fact that is a price is a ratio between quantities exchanged, and the matter of fact that is a production ratio is a ratio between quantities produced.

Production ratios are sufficient to determine what is to be produced in what quantities in the sense that they give a determinate productive process. But the exchange economy endeavors to meet a further issue, namely, Is the pattern of quantities under production the pattern of quantities that happens to be wanted? No doubt producers' marginal comparative valuations select the pattern of quantities that producers prefer; but is it also the pattern of quantities that consumers and workers and owners of the sources of raw materials prefer?

This question the exchange economy answers by rewarding the contributions of property, labor, and management with monetary income for the purchase of the goods and services resulting from these contributions. Now income sets another problem of alternative quantities, for the more one buys of any object *i*, the less one can buy of other objects *j*, *k*, ... Thus there is another differential equation to be solved, say,

$$0 = B_i dm_i + B_j dm_j + B_k dm_k \ldots \tag{26}$$

where the coefficients are again all positive, so that the more one spends on any object the less one can spend on other objects. The solution of this equation sets up another set of marginal comparative valuations, say,

$$m_i = m_z s_{iz} \tag{27}$$

$$m_j = m_z s_{jz} \tag{28}$$

and so on, where m_z is a known quantity, and s_{iz}, s_{jz}, ... are known ratios, which may be called spending ratios.

Thus, corresponding to the production ratios determined by the decisions of sellers, there are spending ratios determined by the decisions of buyers. If one could postulate a preestablished harmony guaranteeing the continuous congruence of both sets of ratios – and such a postulate is implicit in the benevolent forms of socialism in which the planning board supplies just what people want – then there would be no need for the pedestrian trial and error of supply and demand. Without such a preestablished harmony and without authoritarian solutions on what the standard man is and what he is going to want, whether he likes it or not, supply and demand are inevitable. For supply schedules are production ratios determined with respect[2]

8 Prices

Any exchange involves a ratio between the quantities of the objects exchanged. When x_i units of an object *i* are traded for x_j units of an object *j*, then there is always some ratio, say p_{ij}, such that

$$x_i = p_{ij}x_j \tag{8}$$

The ratio p_{ij} is named a price: it is a ratio between quantities of objects exchanged; and it is defined by equation (8) as a multiple of the number of units of the second object, *j*. When prices are expressed as multiples of the units of some standard object, that object is named a money; the subscripts *j* of equation (8) may then be understood, and one may write

$$x_i = p_i x \tag{9}$$

so that p_i is the price of the object *i* in monetary units.

The price of the same object at the same time is the same in all exchanges of that object. The statement is methodological. It is a definition of 'same object' and 'same time.' Thus, if what seems to be the same object is traded at different prices, the larger price is larger because it includes, besides the price of the object, the price of something else: for instance, between different places, this price of something else would be the price of information, transportation, the use of agents, and the like; again, in the same locality, this price would be the price of special services, more agreeable circumstances, ignorance, gullibility, pride of purse, and the like. In other cases the apparent divergence is a divergence between clock time and economic time: the new price has not yet become operative at a more remote market.

2 This section ends in midsentence at the bottom of a page of typescript. There could, then, be missing pages.

The significance of prices is not limited to formal exchanges. This appears at once if equation (8) is differentiated on the supposition that the price p_{ij} is a constant. Then,

$$dx_i = p_{ij}\, dx_j \tag{10}$$

which is the same equation and admits the same varieties as equation (7), namely, the marginal comparative valuations that make the quantities of the productive process determinate. Hence constant prices and determinate quantities in process are concomitant: if the one, then also the other. Which is cause and which is effect is a further question. But one has at once that if either exists, the other also exists. Now the possibility of determinate quantities is not limited to exchange economies. Hence, the ratios that emerge as prices in exchanges are a more universal reality than exchanges.

In an exchange, then, it is necessary to distinguish between two aspects: there is the aspect of free consent; there is also a pragmatic equivalence between different quantities of different objects. The aspect of free consent consists in the fact that an exchange occurs when there is a coincidence of two opposite decisions; one party prefers x_i of i to x_j of j; the other party prefers the opposite; and the two come to terms. On the other hand, the aspect of pragmatic equivalence lies entirely in the coming to terms, in the objective effect of the exchange. This objective effect may exist regardless of preferences or free consents. There is a pragmatic equivalence between the work and the upkeep of slaves; it exists independently of their estimated demand; demand schedules are spending ratios determined with respect to hypothetical prices; and actual prices are the solutions, when they exist, of consequent demand and supply functions. They are the solutions at the point at which the least eager buyer and the least eager seller come to terms, and at which the maximum quantity that could be sold with consistent prices and given conditions is sold as a matter of fact.

One now may say in what sense prices are the marginal comparative valuations of the community. The statement does not mean that the least eager buyer and seller are the representatives of the community. The least eager buyer may be a monopsonist; the least eager seller a monopolist; and both monopsonists and monopolists need represent no one but themselves. In a first sense, prices are the work of the community insofar as prices are the method chosen by the community for determining its marginal comparative valuations. In a second sense, prices are the work of the community insofar as this method of determining marginal comparative valuations does not make economics a department of politics, operates more through desire than through fear, does not of itself restrict initiative, provides a continuously effective weapon against producing what is not wanted (in this line the genius of technical experts is without limit), and provides a continuous incentive to produce in the most efficient manner precisely what is wanted.

f) The Dialectic of Prices. Within the last hundred years economic thought has moved steadily away from the view that fluid prices and competition are the panacea for all economic ills and the guarantee of ever greater benefits. Underlying this change of thought there is the very simple fact that, while the price system is an exquisite mechanism, still it is not a mechanism into which one can put little knowledge and less wisdom and then reasonably expect to receive notable amounts of both. The price system will strike a balance of any present set of preferences; but it will not make the preferences wise, nor will it make the expectations on which they are based turn out to be true. On the contrary, it will find the economic mean, so to speak, of wise and stupid, intelligent and foolish preferences; it will weight true and false expectations with the money that backs them; and with a relentless accuracy it will work out the anomaly one may expect a machine so controlled to yield. In the long run one is presented with a dilemma: either eliminate from every strategic post in the economy the unenlightened freedom of choice that works ruin through exchanges and through prices, or else, if you would preserve that freedom, take effective steps to enlighten it. The alternatives are socialism or an enlightenment of insufficiently enlightened self-interest.

By a dialectic of prices is meant, not subscription to the doctrines of the more absurd philosophic systems, but simply the historical see-saw that marches ineptly from the insufficiency of rugged individualism to the insufficiency of rugged collectivism. In a first period fluid prices and competition bring obvious benefits: markets enforce the consistency of prices; first, the economies of the nations, then the nations of the world, are worked into a unified system; the prices of inconsistency tend to be reduced to a minimum, and with them the payments for mere inconsistency. This enforcement of consistency affects not merely actual processes in themselves but also the actual with respect to the potential; the entrepreneur emerges to set up a procession of new and more efficient combinations of production factors; there is an industrial revolution; there are new ideas, new men, new firms, new ways of doing things, new capital equipment, and, as the acceleration works through the surplus stages to reach the basic, eventually a rising standard of living.

But upon the first period there superposes a second. Supply and demand are harsh masters. The elasticity of fluid prices will adjust the x_i, x_j, x_k, ... of quantities produced to the q_i, q_j, q_k, ... of quantities sold. The trial and error of windfall profits and losses will tend to bring competitive producers to the acceptance of minimum profits and to an ever better knowledge of an ever more elusive equilibrium. Still, competitive producers are ever victims of the unforeseen, and, what is worse, even when they do foresee, their foresight will not avail them unless they also combine. Why not combine? Is not the doctrine of competition merely an embargo upon one of the more valuable types of new idea, namely, new ideas in organization? The trouble is that that is true. The age of corporations begins. It reorganizes industry. It organizes labor. It reaches out to tame the individualism of small producers of basic materials for world markets, producers of wheat, of cotton, of coffee. It forms cooperatives to link in united fronts of monopolists and monopsonists little sellers and buyers of any description. Issues cease to be merely economic. They are also political in a stretch of legislation that began with the Factory Acts and does not culminate even with Social Security. For such a growth of political interference has its premise in the inadequacy of competition and fluid prices to meet economic issues. It cannot but continue until it absorbs the whole sphere of economics or, alternatively, until economics finds a new charter. Already, with the increasing generalization of monopoly and monopsony, both competition and fluid prices are becoming dead letters.

If one attempts to break the impasse of government settling the terms upon which monopolists and monopsonists are to agree, and if one proceeds along the existing line of development, one reaches socialism. There is no longer ownership of means of production, but the use and the production of them is dictated to civil servants by the wise and learned men on the planning board. On the supposition that their wisdom and learning is not overbalanced by a fanatical streak, that the liquidation of classes does not prove necessary, that the universal enthusiasm for the system precludes the use of secret police and terrorism, one may expect an economy that presents the advantage of being free from booms and slumps of the old type[3]

3 The text ends abruptly, early in a page. It seems a case, not of missing pages, but of an abandoned effort.

13

Superposed Circuits

14 Superposed Circuits

The foregoing account of profits, price spreads, and the increment of basic income has now to be complemented with an account of superposed circuits. At any stage of the cycle, there may be superposed upon the main economy a subsidiary movement which adds, say, Z' to basic activity and Z'' to surplus activity per interval. This subsidiary movement, apart from its own fluctuations, has no general dynamic implications. In that respect it differs from the rate of investment balancing profits. On the other hand, it is the general form of profit as a monetary phenomenon, for it is the general case of a compensated rate of transference to and from the redistributive function entering into and modifying the movements of the circuits. First, we shall consider the route of the superposed circuits; second, we shall indicate its concrete interpretations in the favorable and the unfavorable balances of trade, in government deficit spending and the payment of public debts, and incidentally in the second-hand trade.

The route of the superposed circuits may be described most simply by adding Z' and Z'' to elements in the diagram of rates of payment and transfer. It consists of the following four elements:

(1) $DD' + Z'$ and/or $DD'' + Z''$

(2) $DE' + Z'$ and/or $DE'' + Z''$

$$(3)\ G'DO' + Z' \text{ and/or } (1 - G'')DO'' + Z''$$

$$(4)\ DD'' - Z' - Z''$$

Apart from lags, Z' is the same quantity in each case, and similarly Z'' is the same quantity in each case; the 'and/or' means that in any given situation Z' or Z'' may be zero; however, neither Z' nor Z'' is ever a negative quantity.

The four elements of the superposed circuits are circular: in interpreting them one may begin anywhere and move round the circuit in either direction. Element (1) is a transfer per interval from the redistributive function of Z' to basic demand and Z'' to surplus demand. Element (2) is an additional basic expenditure of Z' and an additional surplus expenditure of Z''. Element (3) is the emergence of these expenditures in surplus income: Z' is added to basic outlay going to surplus demand; Z'' is added to surplus outlay going to surplus demand. Element (4) is the transference of both Z' and Z'' from surplus demand to the redistributive function. Since there is a circuit, the process so represented can be repeated indefinitely as long as a concrete meaning to each element in the circuit can be given.

To apply the superposed circuit as an interpretation of the favorable balance of foreign trade, we have to drop the assumption of a closed economy. Let us suppose, then, a number of economies, each with its own basic and surplus circuits and redistributive function. Transactions between economies will be assumed to take place in the respective redistributive functions: thus, goods or services leaving one economy for another are considered to have passed beyond the productive process of the former and to have become redistributive goods or services sold on a redistributive market; similarly, goods or services entering an economy enter as redistributive goods or services, even though like second-hand materials they may enter the productive process for further fashioning or for sale in a regular commercial channel.

In the case of a favorable balance of foreign trade more goods and services are produced in a given economy than are sold in it. The excess is the favorable balance, say Z' of basic and Z'' of surplus products per interval. The favorable balance of trade appears as a credit item in the balance of payments, and this credit item will be $Z' + Z''$ per interval. It may be a gold import, a rate of foreign lending, a rate of paying foreign debt whether interest or principal. In any case, element (4) is a rate of surplus income moving from surplus demand to the redistributive function, where it purchases the gold import, or invests in foreign securities, or transforms a foreign debt into a domestic debt. Element (1) is the reception of this money, $Z' + Z''$, in return for the gold, for the sold securities, for the extinguished debt, and, further, its movement to basic and surplus demand respectively to purchase currently produced goods and services. Element (2) is the purchase of currently produced goods and services, not out of domestic income but by foreign traders. Hence there follows element (3): $Z' + Z''$ is a surplus in income over and above requirements in domestic income to purchase what is for sale on the domestic markets.

The favorable balance of foreign trade is of greatest significance for the accelerating economy. It yields a rate of pure surplus, $Z' + Z''$, per interval. Concomitantly, it effects a price spread or inflation of purchasing power of current income: the economy is doing more work, using more materials, but not to the advantage of its own standard of living. Above all, it provides an outlet to expansion without raising basic income: if the economy can sell abroad the increment in production resulting from acceleration, then it does not have to sell this increment at home; and not having to sell it at home, it does not have to raise lower incomes and lower higher incomes. Thus, the favorable balance of foreign trade cushions the profit cycle. It makes it possible to conduct an economy simply on the precepts of thrift and enterprise, precepts that pertain only to the initial phase of the expansion, but remain valid in later phases insofar as the unpleasantness of the 'squeeze' can be avoided by directing the increment in production beyond domestic frontiers.

The inverse phenomenon is the unfavorable balance of foreign trade. Then the economy is selling more than it is producing, say $Z' + Z''$ per interval. In the balance of foreign payments, $Z' + Z''$ appears as a debit item: it may be an export of gold, a rate of foreign borrowing, a rate at which a creditor nation is receiving interest or principal from debtors. In return there emerge goods or services in the redistributive function. Their purchase by entrepreneurs for further fashioning or for sale is represented by element (4). The proceeds of the sale – payments for further fashioning and for the activity of selling are purely domestic phenomena – yield surplus income as in element (3). The purchase of the excess import by the domestic public gives element (2). The possibility of this purchase by the domestic public is a transfer to demand from the redistributive function as in element (1). This last is the catch. It is the inverse to the cushioned profit cycle of the favorable balance.

There is, of course, the money available in the redistributive function for this transfer. Entrepreneurs are paying $Z' + Z''$ for the excess import; and this is received by those selling gold for export, or by those borrowing abroad, or by the recipients of the interest or principal of earlier foreign investments. Willingly enough, if prospects are bright, these gentlemen will make their funds available for investment to give the surplus part, $DD'' + Z''$, of element (1). However, there is a difficulty about prospects being bright: for the economy with the unfavorable balance to have a rate of profit, it must have a rate of investment in new firms or new fixed capital over and above the rate Z''; Z'' itself does not yield a rate of profit but only a rate at which domestic dealers purchase an excess import of foreign surplus goods or services; on the other hand, Z'' will combine with other investment to accelerate the domestic productive process and so hasten the day when the domestic economy will be able to sell abroad more than it borrows. While this is a great advantage to the backward economies, it is no advantage to the creditor nation with an unfavorable balance of trade; for the creditor nation will have a world full of competitors when, after having passed from a favorable to an unfavorable balance, it attempts to return to a favorable balance.

Even more intractable is the basic part of element (1), namely, $DD' + Z'$ per interval. The possibility of this may be illustrated by oriental princes dehoarding gold to purchase occidental trumperies, by a rentier class maintaining its standard of living by the interest or dividends from its foreign investments. But these may easily prove insufficient. If so, there immediately follows a contraction of the circuits: for there is insufficient income derived from domestic production to purchase both domestic products and the excess import; prices fall; scales of operation are curtailed; labor becomes unemployed; and this continues indefinitely as long as the unfavorable balance of trade is throwing goods on the domestic market but not generating the income to buy them. The state has to intervene. Huge income taxes transform unspent rentier income into a dole to complement the upper leisure class with a lower leisure class of unemployed. Nor, in the long run, will income taxes suffice. When foreign debtors begin paying the principal of their debt, provided they are allowed to do so, then the income tax has to become a capital levy, unless the rentier class is willing to go on a spree and spend their capital. Obviously, an economy that has worked itself into so unhealthy and demoralizing a situation is not regarded as a model for imitation by other economies more fortunately placed; its 'social security' programs may be defensible from the viewpoint of its domestic problems; but they are not for export to entirely different situations.

Deficit government spending and its consequent, paying off public debt, repeat the same phenomena in another mode. The deficit spending by the government (federal, state or provincial, municipal) gives at once element (1) $DD' + Z'$ and $DD'' + Z''$ and, as well, element (2) $DE' + Z'$ and $DE'' + Z''$. This spending takes over for public use or waste a section of current production, $Z' + Z''$, per interval; as this production generates equal income, which has not to be spent by individuals on current products, there results the pure surplus of element (3), which moves from surplus demand to the redistributive function, where it purchases government securities and so constitutes element (4).

While this movement is exactly parallel to the favorable balance of foreign trade, it has to be accompanied by another movement that is exactly parallel to the unfavorable balance of foreign trade. Deficit spending has to meet its current interest charge, and, on sound principles, it has to build up a sinking fund as well. Now, if the public debt has been mounting at the rate of $Z'_i + Z''_i$ per interval, then it has reached the proportions of $\Sigma (Z'_i + Z''_i - Z'_i - Z''_i)$ where $Z'_i + Z''_i$ per interval is the rate of accumulation in the sinking fund. Let $X'_i + X''_i$ be the debt service per interval, so that, where r is the rate of interest per interval

$$X'_i + X''_i = Z'_i + Z''_i + r.\Sigma(Z'_i + Z''_i - Z'_i - Z''_i) \qquad (30)$$

where it is supposed that the rate of interest on money in the sinking fund just cancels the interest on an equal portion of the debt. On the supposition of a consolidated or permanent public debt, there is no sinking fund but only a permanently large sum to be paid in interest.

Now there must be debt servicing, else even the emergency use of deficit spending is jeopardized. Thus only a revolutionary policy, aimed at the destruction of existing institutions and predicated on the hope of being able to restore confidence by the liquidation of the intelligent and by the psychological conditioning of the masses, would be opposed to debt servicing. Further, debt servicing can hardly be carried on by capital levies: the creditors would be among the chief victims of the levy; and a government could not both maintain confidence in its bonds and pay principal and interest by confiscating them. Hence the $X' + X''$ per interval has to come from the circuits, and the condition of its coming from the circuits without causing a general contraction is that by another route it is also going to the circuits. To make it go to the circuits is the difficulty. X' has to be a rate of rentier standards of living or, alternatively, of taxation on rentier income transferred to a dole, social security, or the like. X'' has to be a rate of investment, which, however, yields no profit but merely balances a rate of taxation, though it has the accelerating effects on the economy of ordinary investment in new fixed capital. Granted the first element, $DD' + X'$ and $DD'' + X''$, the rest follows. The second element is $DE' + X'$ and $DE'' + X''$; the third is the emergence of surplus income, since the products sold in the previous element generate income not needed for their sale; the fourth element is the removal by taxes of this surplus from the circuits, the payment of the rentiers, and the building up of the sinking fund.

The effects of deficit government spending, then, have to be the compound resultant of both the spending itself and the debt servicing. Using Z', Z'' to denote the spending, X', X'' to denote the servicing, the four elements of these superposed circuits are

(1) $DD' + Z' + X'$ and $DD'' + Z'' + X''$

(2) $DE' + Z' + X'$ and $DE'' + Z'' + X''$

(3) $G'DO' + Z' + X'$ and $(1 - G'')DO'' + Z'' + X''$

(4) $DD'' - Z' - Z'' - X' - X''$

To take the elements in inverse order, in the fourth element, $Z' + Z''$ is a rate of purchase of government bonds, while $X' + X''$ is a rate of taxation on surplus income. In the third element, $Z' + Z'' + X' + X''$ is a rate of surplus income, generated by current production, but paid in to the government for its wise spending. In the second element, $X' + Z'$ measures the inflation of labor income: labor, capital, management are producing that much per interval but not for their standard of living; except insofar as capital and, to some extent, management receive surplus income and purchase bonds which yield interest that increases their standard of living. Z' goes to public consumption, X' goes to the rentier class or its substitutes through a dole or social security. The other side of the second element, $DE'' + Z'' + X''$, reveals government purchases of capital goods at the rate Z'' per interval and further purchases of capital goods by borrowers from rentiers or from the sinking fund (indirectly) at the rate X'' per interval. Thus, $Z'' + X''$ gives a minimum rate of surplus expenditure on new fixed capital, and it is only additional expenditure on new fixed capital that yields a profit: X'' pays taxes; Z'' is a restricted profit inasmuch as it has to buy bonds.[1]

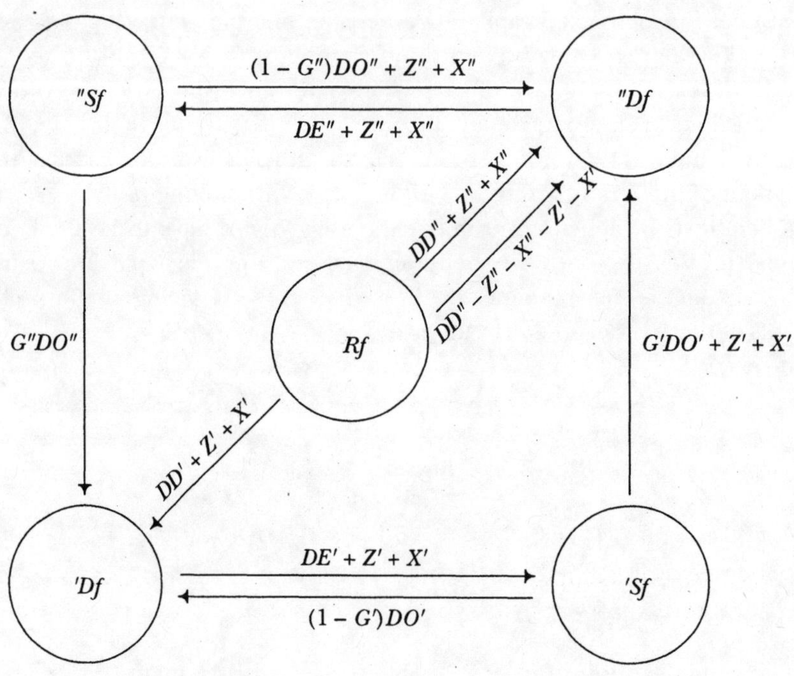

1 The diagram to follow is supplied by the editor; it was not part of the original text. The only diagrams of this period of Lonergan, and so until 1978, are those of section 34, Part One, and section 8, chapter 16, of Part Three. From these it is evident that there was nothing sacred about the positioning of the parts of the diagram. CWL 15 discusses further variations of the diagrams, in the Appendix. Diagrams such as the one above were developed in the McShane presentation of *Circulation Analysis* in Boston, 1977. A range of such diagrams are reproduced in Philip McShane, *Economics for Everyone. Das Jus Kapital* (Halifax, Axial Press, 1998).

14

Random Pointers[1]

[The Editor's Introduction indicated the selective nature of the present chapter. Furthermore, the fragments presented here are not presented in chronological order. It would be very difficult to determine that order: at best one can claim that the fragments, including the piece regarding Schumpeter in section 4, would seem to span two years of work in 1942–1944. So, the order and selection is geared, rather, to open the reader to a better comprehension of what Lonergan was attempting in his various efforts of economic analysis.]

1 The Fundamental Aspiration

[The first fragment presented here happens to be a candidate for final scribbles by Lonergan before he put his work aside for, perhaps, more than two decades.[2] The fragment consists of two pages, one of which has been used at the opening of this volume (p. xiv). The second page contains only three handwritten lines:]

Part I Define what cycle is inevitable
Part II Work out the conditions of this
cycle not being a 'trade cycle.'

1 Editorial comments will appear in the text of this chapter, in square brackets. Curly brackets, { }, in Lonergan text indicate obscurity of handwriting.
2 See below, p. 204, and CWL 15, Editors' Introduction.

[The text of the first page will be presented here immediately. The two pages would seem to be in the right order: they were so found by McShane at the end of the pages that provide the content of the previous chapter. While that chapter can be plausibly identified as a treatment of superposed circuits that predates the version of *Circulation Analysis*, the two pages that are considered here very likely postdate the conclusion of that analysis. If so, we have a date for Lonergan's change of interest in 1944: the first page is dated March 23, 1944. It is, in fact, the only precisely dated page in the various versions of the economics. While the significance of these two pages may be left to the reader and to future interpreters, it seems worthwhile to suggest that Lonergan was entertaining the possibility of a further attempt at analysis, one that would exploit the related mathematical presentation of *Circulation Analysis*.[3] The text of the first page is as follows:]

The Inevitable Cycle
March 23/1944

Let $Q' = f_1(t)$
$Q'' = f_2(t)$

Then $K_1 f_1'(t) - A_1 = f_2(t-a)$
$K_2 f_2'(t-a) - A_2 = f_3(t-b)$
$K_3 f_3'(t-b) - A_3 = f_4(t-c) \qquad a < b < c$

where A_1 A_2 A_3 are positive when lower stage goes in for short-term acceleration negative numerals as higher stage is merely maintaining
K_1 K_2 K_3 are linear functions relating output of higher stage with rate of increase of lower – ~~over~~
on average constants
not systematic variables

$a < b < c$ are time lags.

$$f_4(t-c) = K_3 f_3'(t-b) - A_3$$
$$= K_3[K_2 f_2''(t-a) - dA_2] - A_3$$
$$= K_3\{K_2[K_1 f_1'''(t) - D^2 A_1] - dA_2\} - A_3$$

Condition of non-cycle is Q''/Q' = a constant

3 See below, p. 244.

$$\text{i.e. } \frac{f_2(t) + f_3(t) + f_4(t) + \ldots}{f_1(t)} = \text{a constant}$$

2 Some Transitional Searchings

[The fragments in this section belong with the text presented in chapter 8 above. Facsimiles of the first and last page of the relevant archival file, pages G74 and G131, are included at this chapter's end (**1** and **2**) so that the reader may better assess the text of G74, to follow immediately, and the text of G131 that should conclude, in some form, the incomplete text of chapter 8. A typed version of G74 follows. Handwritten additions to Lonergan's typescript are shown in smaller type.]

Essay towards a Pure Theory of Social Economics

1. *Economic Activity.* → fulfilment of material conditions of human life
S.L. = human life as ~~lifted from economic~~
materially conditioned and sustained

Society
Man = potency to human life
material conditions of actuation of potency
E.A. fulfilment of material conditions
S.L. measure of this fulfilment

Economic activity is an ordered and variable process towards a standard of living.

economic {deposit} of human life as lived

The fundamental fact is the *standard of living.* In any given area over any period of time there exists some standard of living, some quantitative rate at which people are obtaining food, clothing, shelter and the implements of amusement, art, education, law, medicine, politics, religion, research and war. Measurement of this standard is not possible immediately, for as yet no yard-stick has been determined. But even without such a determination, we can and do know that there is such a thing as a standard of living, that it is quantitative now standing at a higher level and now at a lower, and that it is a rate, not 'goods and services' but a 'flow of goods and services,' not a 'so much' but a 'so much every so often.'

To effect the standard of living continuous human effort is required. For between the potentialities of nature, whether physical, chemical, vegetal, animal or human, and on the other hand the standard of living, there is a gap to be bridged. Even South Sea islanders have some effort to make. Such an effort is termed *economic activity*. It may be anything from digging ditches to signing slips of paper, from tending machines to clipping coupons. But it exists always, for the world's work is never done. Like the standard of living itself, it is not a 'so much' but a 'so much every so often.' It is an endless series of repeated routines. It is a flow, not indeed

[The significance of G74 is that it seems to be a transition page in Lonergan's thinking. It seems plausible that the handwriting on the page, including the title, 'Essay ...,' were added when the page was complete. There are no further pages of this text and, as was noted already, the page was used to wrap the contents of file 60 of his notes. Did he move on from this page to the analysis given in that file, reproduced here in chapter 8? At all events, that analysis represents a more precise focus on 'pure economic analysis.' This is most easily seen by comparing the approach of this analysis with the broader sweep of 'For a New Political Economy.' The text of G131 reads as follows:]

activity does more to raise prices than anything else. No one of the three arguments is peremptory, but the three combined tend to limit positive action by *DD′* to a stimulation of the quantity acceleration and to leave *DS′* the main part of the work of providing the increased quantities of money for the increased turnovers.

Stimulating action on the part of *DD′* is not, of course,

The immediate stimulation of basic supply

necessary. ~~Its origin~~ we shall find later in cross-over disequilibrium. Meanwhile it will be interesting to note a correlation between the rise in prices, *DP′*, and the rate of acceleration, *DQ′*, when *DD′* is zero. For any rate of acceleration of goods and services, *DQ′*, there is an excess of goods in production over goods at the final market; the former is increasing ~~incomes~~ outlays and so also incomes while the increase in goods for expenditure lags; corresponding to this lag

[Lonergan canceled line 1 from 'does' to 'else.' and replaced this in handwriting thus:]

is apt to raise price levels and so multiply the need for more money throughout industry and commerce.

[Lonergan also canceled the entire paragraph, 'Stimulating ... to this lag,' and replaced it in handwriting thus:]

Mutatis mutandis, the same arguments that hold at the beginning of an acceleration hold throughout its duration. For any rate of acceleration of goods and services, DQ', ~~there is a lag but~~ goods in production are in advance of goods on the final market, and ~~income~~ increasing income is in advance of the possible basic expenditure at initial prices. This lag is a function of DQ', increasing with its increase, and decreasing with its decrease; and corresponding to the size of this lag there is some single advance in prices, DP', that clears the basic market with DD' at zero. When the lag changes another change in prices is necessary if DD' is still zero. But then when the acceleration DQ' eventually becomes zero, a positive DD' is for the first time desirable, namely, to prevent the negative DP' implied in the disappearing lag

[The third page-fragment made available in this section is a page that Lonergan put aside carefully. It is the single page that is contained in folder 51 of Lonergan's notes. There is, in fact, another copy of that page in the archival material. It does not seem to have been preserved with serious deliberation: it is on the reverse side of a *Gratia Operans* typescript.[4] The page corresponds to a page, G90, of the text of chapter 8, to be found above, beginning line 30, p. 123, with the words 'decreasing. Finally ...' The page is significant in that it represents a change in direction, a decision not to enter into detail with regard to variations in crossovers such as are expressed in the array of numbers on this page. A corresponding array occurs on page 55 above, of section 29 of 'For a New Political Economy,' and the text of that section adds an enlightening context to the treatment that replaced this rejected page. Above all, these arrays and their contexts help the reader to appreciate the concrete complexity of Lonergan's perspective, a complexity hidden by his compact prose. The relevant fragment is as follows:]

decreasing. Finally, in the compound expansion and the compound contracting, when both DO' and DO'' are varying in the same direction, one cannot say at once whether crossover equilibrium requires DH to be positive, zero, or negative; later it will be argued from general considerations that the tendency of a compound expansion is to require DH to be negative in the first period and positive in the second, while the tendency of the

4 The Lonergan Archives reference is A314. I am indebted here and in section 3, and also for the retrieval of the scribbles on Keynes referred to at note 7 below, to the research of Michael Shute.

compound contraction is to require *DH* first to be positive and then negative.

The change in *DH* required per interval in the different phases if the crossover equilibrium is to be maintained, is indicated in the third column of the table of names and definitions of the phases (see above). Whether the change in *DH* is effected by a change in G' or a change in G'' is immaterial; but it is worth noting that a small change in G' does as much as a greater change in G'', for G' is the denominator in G''/G'. The point is illustrated in the following table.

G' \ G''	95%	90%	85%	80%	75%	70%	65%	60%
5%	19	18	17	16	15	14	13	12
10%	9.5	9	8.5	8	7.5	7	6.5	6
15%	6.3	6	5.6	5.3	5	4.6	4.3	4
20%	4.75	4.5	4.25	4	3.75	3.5	3.25	3
25%	3.8	3.6	3.4	3.2	3	2.8	2.6	2.4
30%	3.16	3	2.83	2.6	2.5	2.3	2.16	2
35%	2.7	2.57	2.43	2.28	2.14	2	1.85	1.7
40%	2.37	2.25	2.12	2	1.87	1.75	1.62	1.5

The independent variables are G' and G'' given in percentages, G' of DO' and G'' of DO''; the corresponding value of G''/G' is found at the intersection of the row and column marked by the percentage.

[The fourth fragment, a few pages of typescript in length, represents another direction abandoned. The text presented in chapter 8 goes from G114 to G119, as indicated in note 3 of that chapter. Lonergan would seem to have abandoned this other line of discussion because of the need for a fuller treatment of the topic. The pages abandoned (but in fact left with the text of chapter 8) are as follows:]

Equations (36) and (37) tacitly assume that the increased quantities of money involved in increased turnovers are derived exclusively from the net transfer to basic supply, DS'. This tacit assumption has now to be corrected: the quantity of money in the basic circuit may increase or decrease in three ways, by a net transfer to basic supply, by a net transfer to basic demand, and by a crossover disequilibrium. Let DM' be this increase in quantity of money in a given interval, so that

$$DM' = DS' + DD' + DG \tag{39}$$

where the parallel equation for the surplus circuit would be

$$DM'' = DS'' + DD'' - DG \tag{40}$$

since a positive DG empties the surplus circuit in favor of the basic while a negative DG empties the basic circuit in favour of the surplus (cf. equation 4 above).

The next question is whether DM' may replace DS' in equations (36) and (37). The answer involves some determination of the concept of income velocities. Let us write

$$DD' = DE' - DI' \tag{41}$$

so that savings are in the redistribution function: when people spend less than they earn, the difference gives a negative DD'; and when they spend more than they earn, they are drawing on savings in the redistribution function and effecting a positive DD'. The effect of this equation, (41), is to eliminate the concept of income velocities. There is a rate of income, DO'; there is a rate of expenditure, DE'; but between these two there is no rate but only a quantity of money which DD' increases or diminishes in a manner that equilibrates the two terminal rates, DO' and DE'. This device assimilates the analysis of velocity in basic demand to the analysis given for basic supply: for in supply there are posited no velocities of money between payments, but simply rates of payment with quantities of money between them and DS' as the proximate source of variations in these quantities.

A further effect of equation (41), more relevant to the present issue, appears on recalling that

$$DI' = DO' + DG \tag{7}$$

so that

$$DE' = DO' + DG + DD' \tag{42}$$

so that basic expenditure equals basic outlay plus the crossover difference plus the net transfer to basic demand. But basic expenditure is also basic receipts, that is, the receipts of the entrepreneurs who deal immediately with consumers. Now such receipts over an interval may be equal to or greater than or less than the payments, initial and transitional, of these entrepreneurs over the interval. Let us assume that at the end of each interval these entrepreneurs make up their books, transfer a positive difference to the redistribution function to give a negative element in DS', or make good a negative difference by effecting a positive transfer from the redistribution function. Then,

$$DM' = \sum (ds_i + dr_i) \tag{43}$$

and on the suppositions of equation (37)

$$DM' = \sum (1 + v_i)\, dr_i \tag{44}$$

The foregoing results may be put more precisely. It will be recalled that $r_i n_i$ *and* $s_i n_i$ are approximate average figures over the interval and that dr_i, ds_i, dn_i are increments found by comparing the averages of two intervals. However, there is another notation, already mentioned, that makes r_{ij} the exact initial payments and s_{ij} the exact transitional payments of the *i*th entrepreneur in his *j*th turnover or fractional turnover during the interval. Let us define dr_{ij} and ds_{ij} as the increments emerging from the comparison of two successive turnovers, figures being taken from complete and not from fractional turnovers. Further, let DM' be the quantitative increment of money in the circuit during the same interval and not, as hitherto, the increment in the second of two intervals under comparison. Then, on the suppositions of equations (42) and (43)

$$DM' = \sum\sum (dr_{ij} + ds_{ij}) \tag{45}$$

and since it is always possible to find numbers u_{ij} such that

$$\sum\sum ds_{ij} = \sum\sum u_{ij} dr_{ij} \tag{46}$$

one can also write

$$DM' = \sum\sum (1 + u_{ij})\, dr_{ij} \tag{47}$$

where all summations are taken first with respect to turnovers *j* and then with respect to entrepreneurs *i*. In this notation varying velocities, i.e. turnover frequencies, appear in the number of terms in the summations with respect to *j*.

3 Economic Control

[The short fragment included here comes from the reverse side of a typescript on *Gratia Operans*.[5] Its preservation is important in that, while Lonergan discussed economic measurements in *Circulation Analysis*,[6] and was quite clear there on the irrelevance of quantifying indeterminacies,[7] he was not explicit on strategies of economic control. This piece gives some guidance to his thinking. It begins in mid-sentence at the top of a first page, evidently working through an extended analogy between the bases of the baseball diamond and the functional zones of his economic diagram. The fragment ends in the middle of a second page with the roundedness of a definite conclusion. The fragment reads as follows:]

third to second is $(1 - G'')DO''$, from third to home is $G''DO''$. As far as these movements are concerned, at the end of each interval the groups at home and first have DG more balls than at the beginning of the same interval, while the groups at second and third have DG less balls at the end of each interval than at the beginning of the same interval, where

$$DG = G''DO'' - G'DO'$$

and so DG may be positive, zero, or negative. However, the group at the pitcher's box is far from idle. In the course of the interval it has made DD' more throws to home than the group has made to it, DS' more throws to first than first has made to it, DD'' more throws to second than second has made to it, and DS'' more throws to third than third has made to it. The result of these movements is that at the respective bases there have been added to the home-first circuit $(DD' + DS')$ balls during the interval and also there have been added to the second-third circuit $(DD'' + DS'')$ balls during the interval, where however any of these quantities may be positive, zero, or negative.

Evidently, there is a high degree of indeterminacy to events within such

5 Lonergan Archives, A42.
6 See below, pp. 268–74.
7 The relevant discussion is chapter 15, section 5. Note especially the conclusion in relation to such problems as the measurement of capital.

a dynamic structure. All one can say is the game may go all awry. A large and positive crossover difference uncompensated by action from the pitcher's box will result sooner or later in depriving the groups at second and third bases of all their balls, or if the crossover difference is large and negative, it will result in depriving the groups at home and first of all their balls. Similarly if the group at the pitcher's box makes up its mind to accumulate balls, tossing back fewer than they receive, the groups at the bases will again find themselves without balls eventually. But without further information one cannot say how rapidly the ultimate event of being without balls will arrive. Further, the players at the bases may make up, by a greater efficiency in pitching and catching what balls they have, for any loss of balls they may suffer, up to the ultimate moment when they have no balls at all.

But despite this almost baffling indeterminacy, it remains that there is a definite dynamic structure. There are hypotheses on which the game can go awry; and this possibility constitutes a fundamental indeterminacy for the structure. On that basis either by adding further information about the nature of the game or by adding further suppositions, a still greater determinacy may be built.

4 Schumpeter, Keynes

[At the time of Lonergan's early work in economics, Keynes was the big name. More recently, Schumpeter is being acknowledged as a, or perhaps the, significant economist of the early century.[8] Lonergan mentions Keynes regularly in his work; indeed the introductory page of *Circulation Analysis* relates the analysis very definitely to Keynes. Schumpeter is mentioned less regularly, but it is evident that Lonergan had a great respect for Schumpeter's work. A third figure of the early century who is regarded by many as having been a better Keynsian than Keynes is M. Kalecki, who arrived in Cambridge from Poland in the mid-thirties. Kalecki was not known to Lonergan in the pre-1945 period of his work.[9]

8 Succinctly, Peter Drucker, 'Schumpeter and Keynes,' *Forbes*, 23 May 1982, pp. 300–304; Robert Heilbroner, 'Was Schumpeter Right After All?' *Journal of Economic Perspectives* 7 (1993) 87–96.

9 Lonergan got to know Kalecki's work in his later years and used the Kaleckian quip, 'capitalists get what they spend; workers spend what they get.' While Kalecki is not mentioned in the texts of this volume, I have nonetheless included 'Kalecki' in the index: from the references the reader may gather to

Lonergan's analysis is implicitly critical of Keynes, less critical of Schumpeter. The content of such criticism is a task for later studies, but it is of interest to reproduce here two brief extracts from Lonergan's scribbled notes, one giving a brief comparative comment on 'Schumpeter and Lonergan,' the other sketching parallels between Lonergan and Keynes. A facsimile of both scribbles is given on a single page here (3), although the two notes are from quite separate parts of the archives.[10] The Schumpeter extract follows.]

Schumpeter and Lonergan:
My real and my circulation phases involve no distinction between growth (mere increase in size) and development (new productive combinations). For Schumpeter these two are specifically distinct – the new production functions create new situations that increase enormously the average of error and bring about the cycle(s).

However, the ideas of capital, credit, interest, etc., that Schumpeter advances appear more clearly and more generally and in more detailed a fashion. The relevance of Schumpeter's insistence on development as opposed to growth is in the concatenation of the phases, e.g. Schumpeter's development can take place in my static phase if $DQ_n'' > 0$ and if the new combinations are continuously offset by equal liquidations of former enterprises.

[Keynes and Lonergan

The comments on Keynes are a few lines of comparison located between two equations, which can be traced back to 'For a New Political Economy,'[11] and, upside-down, a reference to a book which must have been recently published or reviewed at the time: '*The Managerial Revolution.* John Burn-

---

what extent Lonergan anticipated, in his fuller thematic, some of Kalecki's central insights. It should certainly lead to a new twist on twentieth-century economics: 'Kalecki has received general acclaim as a great economist of the twentieth century; the man who arguably discovered the theory of effective demand prior to and independently of Keynes' (Andrew B. Trigg, 'On the Relationship between Kalecki and the Kaleckians,' *Journal of Post-Keynesian Economics* 19 [1994] 92). Lonergan's view of effective demand is a much richer achievement.

10 The quotation regarding Schumpeter is among the handwritten notes of folder 60 of Lonergan's economic writings. The Keynes material is labeled A44 in the Lonergan Archives, the reverse of A42.

11 See the beginning of chapter 6, above.

ham. John Day Co., Inc. 1941 New York 285pp Boston & Montreal $3.00.' This, of course, helps to date 'For a New Political Economy' as being about 1942.

Why did it occur to Lonergan, if it did, to comment on Keynes in connection with the equations jotted down on the same page? What is the significance of his correlations? It is best to leave these questions to the reader. The typescript of the jottings is as follows:]

$$P'DQ' = C' \, [p'Dq' + p''Dq'']$$

$$P' = \frac{C'p'dq'}{DQ'} + \frac{C'p''Dq''}{DQ'}$$

Keynes

$E = DI' + DI''$
$I' = DI''$
$E - I' = DI'$
$0 = DQ' + DQ''$
$R = DQ'$
$C = DQ''$
$P = P'$
$S = DE''$

5 Some Scribbled Searchings

[Two blocks of jottings are presented here. Both are also given in facsimile (4 and 5), since the handwritten versions supply the reader both with a check on the version here and with an impression of Lonergan's creative energy and style of work. The first block is from the reverse side of two sequential pages of the material presented above in chapter 12, p. 192, beginning '8 Prices.' The second block is from the reverse sides of some late rejected half-typed pages of the text presented in chapter 8 above. The order in which they are presented here is not a judgment on the order of their composition, although it is likely the right chronological order. They are presented in this order because they convey to the reader two extremes of Lonergan's efforts, the first more easily comprehensible. The first block represents the large sweep that still reaches the details, the concrete; the second block gives a sense of his focus on detail within the sweep of his broad searchings. The first two pages, on prices, follow.]

[Page 1]

One may reflect that all this has been said before. But over one hundred years, practice followed in the wake of theory, has moved away from the view that fluid prices and competition are the panacea for all economic ills and the guarantee of ever greater benefits. No doubt that view provided an effective means for enforcing the consistency of prices: it worked the whole world into a single market place. Again, it gave a free hand to the entrepreneur ...

But it eliminated itself. ~~Competition is no more than an embargo upon a very valuable type of new~~

~~Too harsh~~ Competition an embargo
Too harsh
the age of corporations

Neither fluid prices nor competition
But with {praise} of fluid prices and <u>competition</u>. Review statements ≡
Not a norm but a mechanism. Definition –

Result __ __ But the idea of mechanism: handle the
merely empirical __ Postulate and effect enlightenment

[Page 2]

<u>for handling the merely empirical</u>
↑

~~But mere prices~~

<u>Prices: Mechanism or Norm</u>

<u>Prices and Acceleration</u>

<u>Competition & Fluid Prices</u>
actual & potential consistency
monopoly vs. potential competition

inertia
1) <u>The ~~rigidity~~ of real prices</u>

~~$q_i = q_j dp_{ij}$~~

$q_i = q_j$ ~~dp~~p_{ij}

$dq_i = q_j dp_{ij} + p_{ij} dq_j + dp_{ij} dq_j$

suppose $dq_i = 0$
then dp_{ij} and dq_i have to be opposite in sign
more means a lower real price
less means a higher real price
And everything cannot accelerate at once

2) The problem of 'more money'

   1) Mercantilism
   2) Bills of exchange, banking
   3) Gold standard
   4) No gold standard

3) Booms an artificial acceleration
   Slumps cutting out the artific— propensity to consume max
   for zero acceleration

[There follow scribbles on outlay and accelerations. These four pages of scribbles (**6** to **9**) all belong with the text reproduced in chapter 8 above. The first, on outlay, is the reverse of the page named G118; the other three come in sequence, the reverse of the pages G127–9.]

[The Outlay Page]

Outlay DO'

$$DO' = \sum_i [(\alpha_{io} + j - 1 + \alpha_{ij}) r_{io} + \sum_{n=1}^{n=n} (j - n + \alpha_{ij})\, dr_{in}]$$

where $\alpha_{io}\, \alpha_{ij}$ are constants for each "i"
α_{io} the fraction of the zero turnover left over from last turnover
α_{ij} the fraction of last turnover found in this one
$j+1$ is the number of turnovers counting both fractional turnovers
dr_{in} is the difference in outlay between the nth and
the $(n-1)$th counting the first complete turnover
as the first

[The 'Acceleration' Pages]

[Page 1]

Negative acceleration
$DM' = -K$
General squeeze – falling prices
if at once & universal, solution
de facto, falling prices and reducing production
– which augments – DM' – makes
it systematic – & does not provide a solution

Return from positive acceleration to zero acceleration on acquired higher level

I [Acceleration – proportionate lag
initial (struck out)
– unless – DD', maintained (struck out) then + DP'
lag ends –
End of acceleration – unless + DD', then – DP'
can't take it, because unorganized for general price drop and {crash} can't be avoided, because unorganized for – DD']

II No – DS' – if expansion on ^increasing volume of loans
then remaining at peak of expansion
means remaining at peak of volume of loans
to pay the loans off and not renew them – reduces volume – gives – DS', gives reduced turnover size.

[Page 2]

Abortive Accelerations

~~1 Profit and loss~~ corrected 1/ index of expansion or contraction
1 Varying inventories 2/ acceleration starts and finishes without going around.
uncorrected

2 Windfall profits & losses
X makes outlay – Y gets it in addition to his own outlay
Y' gets it & makes a – DD'
X' spends + DD' – Y uses it to decrease c.cap. on short term loans

Successful acceleration & increase of prices

~~wrong to put $DE' = DO'$~~
~~DO' at beginning of expansion – a saving needed to meet – DR~~

successful process says a good deal more
[DP' DD' at beginning and end
DS' + no repayment of principal]

[Page 3]

Surplus Circuit

1) Repeat all said about basic

2) Case of *DD″* different

Investments
- 1/ Redistributional
- 2/ Services of financial houses
- 3/ New Capital equipment *DD″*
- 4/ New monetary circulating capital, *DS′ DS″*

3) Difference α Once expansion in process

same

then *DI″* – *DE″*

purchase of more capital equipment at *DD″* = 0

ß different

DO″ can be positive over long periods

~~less danger of raising price level~~

& this positive gives crossover disequilibrium

a new complication of basic circuit

Conclusion

[The sample of fragments presented here, illustrating a masterly reach for the norms of control of economic detail, provide a significant additional context of respect for the final product of those years of effort, the *Essay in Circulation Analysis* that is the topic of the final section of this volume.]

Essay towards a Pure Theory of Social Economics

1. Economic Activity.

Economic activity is an ordered and variable process towards a standard of living.

The fundamental fact is the standard of living. In any given area over any period of time there exists some standard of living, some quantitative rate at which people are obtaining food, clothing, shelter and the implements of amusement, art, education, law, medicine, politics, religion, research and war. Measurement of this standard is not possible immediately, for as yet no yard-stick has been determined. But even without such a determination, we can and do know that there is such a thing as a standard of living, that it is quantitative now standing at a higher level and now at a lower, and that it is a rate, not "goods and services" but a "flow of goods and services," not a "so much" but a "so much every so often."

To effect the standard of living continuous human effort is required. For between the~~p~~ potentialities of nature, whether physical, chemical, vegetal, animal or human, and on the other hand the standard of living, there is a gap to be bridged. Even South Sea islanders have some effort to make. Such an effort is termed economic activity. It may be anything from digging ditches to signing slips of paper, from tending machines to clipping coupons. But it exists ~~invariab~~ always, for the world's work is never done. Like the standard of living itself, it is not a "so much" but a "so much every so often." It is an endless series of repeated routines. It is a flow, not indeed

1

throughout industry
is apt to raise price levels and so multiply the need for more money
activity ~~does more to raise prices than anything else.~~ No one of the three arguments is peremptory, but the three combined tend to limit positive action by DD' to a stimulation of the quantity acceleration and to leave to DS' the main part of the work of providing the increased quantities of money for the increased turnovers.

~~Stimulating action on the part of DD' is not, of course, necessary. Its origin~~ The immediate stimulation of basic supply we shall find later in cross-over disequilibrium. Meanwhile it will be interesting to note a correlation between the rise in prices, DP', and the rate of acceleration, DQ', when DD' is zero. For any rate rate of acceleration of goods and services, DQ', there is an excess of goods in production over goods at the final market; the former is increasing ~~incomes~~ outlays and so also incomes while the increase in goods for expenditure lags; corresponding to this lag

Mutatis mutandis, the same arguments that hold at the beginning of an acceleration hold throughout it during. For any rate of acceleration of goods & services, DQ', ~~there is an~~ ~~[illegible]~~ goods in production are in advance of goods on the final market, and ~~income~~ increasing income is in advance of the possible basic expenditure at initial prices. This lag is a function of DQ', increasing with its increase, & decreasing with its decrease; and corresponding to the size of this lag there is some single advance in prices, DP', that clears the basic market with DD' at zero. When the lag changes ~~[illegible]~~ another change in prices is necessary if DD' is still zero. But then when the acceleration DQ' eventually becomes zero, a positive DD' is for the first time desirable, namely, to prevent the negative DP' implicit in the disequilibrium

Schumpeter & Lonergan

My real as my circulation phase wisdom no distinction between growth (mere increase in size) and development (new production combinations)

For Sch. these two are specifically distinct – the new production functions create new situations that increase enormously the average of error & bring about the cycle.

However, the ideas of capital, credit, interest, etc., that Schum. advances appear more clearly & more generally & in more detailed a fashion – the relevance of Sch. insistence on development as opposed to growth is in the concentration of the phases – eg. Sch development can take place in any static phase if $DQ''n > 0$ and if the new combinations are continuously offset by equal liquidations of former enterprises

$$p' DQ' = c'[p' Dq' + p'' Dq'']$$

$$P' = \frac{C' p' Dq'}{DQ'} + \frac{C' p'' Dq''}{DQ'}$$

Keynes

$$E = DI' + DI''$$

$$I' = DI''$$

$$E - I' = DI'$$

$$O = DQ' + DQ''$$

$$R = DQ'$$

$$C = DQ''$$

$$P = P'$$

$S =$ [illegible]

One may reflect that all this has been said before. But one hundred years' practice followed in the wake of theory, has moved away from the view that fluid prices and competition [are] the panacea for all economic ills and the guarantee of ever greater benefit. No doubt that view provided an effective means for enforcing the consistency of prices: it worked the whole world into a single market place. Again it gave a free hand to the entrepreneurs — . —

But it eliminated itself. ~~Competition is no more~~ ~~a very valuable type of ...~~ ~~Human embargo upon~~

~~Too harsh~~ Competition an embargo

Too harsh

An age of corporations

Neither fluid prices nor competition

But not praise of fluid prices or competition. Review statements =

Not a norm but a mechanism. Definition —

But the idea of mechanism: handle the

Result — —

merely empirical — Postulate & effect enlightenment.

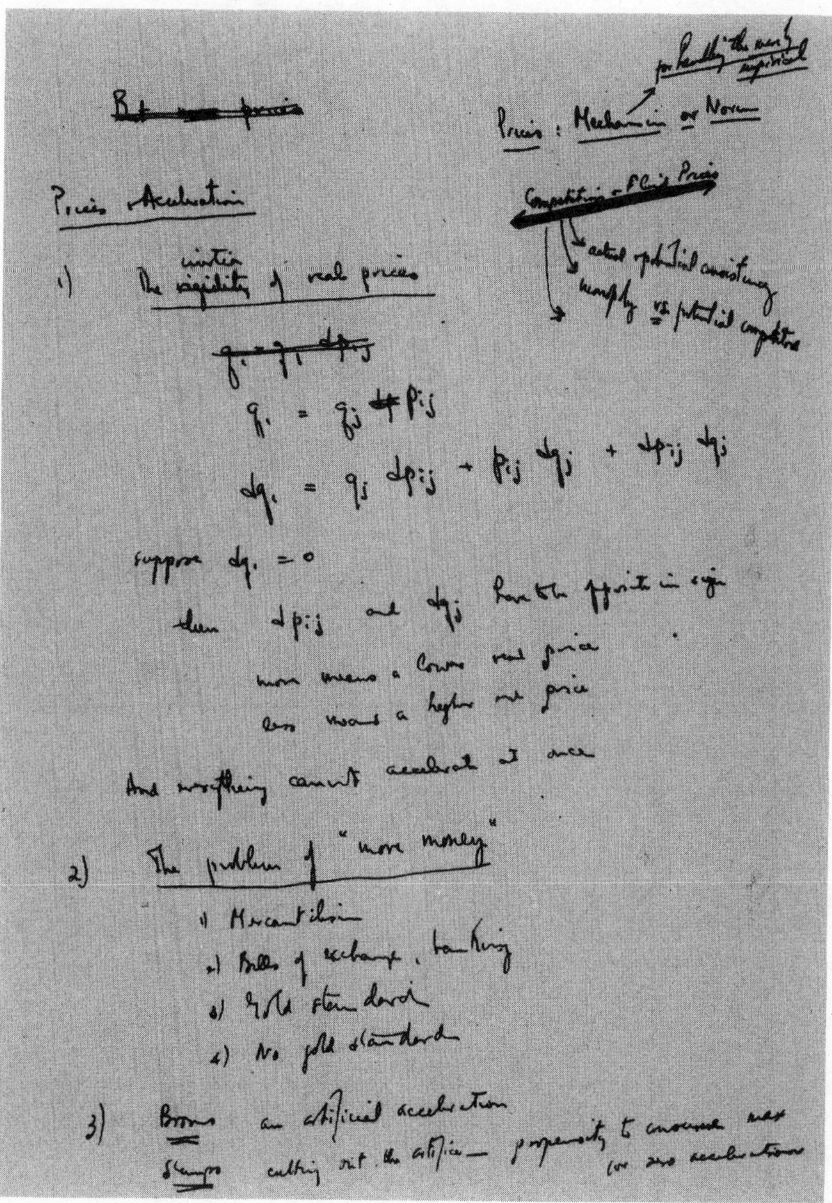

~~Rt ... prices~~

Prices : Mechanism or Norm → for handling the merely empirical

Prices & Acceleration

Competition – Flexible Prices
→ actual & potential consistency
→ monopoly vs potential competition

1) The rigidity [inertia] of real prices

$$q_i = q_j \, p_{ij}$$

$$dq_i = q_j \, dp_{ij} + p_{ij} \, dq_j + dp_{ij} \, dq_j$$

suppose $dq_i = 0$

then dp_{ij} and dq_j have the opposite in sign

more means a lower real price

less means a higher real price

And everything cannot accelerate at once

2) The problem of "more money"

1) Mercantilism
2) Bills of exchange, banking
3) Gold standard
4) No gold standard

3) Booms an artificial acceleration

Slumps cutting out the artifice — propensity to consume max for zero acceleration

5

Outlay DO'

$$DO' \quad \sum_i \left[(d_{i0} + j - 1 + d_{ij})\, r_{i0} + \sum_{n=1}^{now} (j - n + d_{ij})\, dr_{in} \right]$$

where d_{i0} d_{ij} are constants for each "i"

d_{i0} the fraction of the zero turnover left over from last

d_{ij} the fraction of last turnover found in this one

$j+1$ is number of turnovers counting both fractional ones

dr_{in} is the difference in outlay between the n'th and the (n−1)th counting the first complete turnover as the first

6

Negative acceleration

$DM' = -K$

General squeeze – falling prices

if at once + universal, shutdown de facto, falling prices + reducing production – which augments $-DM'$ – makes it systematic – + does not provide solution

Return from positive acceleration to zero acceleration on acquired higher level

I Acceleration – proportionate lag – unless $-DS'$, inadvertently then $+DP'$

End of acceleration lag ends – unless $+DP'$, then $-DP'$

can't take it, because unorganized for general price drop

and cause can't be avoided, because unorganized for $-DP'$.

II No $-\frac{DS'}{2}$ – if expansion on increasing volume of loans

then remaining at peak of expansion

means remaining at peak of volume of loans

to pay the loans off + not renew them – reduce volume –

gives $-DS'$, gives reduced turnover size.

Abortive Accelerations

your profits & losses as corrected (i) index of expansion or contraction

(i) Varying inventories [(ii) acceleration starts of ... without going round.

uncorrected

(ii) Windfall profits & losses

X makes outlay & Y gets it in addition to his own outlay

Y puts it & makes a $-DD'$

X' spends $+DD'$ — Y' uses it to decrease c. cap. on short term loans

Successful acceleration & success of process

Wrong to put $DE = DD'$ ...

$-DD'$ at beginning of expansion ...

successful process says a good deal more

DP' DD' at beginning & end

DS' & no repayment of principal

8

Surplus Circuit

1) Repeat all said about basic

2) Case of DD'' different

Investment
1) Redistributional
2) Increase of financial loans
3) New capital equipment DD''
4 New monetary circulating capital, DS' DS''

3) Difference 1. Once expansion in process
then DS'' = DE''
purchase of new capital equipment at DD'' = 0

2. different DD'' can be positive over long periods
~~[illegible]~~
& this positive gives cross-over disequilibrium
a new complication of basic circuit

PART THREE

Circulation Analysis

15

The Productive Process

Outline of the Argument

The present inquiry is concerned with relations between the productive process and the monetary circulation. It will be shown (1) that the acceleration of the process postulates modifications in the circulation, (2) that there exist 'systematic,' as opposed to windfall, profits, (3) that systematic profits increase in the earlier stages of long-term accelerations but revert to zero in later stages – a phenomenon underlying the variations in the marginal efficiency of capital of Keynesian *General Theory*, (4) that the increase and decrease of systematic profits necessitate corresponding changes in subordinate rates of spending – a correlation underlying the significance of the Keynesian propensity to consume, (5) that either or both a favorable balance of trade and domestic deficit spending create another type of systematic profits, (6) that while they last they mitigate the necessity of complete adjustment of the propensity to consume to the accelerations of the process, (7) that they cannot last indefinitely, (8) that the longer they last, the greater becomes the intractability of ultimate problems. From the premises and conclusions of this analysis it then will be argued (9) that prices cannot be regarded as ultimate norms guiding strategic economic decisions, (10) that the function of prices is merely to provide a mechanism for overcoming the divergence of strategically indifferent decisions or preferences, and (11) that, since not all decisions and preferences possess this indifference, the exchange economy is confronted with the dilemma either of eliminating itself by suppressing the freedom of exchange or of certain classes of exchanges, or else of effectively augmenting the enlightenment of the enlightened self-interest that guides exchanges.

4 The Productive Process

The term 'productive process' is to be used broadly. It denotes not merely 'making things' but the extraction or cultivation of raw materials, their transportation and assembly, the planning and designing of products, processing and distribution. It includes not only activities upon material objects but also services of all kinds, not only labor but also management, and not only production management but also sales management. In brief, it is the totality of activities bridging the gap between the potentialities of nature, whether physical, chemical, vegetable, animal, or human nature, and, on the other hand, the actuality of a standard of living. Such activities vary with the conditions of physical geography and with the cultural, political, and technical development of the population. They range from the simple and fixed routines of primitive hunters and fishers to the highly complex and mobile routines of modern Western civilization. Yet in every case there is one effect: the potentialities of nature become a standard of living. And in every case this effect is attained in the same way: it is attained not once and for all but only by a continuous succession of activities, by a rhythmic repetition of constant or mobile routines, by a process.

The productive process is, then, the aggregate of activities proceeding from the potentialities of nature and terminating in a standard of living. Always it is the current process, and so it is distinguished both from the natural resources, which it presupposes, and from the durable effects of past production. To draw sharp lines of demarcation is not possible immediately, but it will be possible later. Meanwhile it will be sufficient to advert to the fact that the current process is always a rate of activity, that this rate of activity differs from the potentialities of nature, from which it proceeds, and that it differs from its finished products, which, *ex hypothesi*, are no longer in process but already produced. No doubt the three are closely related, but relation presupposes distinction, and before relations can be grasped adequately, the distinctions must be grasped. Goods that have been completed are not goods in process; services that have been rendered are not services being rendered. Again, goods in process are not the natural resources from which they are derived; and services being rendered are not the natural potentialities from which they are derived. There can be resources and potentialities without goods or services being derived from them; and while they are in process of being derived, the goods are not yet produced and the services not yet rendered.

Thus the productive process is a purely dynamic entity. We began by saying how broadly the term was to be taken. But it is also necessary to insist how narrowly. It is not wealth, but wealth in process. It is none of the potentialities of nature, whether physical, chemical, vegetable, animal, or human. It is none of its own effects, if by effects are understood what has been completed. It is neither the existence nor the use of durable consumer goods, of clothing, houses, furnishings, domestic utensils, personal belongings, or indeed any item of private or public property that can be listed as a consumer good and has passed beyond the process to become an element of the community's standard of living. On the other hand, with regard to producer goods a distinction has to be drawn: they are in the process as means of production; they are in the process in the sense that labor is in the process or that management is in the process, namely, their use forms part of the process; but once they are completed they no longer are under process, any more than labor or management is under process and being produced. A ship under construction is part of the process; but once the ship is completed and begins to transport ocean freight, it is not the ship but only the use of the ship that is part of the process. The same distinction is to be made with regard to every other item of producer goods: factories and machinery, railways and power units, warehouses and offices are in the productive process only while being produced; once they are produced, they themselves have passed beyond the process to enter the category of static wealth, even though their use remains as a factor of production.

Thus the productive process, which proceeds from the potentialities of nature, terminates in a standard of living in two distinct ways. It terminates in a standard of living inasmuch as the goods and services it renders become elements in a standard of living. But it may also terminate indirectly in a standard of living inasmuch as the goods and services it renders complement the potentialities of nature to make the process capable of effecting a higher standard of living. Consumer goods and services enter directly into a standard of living. Producer goods and services enter indirectly into a standard of living: directly they are improvements upon nature that facilitate the productive process and increase its power and efficacy; and only indirectly, through this increased power and efficacy, do they affect the standard of living by improving and increasing the supply of consumer goods and services.

5 Division of the Productive Process

The foregoing section isolated the productive process as a purely dynamic entity, and drew a distinction between consumer goods that enter the standard of living and producer goods that raise the standard of living. That distinction must now be examined more fully. It is to be shown that the correspondence between elements in the productive process and elements in the standard of living may be a point-to-point, or a point-to-line, or a point-to-surface, or even some higher correspondence.

There exists, then, a point-to-point correspondence between bushels of wheat and loaves of bread, between head of cattle and pounds of meat, between bales of cotton and cotton dresses, between tons of steel and motorcars. In each case the elements in the standard of living are algebraic functions of the first degree with respect to elements in the productive process. These functions are not immutable. There can be more or less wheat in a loaf of bread, more or fewer pounds of meat from a head of cattle, more or fewer cotton dresses from a bale of cotton, more or fewer motorcars from a ton of steel. One can, for instance, spin the cotton more loosely, weave it more broadly, cut it more skillfully, shorten skirts, eliminate sleeves, and perhaps find other devices to make more dresses out of fewer bales of cotton. But such efforts only serve to emphasize the existence of an inexorable law of limitation. No matter how one makes the dresses, one cannot get more cotton in the dresses than one had in the bales. No matter how one arranges the points, the point-to-point correspondence remains. For in the totality of such instances there is an identity of elements: the very material elements that were in the productive process enter into the standard of living; and the affirmation of a point-to-point correspondence is no more than the affirmation of the permanence of this material identity.

However, not all material objects in the productive process are limited to a point-to-point correspondence with elements in the standard of living. When a primitive hunter makes a spear, he makes it to kill not one wild animal, nor ten, nor fifty, but just as many as he possibly can get. Similarly, the primitive fisher makes his net not for one but for an indeterminate series of catches of fish. The shipbuilder constructs ships not for one but for an indeterminate number of voyages. And in our industrial age machines are built and factories rise not for each batch of manufactured products but for an indeterminate series of batches. There is a new piece of leather, but not a new shoe factory, for every new pair of shoes. There is a new lot of metals, but not a new plant, for every new motorcar. In each of these instances the point-to-point correspondence is escaped because it is not the product but some ulterior effect of the product that enters into the standard of living. Spears, nets, ships, factories, machines end up as means of production. They enter the standard of living, not in themselves, but in their effects of pounds of meat and fish, ocean voyages, shoes, and motor-cars. Such a correspondence may be named point-to-line: elements in the productive process correspond not to single elements in the standard of living but to indeterminate series of the latter.

Higher correspondences are possible. The machines that make shoes are made by machine tools. Since the former are in a point-to-line correspondence with elements in the standard of living, the latter by that very fact are in a point-to-surface correspondence. Again, the machines used in shipbuilding are made by machine tools: the ships are in a point-to-line correspondence with elements in the standard of living; the machines making ships are in a point-to-surface correspondence; the machine tools making the machines used in making ships are in a point-to-volume correspondence.

Now there exist the same types of correspondence between elements of activity or services in the productive process and elements in the standard of living. The matter is clear when the services are, as it were, incorporated in a material product. All the services involved in growing wheat, storing it, transporting it, milling it, making bread, distributing bread are proportionate to the supply of bread. They are repeated as often as wheat is grown and bread supplied. No doubt, they are variable functions of the wheat-to-bread process: more or less activity, a greater or less efficiency, may be involved. But the correspondence remains point-to-point, for there is no possibility of these services being done once and then the wheat-to-bread process being repeated an indeterminate number of times. Even if robots were employed, the robots would have to go through the motions every time wheat grew and was processed into bread. In like manner the activities and services involved in making ships are repeated as often as ships are made but not as often as ships are used. Their correspondence remains point-to-line. And the same holds for the activities and services incorporated in the making of machine tools. Their correspondence is point-to-surface, or point-to-volume, or at times even higher; they are repeated when the making of machine tools is repeated; they are not repeated when the use of machine tools is repeated; and much less are they repeated when the use of the products of the machine tools is repeated.

However, not all activities and services are coincident with the process of material objects to take their correspondence from that of the objects. It remains that the same general types of correspondence may be discerned. There is a point-to-point correspondence between movements of trains and passenger-miles, not indeed in the sense that there is some fixed ratio between train-miles and passenger-miles, but in the sense that the train has to move as often and as far as passengers move. From instance to instance, a train may have more or fewer passengers, to vary the ratio between train-miles and passenger-miles; but the ratio is always some definite ratio; it is something determinate in the present of each instance. In fact, it is but another form of the flexibility of the point-to-point correspondence: as there may be more or less cotton in a cotton dress, as there may be greater or less efficiency in the operations coincident with growing wheat and making bread, so there may be greater or less efficiency in the transportation of passengers. The flexibility does not eliminate but rather emphasizes the point-to-point correspondence.

Train journeys illustrate one type of service that is not incorporated in material objects. Another ambiguous type is the maintenance of capital equipment. Strictly one may regard maintenance, like replacements, as a prolongation of the process of production of the capital equipment. On the other hand, one might prefer to consider it as a condition of the use of the equipment, and so to classify it along with the power that drives the equipment, the labor that operates it, the management that directs the operations. In fact, maintenance is an accountant's unity, and it comprises quite different realities. There are types of maintenance that are part and parcel of use; there are others that arise whether or not the equipment is in use; and it should seem best to distinguish, at least in a theoretical discussion, according to concrete circumstance, and sometimes count maintenance in the lower correspondence in which the equipment is used, sometimes in the higher correspondence in which the equipment is made.

So much, then, for the division of the productive process. In the previous section it was defined as a purely dynamic entity, a movement taking place between the potentialities of nature and products. In the present section, there has been attempted a dynamic division of that dynamic entity. Elements in the process are in point-to-point, or point-to-line, or point-to-surface, or even some higher correspondence with elements in the standard of living. Some general reflections are now in order.

The division is not based upon proprietary differences. It is not a difference of firms, for the same firm may be engaged at once in different correspondences with the standard of living. Again, it is not a division based upon the properties of things: the same raw materials may be made into consumer goods or capital goods; and the capital goods may be point-to-line or point-to-surface or a higher correspondence; they may have one correspondence at one time and another at another. Similarly, general services such as light, heat, power, transportation may be employed in any correspondence, and in different proportions in the several correspondences at different times. The division is, then, neither proprietary nor technical. It is a functional division of the structure of the productive process: it reveals the possibilities of the process as a dynamic system, though to bring out the full implications of such a system will require not only the next section of the process but also a later section on cycles.

There remains, however, a more immediate question. The point-to-line and higher correspondences are based upon the indeterminacy of the relation between certain products and the ultimate products that enter into the standard of living. Now such indeterminacy does not seem to be a fact. Granted that there is not a new shoe factory for every new pair of shoes, still every factory has a calculable life, and the same holds for every piece of machinery; in advance one can estimate, and in historical retrospection one could know, exactly how many pairs of shoes are to be produced or were to be produced by the given equipment. Hence the whole division breaks down. There is no real difference between point-to-point, point-to-line, and the higher correspondences.

The objection is shot from a double-barreled gun: the indeterminacy is not a fact, first, because at some date, in a more or less remote future, determinate information is possible, and second, because here and now a very accurate estimate is possible. It should seem that the indeterminacy is very much a present fact. One has to await the future to have exact information. And while estimates in the present may be esteemed accurate, the future has no intention of being ruled by them: owners do not junk equipment simply because it has outlasted the most reliable estimates; nor are bankrupts kept in business because their expectations, though mistaken, are proved to have been perfectly reasonable. The analysis that insists on the indeterminacy is the analysis that insists on the present fact: estimates and expectations are proofs of the present indeterminacy and attempts to get round it; and, to come to the main point, an analysis based on such estimates and expectations can never arrive at a criticism of them; it would move in a vicious circle. It is to avoid that circle that we have divided the process in terms of indeterminate point-to-line and point-to-surface and higher correspondences.

6 The Basic and Surplus Stages of the Productive Process

In the fourth section the productive process was isolated as a dynamism proceeding from the potentialities of nature and terminating in a standard of living. In the fifth section the dynamism itself was subjected to analysis: different types of correspondence were found to exist between elements in the process and elements in the standard of living. The purpose of the present, sixth, section is in the main to collect results.

Let us assume as known what is meant by the term 'standard of living.' Let the term 'emergent standard of living' be defined as the aggregate of rates at which goods and services pass from the productive process into the standard of living. Then each of these rates will be a 'so much every so often'; for instance, so much bread a year; so much meat a year; so much clothing a year; so many motorcars a year; so many passenger-miles a year; and so forth throughout the whole catalogue of elements entering into the standard of living. It follows that the emergent standard of living, the aggregate of such rates, is a variable with respect to intervals of time; for instance, in a comparison of successive years, one may find two types of difference: the catalogue of elements may change, some items being dropped and other new items added; further, the rates with respect to the same items may change, becoming greater or less than in the previous year. Thus the emergent standard of living is an aggregate of rates that are both qualitatively and quantitatively variable with respect to successive intervals of time.

Next, let the basic stage of the productive process be defined as the aggregate of rates of production of goods and services in process and in a point-to-point correspondence with elements in the emergent standard of living. As explained in section 4, goods and services are in process when they are neither the mere potentialities of nature nor on the other hand finished products. As explained in section 5, goods and services are in a point-to-point correspondence with elements in the standard of living when they are some determinate, though not immutable or unvarying, algebraic function of the first degree with respect to elements in the standard of living. Finally, just as the aggregate of rates constituting the emergent standard of living is an aggregate of instances of 'so much every so often,' so also is the aggregate of rates of production in the basic stage of the process; and again, as the emergent standard of living, so also the basic stage of the process is an aggregate of rates that are qualitatively and quantitatively variable with respect to successive intervals of time.

It is to be noted that the emergent standard of living and the basic stage of the process are not identical aggregates of rates. The basic stage of the process is, in its pure form, an aggregate of rates of labor, of managerial activity, of the use of capital equipment, for the sake of the goods and services that enter the standard of living. Let us say that some ultimate product, whether service or material object, is Q_i; that *j* enterprises contributed each a respective Q_{ij} to the emergence of Q_i; that in each of these enterprises *k* factors of production, such as labor, management, capital equipment in use, contributed each a respective Q_{ijk} to the emergence of Q_i; then the ultimate product Q_i is a double summation of the contributions of the factors of production Q_{ijk}. For the ultimate product is the summation of the contributions of the several enterprises to the ultimate product; and the contribution of each enterprise is a summation of the contributions of each of its factors of production; so that there is some sense in which

$$Q_i = \sum_j \sum_k Q_{ijk} \tag{1}$$

the summations being taken, first, with respect to all instances of *k* and, secondly, with respect to all instances of *j*. But if the ultimate product Q_i is related by a double summation to the contributions of factors of production Q_{ijk}, then the rate of emergence of Q_i, say dQ_i, is also related by a double summation to the rates of the contributions of the factors of production dQ_{ijk}, where both dQ_i and dQ_{ijk} are instances of the form 'so much or so many every so often.'

Since the form of the relation between them is a double summation, the emergent standard of living and the basic stage of the process are not identical aggregates of rates. On the other hand, precisely because the relation is a double summation, they are equivalent aggregates of rates. However, this statement requires three qualifications. First, mistakes are made in the productive process: there are activities that are useless in the sense that they do not contribute to any of the goods and services that enter the standard of living; materials are wasted; production is begun but not completed; operations are performed wrongly and have to be begun over again. Second, there is an extremely complex and somewhat variable pattern of lags between the time of the contribution made by the factor of production and the time of the emergence of the ultimate product; to select the time limits of the elements Q_{ijk} relevant to a given Q_i would be a

Herculean task that would have to be repeated on every occasion on which there was a variation in the pattern of the lags; however, though a Herculean task, it would not be an impossible task, in the sense that such time limits are not objectively determinate in the present and past, for every contribution to Q_i which now exists did take place during a determinate period of time. The third qualification is with regard to the meaning of the equivalence: the symbolic expression (1) is not a mathematical equation and it cannot be until a common measure is found for ultimate products and contributions to ultimate products; such a common measure is not had until the measure of exchange value is introduced; for the present, then, the equivalence in question is not a mathematical equality but a form of correlation, a double summation, that can become a mathematical equality.

Hence, both the emergent standard of living and the basic stage of the productive process are aggregates of rates that are quantitatively and qualitatively variable with respect to successive intervals of time; and further, when allowance is made for lags and for mistakes in production, the relation between these two aggregates of rates is a double summation.

The basic stage is only part of the current productive process. Besides it, there is a series of surplus stages. Each of these surplus stages is an aggregate of rates of production of goods and services in process and in a point-to-line, or point-to-surface, or higher correspondence with elements in the standard of living. As before, each of these rates is a 'so much or so many every so often'; again, each is qualitatively and quantitatively variable with respect to successive intervals of time; and finally, the relation between an ultimate product, Q_i, of any surplus stage and the contributions of factors of production in that stage with respect to that product, Q_{ijk}, is again a double summation in which allowance must be made for lags and for mistakes in production.

However, there is this difference between the basic stage and the surplus stages. The ultimate products of the basic stage, whether goods or services, enter into the standard of living. The ultimate products of the surplus stages, whether goods or services, do not enter into the standard of living. From being under process themselves they pass into use in a lower stage of the process: they become means of production or the replacement or the maintenance of means of production, where production is understood in the broad sense already defined. Thus, as the emergent standard of living is consumer to the basic stage of the process, so the basic stage in turn is consumer to the lowest of the surplus stages, and each lower surplus stage is consumer to the next higher surplus stage. In other words, producer goods and services are goods and services consumed by producers. Not passengers but railway companies consume rolling stock and rails. Passengers consume transportation. And similarly in similar cases.

But if the ultimate products of the surplus stages do not enter into the standard of living, nonetheless they are related to it. To determine that relation a distinction has to be drawn between short-term and long-term accelerations of the productive process. A short-term acceleration is an increase in rates of production due to a fuller use of existing capital equipment, to a greater efficiency of labor and management, to a decrease in stocks of goods. A long-term acceleration is an increase in rates of production due to the introduction of more capital equipment and/or more efficient capital equipment. The latter is termed a long-term acceleration because it changes the basis on which the short-term acceleration works: the short-term acceleration makes the best of existing equipment; the long-term improves and increases the equipment which a corresponding short-term acceleration will use in the fullest and most efficient manner.

Now, as is apparent from the definitions, the several stages of the process may have, independently, short-term accelerations. But long-term accelerations take place in virtue of the dependence of each lower stage on the next higher stage. More, and more efficient, capital equipment is had in the basic stage by procuring more, and more efficient, equipment from the lowest of the surplus stages. If the demand in the basic stage is strong enough, the lowest of the surplus stages will have to go into a long-term acceleration to obtain for itself more, and more efficient, capital equipment. Similarly, the next stage may need a long-term acceleration to meet its demand, and so on until the highest of the surplus stages is reached; and there only a short-term acceleration is possible. Thus the structure of the productive process is a series of stages, where each stage is an aggregate of rates of production, and each lower stage receives from the next higher stage the means of long-term acceleration of its rates.

The phenomena of a generalized long-term acceleration of the whole productive process are well known. They may occur in a backward economy that is copying the achievements of an advanced economy, and then one gets a series of five-year plans. They may occur in an economy that is pioneering advance for the rest of the world, and then one gets an industrial revolution. In either case there is a transformation of the capital equipment of the economy. There are continuous migrations of labor as it is displaced by more efficient equipment and turns to operating more equipment. There is first a period in which the consumption of materials and the quantity of labor mount with no corresponding increase in the standard of living; and after this period of transformation, of equipping industry and commerce anew, there follows a period of exploitation in which the fruits of the long-term acceleration finally reach the basic stage of the process and the standard of living rises to a new level. Thus a cycle[1] is inherent in the very nature of long-term accelerations of the productive process.

To cycles the argument returns later. The one point to be observed at present is that long-term accelerations are limited. With respect to a given field of natural resources and population, and on the supposition of a given level of cultural, political, and technical development, there is a maximum rate of production for the process. The ground of the limitation is that both the greater complexity of more efficient equipment and the greater quantity of more equipment postulate proportionate rates of replacement and maintenance. The process accelerates against an increasing resistance, so that every element of acceleration reduces the room for further accelerations. In the limit the whole effort of the surplus stages is devoted to replacement and maintenance of capital equipment, and then the only possibility of further acceleration is to depart from the assumption of a given level of cultural, political, and technical development. For with better men, a better organization of men, and better practical ideas, it becomes possible through the short-term accelerations to introduce more efficient equipment, displace labor, devote the displaced labor to a greater quantity of equipment, and so recommence the cycle of long-term advance.

7 Cycles of the Productive Process

The cycle that is inherent in the very nature of a long-term acceleration of the productive process is not to be confused with the familiar trade cycle. The latter is a succession of booms and of slumps, of positive and then negative accelerations of the process. But the cycle with which we are here concerned is a pure cycle. It includes no slump, no negative acceleration. It is entirely a forward movement which, however, involves a cycle inasmuch as

1 Here, and elsewhere, Lonergan changed 'cycle' to 'wave or cycle' in the 1982 version. In McShane, *Economics for Everyone. Das Jus Kapital* (Halifax: Axial Press, 1998), 'surge' is used as capturing better the sense of the normative productive shift.

in successive periods of time the surplus stage of the process is accelerating more rapidly and, again later, less rapidly than the basic stage. When suitable classes and rates of payment have been defined, it will be possible to show that under certain conditions of human inadaptation this pure cycle results in a trade cycle. However, that implication is not absolute but conditioned, not something inevitable in any case but only something that follows when human adaptation is lacking.

These further consequences are not to the present point. For the present issue is whether the pure cycle is itself inevitable on the supposition of long-term acceleration. Would it not be possible to have a long-term acceleration and yet 'smooth out' the pure cycle? Or must one say that, in view of the dynamic structure of the productive process, pure cycles become inevitable if long-term accelerations are attempted? A discussion of this issue turns upon two main points. What is involved in a long-term acceleration of the productive process? What is involved in a pure cycle? These will be discussed in turn.

There are three reasons for expecting a long-term acceleration to be a massive affair. In the first place, it is a matter of long-term planning: the utility of capital formation emerges only over long periods; hence long-term planning is involved in capital formation, and since one is settling one's fate for years to come, it is generally worth while to do so in the best manner possible. In the second place, the introduction of more, or more efficient, units of production is not to be expected to take place in random fashion: the supply of a single product depends upon the activities of many units, so that it is worth while for many units to develop when it is worth while for any one of a series to develop; on the other hand, increased demand does not concentrate upon some one product but divides over several products, so that if there is an increased demand for one, there will be an increased demand for many; and as the increased demand for one justifies development in a series of productive units, so the increased demand for many justifies development in a series of series of units. There is a third consideration of a more abstract character. The emergence both of new ideas and of the concrete conditions necessary for their practical implementation forms matrices of interdependence: any objective change gives rise to series of new possibilities, and the realization of any of these possibilities has similar consequences; but not all changes are equally pregnant, so that economic history is a succession of time periods in which alternatively the conditions for great change are being slowly accumulated and, later, the great changes themselves are being brought to birth.

7bis Cycles in the Productive Process

It will be well to state systematically the foregoing conclusion that cycles are inherent in the very nature of a long-term acceleration of the productive process. Consider the following four series of continuous functions of time, namely,

$$f_1'(t), f_2'(t), f_3'(t), \ldots$$
$$f_1''(t), f_2''(t), f_3''(t), \ldots$$
$$A_1, A_2, A_3, \ldots$$
$$B_2, B_3, \ldots$$

The suffixes 1, 2, 3, ... refer respectively to the basic stage of the productive process, the lowest of the surplus stages, the next to lowest of the surplus stages, and so forth. Expressions of the type $f_n'(t)$ measure the rate of production on the *n*th level, while the derived functions $f_n''(t)$ measure the acceleration of the rate of production. Again, the functions A_n measure the short-term acceleration of the rate of production on the *n*th level, so that the long-term acceleration is $f_n''(t) - A_n$. Finally, the functions B_n measure the rate of production that is effecting merely replacements and maintenance on the next lower stage, so that the rate of production effecting long-term acceleration on the next lowest stage is given by $f_n'(t) - B_n$.

Now let a, $b - a$, $c - b$, ... be time lags, and let k_2, k_3, ... be multipliers that connect the rate of production effecting long-term acceleration and the rate of acceleration so effected. Then, since this effect emerges with a time lag, one has

$$\begin{aligned} k_2[f_2'(t-a) - B_2] &= f_1''(t) - A_1 \\ k_3[f_3'(t-b) - B_3] &= f_2''(t-a) - A_2 \\ k_4[f_4'(t-c) - B_4] &= f_3''(t-b) - A_3 \end{aligned}$$

The equations are simply symbolical expressions of the analysis to the effect that any stage may accelerate in either of two ways: by a short-term acceleration in the stage itself when A_n becomes greater than zero and so $f_n''(t)$ increases equally; or in virtue of the fact that on the next higher stage the rate of production is greater than a rate of mere replacement and maintenance and so is bringing about, with a time lag, a long-term acceleration of the next lower stage.

The advantage of such symbolical expression is that its brevity makes its implications more obvious. Thus it is evident that any level of the process can accelerate on its own in short-term fashion, but if such acceleration occurs on any level but the lowest, then, since a small increase in $f_n''(t)$ is identical with a great increase in $f_n'(t)$, there will have to be great increases in replacements and maintenance, in B_n, if there is not to be, with a time lag, a great long-term acceleration of the next lowest stage. If such an acceleration occurs, the same argument re-occurs to give a still greater long-term acceleration on the next lower stage. Hence, if on any level of the process except the lowest there occurs a short-term acceleration, then unless this rate of production is totally absorbed by increasing rates of replacement and maintenance, there is released a series of expansive movements in which each successive movement measures the acceleration of the next. It is as though an airplane were so difficult to accelerate that its accelerator were not a simple lever but a wheel turned over by a motor; and this motor in turn had its accelerator run by another motor; and so on.

This dynamic structure has now to be connected with the idea of cycles. Let us distinguish two totally different types. There is the familiar trade cycle which is characterized by a succession of positive and negative accelerations of the productive process; there are booms and then there are slumps. Quite different from this trade cycle one may conceive a pure cycle that has no necessary implications of negative acceleration. A pure cycle of the productive process is a matter, simply, of the surplus stage accelerating more rapidly than the basic, then of the basic stage accelerating more rapidly than the surplus.

16

Monetary Flows

7ter Classes of Payments

In any economy with a degree of development beyond that of primitive fruit-gathering, it is possible to verify the existence of a productive process with one or more surplus stages, a basic stage, and an emergent standard of living. Equally may one verify the facts that as the emergent standard of living is consumer to the basic stage, so the basic stage is consumer to the lowest surplus stage, and similarly up the hierarchy of stages. Again, in each case this rate of consumption stands, with due allowances, as a double summation of the activities constituting the product to be consumed. Finally, while each higher stage is for the long-term acceleration of the next lower stage, the basic stage is for the standard of living, and the standard of living for its own sake.

These differences and correlations have now to be projected into their monetary correlatives to set up classes of payments. Thus a restrictive supposition is introduced into the argument. The productive process is now to be envisaged as occurring in an exchange economy. It will be supposed to be an economy of notable size, complexity, and development, with property, exchange, prices, supply and demand, money. However, to obviate considerations irrelevant for the moment, it will be convenient to suppose that foreign trade and foreign payments do not exist; and this supposition is to be maintained until notice to the contrary is given.

The supposition of an exchange economy is a supposition of a relation to sales. Thus, along with the productive process of the exchange economy in a given geographic area, there may exist other productive processes. Any individual may set up his own Robinson Crusoe economy in which he is both monopolist seller and monopsonist buyer in transactions which occur only in his mind. One may go to a barber or shave oneself. One may live in maximum dependence upon the goods and services of the exchange process, or one may pursue an ideal of autarky on a farm. There results from such decisions a difference in the size of the exchange economy, and this difference in size is constituted by setting up another complete or partial economy distinct from the main exchange process or, on the other hand, by eliminating such withdrawals.

It follows that the productive process of the exchange economy is a process of production for sale. Already it was remarked that the productive process included sales management as well as production management. The remark has now to be completed. The productive process includes not only sales management but the sales themselves. What is produced and not sold either does not appertain to the exchange economy at all or else it is an unfinished product. Inversely, in any section or stage of the productive process, goods and services are completed only if they are sold and only when they are sold. For in the exchange economy production is not a matter of art, of doing or making things for the excellence of the doing or the making; it is a matter of economics, of doing and making things that other people want and want badly enough to pay for.

This gives a fundamental division of exchanges into operative and redistributive. Some exchanges are operative: they are part and parcel of the productive process; they mark the completion of an element at some section or stage of the process; they not merely mark that completion but constitute it; for without the exchange the element remains an unfinished product. Because they are intrinsic to the process and partial constituents of the process, operative exchanges form a network that is congruent with the proprietary network flung over the process itself. Thus they recur with the recurrence of its routines. In general, they are proportionate to the volume of these routines, to set up the immanent manifestation of their success and the only immediate common measure of their magnitude. Finally, there is a correlation of operative exchanges based upon the technical correlations involved in the physical productive process.

While this description of operative exchange is derived from a deduction of the idea of production for sale, the meaning of the description may be made clearer by an example. Consider in broad outline the production of shoes. It involves in an exchange economy payments by consumers to shopkeepers, payments by shopkeepers to wholesalers, payments by wholesalers to manufacturers, payments by manufacturers to tanners, to spinners, to makers of nails, payments by each of these to their sources of supply. It also involves a host of other categories of payments, but our purpose is not a study of the shoe industry but an illustration of the idea of operative payments. Now the payments listed above are part and parcel of the production of shoes in an exchange economy. They occur at proprietary frontiers. They are repeated at regular intervals as long as the process is maintained. They increase and decrease with the volume of the shoe trade. They are the index of its prosperity as also of its misery. They provide the one common measure of all its elements, a measure that is intrinsic to the element as completed. Finally, they are correlated with one another along lines of interconnection that are congruent with the correlations involved by a process from leather, cotton, and iron into shoes.

Redistributive exchanges form a remainder class. They are all nonoperative exchanges. Like operative exchanges they transfer ownership; but unlike them, they are not constitutive elements of the current productive process. They are with respect to the natural resources that are presupposed by current production. They are with respect to the durable products of past production, provided these have not reentered the current process as happens in some cases of the secondhand trade. Finally, they may be with respect to money, that is, they include exchanges in which money is not only what is paid but also what is paid for. No doubt, redistributive exchanges may be related intimately to operative exchanges; no doubt, this relationship is at times highly significant; but, without metaphysical digressions, it perhaps may be taken for granted that it is one thing to be related to another type of exchange, and that it is something quite different to be an instance of that other type. Again, borderline cases exist in which one has to attend closely to the definitions if one is to apply them correctly; but that is a misfortune that is common to every effort to place data in the categories of a classification; and it will be more convenient to postpone a study of a few such problems until operative exchanges have been identified more fully by their division into basic and surplus, and by the division of both basic and surplus into initial, transitional, and final payments.

Operative exchanges are intrinsic to the current productive process; but that process divides into basic and surplus stages; hence operative exchanges also divide into basic and surplus. For every element under process becomes a completed product only when it is sold. Again, every element under process stands in a point-to-point, or a point-to-line, or some higher correspondence with the emergent standard of living. There are, then, operative payments completing basic elements, and these may be termed basic operative payments. There are also operative payments completing surplus elements, and these may be termed surplus operative payments. The division of operative payments into basic and surplus is but a corollary of the division of the productive process into basic and surplus stages.

Further, it has been argued that the products, whether goods or services, of any stage of the process stand as a double summation of the activities of that stage. There is a first summation with respect to factors of production within a given entrepreneurial unit. There is a second summation with respect to the contributions of several entrepreneurial units towards the same product. This formal structure of any stage of the process gives the division of payments of that stage into initial, transitional, and final. Initial operative payments are to the factors of production within a given entrepreneurial unit; they reward each contribution to the process and are with respect to that contribution; they are wages and salaries, rents and royalties, interest and dividends, allotments to depreciation, to sinking funds, to undistributed profits. Initial payments are the payments of the first summation. Now the second summation may emerge, not all at once, but gradually: sources of raw materials are paid by dealers, dealers are paid by manufacturers, manufacturers are paid by wholesalers, wholesalers by retailers; again, any one of these may pay the contributions of transportation companies, of public utilities, and so forth. But in any such case, the second summation is only in process. Payments that regard the second summation in process are termed transitional. They are from one entrepreneurial unit to another as operating in the same stage of the process. In any particular case, the entrepreneurial unit might be fully self-sufficient and on its stage of the process reach from raw materials to final buyer; then transitional payments are a zero class; for then the second summation takes place not gradually but all at once. Lastly, whether the second summation takes place gradually or all at once, it must be completed; else we are outside the supposition of an exchange economy; production becomes like art, for itself and not for sale. The payments with respect to the completed second summation are termed final payments. They are final in the sense that they are the last payments that are operative with respect to that product. They are final in the sense that any subsequent resale involves not an operative but a redistributive payment. They are final in the sense that they define the limit of the current process; for once these payments are made, the product is no longer under process but a product of past production.

So much then for the classes of payments. With respect to any exchange one has to ask, Is it a constitutive element of current production, recurrent with the recurrence of productive routines, in correlation with other similar payments along lines defined by the physical and technical dependence of products upon their sources? If the answer is negative, the payment is redistributive. If the answer is affirmative, the payment is operative, and further questions arise. Is the element, economically completed by this payment, in a point-to-point correspondence with elements in the emergent standard of living? If the answer is affirmative, the payment is a basic operative payment. If the answer is negative, the payment is a surplus operative payment. In either case, further questions arise. The lines defined by the physical and technical dependence of products on their sources have the structural form of a double summation. If the given basic or surplus operative payment is an item that is added in the first summation, a cost in the broadest sense but in its primary form, then the payment is initial. Next, if the payment occurs as the second summation gradually adds together the results of the first summation, then the payment is transitional. Lastly, if the payment occurs in the completed second summation, the payment is final.

The divisions of the process into basic and surplus stages, and the formal structure of the stages as double summations of activities, have been discussed previously. The troublesome borderline cases arise from the fundamental distinction between operative and redistributive payments, and, as is to be expected, they occur at the frontier of final operative payments. Four types of instances are discussed: the resale of durable basic products, the resale of durable surplus products, such resales when there is an organized secondhand trade, and financial operations.

First, the resale of durable basic products where no secondhand trade is involved gives a redistributive payment. Mr Jones has a private home constructed for his personal use. He pays the construction company for it. His payment is the final operative payment on that product. If he did not pay, the company would have the home on its hands, an unfinished product in the sense of an unsold product. When he does pay, his payment is submitted to the analysis of a double summation: the construction company is given the means of carrying on its own internal, and so initial, payments, and further, by transitional payments it gives other companies the means of carrying on their internal and so initial payments. Next, Jones sells the home to Brown. This may occur after forty years or it may occur immediately. In either case Brown's payment is redistributive. It changes titles to ownership. However relevant to current production – for otherwise Brown might have had a house of his own built – Brown's payment is not a constituent of current production.

Second, the case is exactly the same if Jones had a factory built instead of a home. The final operative payment on the factory is the payment made by Jones. Any subsequent resale involves not an operative but a redistributive payment. Objection, however, may be made to calling Jones's payment final. Does he not intend to get his money back? Does not the consumer pay? But the question is not whether the consumer pays for the factory in some virtual sense. The only question is whether the consumer comes to own the factory. Evidently, the consumer does not. There is no question of the consumer owning the factory, because there is no question of the consumer buying the factory. What the consumer buys are products made in the factory. Again, the question is not whether Jones intends or hopes to get his money back. No doubt, he has such intentions and hopes; but they are not intentions and hopes of anything so elementary as getting the money back by reselling the factory; they are the more sophisticated intentions and hopes of getting the money back, and more, and still remaining owner of the factory. The final operative payment made upon the factory was made by Jones when he bought it from the construction company. That payment completed an element in current production. But the production Jones will carry on in the factory, though current, will not be production of the factory but of something else. The profits Jones garners or fails to garner in will be operative payments, not in the process that built the factory, but in the process in which the factory is used. Finally, should Jones happen to sell the factory to Brown, that event occurs neither in the process that built the factory nor in the process in which the factory is used; it involves a redistributive payment outside the process.

In the third place, it will be best to consider financial operations, that is, any exchange in which a sum of money is paid for a sum of money to be received. Now either the two sums of money are equal, or else one is greater than the other. If the two are equal, the transaction is purely redistributive. If one is greater than the other, then, generally speaking, the difference is the payment for a service of some specific type; rendering such services is as much a part of current production as rendering any other service; while the payment will be divided up, perhaps among different entrepreneurial units, and commonly in initial payments of wages, salaries, rents, dividends, reserve funds, and so forth. In other words, financial operations are partly redistributive payments and partly payments for services rendered; thus in banking, payments of principal are redistributive, but payments of interest are operative, with interest paid to the banks as a final operative payment and interest paid by the banks to depositors an initial operative payment; again, in insurance the payment of policies is redistributive, but the payment of premiums on policies is partly redistributive and partly operative; it is redistributive to the extent it balances the payment of policies; and it is operative to the extent it pays insurance companies for their services.

There remains the secondhand trade. As a trade with recurrent routines of varying volume, it is part of current production of services; but what is traded belongs to past production or, as is the case with the indestructible properties of the soil, never was a human product. Thus, with regard to the secondhand trade, one again must distinguish between payments for the object traded and payments for the services of the trader; the former are redistributive; the latter are operative. The analysis applies of course not only to old watches and jewelry, books and motorcars, but equally well to real estate, and, except in the first instance of investment, to the resale of stocks and shares. Investment itself is a complex payment, but its analysis may be left until later. However, there is a special instance of the secondhand trade in which an old product is brought back into the process as a raw material or semifinished product; in such a case the payment causing reentry into the process is redistributive but subsequent payments are operative.

8 Rates of Payment and Transfer

A baker's dozen of classes of payments have been defined by the relation of the payments to the productive process. The argument now moves from classes of payments to rates of payment, and from the rates of payment to the circulatory interdependence of the rates. Just as there is a dynamic structure of the productive process, so also there is a dynamic structure of the circulation. The classes of payments provide the link between the two: the classes are based upon the dynamic structure of the process; the rates, constructed from the classes, aim at an analysis of the circulation.

Eight rates of payment form the main points of reference in the circulatory process. They will be denoted by the symbols DE', DE'', DR', DR'', DO', DO'', DI', DI''. The initial upper-case D is used in each case to emphasize the fact that we deal not with a static quantity but with a rate, a 'so much every so often.' The dashes (′) and (″) indicate basic and surplus rates respectively. Upper-case *E* stands for expenditure, *R* for receipts, *O* for outlay, *I* for income. All rates refer to some standard interval of time: a day, week, month, quarter, half-year, year, as the subject matter of the issue may permit or demand. The rates of successive intervals may be distinguished by suffixes: thus DE_1', DE_2', DE_3', ... denote the rate DE' in three successive intervals.

The rates DE' and DR' are the two aspects of final basic operative payments. DE' is the expenditure of consumers purchasing the emergent standard of living of the given interval; DR' is the receipt of this expenditure by the final agents of basic supply.

The rates DE'' and DR'' are the two aspects of final surplus operative payments. DE'' is the expenditure of producers purchasing surplus products: it includes the payments of basic producers to the final agents of the lowest stage of surplus supply; the payments of producers in the lowest stage of surplus supply to the final agents of [the] next to lowest stage of surplus supply; and so on up the dynamic ladder of the productive process. On the other hand, DR'' is the receipt of such expenditure by the final agents of surplus supply, no matter what level of surplus supply they may represent.

Next, both DR' and DR'' stand as double summations to activities in basic and surplus industry, respectively. The analysis leaps across the double summations to the initial elements. DO' is the aggregate of initial basic payments during the given interval; DO'' is the aggregate of initial surplus payments during the same interval. These rates may be named basic outlay and surplus outlay, respectively; they are payments of wages and salaries, rents and royalties, interest and dividends, and allocations to depreciation, sinking funds, undistributed profits; they are the rewards of the ultimate factors of production in the basic stage and in the surplus stage, respectively, of the productive process.

Now while DR' is identical with DE', and DR'' is identical with DE'', not only is DO' not identical with DR' nor DO'' with DR'', but it usually happens that it is greater or less. One is not to think of DO' as the distribution of DR' among the factors of production. DO' is simultaneous with DR', an aggregate calculated with respect to the same time interval as DR'. A present DO' is an aggregate of initial payments that at a series of future dates will reach their place in a double summation to become elements in some DR'; similarly, a present DR' is a double summation with respect to initial payments occurring at a series of past dates. The same is true of DR'' and DO''.

Six of the eight rates of payment have been defined. Before defining basic income, DI', and surplus income, DI'', it will be necessary to introduce the idea of monetary functions. Thus, the argument takes a further step towards defining a circulation of money. For a circulation of money is not a rotational movement of money. Rather it is a circular series of relationships of dependence of one rate of payment upon another. Money moves only at the instant of a payment or transfer. Most of the time it is quiescent. It may be totally quiescent, as when it is held in reserve for no purpose whatever. But it may also be dynamically quiescent, held in reserve for some definite purpose.

Money held in reserve for a defined purpose will be said to be in a monetary function. Five such functions are distinguished: basic demand, basic supply, surplus demand, surplus supply, and a fifth, remainder, redistributive function. Money held in reserve for basic expenditure and so on its way to entering DE' will be said to be in the basic demand function. Money held in reserve for surplus expenditure and so on its way to entering DE'' will be said to be in the surplus demand function. Again, money on its way from DR' to DO', from final basic operative payments to initial basic operative payments, will be said to be in the basic supply function. Similarly, money on its way from DR'' to DO'' will be said to be in the surplus supply function. Finally, money held in reserve for redistributive payments, or for no specific purpose whatever, will be said to be in the redistributive function.

Now initial payments are income. They may be supposed to be, at least for an instant, in the basic or surplus demand functions. Hence one may write, without affecting the generality of the analysis,

$$DO' + DO'' = DI' + DI'' \qquad (2)$$

where DI' are the initial payments entering basic demand, and DI'' are the initial payments entering surplus demand during the given interval of time. Let us now introduce two crossover ratios: G' is the fraction of DO' that moves to surplus demand, and G'' is the fraction of DO'' that moves to basic demand. Hence one may replace equation (2) by two equations, namely,

$$DI' = (1 - G')DO' + G''DO'' \qquad (3)$$

$$DI'' = (1 - G'')DO'' + G'DO' \qquad (4)$$

These equations may be given a simpler form in two ways. One may introduce a rate of crossover difference, DG, where

$$DG = G''DO'' - G'DO' \tag{5}$$

so that equations (3) and (4) may be written

$$DI' = DO' + DG \tag{6}$$

$$DI'' = DO'' - DG \tag{7}$$

Again, one may introduce the supposition that

$$G'' = 1 - G' \tag{8}$$

namely, the movement of money to basic demand disregards its source, so that generally the same proportion of both basic outlay and surplus outlay move to basic demand. Hence one has

$$DI' = (1 - G')(DO' + DO'') \tag{9}$$

$$DI'' = G'(DO' + DO'') \tag{10}$$

and the definition of crossover difference becomes

$$DG = (1 - G')DO'' - G'DO' \tag{11}$$

It is to be remembered that equations (2) to (7) are perfectly general, while equations (8) to (11) involve a restrictive supposition.

Movements between four of the monetary functions have now been named and defined. They form two circuits connected by a crossover. There is a basic circuit of basic expenditure DE', becoming basic receipts DR', which move towards basic outlay DO', which with allowance made for the crossover difference DG becomes basic income DI'. There is a similar surplus circuit of surplus expenditure DE'', becoming surplus receipts DR'', which move towards surplus outlay DO'', which with allowance made for the crossover difference DG becomes surplus income DI''.

Now the redistributive function is to be studied only in its relations to these two circuits. These relations are basically to be derived from changes of the quantity of money in the circuits. Let DM' be the quantity of money added to the basic circuit during the interval, and DM'' be the quantity of money added to the surplus circuit during the interval. Further let us write

$$DM' = DS' + DD' + DG \tag{12}$$

$$DM'' = DS'' + DD'' - DG \tag{13}$$

where any of the rates involved may be positive, zero, or negative. DG has been defined already. DS', DS'', DD', DD'' are quantities of money per interval transferred from the redistributive function to basic supply, surplus supply, basic demand, surplus demand, respectively. These quantities per interval are net quantities, that is, the net result of all transferences in either direction. DS' and DS'' are the quantities added to, or if negative subtracted from, the quantity of money moving from basic receipts to basic outlay (DR' to DO') and from surplus receipts to surplus outlay (DR'' to DO''), respectively, during the interval. DD' and DD'' are the quantities added to, or if negative subtracted from, the quantity of money moving from basic income to basic expenditure (DI' to DE'') and from surplus income to surplus expenditure (DI'' to DE''), respectively, during the interval. Hence equation (12) states that the total quantity of money added to the basic circuit during the interval, DM', is equal to the quantity added from the redistributive function to basic supply, DS', plus the quantity added from the redistributive function to basic demand, DD', plus the quantity added from the other circuit by the crossover difference DG. Similarly, equation (13) states that the total quantity of money added to the surplus circuit during the interval, DM'', is equal to the quantity added from the redistributive function to surplus supply, DS'', plus that added from the redistributive function to surplus demand, DD'', minus the quantity contributed to the other circuit by the crossover difference DG. Any of these seven quantities per interval may be negative; and when they are negative, 'added' is to be replaced by 'subtracted' in the above statement.

It is to be observed that there is no simple correlation between rates of payment per interval, DE', DR', DO', DI', G', DE'', DR'', DO'', DI'', G'' and, on the other hand, changes in the quantity of money per interval, DM', DS', DD', DM'', DS'', DD''. Rates of payment are products of quantity and velocity of money. Hence without suppositions regarding the velocity of money, changes in quantity yield no conclusions about rates of payment. Inversely, with velocities undetermined, changes in rates of payment yield no conclusions about changes in quantities.

This section may be resumed by explaining the diagram of transfers on the following page. There are five monetary functions: a redistributive function R, basic supply S', basic demand D', surplus supply S'', and surplus demand D''. In a given interval, the action of the redistributive function changes the quantity of money available in the other four functions by DS', DD', DS'', DD'', respectively. These changes may be positive, zero, or negative. In the same interval, basic supply makes basic initial payments of $(1 - G')DO''$ to basic demand and of $G''DO''$ to surplus demand; similarly, surplus supply makes surplus initial payments of $(1 - G'')DO''$ to surplus demand and of $G''DO''$ to basic demand. In the same interval basic demand makes final basic payments DE' to basic supply; and surplus demand makes final surplus payments DE'' to surplus supply. The other rates of the analysis are defined in terms of the foregoing, as follows:

$$\begin{aligned} DR' &= DE' \\ DR'' &= DE'' \\ DI' &= (1 - G')DO' + G''DO'' = DO' + DG \\ DI'' &= (1 - G'')DO'' + G'DO' = DO'' - DG \\ DG &= G''DO'' - G'DO' \\ DM' &= DS' + DD' + DG \\ DM'' &= DS'' + DD'' - DG \end{aligned} \tag{14}$$

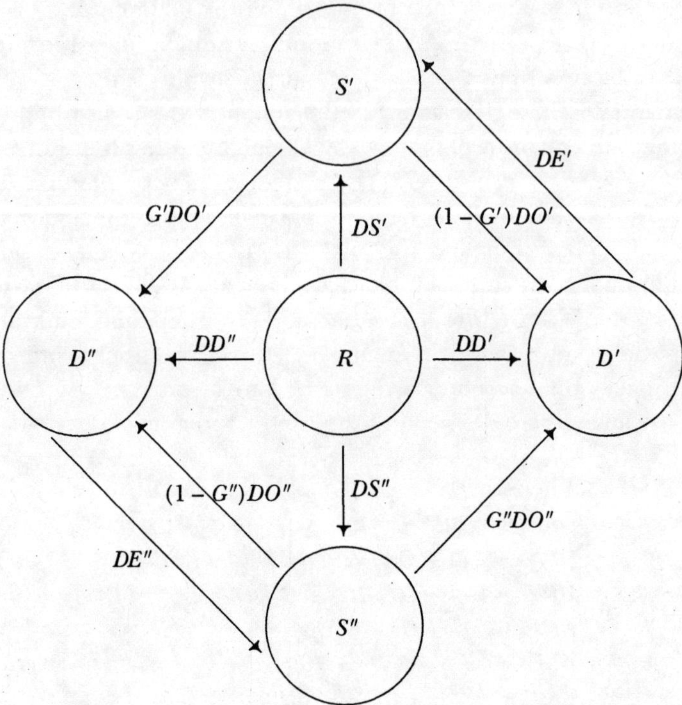

Diagram of Transfers between Monetary Functions

17

Accelerations, Cycles, Phases

9 Circuit Acceleration

The foregoing section defined two circuits of expenditure, receipts, outlay, and income, a pair of crossovers, and two pairs of transfers from the redistributive function to the demand and the supply functions. The present section is concerned to watch the circuits in motion, and more particularly to inquire into the conditions of their acceleration. The inquiry is conducted in three steps: first, one asks what is the possibility of circuit acceleration when DS', DS'', DD', DD'', and DG are each zero; secondly, one asks what is the possibility of acceleration when DS' and DS'' are positive or negative but DD', DD'', and DG remain zero; thirdly, one asks what are the effects of DD', DS'', DG not being zero.

On the first and largest assumption the quantity of money in each circuit remains constant, interval by interval, over an indefinite series of intervals. The possibility of acceleration, accordingly, arises from the possibility of changes in the velocity of money. However, not any change in velocity is relevant: a change in the rapidity with which money changes hands is in itself impotent to effect a circuit acceleration; what is needed is a change in the circuit velocity of money, in the rapidity with which money performs a circuit of work moving, say, from expenditure through receipts, outlay, income back to expenditure. This difference is important. For, while the rapidity with which money changes hands is a highly indeterminate concept, the rapidity with which money performs a circuit of work may be correlated exactly with the turnover frequencies of industry and commerce.

To clarify the notion of turnover frequency, let us define the unit of enterprise as any integrated and determinate contribution to the basic stage or to the surplus stage of the productive process. A contribution is considered 'integrated' when it is not the effect of labor alone, or capital alone, or management alone, but of all three taken together. A contribution is considered 'determinate' when it answers the specification to be found, say, in a catalogue, an order, a contract, and, further, the functional distinction is drawn between basic and surplus. Thus a contribution is any good or service sold at any transitional or any final market by any entrepreneur; it is exclusively the contribution of that entrepreneur, even though what is sold includes the contributions of earlier entrepreneurs in the production series; finally, though exclusively the contribution of the entrepreneur in question, it is not specified by the personality of the entrepreneur, who may conduct simultaneously several units of enterprise, but by the description found in a catalogue, order, or contract, along with the added determination of basic or surplus.

Now every unit of enterprise involves a turnover magnitude and a turnover frequency. The statement would be merely a truism if it meant no more than that the rates of payments received and made by the unit of enterprise involved quantities and velocities of money; for obviously all rates of payment are products of quantity and velocity. But the statement is not a truism, for it involves a correlation between the quantities and velocities of rates of payment with the quantities and velocities of goods and services.

The existence of this correlation may be seen readily enough. To double, say, rates of payment, either one may double the sums of money in each payment in the rate or one may double the frequency with which each payment is made. Similarly, to double a rate of production, one may double the number of items handled at once by a unit of enterprise or one may double the frequency with which this number is produced and sold. There are, then, alternatives between quantity and velocity in both rates of payment and rates of production. But the quantity alternative in the rates of payment is conjoined with the quantity alternative in the rate of production, and the frequency alternative in the rate of payment is conjoined with the frequency alternative in the rate of production. The two cases of quantity-velocity are not only parallel but also correlated.

The point may be illustrated by simple examples. Suppose a shipbuilder to have four ships under construction at once, and to finish a ship every two hundred days. Let demand be doubled. Then the builder may put eight ships under construction at once or he may study Henry Kaiser's methods and learn to complete a ship in one hundred days. In either case his rate of production is doubled, and, we may suppose, his rates of payments received and made are doubled, that is, the selling price of each ship remains the same, and payments made include profits. But the doubling of the rates of payments takes place in different ways. If he has eight ships instead of four under construction at once, then the magnitude of payments in the rates is doubled: every two hundred days his payments received amount to the value of eight ships, and his payments made amount to the value of eight ships, where before the payments received and made with the same frequency amounted to the value of only four ships. If, on the other hand, he has only four ships under construction but completes a ship in one hundred days, the magnitude of his payments received and made amounts to the value of four ships, but their frequency is doubled since these payments take place every hundred days instead of every two hundred days.

Now it might be thought that this distinction between turnover magnitude and turnover frequency was valid in such discontinuous production as shipbuilding but broke down as production approximated to continuity. It happens, however, that while production may approximate to continuity, sales do not, and that the relevant period to turnover frequency is not simply the production period but the period of production and sales. The perfect example of productive continuity is the supply of electric power, in which the generation, the distribution, and the consumption of the product are practically simultaneous; indeed, on Einstein's definition, they are exactly simultaneous. However, a power company cannot collect payments due as rapidly as it can supply electrical impulses. While conditions of production do not limit the frequency of its turnovers, conditions of collection provide a very palpable limit. A power company might decide to receive smaller payments more frequently, but then it would have to hire more men to read meters and a larger office staff to send out bills; further, this greater cost of collection would not yield a higher turnover frequency unless people responded and paid their bills at shorter intervals.

Similarly, in every unit of enterprise there is some determinate turnover magnitude and turnover frequency. The magnitude of the turnover depends upon the number of items handled at once and the selling price of each item. The frequency of the turnover depends upon the period of production plus any time lag involved in sales or collection. In general, each unit of enterprise first estimates demand, which determines both rate of payments received and rate of supply; in the second place, it estimates turnover frequency from its conditions of production and of sale and, *caeteris paribus*, selects a more rapid rather than a less rapid frequency; in the third place, it finds its turnover magnitude determined by the other two factors. The estimate of demand comes first, because there is no use producing without selling. The estimate of frequency comes second, because a more rapid frequency is, in the main, an advantage but one can never have as rapid a frequency as one pleases. Finally, turnover magnitude is left to be determined by the other two factors, because turnover magnitude is the easiest to control of the three.

Now, if in each unit of enterprise the magnitude and frequency of payments depend upon the magnitude and frequency of turnovers, it follows that with respect to the aggregate of basic units and again with respect to the aggregate of surplus units we have quantities and circuit velocities of money determined by turnover magnitudes and frequencies. Hence to say that the circuits accelerate in virtue of greater, or less, circuit velocities of money is to postulate an aggregate change in turnover frequencies. Either production periods are shortening, or lengthening, or the lag of sales or collection is shortening, or lengthening. The question before us, then, is the possibility of changes in turnover frequency when there are no changes in the aggregate quantities of money available in the circuits.

First, one may expect a general increase in turnover frequencies in the brisk selling of a boom, and similarly one may expect a general decrease in turnover frequency in the lagging sales ushering in a slump. But whether one may expect either a boom or a slump without changes in the aggregate quantity of money available in the circuits, that is another question; and to it we shall give an answer that is negative. In the second place, there is the increment in turnover frequency due to reduced, or increased, production periods. Now there are variations in production periods to meet variations in demand, for at times it is simpler to vary the production period than the used capacity; but one may expect such variations to cancel; they may be as much one way as another; they provide more a means of adaptation than a general principle of acceleration. In the main, variations in production periods result from the application of new ideas: these may introduce more efficient machinery, more efficient organization, more efficient labor, more efficient selling. The effect of such changes may be very great. But they are all long-term changes. In the short run they occur in random units of enterprise. Further, under the limitation we are considering, namely, unchanged quantities of money in the circuits, the acceleration possible from these increased frequencies is limited by the irregularity of their incidence. All units of enterprise contributing in a series to one final product have to keep in step. Unless all the units in the series simultaneously increase frequency from reduced turnover periods, there cannot be a general acceleration due exclusively to increased frequency; the units with increased frequency have to reduce their turnover magnitudes to allow other units in the series without increased frequency to accelerate by increased turnover magnitudes.

This brings us to the conclusion of the first step in the inquiry. On the assumption that

$$0 = DS' = DS'' = DD' = DD'' = DG$$

there is a possibility of circuit acceleration but that possibility is quite limited. It is a matter of acceleration with quantities of money in the circuits unchanged in the aggregate but with circuit velocities increasing or decreasing. This change in circuit velocities involves a change in turnover frequencies, which of course are determined not merely by the supply functions but, since they depend on sales and are lengthened by a lag of sales, no less upon the demand functions. Now turnover frequencies are the least controllable of the factors in the rates of production and sales. Each unit of enterprise tends to be already at its greatest turnover frequency and to depend upon the emergence of more efficient methods for increments of frequency. Further, units in a series have to keep their rates of production adjusted, and since increments in frequency occur at random, the supposition of constant aggregate quantities of money cuts down the acceleration effect of increased frequencies by making necessary simultaneous reductions of turnover magnitude in the units with greater frequency. Finally, while booms and slumps effect a general increase or decrease of frequencies by shortening or lengthening the lag of sales, still one must have the booms or slumps before one can have the frequency changes that result from them.

If now one turns to the second step in the inquiry, the question is, What is the possibility of circuit acceleration when

$$0 = DD' = DD'' = DG$$

so that DS' and DS'' may be positive or negative? Now there is a sense in which this supposition is contrary to the common assumption of investment equaling savings, but a discussion of that issue had best be reserved until we have given a definition of savings and of investment. As to the fact of aggregate increments in the quantity of money in the circuits, there should seem to be no doubt. The whole history of the development of money points to that conclusion. Mercantilism is among the earliest of the products of economic thinking; it arose when inquiries into the prosperity of some and the poverty of other principalities and republics of the early Italian Renaissance led to the conclusion that prosperity depended on an abundance of gold; for centuries nations endeavored to buy abroad less than they sold that they might have a favorable balance of gold payments. Further, by the time mercantilism became discredited, other means had been found to provide the circuits with greater quantities of money. Idle money had been decried. Laws against interest and usury had been attacked successfully. Bills of exchange and discounting houses flourished. Banking developed. There followed the fundamental increase in means of payment by the introduction of a gold standard and fiduciary issue. And in our own day we have witnessed the elimination of gold, even as a constitutional monarch, and the substitution of a managed money, that is, a money managed according to the requirements of industry and commerce and not according to rules of thumb and a gold reserve. Now unless the operative circuits have an appetite for ever greater means of payment, this whole development appears meaningless. On the other hand, the supposition that circuit acceleration to some extent postulates increments in the quantities of money in the circuits accounts both for mercantilism and for the substitution of more elegant techniques in place of mercantilism. Further, it points to excess transfers to supply, to *DS′* and *DS″*, as the mode in which increments in quantities of money enter the circuits.

The effect of excess transfers from the redistributive function to the supply functions, of *DS′* and *DS″*, is twofold. Primarily it is a matter of aggregate increments in monetary circulating capital; secondarily it is a matter of absorbing windfall losses and profits. As to the primary effect, the function of monetary circulating capital is to bridge the gap between payments made and payments received; as goods and services are in process, the unit of enterprise makes payments to earlier units in the production series and to its own factors; only when goods and services are sold are payments received. Now this gap increases with increments in turnover magnitude: the greater the number of items the unit of enterprise handles at once and the greater the price per item handled, the greater the need of monetary circulating capital. Thus, at a first approximation, *DS′* and *DS″* are positive when turnover magnitudes in the aggregate are increasing, and they are negative when turnover magnitudes in the aggregate are decreasing. There is, however, a second approximation to be made. Payments received are subject to windfall losses and profits, and these may not be passed on to decreased or increased initial payments made. For the entrepreneur may prefer to allow windfall losses and profits to average out to zero over a series of intervals; then fluctuations in payments received are smoothed out by transfers from or to a reserve fund in the redistributive function, so that payments made vary only with changes in the scale of operations or in prices; in this fashion windfall losses are covered by positive elements in DS' and DS'' while windfall profits yield negative elements in DS' and DS''. Evidently enough, this second effect of transfers to supply, insofar as it exists, should be small in the aggregate of basic units and in the aggregate of surplus units unless, as perhaps in a boom or slump, windfall effects tend to be generalized either as profits or as losses.

Now on the supposition of increasing quantities of money in the circuits due to positive values of DS' and DS'', there follows an acceleration of turnover magnitudes proportionate to the magnitude of DS' and DS'', and to this may be added any acceleration of turnover frequency that occurs. Interval by interval the rates of basic outlay, basic income, basic expenditure, and basic receipts are stepping up; similarly, interval by interval the rates of surplus outlay, surplus income, surplus expenditure, and surplus receipts move upwards. Inversely, when DS' and DS'' are negative there is a similar deceleration of the circuits; turnover magnitudes are decreasing proportionately to the magnitude of the negative values of DS' and DS''; and these decreasing magnitudes will tend to effect decreasing frequencies both because of lagging sales and because units of enterprise cannot be run at their optimum capacity.

So much for the first two steps of the inquiry. With all five rates of transfer, DS', DS'', DD', DD'', DG each at zero, circuit accelerations are possible in virtue of changing turnover frequency but limited because aggregate turnover magnitudes remain constant. With only DD', DD'', DG each at zero, there are accelerations in aggregate turnover magnitudes, and these may easily be accompanied and reinforced by similar accelerations in turnover frequency. There remains the question, What happens when DD', DD'', DG are not zero?

The immediate answer aims at no more than postponing the issue by defining different cases. First, there is the case of the superimposed circuit, when in addition to basic and surplus circuits there is a third circuit involving the redistributive function; this phenomenon arises when, say, *DD'* and *DD''* are opposite in sign; it will be discussed when we treat the circulatory effects of a favorable balance of foreign trade or deficit government spending.

Second, with *DG* at zero, positive or negative values of *DD'* or *DD''* belong to the theory of booms and slumps. For such positive or negative values are changes in aggregate basic or aggregate surplus demand. Entrepreneurs are receiving back more, or less, than their outlays (which include profits of all kinds). The immediate effect is upon the price levels at the final markets, and to these changes in price enterprise as a whole responds to release an upward or downward movement of the whole economy. Obviously one may not simply suppose *DD'* or *DD''* not to be zero, for that would be postulating rather than accounting for booms or slumps.

Third, when *DG* is not zero, then one circuit is being drained to augment the quantity of money in the other circuit. Further, this increment in quantity of money appears at the final markets, so that its immediate effect is upon prices, except insofar as it is offset by equal and opposite action by *DD'* and *DD''*. Again one has to deal with cyclic phenomena and not the general case of circuit acceleration.

Thus, the general theory of circuit acceleration is that it takes place, in a constrained and limited way when quantities of money in the circuits are constant, but without let or hindrance when quantities of money are variable. Further, the normal entry and exit of quantities of money to the circuits or from them is by the transfers from the redistributive to the supply functions. Finally, provided *DD'*, *DD''*, *DG* vary only slightly from zero, so that their action is absorbed by stocks of goods at the final markets, they exercise a stimulating effect in favor of a positive or a negative circuit acceleration; otherwise their action pertains either to the superimposed circuits of favorable balances of foreign trade and deficit government spending, or else to the cyclic phenomena of booms and slumps.

Appendix to Section 9

On the assumption that all units of enterprise begin turnover 1 simultaneously and end turnover *n* simultaneously, it is possible to construct a simple mathematical model of circuit acceleration. One may write

$$DR' = \sum_{i'} \sum_{1}^{n} f_{ij}$$

$$DO' = \sum_{i'} \sum_{1}^{n} o_{ij}$$

$$DS' = \sum_{i'} \sum_{1}^{n} s_{ij}$$

where the unit of enterprise i, in turnover j, increases its monetary circulating capital by s_{ij}, makes initial payments o_{ij}, and receives final payments f_{ij}, and each double summation is taken in each unit of enterprise from turnover 1 to turnover n and then with respect to all basic units of enterprise i'.

Now f_{ij} is zero in all units of enterprise that do not deal immediately with final buyers. Let T_{ij} be transitional payments received and t_{ij} be transitional payments made by the unit of enterprise i, in turnover j. Further, let j' denote the turnover immediately preceding turnover j. Then, since the increment in monetary circulating capital may be equated to the excess of payments made in turnover j, over payments received in turnover j', one has

$$f_{ij'} + T_{ij'} = o_{ij} + t_{ij} - s_{ij}$$

Submitting this equation to a double summation, one has

$$\sum_{i'} \sum_{0}^{n-1} (f_{ij} + T_{ij}) = \sum_{i'} \sum_{1}^{n} (o_{ij} + t_{ij} - s_{ij})$$

where the difference between turnovers j' and j is covered by the difference of the limits. However, the limit on the left-hand side may be assimilated to that on the right-hand side by introducing dR' and dT' defined by the equations

$$dR' = \sum_{i'} (f_{in} - f_{i0}) \text{ (so that } \sum \sum_{1}^{n} f_{ij} - \sum \sum_{0}^{n-1} f_{ij} = dR'\text{)}$$

$$dT' = \sum_{i'} (T_{in} - T_{i0})$$

where, since turnover o is the last turnover of the previous interval, dR' is the difference in the turnover magnitude of basic final payments at the beginning and at the end of the interval; and dT' is the similar difference in the turnover magnitude of basic transitional payments. Further, since in the aggregate, transitional payments made are identical with transitional payments received, one has

$$0 = \sum_{i'} \sum_{1}^{n} (T_{ij} - t_{ij})$$

so that all summations may be eliminated and one may write

$$DS' = dT' + (DO' - DR') + dR' \tag{15}$$

and by changing (′) to (″), one has a parallel equation for the surplus circuit.

With DG at zero and DD' at zero, $(DO' - DR')$ can be no more than a lag, and as will appear later, this lag unfortunately tends to be zero. Again, dT' and dR' will be of the same sign: final payments are not increasing when transitional payments are decreasing, nor vice versa. Thus, excess transfers to or from supply, DS', tend to equal the sum of the increments of aggregate turnover magnitudes in final payments and in transitional payments. Of these two, the increment in transitional payments will be the larger, since for each sale at the final market there commonly is a sale at a number of transitional markets.

In the summations, turnover magnitudes appear directly but turnover frequencies only indirectly, inasmuch as the number of turnovers, n, per interval increases in the case of any given unit of enterprise. An increase of the number of turnovers per interval would have a great effect on DR' and DO', since it increases the number of instances of f_{ij} and o_{ij} to be summated. But it need have no effect on DS', since s_{ij} may be positive or negative and so cancel in the aggregate of instances. Finally, increasing turnover frequency, of itself, has no effect on dR' or dT', since these terms represent the difference between two turnover magnitudes, and increasing frequency only puts further apart the two magnitudes compared.

Thus, in pure theory DO' and DR' might accelerate to any extent while DS', dR', dT' each remained at zero. It would be a pure frequency acceleration. The contention of the preceding pages was that such pure frequency acceleration has conditions that are difficult to realize, and that the history of the development of money points to a preponderant role of increasing turnover magnitude in circuit accelerations.

10 The Theoretical Possibility of Measurement of the Productive Process

In the three preceding sections classes and rates of payment were defined to make possible a statement of conditions of acceleration of the monetary circuits. Evidently it is desirable to complete this list of conditions by bringing in a consideration of the underlying acceleration of the productive process itself. But before this can be done, at least a method of defining the measurement of such acceleration must be provided. It is not necessary that any actual measurement be undertaken, or even that a method which statisticians would find practicable be assigned. But it is necessary that we have a clear and definite idea of what we are discussing when we speak of an acceleration of the productive process.

The problem of the present section may be put as follows. Consider two successive and equal intervals of time, long enough to be representative, yet not so long that much averaging is required. Suppose that in the first of the two intervals, objects of a class i were sold in the quantity q_i and at an average price p_i, and in the second interval objects in the same class were sold in the quantity $q_i + dq_i$ and at the average price $p_i + dp_i$. Suppose, further, that there are n such classes, that the aggregate payment for them in the first interval was DZ and in the second interval was $DZ + D^2Z$ so that

$$DZ = \Sigma\ p_i q_i \tag{16}$$

$$DZ + D^2Z = \Sigma\ (p_i q_i + p_i dq_i + q_i dp_i + dp_i dq_i) \tag{17}$$

where all summations are taken with respect to all instances of i from 1 to n. The question is, How much does the increment in the rate of payment D^2Z result from price increments dp_i, and how much does it result from quantity increments dq_i? In other words, can one define two numbers, say P and Q, such that P varies with a set of numbers $p_1, p_2, p_3, \ldots$ and Q varies with another set of numbers $q_1, q_2, q_3, \ldots$?

A universally valid answer to this question may be had when P and Q are not mere numbers but vectors in an n-dimensional manifold. Let P and Q be the vectors from the origin to the points $(p_1, p_2, p_3, \ldots)$ and $(q_1, q_2, q_3, \ldots)$, respectively. Then any variation in the price pattern, that is, in any ratio of the type p_i/p_j, will appear as a variation in the angle between the projection of P on the plane ij and the axis j. Similarly, any variation in the quantity pattern will appear as a parallel variation in an angle made by a projection of Q. But besides such variation in price pattern or in quantity pattern there may be general increases or decreases in prices or in quantities. The latter appear as positive or negative increments in the absolute magnitudes of the vectors, for

$$P^2 = \Sigma\, p_i^2 \tag{18}$$

$$Q^2 = \Sigma\, q_i^2 \tag{19}$$

that is, the length of the vector P is the square root of the sum of all prices squared, and the length of the vector Q is the square root of the sum of all quantities squared. Thus one may suppose two n-dimensional spheres of radii P and Q, respectively. The vector from the origin to any point in the first 'quadrant' of the surface of such spheres represents a determinate price pattern or quantity pattern. On the other hand, variation in P and Q is variation in the size of the spheres.

Now there is a well known theorem, called the dot product, which enables us to equate DZ with P and Q, whence

$$DZ = \Sigma\, p_i q_i = PQ \cos A \tag{20}$$

where A is the angle between the vectors P and Q. Thus variation in DZ depends not only on the magnitude of P and Q but also on the price and quantity patterns as represented by the angle A between the vectors. This is evident enough, since it makes a notable difference in DZ whether large or small instances of p_i combine with large or small instances of q_i, and such combination is ruled by the relative price and quantity patterns, to appear ultimately in the angle A.

Next, consider the second interval in which the vector P increases to $(P + dP)$, the vector Q to $(Q + dQ)$, and the angle A to $(A + dA)$. Then

$$(P + dP)^2 = \Sigma\, (p_i + dp_i)^2 \tag{21}$$

$$(Q + dQ)^2 = \Sigma\, (q_i + dq_i)^2 \tag{22}$$

$$DZ + D^2 Z = (P + dP)(Q + dQ) \cos (A + dA) \tag{23}$$

From equations (20) and (23) one obtains for $D^2 Z$ the expression

$$D^2 Z = PQ[(dP/P + dQ/Q + dPdQ/PQ) \cos (A + dA) - (\sin A \sin dA/2)/(dA/2)] \qquad (24)^1$$

1 This equation has to be corrected to read:

$$D^2 Z = PQ[dP/P + dQ/Q + dPdQ/PQ) \cos (A + dA) - 2 \sin (dA/2) \sin (A + dA/2)].$$

Thus D^2Z depends not only on the initial quantities P, Q, A, and the increments in absolute magnitude dP and dQ, but also upon changes in the relative price and quantity patterns as represented by the angle dA.

From equations (18) to (20) it can be shown that if all prices and all quantities change in the same proportion, then there is no change in cos A, so that the angle dA is zero. Further, dA is again zero whenever there is compensation for deviation of change from the same proportion, inasmuch as some prices or quantities change more and others less than a strictly proportionate change would require. But whenever dA is zero or very small one may write

$$D^2Z = PQ[(dP/P + dQ/Q + dPdQ/PQ) \cos A - \sin A] \qquad (25)^2$$

so that the increment D^2Z then depends solely on the increments dP and dQ and the initial quantities P, Q, A.

Now the significance of the foregoing is purely theoretical. The question has been about the possibility of price and quantity indices. The only relevant common measure of tons of iron ore, ton-miles of transportation, kilowatt hours, and so on, lies in their prices; but prices themselves are subject to change; hence if it is possible to measure the acceleration of the productive process, it has to be possible to differentiate between price variation, price pattern and quantity pattern variation, and the pure quantity variation of the productive process. The foregoing discussion has aimed at showing that, without ever lapsing into meaninglessness, it is always possible to make such distinctions.

However, the definitions that have been given are rather elaborate. When change is gradual, it will be sufficient to use the following approximate definitions of P, Q, dP, and dQ, namely,

$$PQ = \Sigma\, p_i q_i \qquad (26)$$

$$PdQ = \Sigma\, p_i dq_i \qquad (27)$$

$$QdP = \Sigma\, q_i dp_i \qquad (28)$$

$$dPdQ = \Sigma\, dp_i dq_i \qquad (29)$$

2 This equation has to be corrected to read:

$$D^2Z = PQ[(dP/P + dQ/Q + dPdQ/PQ) \cos A].$$

so that

$$D^2Z = PQ''dP/P + dQ/Q + dPdQ/PQ) \qquad (30)$$

as results by referring back to equations (16) and (17) which pertain to the statement of the problem. On this definition one obtains different values for P and Q, and they may be termed 'weighted averages' as opposed to the previous 'vectorial averages.' The difference is most apparent in the respective equations for D^2Z: equations (24) and (25) contain all the relations of equation (30) but add to the latter a qualification by introducing a trigonometric function of the angle A.

The greater simplicity of the weighted averages is not without its drawbacks. Equations (26) to (29) have to be taken simultaneously; to be taken simultaneously they must be consistent; it follows that as the four left-hand-side expressions are in a fourfold proportion [$PQ/PdQ = QdP/dQdP$], so also, for consistency, the four right-hand-side summations must be in a fourfold proportion. This condition obviously restricts the validity of the definition by weighted averages: in the rare cases when the summations are proportionate, the definition is exact; when the summations are approximately proportionate, the definition is no more than an approximation; when the summations are not even approximately proportionate, the definition involves a contradiction and so is meaningless.

Naturally, a theorist is ill at ease when dealing with objects whose definition can lapse into meaninglessness and usually is at best approximate, especially when there is no saying what it approximates to. On that account one may well prefer to regard equation (30) as an alternative expression for equation (25): both of these equations have parallel variables (D^2Z, dP, dQ), though the latter adds a further initial quantity, A, to P and Q; apart from the additional initial quantity of (25), both relate variables and initial quantities in the same way; both are in the general case approximations; and both have parallel conditions of approximation, namely, a fourfold proportion involving sets of prices, quantities, price increments, and quantity increments. This parallelism should seem sufficient to provide an answer to the embarrassing question, To what do the weighted averages approximate? One may say that they are a simplified approach to the conceptually exact vectorial averages. So much, then, for the theoretical problem of the measurement of the acceleration of the productive process: from rates of payment DZ and their increments D^2Z, it is possible to proceed to rates of production Q and their increments dQ.

There remains the question of the application of this method of measurement to the basic and surplus stages of the productive process. In general the discussion will center on hypothetical smooth trends of expansion, so that instances of dp_i and dq_i will all be relatively small and the definition in terms of weighted averages will be available. The main indices to be employed will be P', the basic selling price index, and dP' its increment; Q', the index of basic quantities sold in the given interval, and dQ' its increment; P'', the surplus selling price index, and dP'' its increment; and Q'', the index of surplus quantities sold, and dQ'' its increment. These indices are calculated from rates of payment at the basic and surplus final markets, as follows.

$$DE' = P'Q' \tag{31}$$

$$D^2E' = P'Q'[dP'/P' + dQ'/Q' + dP'dQ'/P'Q'] \tag{32}$$

$$DE'' = P''Q'' \tag{33}$$

$$D^2E'' = P''Q''[dP''/P'' + dQ''/Q'' + dP''dQ''/P''Q''] \tag{34}$$

At times of great and abrupt change, when weighted averages cease to have a meaning, the meaning of the indices may be salvaged by shifting to the definition in terms of vectorial averages and adding to equations (31) to (34) the appropriate trigonometric functions of A and dA. On the other hand, in discussing equations of the type of (32) and (34), one may ignore the third quotient on the right-hand side, often because it is relatively small, always because it is merely the product of the first two quotients and so does not add a further factor of variation that is different in kind.[3]

Since Q' and Q'' refer to quantities sold at the final markets, they have to be corrected by acceleration coefficients, a' and a'', to give quantities under production during the contemporaneous interval. Thus, when basic quantities sold are Q', basic quantities under production will be $a'Q'$; similarly, when surplus quantities sold are Q'', surplus quantities under production will be $a''Q''$. Estimates of the acceleration coefficients proceed in two steps. First, one considers the series of indices for final sales over a number of intervals, say, Q'_1, Q'_2, Q'_3, ... If these are about equal, the acceleration

3 See above, pp. 129–31, where there is a lengthier consideration of the problems associated with this.

coefficient will be unity; if they are an increasing series, then a'_1 will be greater than unity; if they are a decreasing series, then a'_1 will be less than unity. Second, one adverts to the influence of speculative anticipations: the current rate of production is based not on actual but on anticipated future rates of final sales; further, when prices are rising, there is an advantage in buying long in advance, and when prices are falling, the advantage lies with minimum inventories; finally, there is a cumulative effect whenever there is a series of transitional markets, for each successive market tends to count the speculative increments of demand of later markets as part of the objective evidence, to add on a further speculative increment, and to pass on a cumulatively inflated or deflated demand to earlier markets. Hence one may characterize the acceleration coefficients as greater or less than unity according as the stages of the process are accelerating or decelerating, as notably greater than unity when current production is expanding speculatively, and perhaps as tending to be notably less than unity in the liquidation of a crisis.

11 The Cycle of the Productive Process

By a cycle is meant a more or less necessary succession of phases. By a phase is meant a series of intervals in which certain defined characteristics are verified. By a cycle of the productive process is meant a concatenation of phases defined by relations between quantity indices and their increments. The following table explores the possibility of different types of phases.

	dQ'', dQ'	$dQ''/Q'' > dQ'/Q'$	$dQ''/Q'' = dQ'/Q'$	$dQ''/Q'' < dQ'/Q'$
	Unspecified	Surplus Advantage Phase	Proportionate	Basic Advantage
II.	Neither negative	Surplus Expansion	Proportionate Expansion	Basic Expansion
III.	Neither positive	Surplus Contraction	Proportionate Contraction	Basic Contraction
IV.	Both zero	–	Static Phase	–
V.	One positive and one negative	Mixed Phase	–	Mixed Phase

The foregoing is simply a complete list of possibilities of a given type.[4] The main criterion of division is derived from the relation between basic and surplus acceleration. In any given interval, dQ''/Q'' must be greater than, or equal to, or less than dQ'/Q'. If one does not specify whether dQ' and dQ'' are positive, zero, or negative, one has three generic types of phases named respectively the surplus advantage, the proportionate phase, and the basic advantage. If however one specifies that neither dQ' nor dQ'' is negative, *in the sense that at least one is positive,* the phase is respectively a surplus expansion, a proportionate expansion, or a basic expansion. On the other hand, if one specifies that neither dQ' nor dQ'' is positive, *in the sense that at least one is negative,* the phase is respectively a surplus contraction, a proportionate contraction, or a basic contraction. Finally, if both dQ' and dQ'' are zero, there is a static phase, and if one is positive and the other negative, there is a mixed phase; the static phase and the mixed phase are likely to be mere theoretical possibilities.

The significance of the table is that it makes possible a distinction between different types of cycle. The trade cycle is a succession of expansions and contractions: it certainly is a movement up and down the table, and it may or may not also involve movements across the table. The contention of the present analysis is that there is a pure cycle at the root of the trade cycle. By a pure cycle is meant a movement across the table with no implication of a movement up or down the table. Thus the succession of surplus expansion, basic expansion, proportionate expansion, repeated as often as you please, would give a pure cycle. Of itself, it would not involve any con-

4 It is helpful to relate this list to the lists of Part Two (see pp. 122, 152, 156) and the discussions there. A simple way of envisaging the relation is to locate the nine members of the previous lists in a display that parallels the above display of possibilities II–V:

II	+″ *o*′	+″ +″	*o*″ +″
III	−″ *o*′	−″ −′	*o*″ −′
IV		*o*″ *o*′	
V	+″ −′		−″ +′

What Lonergan is seeking, in all these related sections, is a general characterization of cycles in terms of the substructures, 'phases,' themselves consisting of intervals that are related to each other by 'trends ... determinate relations between successive intervals' (pp. 152, 155). So, for example, there is the pure cycle (II, straight across), with a first phase the intervals of which are characterized by an increasing of Q'' per interval. That phase pulses forward to a phase of proportionate expansion followed by a phase of basic expansion. Again, III, straight across, illustrates a similar cycle of contraction: the focus is on magnitudes, not on negatives.

traction. It would be simply a matter of the intermittent emergence of acceleration lags in a general movement of expansion. Such a pure cycle can be shown to have an exigence for rather vigorous adaptation on the part of human agents as one phase succeeds another. It can further be shown that the lack of such adaptation transforms the pure cycle into a trade cycle: the free economies of the present day are overadapted to the surplus expansion, which they exaggerate into booms, but underadapted to the basic expansion, which they convert into slumps. Lack of adaptation thus transforms a movement across the table into a movement that also is down the table. So much, then, for the general drift of the argument in subsequent sections; present concern is the probability or necessity of pure cycles.

A first preliminary point is a distinction between the several functions of surplus final products. The aggregate of surplus final products in any given interval is measured by Q''. But of this aggregate, part goes to supplying mere replacements and maintenance of existing capital equipment, while the remainder goes to supplying additional and/or more efficient equipment. Thus while part of Q'' has no tendency to accelerate the process, the remainder tends to effect a long-term acceleration in either a surplus stage or in the basic stage. Let us say that in any given interval, $(1 - H)Q''$ has no accelerating effect, $H''Q''$ accelerates the surplus stage, and $H'Q''$ accelerates the basic stage, where $H = H' + H''$.

There immediately follows a distinction between two significantly different situations. At any given time the coefficient H may be great or small. If it is small, the possibility of a long-term acceleration of the process requires that first the surplus stage accelerate itself to make Q'' and H great before turning to the long-term acceleration of the basic stage. On the other hand, if H already is great, the surplus stage may proceed at a constant rate yet have a great $H'Q''$ to effect a notable long-term acceleration of the basic stage; and in this case the basic stage will accelerate first uniformly and then with decreasing rapidity, as the lag in additional replacement requirements gradually is overcome and H decreases.

This distinction between a high and a low potential for long-term acceleration, according as H is great or small, is to be complemented with a parallel distinction between a high and a low potential for short-term acceleration. The two types of acceleration differ, it will be recalled, inasmuch as the short-term acceleration is through the more intense and more efficient use of existing capital equipment, while the long-term acceleration is through the introduction of additional and/or more efficient equipment; thus, the short-term acceleration is a consequent of a previous long-term acceleration and consists in exploiting it to the full; inversely, one may say that the long-term acceleration changes the basis on which short-term accelerations operate. Now at any given time the potential of the economy for short-term acceleration may be high or low. One may presume it to be high when a long-term acceleration is well advanced: then there is much new equipment; many new combinations of production factors have recently emerged; and one may expect that the full potentialities of this new situation have not yet been discovered and exploited. Again, one may expect short-term potential to be high after a crisis: for then there has been a sudden contraction of rates of production, so that the material means for increasing these rates greatly are still in existence. On the other hand, short-term potential is low if a long period has elapsed since the last long-term acceleration has taken place. For if the expansion of the process has been maintained, the potentialities of short-term acceleration will in time be exhausted; and if the expansion has not been maintained but has degenerated into a slump, the potentialities of short-term acceleration will in time be destroyed by obsolescence and liquidations.

This pair of distinctions between high and low long-term and short-term acceleration potential sets the stage for a pure cycle. But the issue has yet to be clarified by further considerations. It is to be expected, in the first place, that either a long-term acceleration does not occur at all or else it occurs in a massive fashion. There are three main reasons grounding such an expectation. First, a long-term acceleration is a matter of long-term planning: capital formation is not worth while unless one can foresee a long period of utility for it; on the other hand, if such an anticipation is possible, then it is worth while to do the job properly while one is about it, for one is settling one's fate for years to come. Second, the introduction of additional or more efficient capital equipment will not take place in isolated units here and there in the productive process; the supply of a single product depends upon the activities of many units; and if it is worth while for one of them to go in for an expansion, it is worth while for a series to do so. Third, in a long-term acceleration, demand is not for some single type of surplus product but for a ramifying variety of products; thus one may expect not merely series of units but series of series of units to expand. These considerations do not make long-term accelerations inevitably massive, but they do reveal an objective logic which is verified no less in socialist planning than in capitalist free enterprise.

In the second place, the more massive the long-term acceleration the greater will be the expansion of surplus activity. Surplus activity supplies capital equipment to the surplus stages and to the basic stage. Hence a massive long-term acceleration is a massive development of surplus activity. Further, one is not to think of this increment in Q'' as concentrated in firms of certain types. The distinction between basic and surplus is not a material nor a proprietary but a functional distinction. There are types of enterprise that in themselves are indifferently basic or surplus and turn from one stage to the other according to the use to which their products are put: such are the extraction or production of raw materials, transportation, the supply of light, heat, power, and a variety of general services. As the quantity of surplus activity expands, there is not merely a great increase in the supply of tools and machines, and so on, but also a great diversion of indifferent activities to the surplus stage.

In the third place, it is to be observed that a series of intervals in which dQ''/Q'' is constant and positive is not a series of intervals with the surplus stage undergoing uniform acceleration. For dQ''/Q'' to be constant, Q'', interval by interval, has to be increasing in a geometrical progression. Thus, if in an initial interval surplus activity is Q'' and over a subsequent series of intervals dQ''/Q'' equals $k-1$, then the series of values for surplus activity will be Q'', kQ'', k^2Q'', ... k^nQ''. Inversely, if surplus activity accelerates uniformly over a series of intervals, then dQ''/Q'' is decreasing in geometrical progression; successive values of the ratio will be rdQ''/Q'', r^2dQ''/Q'', ... r^ndQ''/Q'', when the initial value of dQ''/Q'' is $1/r-1$.[5] Now, when the surplus stage of the process is effecting a long-term acceleration of surplus activity but as yet not affecting basic activity, one may expect successive values of Q'' to increase in a geometrical progression. This gives an initial period, in which the graph of dQ''/Q'' is approximately a level straight line. Next, as the surplus expansion develops and devotes more and more of its activity to the long-term acceleration of the basic stage, one may expect no more than a uniform acceleration of the surplus stage. This gives a second period, in which dQ''/Q'' is curving downwards with successive values in a decreasing geometrical progression. Thirdly, as the expansion approaches its maximum in the surplus stage, dQ'' reverts to zero and Q'' becomes constant. In this third period dQ''/Q'' is again a level straight line but now coincident with the x-axis; H'' is zero, but $H'Q''$ may be great for a notable period to effect a long-term acceleration of the basic stage which, however, gradually declines as replacement requirements begin to mount.

5 This was changed, from 1978, to read: 'then dQ''/Q'' is decreasing and successive values of the ratio will be rdQ''/Q'', $[r/(2-r)](dQ''/Q'')$, ... $\{r/(n-1)-(n-2)r]\}(dQ''/Q'')$, when the initial value of dQ''/Q'' is $1/r-1$.'

The same general principles hold with regard to dQ'/Q'. When Q' accelerates in a geometrical progression, dQ'/Q' is constant. When Q' accelerates uniformly, dQ'/Q' decreases in a geometrical progression.[6] Further, one may expect the aggregate sum of values of the increments, dQ', over a long series of intervals to be approximately in the ratio Q'/Q'' to the aggregate sum of values of the increments, dQ'', over the same long series of intervals. It is indeed true that Q' is very much larger than Q'', since basic activity is to surplus as, say, volume to surface. But one may expect the increment of a volume to stand to the increment of a surface as the volume does to the surface. To suppose the contrary leads to absurd conclusions. If, for instance, dQ''/Q'' were on a long-term aggregate much greater or much less than dQ'/Q', then a series of long-term periods would make this difference multiply in geometrical progression to effect a convergence of Q'' and Q' or else a geometrically mounting divergence.[7] Such a convergence or divergence would imply that the more roundabout methods of capitalist progress were increasingly less efficient or increasingly more efficient in expanding the supply of consumer goods. Neither view is plausible. New ideas and new methods increase existing efficiency in both the surplus and the basic stages; the ratio between the quantity of surplus and the quantity of basic products per interval is not a matter of efficiency but of the point-to-line correspondence involved in any more roundabout method, in the fact that a single surplus product gives a flow of basic products. In a word, while any concrete realization of the capitalist idea is subject first to increasing and then to decreasing returns, the series of new capitalist ideas cannot be said to be subject to either.

There is a final observation to be made. So far attention has been directed to the latter parts of the graphs of dQ''/Q'' and dQ'/Q'. It has been said that when the surplus stage devotes all its energies to self-acceleration, then Q'' will be increasing in geometrical progression and dQ''/Q'' will be a level straight line. When this period of gestation is coming to an end, the acceleration of Q'' tends to become uniform, and then gradually to decrease to zero; when it is uniform, dQ''/Q'' is decreasing in a geometrical progression,[8] and when it is zero, dQ''/Q'' is zero. Now, when the acceleration of Q'' is uniform, the long-term potential of the surplus stage

6 Following the change of note 5, the sentence should end at 'decreases.'

7 Following the change of note 5, the end of the sentence should read 'or else a mounting divergence.'

8 Following the change of note 5, 'in a geometrical progression' should be omitted.

is increasing, and so the surplus stage is devoting more and more of its efforts to the long-term acceleration of the basic stage; then Q' will be increasing at an increasing rate, and the time series of its values may stand in a geometrical progression to make dQ'/Q' a level straight line. When, however, Q'' becomes constant, the acceleration of Q' becomes uniform, and then dQ'/Q' will curve downwards in geometrical progression;[9] and as replacement requirements begin to mount, this downward curve is accentuated until dQ' reverts to zero. Thus, both dQ''/Q'' and dQ'/Q' are described as initially level straight lines that eventually curve downwards till the acceleration ratios become zero. One well may ask an account of the movement of the acceleration ratios from their initial zeros to the level straight lines.

There are two factors in such a movement: short-term acceleration and the period of generalization of a long-term acceleration. Now any long-term acceleration has to begin as a short-term acceleration. New capital equipment does not begin to accelerate rates of production until it has been produced; its production in a series of initial cases has to be a matter of the more intense or more efficient use of existing facilities, in brief, a short-term acceleration. Further, once long-term acceleration is under way, rates of production increase increasingly; their graphs are concave upwards; but the curvature moves from being flatter to rounder as the acceleration is generalized from one section to another throughout the productive process. During this period of generalization, rates of production are not merely increasing in geometrical progression but moving from less to more rapid geometrical progressions.

In one very important aspect, however, the initial period of dQ'/Q' differs from the initial period of dQ''/Q''. For reasons that will appear later, the basic stage will begin a short-term acceleration as soon as there is an appreciable surplus expansion. But while the short-term acceleration of the surplus stage passes automatically into a generalizing long-term acceleration, there is bound to be a lag, equal to the surplus period of gestation, before long-term acceleration can emerge in the basic stage, and a further lag before it can be generalized there. Thus, the initial period of the long-term expansion will approximate to a proportionate expansion with dQ'/Q' roughly equal to dQ''/Q''. But the surplus expansion would have to be

9 Following the change of note 5, 'in geometrical progression' should be omitted.

quite small, or the basic potential for short-term acceleration quite great, for this proportionate expansion to be maintained. Short-term acceleration can move dQ'/Q' up to a peak but it cannot keep it at the peak; it can move it to a peak by generalizing itself throughout the basic stage; it cannot keep it at the peak, because once it is generalized, it is apt to be exhausted, and even if it is not exhausted, it cannot make the time series of values of Q' a great geometrical progression. Thus, though dQ'/Q' initially moves to a peak, it immediately begins to descend even though Q' continues to expand at a uniform time-rate of increase. It follows that the initial proportionate expansion is succeeded by a surplus expansion: dQ''/Q'' is constant, because Q'' is increasing in some geometrical progression; dQ'/Q' is falling from a peak, even though Q' is increasing. This situation, however, is bound to be temporary; its existence is the lag between the generalized long-term acceleration of the surplus stage and that of the basic stage. When that is overcome, dQ'/Q' moves again to a peak and remains there; and by the same token, dQ''/Q'' will begin to decline. The surplus expansion is followed by a basic expansion. Finally, as replacement requirements begin to mount, the factor H in the product HQ'' begins to decline; the rate at which the surplus stage accelerates the basic accordingly declines; and so the basic expansion approaches its end. The ultimate situation is a static phase in which dQ' and dQ'' are both zero, Q' and Q'' are on new high levels but constant, and further development is awaiting new ideas, new methods, new organization.

So much for the outline of an expansive pure cycle. It assumes a long-term acceleration of the productive process and asks how such an acceleration develops. It answers by positing three periods. Generalizing short-term acceleration in both surplus and basic stages gives an initial proportionate expansion. The development of long-term acceleration in the surplus stage and its lag in the basic stage gives a surplus expansion. The emergence and generalization of long-term acceleration in the basic stage, together with the impossibility of maintaining the increasing rate of acceleration in the surplus stage, gives a basic expansion. At first, dQ''/Q'' is equal to dQ'/Q', then it is greater, then it is less. Without urging the necessity of such a cycle, one may say that it is solidly grounded in a dynamic structure of the productive process; and one has only to think of the practical impossibility of calculating the acceleration ratios dQ'/Q' and dQ''/Q'' to smile at the suggestion that one should try to 'smooth out the pure cycle.'

12 The Phases in Circuit Acceleration

On combining equations (31) and (32) and again equations (33) and (34) one obtains[10]

$$D^2E'/E' = dP'/P' + dQ'/Q' \tag{35}$$

$$D^2E''/E'' = dP''/P'' + dQ''/Q'' \tag{36}$$

so that, apart from price-level variations, DE' varies with Q' and DE'' varies with Q''. The question arises, To what extent does price-level variation offset or reinforce the concomitance of DE' with Q' and DE'' with Q''?

In the first place, variations in P' and P'' will not be equal and opposite to variations in Q' and Q'' to leave DE' and DE'' constant. This is evident from the nature of the expressions dP'/P' and dP''/P''. When Q' or Q'' is increasing in geometrical progression, P' and P'' would have to be decreasing in geometrical progression. But it is normal for rates of production to increase in geometrical progression in a long-term acceleration: the greater the rate of production, the greater the capacity to increase that rate. On the other hand, falling prices are a signal for a slump. Prices falling in a geometrical progression would soon inflict enormous losses on every entrepreneur, for entrepreneurs would be making the main part of their outlays at the higher prices but collecting their receipts at the later lower prices. Under such circumstances, the long-term acceleration, if ever it began, would rapidly come to a sudden end. The fact illustrates the value of vulgar notions of money being sound because it is rigid.

In the second place, prices tend to move in the same direction as quantities. Prices rise in a boom, when quantities increase, to fall in a slump, when quantities decrease. However, the causes of such price variation are of two kinds. There is the normal causality of increasing or decreasing scarcity. As rates of production increase, competitive demand for labor and for materials, as well as for general services such as power, transportation, credit, and so on, increase. Inversely, as rates of production decline, demand falls off. On this head, one would expect price levels to mount increasingly as the expansion developed, that is, imperceptibly in the early period, in more marked fashion once expansion becomes generalized, and in a purely infla-

10 The result depends on neglecting the third term in both equation 32 and equation 34.

tionary manner if the maximum rates of production possible were attained yet credit continued to be expanded. Thus, so far from canceling the requirement that DE' vary with Q' and DE'' with Q'', one may expect price levels to reinforce and augment such variation, though in different degrees as the pressure on general markets is slight, notable, or fatuous.

These variations in DE' and DE'' postulate, in turn, parallel variations in DI' and DI''. The normal source of basic expenditure is basic income, and the normal source of surplus expenditure is surplus income. As was argued in section 9, a condition of successful circuit acceleration is that DO', DI', and DE' keep in step, that DO'', DI'', DE'' do likewise, that DD', DD'', and DG remain zero. Thus, the long-term acceleration of the productive process with its successive proportionate, surplus, and basic expansions can be executed successfully only if the variations in the rates of payment follow the phases of the productive cycle. There would be, for instance, a radical maladjustment between circuit and productive acceleration if, when surplus rates of production were increasing more rapidly than basic, basic rates of income were increasing more rapidly than surplus. Then interval after interval, an increasingly excessive amount of monetary income would be moving to the basic final market, and there would follow a rise in prices quite different in kind from the normal rise resulting from increasing scarcity. Such a rise would not be an ordinary scarcity but at once a consequence and, as will appear, a corrective of a disproportion between monetary and real consumer income.

Not only is it true that this second type of price variation is different from the first, but also one must give it a different kind of attention. When prices rise because of real scarcity, one may speak of a requirement for variation in DE' and DE'' over and above the variation postulated by dQ'/Q' and dQ''/Q''. But when prices rise or fall because the distribution of income has not anticipated these requirements correctly, then price variation is not a postulate for variation in DE' and DE'' but rather a spontaneous effort at adjusting what should already have been adjusted. Accordingly, such adjustment variations in prices will be ignored for the moment to be considered more in detail in the next section. Present concern will be for the type of adjustment that the successive phases of the pure cycle postulate.

The central adjustment is variation in the rate of saving. This rate may be defined, conveniently for present purposes, as the ratio of surplus income to total income. Assuming that the rate of saving will not differ appreciably because income is derived from basic or surplus outlay, we may denote this rate by the symbol G, write

$$G = G' = 1 - G'' \qquad (37, \text{see } 8)$$

so that

$$G = DI''/(DI' + DI'') \qquad (38, \text{see 2 and } 10)$$

The condition that G is increasing, constant, or decreasing is that surplus income is increasing, in proportion to its size, more rapidly than basic, or at the same rate, or less rapidly. Symbolically, if one assumes a smooth trend and differentiates equation (38), the numerator on the right-hand side will be $D^2I''/DI'' - D^2I'/DI'$ which, as it is positive, zero, or negative, makes the differential of G positive, zero, or negative.

Now in a proportionate expansion, dQ''/Q'' equals dQ'/Q'. If price levels are rising at all, one may expect both basic and surplus levels to be rising equally. Hence D^2E'/DE' should equal D^2E''/DE''. Further, since rates of income should keep pace with rates of expenditure, D^2I''/DI'' should equal D^2I'/DI'. It follows that in the proportionate expansion, the rate of saving, G, should be constant.

Again, in the surplus expansion, dQ''/Q'' is greater than dQ'/Q'; if there is any divergence in the variation of basic and surplus price levels, scarcity should be felt more in the surplus than in the basic stage of the process, so that any difference between dP''/P'' and dP'/P' would have a reinforcing and not a canceling effect. It follows, as before, that D^2E''/DE'' should be greater than D^2E'/DE', that D^2I''/DI'' should be greater than D^2I'/DI', and so that the rate of saving, G, should be increasing.

Inversely, in the basic expansion, the preceding argument is turned around to give the conclusion that the rate of saving should be decreasing. Then dQ'/Q' is greater than dQ''/Q'', prices varying from scarcity should, if anything, reinforce this difference, and so basic income and expenditure must be increasing more rapidly than surplus.

To conclude, the acceleration of the productive process, if it is to succeed and not be destroyed by circulation maladjustments, postulates that in a proportionate expansion the rate of saving be constant, that in a surplus expansion it increases, that in a basic expansion it decreases. The implications of this postulate will concern us in subsequent sections on the cycle of basic income, the cycle of pure surplus income, and the cycle of price spreads.

18

Cycles of Incomes and Prices

13 The Cycle of Basic Income

The purpose of this section is to inquire into the manner in which the rate of saving, G, is adjusted to the phases of the pure cycle of the productive process. Traditional theory looked to shifting interest rates to provide suitable adjustment. In the main we shall be concerned with factors that are prior to changing interest rates and more effective.

The simplest manner of attaining a fairly adequate concept of basic income is to divide the economic community into an extremely large number of groups of practically equal income. Among these groups it will be convenient to include a zero-income group composed of dependents, the unemployed, potential immigrants, recent emigrants, the recently deceased, and so on. In any group i let there be at any given time n_i members; let each member receive an aggregate (basic and surplus) income y_i per interval, so that the whole group receives $n_i y_i$; finally, let us say that the group directs the fraction g_i of its total income to the basic demand function, so that basic income per interval is given by the equation

$$DI' = \sum g_i n_i y_i \qquad (39)$$

Next, let g_i increase by dg_i, n_i by dn_i, and y_i by dy_i in the immediately subsequent interval. However, since the number of income groups is extremely large, it should always be possible to represent an increase or decrease of an individual's income by his migration from one group to another. In this manner dy_i may be assumed to be always zero, and so one obtains for the increment per interval of basic income the simpler equation

$$d^2I' = \Sigma\ (g_i y_i dn_i + n_i y_i dg_i) \qquad (40)$$

where the component $y_i dg_i dn_i$ is omitted as containing no new variable.[1] We shall consider in turn variations in basic income in virtue of dn_i and variations in virtue of dg_i.

Since there is a zero-income group one may always regard the addition of members to one group as a subtraction from other groups and vice versa. This, in fact, is always approximately true, but the presence of a zero-income group provides a locus in which all error is concentrated without leading to any misstatement about income. Consider, then, the migration of an individual from any group i to a proximate but higher group j. Three increments are to be distinguished: the increment in the individual's total income, $y_j - y_i$; the increment in his basic income, $g_j y_j - g_i y_i$; and the increment in his surplus income, $[(1 - g_j)y_j - (1 - g_i)y_i]$. Now the higher any individual's total income, the smaller will be the fraction g of total income going to basic expenditure. Hence, in migrations from low to less low income groups, most of the increment of individual total income becomes an increment of basic income; but in migrations from high to still higher income groups, most of the increment of individual total income becomes an increment of surplus income. Evidently, then, suitable migrations are a means of providing adjustments in the community's rate of saving. To increase the rate of saving, increase the income of the rich.[2] To decrease the rate of saving, increase the income of the poor.

The foregoing is the fundamental mode of adjusting the rate of saving to the phases of the productive cycle. It reveals that the surplus expansion is anti-egalitarian, inasmuch as that expansion postulates that increments in

1 See p. 273, note 3. Equivalent problems would occur here. From 1978 Lonergan replaced the phrase 'is omitted as containing no new variable' with the phrase 'where n_i includes the adjustment due to migration.'

2 In CWL 15 this sentence reads, 'To increase the rate of saving [social dividend], increase the income of the rich; while they may be too distant from the current operations of the economic process to judge, at least they can put their money into the bank or bonds or stocks, and perhaps others will see how it can best be used' (at note 190 in the text). Lonergan introduced the phrase 'social dividend' instead of 'rate of saving' in 1979. See note 186, there, for a fuller notion of social dividend.

income go to high incomes. But it also reveals the basic expansion to be egalitarian, for that expansion postulates that increments in income go to low incomes.

However, this fundamental mode of adjustment is complemented by a further mechanism of automatic correction. When savings are insufficient, too much money is moving to the basic final market, and so the basic selling-price level rises; inversely, when saving is excessive, insufficient money moves to the basic final market, and so the basic selling-price level falls. This movement of price levels has a double effect: it contracts or expands the purchasing power of monetary income; and it shifts the distribution of monetary income to the higher or to the lower income brackets. The latter effect is less apparent but essential, for without it there results the upward or downward price spiral.

When, then, prices rise, there is no tendency, at least in the first instance, for quantities to contract. It follows that rates of payment expand proportionately to the rise of prices to give a very large increase to total outlay and income. Again, in the first instance at least, this large increase of income consists in speculative profits of the entrepreneurial class, and as one may suppose this class to be already in the higher income brackets, it follows that the increment of total income resulting from rising prices is an increment in the higher income brackets and so mainly an increment in surplus income. Thus, the mechanism of rising prices involves a shift in the distribution of monetary income in favor of the higher income brackets and so in favor of surplus income. This shift in distribution, of course, is achieved through increasing the money in circulation and not by decreasing the monetary income of other brackets. Nonetheless, the equivalent of that effect is had by the reduction of the purchasing power of monetary income. Now the greater the rise in prices, the greater the increase in monetary income, the greater the increase in surplus income, and the greater the reduction of the purchasing power of monetary income. Hence, a sufficient rise in prices will always succeed in adjusting the rate of saving to the requirements of the productive phase. No doubt, as prices rise, the income groups increase their respective fractions g_i by some positive increment dg_i, and no doubt this involves a positive increment in basic monetary income. But also there is no doubt that as prices rise, the capacity of successive lower income groups to effect positive increments dg_i becomes more and more negligible; the fraction g_i cannot be greater than unity. Hence, as prices rise, real saving is forced upon each lower group;

on the other hand, as prices rise, the consequent increment in speculative profits and so of surplus income is far greater than any greater spending effected by the small numbers in the higher brackets.

The foregoing mechanism provides an automatic adjustment to an increasing rate of saving. However, its operation is conditioned. Unless the quantity of money in circulation expands as rapidly as prices rise and, as well, as rapidly as the productive expansion of quantities requires, there will result a contraction of the process: then, instead of adjusting the rate of saving to the requirements of the productive cycle, the productive cycle is arrested to find adjustment to the rate of saving. Again, unless the increment in total monetary income goes to the higher income brackets and so to surplus income, there will be no adjustment of the rate of saving: the monetary income of the lower groups increases as rapidly as the purchasing power of monetary income contracts; no real saving is forced; and *ex hypothesi*, there is no anti-egalitarian shift in the distribution of income. It follows that basic income continues to be excessive, and so the basic price level continues to rise indefinitely.

These two types of failure of the automatic mechanism are interrelated. Banks are willing to increase the quantity of money as long as there is no appearance of uncontrolled inflation, but they curtail and even contract loans as soon as an upward spiral of prices menaces the monetary system. Thus, the root of the failure of the mechanism is the failure to obtain the anti-egalitarian shift in the distribution of income. In any first instance, rising prices effect that shift. But the trouble is that, in every second instance, organized labor can point to the rising prices as palpable proof of the rising cost of living and further can point to increased profits as proof of industry's capacity to pay higher monetary wage rates. Every delay in granting wage increases is of general advantage. On the other hand, every grant of such increases may indeed shift the burden of forced saving from industrial to other lower income groups, but certainly causes prices to spiral upwards and so hastens the curtailment of credit.

So far we have been considering the adjustment of the rate of saving in a surplus expansion when that rate is increasing. There remains the opposite situation of the basic expansion when the rate of saving is decreasing. Then the problem that arises is that insufficient income is moving to the basic final market. There is at hand the same automatic mechanism as before. Prices fall. This fall has the double effect of increasing the purchasing power of income and bringing about an egalitarian shift in the distribution of monetary income. The increase in purchasing power is obvious.

On the other hand, the egalitarian shift in the distribution of income is, in the main, a merely theoretical possibility. The fall of prices, unless quantities increase proportionately and with equal rapidity, brings about a great reduction in total rates of payment. Receipts fall, outlay falls, income falls. The incidence of the fall of income is, in the first instance, upon the entrepreneurial class, and so in the main it is a reduction of surplus income. Thus we have the same scissors action as before: purchasing power of income increases, and the proportion of basic to surplus income increases; the rate of saving is adjusted to the rates of production as soon as the selling-price level falls sufficiently. But just as there is an upward price spiral to blunt the edge of the mechanism when the rate of saving is increasing, so there is a downward spiral to have the same effect when the rate of saving should be decreasing. Falling prices tend to be regarded as a signal that expansion has proceeded too far, that contraction must now be the order of the day. Output is reduced; the income of lower brackets is reduced; the adjustment of the rate of saving fails to take place; prices fall further; the same misinterpretation arises, and prices fall again. Eventually, however, the downward spiral achieves the desired effect; surplus income is reduced to the required proportion of total income; and then prices cease to fall.

An account of the crisis and slump will concern us later. The present point is a very simple point. Just as the surplus expansion is anti-egalitarian in tendency, postulating an increasing rate of saving, and attaining this effectively by increasing, in the main, the income of those who already spend as much as they care to on basic products, so the basic expansion is egalitarian in tendency; it postulates a continuously decreasing rate of saving, a continously decreasing proportion of surplus income in total income; and it achieves this result effectively by increasing, in the main, the income of those who have the maximum latent demand for consumer goods and services.

Previously I have suggested a lack of adaptation in the free economies to the requirements of the pure cycle. What that lack is can now be stated. It is an inability to distinguish between the significance of a relative and an absolute rise or fall of monetary prices. A relative rise or fall is, indeed, a signal for a relatively increased or reduced production. If the product *i* suffers a greater increment, positive or negative, in price than the product *j*, then more or less of the product *i* than of the product *j* is being demanded. As prices are in themselves relative, insofar as they express demand, so also they must be interpreted relatively with regard to expansion and contraction. When the prices both of *i* and of *j* are falling, and *i* more than j, it may still be true that the production of both should be increasing, though with the production of j increasing more than the production of i. For the fall of prices may be general and absolute; as such it will result not from a change in demand but from a failure in income distribution to adjust the rate of saving to the phase of the productive process; to allow such a general maladjustment to convert a basic expansion into a slump is to cut short the expansive cycle of the productive process because one has confused real and relative prices with monetary and absolute prices. Inversely, the rising prices of the surplus expansion are not real and relative but only monetary and absolute rising prices; to allow them to stimulate production is to convert the surplus expansion into a boom. This, I believe, is the fundamental lack of adaptation to the productive cycle that our economies have to overcome. The problem, however, has many ramifications of which the most important is the relativity of the significance of profits. To this we now turn.

Traditional theory looked to shifting interest rates to provide the automatic adjustment between the productive process and the rate of saving. In brief, the argument was that the rate of interest was the price of money: the higher the rate of interest, the greater the incentive to save and, on the other hand, the less the incentive to borrow; inversely, the lower the interest rates, the less the incentive to save and the greater the encouragement to borrowers; in between these positions, it should always be possible to assign some equilibrium rate of interest equating the supply of money with the demand for it. The difficulty with this theory is that it lumps together a number of quite different things and overlooks the order of magnitude of the fundamental problem. What the surplus expansion calls for is not simply more saving but a continuously increasing rate of saving: the problem is not that the rate of saving, G, has to be bigger in a surplus expansion but that it has to be becoming bigger and bigger all the time; dG is positive as long as $dQ''/Q'' - dQ'/Q'$ is positive. Hence if there is to be any relevance to increments in interest rates, one has to envisage not intermittent increments but rather a rate of increase of interest rates. Again, to speak of interest rates providing an incentive to saving is true enough as far as it goes; but it misses the magnitude of the problem, which is to effect an anti-egalitarian shift in the distribution of income. To increase the rates of interest will effect some modification of instances of dg_i in favor of reduced basic income; but it would take enormous interest rates backed by all propaganda techniques at our disposal to effect the negative values of dg_i that are required interval after interval as the surplus expansion proceeds; what is needed is something in the order of 'incentives to save' that is as rapid and as effective as the reduction of purchasing power by rising prices.

But not only does the concept of an equilibrium rate of interest miss the magnitude of the problem. It also involves an indiscriminate lumping together of quite different things. One cannot identify a reduction of basic income with an increase in the supply of money, for a reduction of basic income is only one source of such supply; moreover, it is neither the normal nor the principal source of such supply; normally, surplus final products are purchased with surplus income, which is just as much a circular flow as the purchase of basic final products by basic income; principally the increase in the supply of money is due to the expansion of bank credit, which is necessary to provide the positive DS' and DS'' needed interval after interval to enable the circuits to keep pace with the expanding productive process. In the concrete problem under examination there is an abundant supply of money for all purposes; the one difficulty is that the division of income into basic and surplus is not parallel to the division of productive activity into basic and surplus; a general operation upon the supply of money seems to be a rather roundabout and inept procedure to correct an error in distribution.

The ineptitude of the procedure arises not only from its inadequacy to effect a redistribution of income of the magnitude required but also from its effects upon the demand for money. Four types of such demand may be distinguished: demand for basic final products; demand for surplus final products; demand for maintaining or increasing the turnover magnitudes of units of enterprise; and demand for redistributional purposes. The effect of rising interest rates on consumer borrowing will be excellent as far as it goes, for it cannot but reduce consumer borrowing; on the other hand, one may doubt if such reduction is very significant, for an inability to calculate is a normal condition of consumer borrowing, and rising interest rates hardly exert a great influence on people who cannot calculate.[3] The effect of rising interest rates on the demand for surplus final products is great: one may say that the initiation of further long-term expansion is blocked; to increase the interest rate from 5% to 6% increases by 10% the annual charge upon a piece of capital equipment paid for over a period of twenty years. Thus rising interest rates end further initiation of long-term expansion; on the other hand, expansion already initiated, especially if

3 An understandable looseness here was corrected in 1978 by Lonergan: 'cannot calculate' was replaced by 'do not calculate.'

notably advanced, will continue inasmuch as an increased burden of future costs is preferred to the net loss of deserting the new or the additional enterprise. The effect of rising interest rates on turnover magnitudes depends upon the turnover frequency of the enterprise. If the frequency is once every two years, 1% increase in the rate of interest is a 2% increase in costs; if the frequency is once every month, 1% increase in the rate of interest is 1/12 of 1% increase in costs. Effects of the latter order are negligible when prices are rising. Indeed, then even a 2% increase might be disregarded; but the combination of the 2% increase in costs with the uncertainty of what prices will be in two years' time is a rather powerful deterrent. The effect on turnover magnitudes, accordingly, is great when the frequency of the turnover is low, but negligible when the frequency is high. Finally, as to the effect on redistributional borrowing, there are a variety of complications: gamblers on the stock market will continue to gamble; new flotations of stock will be discouraged for the same reason as the purchase of surplus products; the international position of the country will be affected, a point from which the argument has prescinded so far and which can be considered only later.

However, the following conclusions seem justified. When the rate of saving is insufficient, increasing interest rates effect an adjustment. This adjustment is not an adjustment of the rate of saving to the productive process but of the productive process to the rate of saving: for small increments in interest rates tend to eliminate all long-term elements in the expansion; and such small increments necessarily precede the preposterously large increments needed to effect the required negative values of dg_i. Finally, the adjustment is delayed, and it does not deserve the name of adjustment. It is delayed because the influence of increasing interest rates on short-term enterprise is small. It does not deserve the name 'adjustment' because its effect is not to keep the rate of saving and the productive process in harmony as the expansion continues but simply to end the expansion by eliminating its long-term elements.

14 The Cycle of Pure Surplus Income

A condition of circuit acceleration was seen in § 9 to include the keeping step of basic outlay, basic income, and basic expenditure, and on the other hand, the keeping step of surplus outlay, surplus income, and surplus expenditure. Any of these rates may begin to vary independently of the others, and adjustment of the others may lag. But any systematic divergence brings automatic correctives to work. The concomitance of outlay and expenditure follows from the interaction of supply and demand. The concomitance of income with outlay and expenditure is identical with the adjustment of the rate of saving with the requirements of the productive process. It follows that one may legitimately project a division of expenditure into a division of income, and it is in this manner that we arrive at the concept of a pure surplus income.

Pure surplus income may be defined, for present purposes, as a fraction of total surplus income. This fraction will be denoted by the symbol H, where H is the fraction of surplus expenditure that goes to new fixed investment. All surplus final expenditure may be termed a 'fixed investment' to distinguish it from the outlay of units of enterprise and their transitional payments, which may be called 'liquid investment.' Further, fixed investment may be divided into the purchase at the surplus final markets of replacements and of maintenance and, on the other hand, new fixed investment. Thus in each interval the rate of surplus expenditure DE'' consists of two parts: one part, $(1 - H)DE''$, goes to the replacement and maintenance of old fixed investment; the other part, $H.DE''$, goes to new fixed investment.

Now, when DI'' is keeping pace with DE'', so that DD'' is zero, one may make a parallel distinction in surplus income, naming $(1 - H)DI''$ as ordinary surplus income and $H.DI''$ as pure surplus income. This pure surplus income is quite an interesting object. When H is greater than zero, it is a rate of income over and above all current requirements for the standard of living, since that is provided by DI', and as well over and above all real maintenance and replacement expenditure, since that is provided by $(1 - H)DI''$. Thus one may identify pure surplus income as the aggregate rate of return upon capital investment: entrepreneurs consider that they are having tolerable success when they are not merely 'making a living,' no matter how high their standard of living, and not merely obtaining sufficient receipts to purchase all the equipment necessary to overcome obsolescence, but also receiving an additional sum of income which is profit in their strong sense of the term. An aggregate profit in that sense is precisely what we have found pure surplus income to be. Further, unlike other income, pure surplus income need not be spent currently without effecting a reduction of total income; it is possible to divert pure surplus from the circuits to the redistributional function without causing a negative DD'' because in the redistributional function there is an organization of promoters, underwriters, brokers, and investors who there mobilize sums of money and move them along DD'' from the redistributional function to the surplus demand function where they are spent as new fixed investment. Thus it is pure surplus income, as a concrete fact, which has given rise to and has sustained the ideal of the 'successful man' in our culture. For the 'successful man' is a man who, of course, enjoys a very high standard of living, but who measures his success in quite other terms, namely, in the industrial power of ownership which he wields, in the financial power of possession of large blocks of readily negotiable securities, and in the social prestige that may be buttressed by the purchase of the most conspicuous products of human art and ingenuity in the past history of man. For there to be successful men of this type and for them to attain their success through industry and commerce, it must be possible to derive from the circuits a rate of income that can be moved, without conflicting with circuit requirements, from the circuits to the redistributional function where alone industrial stocks, negotiable securities, and the products of the process in the remote past are now on sale.

Enough, perhaps, has been said to show that pure surplus income is at the nerve center of free economies. We have now to advert to the fact that it is subject to cyclic variation in the long-term acceleration of the productive process. The symbol H in the product $H.DI''$ has already been met. It is the measure of the long-term acceleration potential of the surplus stage of the productive process. The higher the rate of new fixed investment, the greater the rate at which long-term acceleration of the process is proceeding and, as well, the greater the rate of pure surplus income. But the long-term acceleration of the process involves a cycle, and this cycle cannot but affect the rate of pure surplus income. To this we direct attention.

Let the symbol F denote the ratio of pure surplus income to total income, so that

$$F = H.DI'' / (DI' + DI'') \tag{41}$$

whence by equation (38)

$$F = GH \tag{42}$$

On assuming a smooth trend and differentiating, one finds as a condition for a maximum of F that

$$0 = H.dG + G.dH \tag{43}$$

As long as the right-hand side of this equation is positive, the ratio F is increasing; when it becomes negative, F begins to decrease.

Now the ratio G is at its maximum $(dG = 0)$, when the process turns over from a surplus to a basic expansion: throughout the surplus expansion, G increases; throughout the basic expansion, G decreases. On the other hand, the maximum of H depends upon two somewhat independent factors: (H increases as long as Q'' increases) H begins to decrease either because Q'' begins to decrease or because the rate of replacement requirements begins to rise. On the assumption of the pure cycle, Q'' does not decrease but reaches a maximum and then levels off into a straight line parallel to the time axis; in that case, the maximum of H arises subsequently to the maximum of G when, during the basic expansion, the rate of replacements begins to rise or, if Q'' were still increasing, when the rate of replacements begins to increase more rapidly than Q''. If, however, the surplus expansion was overambitious and expanded the surplus stage of the process excessively, then Q'' is bound to fall sharply at some time or other. This will occur prior to the ordinary maximum of H to bring about a premature maximum of that ratio. It may occur after the maximum of G to make the maximum of F not a smooth turning point but a sharp break and fall. It may occur earlier, bringing G to a premature maximum and suddenly changing F from a rate of rapid increase to a rate of still more rapid decrease. Thus, in general, there are three types of maxima for F. There is the ideal maximum when the turn is due to replacements absorbing the capacity of the surplus stage for effecting an acceleration of the process. There is the slightly premature maximum when the turn is due to an overexpansion of the surplus stage but occurs after the maximum of G when the rate of increase of F is already small. There is the extremely premature maximum of F when the turn is due to a great overexpansion and occurs when the rate of increase of F is still great; in this case the maxima of F, G, and H coincide. By overexpansion is meant simply the fact that the surplus rate of production, Q'', falls.

To visualize this cycle, let us say that f_i is the pure surplus income per interval received by the unit of enterprise i, and that o_i is the outlay per interval of the same unit of enterprise. Then

$$F = GH = \Sigma f_i / \Sigma o_i = f_i / o_i \qquad (44)$$

Here, Σf_i is identical with $H.DI''$ and Σo_i is identical with $(DO' + DO'')$. On the other hand, f_i/o_i may be taken as simply a representative ratio of pure surplus to total outlay among units of enterprise. In any given unit of enterprise, according to its advantages or disadvantages, the particular ratio f_j/o_j will be greater or less than the average, f_i/o_i.

Now in the proportionate expansion at the beginning of the pure cycle, the ratio G is constant: proportionately, the surplus stage is increasing as rapidly as the basic. However, the fraction H will be increasing, for the surplus stage is then increasing its potential for long-term acceleration. It follows that the ratio F and the average, f_i/o_i, are increasing as H increases. Further, since both basic and surplus stages are accelerating, Σo_i is increasing; and so the absolute quantity of pure surplus, Σf_i, is increasing as the product of two increasing factors, namely, H and Σo_i. Insofar as prosperity is measured in terms of pure surplus income, prosperity has begun.

The proportionate expansion is based on the capacity of the process for short-term acceleration. If a great long-term acceleration develops, that is, a transformation of the capital equipment of the surplus stage, then dQ'/Q' will lag behind dQ''/Q'', and a surplus expansion will result. Then both G and H are increasing. The ratio F and the average, f_i/o_i, will be increasing as the product of two increasing factors, namely, both G and H. The absolute quantity of pure surplus income, Σf_i, will be increasing as the product of three increasing factors, namely, G, H, and Σo_i. The rewards of entrepreneurial initiative are munificent.

It is to be observed that this phase has no necessary implication of an inflationary rise in prices. That occurrence is conditioned by the failure of the rate of saving to keep increasing rapidly enough. If the pure surplus is captured by the higher income brackets alone, the anti-egalitarian shift in the distribution of income is being achieved. If not, saving is insufficient; prices rise; total income increases; and this increment, at least in the first instance when it appears as a broader price spread, will go to the higher income brackets to combine an anti-egalitarian shift with a reduced purchasing power which pinches the lower income groups.

However, the surplus expansion is only an acceleration lag. The greater it is and the longer it lasts, the greater the potential for basic expansion that is created. Obviously, it is not created and then left unused. It is put to work as rapidly as possible, and so the basic stage accelerates at an ever greater pace while the surplus stage begins to realize that it has acquired as great a potential as possibly can be used. There results the basic expansion, with the basic stage accelerating, proportionately, more rapidly than the surplus. G has passed its maximum.

In the early part of the basic expansion, F is still increasing though at a reduced rate; for the rate of decrease of G is cutting against the rate of increase of H, which now may be less rapid. It follows that the average, f_i / o_i, is also increasing still. On the other hand, the absolute sum of pure surplus, Σf_i, is increasing as the product of two increasing factors, namely, F and Σo_i. On the supposition of a pure cycle, in which Q'' does not decrease, the maximum of F is intermediate between the maximum of G and the maximum of H. It is a smooth turn that decreases pure surplus, not by diminishing receipts but by changing the function of surplus income from being the 'money to invest' of pure surplus to the mere replacement income that has to be spent on overcoming mounting obsolescence. However, while the ratio F and the average, f_i / o_i, decrease after the smooth maximum of F, the absolute quantity of pure surplus income continues to increase up to the maximum of H, which, *ex hypothesi*, is later. Thus two periods are to be distinguished subsequent to the maximum of F: a first period, in which average pure surplus is decreasing though aggregate pure surplus continues to increase; and a second period, in which both average and aggregate pure surplus income are decreasing. In the second of these periods the ratio F and the average, f_i / o_i, are decreasing as the product of two decreasing factors, namely, G and H; if Σo_i is still increasing, Σf_i will be decreasing at a slower rate; but in any case F, H, and Σf_i are reverting to zero, which they reach as dQ', following dQ'', reaches zero.

The foregoing is an outline of perfect adaptation to the pure cycle of the expanding productive process. However, the actual course of events is governed by the actual lack of adaptation to the pure cycle. This lack of adaptation is multiple, and so we treat successively and as distinct though conjoined phenomena the long, drawn-out depression and the short, violent crisis.

At the root of the depression lies a misinterpretation of the significance of pure surplus income. In fact, it is the monetary equivalent of the new fixed investment of an expansion: just as the production of new fixed investment is over and above all current consumption and replacement products, so pure surplus income is over and above all current consumption and replacement income; just as the products of new fixed investment emerge in cyclic fashion, so also does pure surplus income emerge in cyclic fashion. It is mounting from zero at a moderate pace in the proportionate expansion; it is mounting at an enormous pace in the surplus expansion; but in the basic expansion first average, and then aggregate pure surplus income begin to decline, and eventually they have reverted to zero. Now it is true that our culture cannot be accused of mistaken ideas on pure surplus income as it has been defined in this essay; for on that precise topic it has no ideas whatever. However, the phenomena here referred to by the term 'pure surplus income' are not, as is the term, a creation of our own. The phenomena are well known. Entrepreneurs are quite aware that there are times of prosperity in which even a fool can make a profit and other mysterious times in which the brilliant and the prudent may be driven to the wall. Entrepreneurs are quite aware of the ideal of the successful man, a man whose success is measured not by a high emergent standard of living nor by the up-to-date efficiency of some industrial or commercial unit but by increasing industrial, financial, and social power and prestige. In the old days, when the entrepreneur was also owner and manager, pure surplus income roughly coincided with what was termed profit. Today, with increasing specialization of function, pure surplus income is distributed in a variety of ways: it enters into very high salaries of general managers and top-flight executives, into the combined fees of directors when together these reach a high figure, into the undistributed profits of industry, into the secret reserves of banks, into the accumulated royalties, rents, interest receipts, fees, or dividends of anyone who receives a higher income than he intends to spend at the basic final market. For pure surplus income, as distributed, is the remainder of income that is not spent at the basic final market either directly by its recipient or equivalently through the action of others spending more than they earn. Thus pure surplus income may be identified best of all by calling it net aggregate savings and viewing them as functionally related to the rate of new fixed investment.

The consequence is that net aggregate savings vary with new fixed investment, and the complaint is that there exist, in the mentality of our culture, no ideas, and in the procedures of our economies, no mechanisms, directed to smoothly and equitably bringing about the reversal of net aggregate savings to zero as the basic expansion proceeds. Just as there is an anti-egalitarian shift to the surplus expansion, so also there is an egalitarian shift in the distribution of income in the basic expansion. But while we can effect the anti-egalitarian shift with some measure of success, in fact the egalitarian shift is achieved only through the contractions, the liquidations, the blind stresses and strains of a prolonged depression. Once F has passed its maximum, the average ratio of pure surplus to the outlay of an entrepreneurial unit, f_i/o_i, has to decrease. Once H has passed its maximum, the aggregate of pure surplus, $\sum f_i$, has to decrease. There is operative a general 'squeeze.' There is no mechanism for providing adaptation to this 'squeeze.' There follows chaos.

In the first place, there are a number of sources of pure surplus income, as distributed, that are relatively invulnerable. Individuals may hold fixed claims of income against industrial or commercial units. In any particular case these fixed claims, whether against one or against a number of units, may amount to a claim to surplus income. The obvious instance is had in interest-bearing bonds. But there exists a series of more or less analogous instances of pure surplus income in the form of fees or of salaries, and the less these instances are directly derived from industry, commerce, or financial services, the less they can be controlled by their real though remote sources. The significance of such relative invulnerability is that such instances of pure surplus income are the last to feel the 'squeeze,' and, what is more important, that the pressure of the 'squeeze' is all the stronger and more relentless on other instances.

Besides this first degree of invulnerability there is a second. The same reasons that enabled some units of enterprise to recapture more than an average share of pure surplus income during the surplus expansion now will enable them to resist a proportionately more than average reduction of their share of pure surplus. Thus the 'squeeze' is operative most of all upon the firms that have a less than average share of pure surplus. As it proceeds, it will eliminate not merely any pure surplus they receive but as well their replacement income and part of their basic income. Such relative invulnerability brings the circuits to a distorted quasi equilibrium in which an artificial rate of pure surplus income is sustained by a rate of losses. Individuals continue to receive more income than they spend at the basic or at the surplus final markets. There is no compensating rate of new fixed investment to offset this drain. There results a negative value of DD'', but the 'squeeze' gives positive values of DS'' and particularly DS' as embarrassed entrepreneurs undergo a continuous and equal stream of losses. In this fashion, the required reduction of the rate of savings is effected by creating losses to supply the invulnerable rate of savings. From a different viewpoint one may say that the outlay of some firms exceeds their receipts to enable the outlay of other firms to contain an artificial pure surplus income. But however the matter is expressed, the rate of losses has to equal the emergence of more pure surplus income than the process in the given interval is generating; and if at any time the rate of losses proves insufficient, the familiar mechanism of falling prices, decreased total income, and increased purchasing power comes into play either to decrease the rate of savings or to increase the rate of losses.

Evidently, the systematic requirement of a rate of losses will result in a series of contractions and liquidations. Any particular firm may succeed in strengthening its position. But that only transfers the incidence of the 'squeeze' elsewhere. Any number of firms may go bankrupt and be liquidated. But until the position of the strong is undermined by the general and prolonged contracting, the requirement for the rate of losses continues, and with it the depression.

It is quite true that, were a long-term acceleration to get under way, the situation would be remedied, for sooner or later the weaker firms would begin to obtain sufficient receipts to make ends meet. But the difficulty is that a long-term acceleration has been under way quite recently, that it was approaching completion in the surplus stage of the process, and that it was at least partially completed in the basic stage. Further acceleration of the process, from the nature of the development attained, would be a basic expansion, and it would have to be a short-term basic expansion before it could develop into a long-term basic expansion; things have to be going fairly well before a general movement to transform capital equipment can be initiated. Now, whenever the basic stage accelerates more rapidly than the surplus stage, the rate of savings has to decrease continuously. But in the depression there is already an excessive rate of savings, and only a distorted equilibrium is had through the simultaneous existence of a rate of losses. Further decrease in the required rate of savings only intensifies the problem; spontaneously it will work out through the mechanism of falling prices and contracting total income; that under current inadaptation an expansion could be expected against such difficulties is evidently preposterous. On the other hand, increasing contraction and liquidation tends to reduce the requirement for a rate of losses: with the surplus stage already operating at a minimum, any further reduction of the basic stage means that a zero dQ''/Q'' is greater than a negative dQ'/Q'; this postulates an increasing rate of savings, and under the circumstances, this increase of required savings (since actual savings already are too great) is a reduction of losses. Thus the greater the contraction, the less the rate of losses required; again, the greater the contraction, the weaker the position of the initially invulnerable; in the limit the rate of losses will disappear, and a distorted equilibrium give place to a true equilibrium. Meanwhile, obsolescence will have mounted, and so as orders for replacements begin to increase they will be accompanied by surplus purchases that are new fixed investment; *H* begins to increase, and the proportionate expansion of the revival is under way.

Later we shall consider the effect of a favorable balance of foreign trade or of deficit government spending in mitigating the depression's requirement for a rate of losses. The present point, however, should be repeated. It is that in the later stages of a long-term acceleration, even if there is no crisis or general breakdown, there is required a continuously decreasing rate of net aggregate savings so that, at the end of the expansion and until a new expansion gets under way, net aggregate savings or pure surplus income have to be zero. The phenomena of our depressions can be explained by our lack of any mechanism that will reduce net aggregate savings smoothly and equitably. There results a distorted equilibrium conditioned by a rate of losses. This rate of losses forces the series of contractions and liquidations that characterize the depression. Further, under such circumstances, it is vain to expect a solution or remedy by the emergence of a new cycle of expansion; that might be expected if an extremely premature crisis arose but not if the process gets into difficulties after the surplus expansion has largely been completed; in the latter case, supposing current adaptation, it is only the prolonged contraction undermining the position of the strong and reducing the requirement for an impossibly low rate of net aggregate savings that ends the depression. Even after the distorted equilibrium through a rate of losses has been eliminated, it is impossible for the expansion to begin if the real situation is such as to favor a basic expansion; for that would only renew the old difficulties. But with the passage of time, obsolescence will become great enough to make the situation favor a surplus expansion, a great long-term acceleration; then the trade cycle recommences.

It will be convenient to reserve to the next section an account of the more violent phenomena of the crisis.

15 The Cycle of the Aggregate Basic Price Spread

There is a sense in which one may speak of the fraction of basic outlay that moves to basic income as the 'costs' of basic production. It is true that that sense is not at all an accountant's sense of 'costs': for it would include among costs the standard of living of those who receive dividends but not the element of pure surplus in the salaries of managers; worse, it would not include replacement costs, nor the part of maintenance that is purchased at the surplus final market, nor the accumulation for sinking funds which is a part of pure surplus income. But however remote from the accountant's meaning of the term 'costs,' it remains that there is an aggregate and functional sense in which the fraction of basic outlay moving to basic income is an index of costs. For the greater the fraction that basic income is of total income (or total outlay), the less the remainder which constitutes the aggregate possibility of profit. But what limits profit may be termed cost. Hence we propose in the present section to speak of $(1 - G')DO'$, and as well of $G''DO''$, as costs of production, having warned the reader that the costs in question are aggregate and functional costs in a sense analogous to that in which forced savings are savings.

In any given interval, the rates of outlay, DO' and DO'', are functions, not of the indices of quantities sold at the final markets, Q' and Q'', but of these indices corrected by the acceleration factors a' and a''. Thus, when the productive process is expanding or contracting, DO' is some price-level index multiplied by $a'Q'$, and DO'' is some price-level index multiplied by $a''Q''$. In expansions, a' and a'' are greater than unity, since current production is for future greater sales; in contractions, a' and a'' are less than unity, since then current production is for future reduced sales. Let us now introduce two cost-price indices, p' and p'', which are defined by the equations

$$(1 - G')DO' = p'a'Q' \qquad (45)$$

$$G''DO'' = p''a''Q'' \qquad (46)$$

whence by equation (3)

$$DI' = p'a'Q' + p''a''Q'' \qquad (47)$$

Now, when DD' satisfies general conditions of circuit acceleration by being zero, so that DE' equals DI', then since DE' equals $P'Q'$ one may write

$$P'Q' = p'a'Q' + p''a''Q'' \qquad (48)$$

Dividing through by $p'Q'$ one may write

$$J = P'/p' = a' + a''R \qquad (49)$$

where J is the basic price-spread ratio, being the selling-price index P' divided by the cost-price index p', and R is the ratio of surplus to basic activity indicated by the fraction $p''Q''/p'Q'$. It follows that the basic price-spread ratio J is the sum of the basic acceleration factor a' and of the product of the surplus acceleration factor a'' with the surplus-to-basic ratio R.

Variations in R involve no new elements. At a first estimate R will be increasing during the surplus expansion when Q''/Q' is increasing, but decreasing during the basic expansion when Q''/Q' is decreasing. Taking into account the further quotient p''/p', one would expect it to be constant, inasmuch as cost prices in basic and surplus units have the same general determinants; and inasmuch as there arose any divergence between p'' and p', one would expect it to reinforce our initial estimate; p''/p' would increase, if anything, in the surplus expansion, but would decrease, if anything, in the basic expansion.

The influence of R on the aggregate basic price spread is obvious. The greater the fraction of total basic income that is derived from surplus outlay, the less the fraction of total basic income that is derived from basic outlay. But total basic income becomes basic expenditure and basic receipts. And the source of basic price spread is the difference between basic receipts and the fraction of basic outlay going to basic income. A very rough illustration may be had if we identify basic income with aggregate wages, and aggregate wages with costs of all production and, as well, with the receipts of basic sales. Then the greater the surplus activity, the greater the surplus aggregate wages, the smaller the fraction of total wages paid by basic producers, the smaller the fraction of total costs paid by basic producers, and the smaller the fraction of basic receipts required to meet basic costs.

The influence of the acceleration factors is also easily understood. The greater current production relative to current final sales, then the greater the price spread, provided that all current income is spent for the relatively smaller quantity that is finished and now on sale. The exact behavior of the acceleration factors, however, introduces a new element for our consideration. Introducing the symbol q' as identical with $a'Q'$, and differentiating the consequent identity, one obtains

$$da' = a'(dq'/q' - dQ'/Q') \qquad (50)$$

and by changing (′) to (″) one has the parallel equation for da''. Hence, for the acceleration factor a' to be increasing, it is necessary for da' to be positive and so for $(dq'/q' - dQ'/Q')$ to be positive. (Q', q', and a' are always positive.) This means that the acceleration factor can be positive only when the rate of current production of basic quantities is increasing more rapidly in proportion to its size than the rate of current sales of basic quantities is increasing in proportion to its size. Thus, if one supposes that

q' moves ahead of Q', the acceleration factor moves above unity; but as soon as the quantities under production reach the final market, Q' accelerates; if, then, q' is accelerating at the higher rate proportionate to its greater size, a' will be at a maximum and remain constant as long as the acceleration of q' increases with a'; but as soon as the acceleration of q' ceases to mount ever more rapidly, a' begins to fall. The same holds for the surplus acceleration factor a''. Evidently, the acceleration factors are magnificently unstable. The initial lag of quantities sold behind quantities produced enables them to rise above unity. But merely to keep them constant once quantities sold begin to mount means that quantities under production have to increase in a geometrical progression for the rest of the expansion. Any failure to maintain this brilliant pace means that the acceleration factors, and so the basic price spread, drop.

Now in any expansion it is inevitable that quantities under production run ahead of quantities sold. Current production is with reference to future sales, and if there is an expansion, then future sales are going to be greater than current sales. But in the free economies the acceleration factors are not held down to the minimum that results from this consideration. During the surplus expansion the basic price-spread ratio J will increase from an increase of R, of a'', and also of a'. The advance of the price-spread ratio will work out through a rise of basic price level, and selling prices generally will mount. Now, when prices are rising and due to rise further, the thing to be done is to buy now when prices are low and sell later when they are high. There results a large amount of speculative liquid investment. Each producer orders more materials, more semifinished goods, more finished goods, than he would otherwise. Moreover, he makes this speculative addition to a future demand estimated upon current orders received, so that the further back in the production series any producer is, the greater the speculative element contained in the objective evidence of current orders received, the more rosy the estimate of future demand, and the greater the speculative element he adds to this estimate when he places orders with a producer still further back in the series.

Thus an initial rise in prices sets going a speculative expansion that makes the acceleration factors quite notable, expands the price spread still more, and stimulates a pace of further acceleration that it will be quite impossible to maintain. Differentiating equation (49) one has

$$dJ = da' + Rda'' + a''dR \tag{51}$$

Here the cyclic factors are R and dR: in the surplus expansion, R is increasing and dR is positive; in the basic expansion, R is decreasing and dR is negative. R is a fractional quantity, and dR the increment of a fraction. On the other hand, as long as expansion continues, the surplus acceleration factor a'' will be greater than unity. Upon this background enters the performance of da' and da'', with the former preponderant since the coefficient of da'' is the fraction R.

Now during initial proportionate expansion dR will be zero, but da' and da'' will be positive for a while as a short-term acceleration develops. At least in the basic stage it will prove impossible to maintain a generalized rate of expansion in a geometrical progression, so that da' will become negative. The event will probably take place when the surplus acceleration factor a'' has reached a high-level rate so that da'' is zero. It follows that dJ becomes negative with da', and in this dJ will be all the more negative if there is any faltering in the surplus stage to give a negative da'' as well. Thus the price-spread ratio J contracts; the basic price level falls; speculators are disillusioned. There is a minor crisis: first, speculative assets are frozen as everyone wishes to sell before prices fall further, and no one wishes to buy until they fall further; then there is a period of liquidation as liquid assets are sold for whatever price they will fetch. The gravity of this first crisis will depend exclusively upon the magnitude of the speculative development, the solvency of speculators, and their ability to weather the storm without liquidating their stocks. Whether it is a squall or a tempest, the underlying long-term development soon sets things right. For as the surplus stage generalizes long-term acceleration, R increases and dR becomes positive to expand again the price spread and to keep it expanding. As this proceeds, there develops another speculative boom. The surplus acceleration factor a'' mounts and remains constant at its maximum; the basic acceleration factor a' mounts and then contracts; previous phenomena are repeated with the difference that the negative da' is mitigated by a positive dR, and that throughout this crisis there is at work a positive dR to bring things back to an even keel. When the rate of expansion is restored, the basic stage will move into a general long-term acceleration; for a while yet dR will remain positive and a third speculative boom develops. This boom suffers no restrictions from a limited potential for short-term acceleration, since both stages are now expanding in long-term style. Both acceleration factors can mount to that maxima and remain at the summits with da' and da'' both zero. Further variations of the price spread thus depend exclusively upon dR, and this becomes negative as the surplus expansion gives place to a basic expansion. When then prices begin to fall to effect the continual reduction of the price spread, there follows sooner or later the real and final crash. Speculative embarrassment makes both da' and da'' negative, to augment the rate of contraction of the price spread and intensify the embarrassment. Assets are frozen and then liquidated in a great drop of prices. Worse, there is no recovery; for the remainder of the cycle should be a basic expansion which our ill-adapted economies transform into a depression.

It may be noted that the triple crisis per cycle may perhaps correspond to Professor Schumpeter's combination of three small cycles named Kitchins in one larger cycle named a Juglar, which has a ten-year period.[4] The pattern of six Juglars in one sixty-year Kondratieff would seem to result from the quasi logical connection between successive long-term accelerations. A fundamental transformation of the capital equipment of an economy needs preparatory long-term accelerations that open the way for it; and once the fundamental transformation is achieved, there are other subsidiary transformations that for the first time become concrete possibilities. Such a time series has more affinities with a philosophic theory of history than the merely mechanical structures that we have been examining. A theory of the Kondratieff is in terms of the precise nature of the fundamental transformation, for example, railroads, but the theory of the Juglar and Kitchin that has been developed here depends solely upon the structure of the productive process and the measure of human adaptation to the requirements of an acceleration in that structure.

It is to be recalled that the account given of the cycle of the basic price-spread ratio supposes DD' to be zero throughout. A speculative boom in the stock market which encourages basic spending may be represented by a positive DD': there is an excess release of money from the redistributional function to the basic demand function. Alternatively, it may be represented by an upward revision of the fractions g_i of total current income going to basic demand, while the fact that the surplus final market suffers no contraction then results from the excess of the rate of new fixed investment over the rate of pure surplus income, so that DD'' is positive. In either case, a movement of this type with its basis in redistributional optimism will offset any tendency towards a contraction of the price spread and will reinforce any tendency of the price spread to expand. On the

4 See Joseph Schumpeter, *Business Cycles: A Theoretical, Historical and Statistical Analysis of the Capitalist Process* (New York: McGraw-Hill, 1939; paperback ed., 1964; original German, two vols. 1939) 170–73.

other hand, the subsequent stockmarket break intensifies the crisis of the circuits, removing the props that had hitherto swollen expansive tendencies, and leaving the system with a greater height from which to fall.

19

Superposed Circuits

16 Superposed Circuits

There are sets of phenomena, notably the favorable and unfavorable balances of foreign trade, deficit government spending, and the payment of public debts by taxation, that are analogous to the phenomena of the cycle. It is proposed to deal with them under the general title of 'superposed circuits.' In our general account of the monetary circulation, two circuits, a basic and a surplus, were distinguished. They were interconnected with a crossover. But they involved no regular flow through the redistributive function; that function stood, as it were, outside the circuits, a source of more money for expansions and a refuge for money during contractions, but not a regular stop in the circulation of money as far as the productive process was concerned.

There is, however, no impossibility of the redistributive function becoming a point through which a circuit regularly passes. On the other hand, such a circuit both presupposes and is distinct from the basic and surplus circuits already considered. Hence, the name of superposed circuits, and also the mode of treatment. For any superposed circuit may be represented by rates of payment, DZ' and DZ'', per interval added to variables of the circulation diagram as follows:

(1) $DD' + DZ'$ — $DD'' + DZ''$
(2) $DE' + DZ'$ — $DE'' + DZ''$
(3) $G'DO' + DZ'$ — $(1 - G'')DO'' + DZ''$
(4) $DD'' - DZ' - DZ''$

The foregoing additions and, in the last case, subtractions are supposed to be made to or from the other rates, *DD′*, *DD″*, *DE′*, *DE″*, and so on, as they are determined generally. No doubt the additions or subtractions modify these rates, reinforce or counteract the tendencies of whatever phase may be in progress. Our purpose in representing them as above is not at all to deny such interaction but rather to gain a viewpoint from which such interaction may be studied. The viewpoint adopted is that of the circuit: the circular route of *DZ′* and *DZ″* is a different route from that of basic or surplus expenditure, outlay, or income; there exists a partial coincidence, but its significance varies with the nature of the superposed circuit; and there is never a total coincidence since the redistributive function is a regular port of call in the superposed circuit.

In any given interval, *DZ′* is the same value no matter whether it is added to *DD′* or *DE′* or *G′DO′* or subtracted from *DD″*. Further, the addition or subtraction always occurs in each of the four cases. These two conditions are necessary to have a circular movement of a sum of money, *DZ′*, per interval. The same holds for *DZ″*. On the other hand, from one interval to another, the quantity represented by *DZ′*, or by *DZ″*, may vary. However, since our interest is to examine the superposed circuit in itself rather than the effect of its variations, in general it will be convenient to suppose that *DZ′* and *DZ″* are constant over a series of intervals. Finally, there never is any need of *DZ′* and *DZ″* being equal.

As represented by the list of additions to the circuit diagram, a superposed circuit consists of the following eight movements per interval: from the redistributive function, *DZ′* to basic demand and *DZ″* to surplus demand; from basic demand, *DZ′* to basic supply, and from surplus demand, *DZ″* to surplus supply; from basic supply, *DZ′* to surplus demand, and from surplus supply, *DZ″* to surplus demand; from surplus demand, *DZ′* and *DZ″* to the redistributive function. In any given interval either *DZ′* or *DZ″* may be zero; but if both are zero, there is no superposed circuit.

In studying the superposed circuits one may begin at any function to move in either direction. One may begin anywhere because the total movement is circular. One may move in either direction, for one may ask where the money goes or where it is coming from. Finally, one may regard the eight movements as simultaneous: they all occur within the same interval; the condition of a circulation is satisfied if they occur within the interval; and the condition of a circulation is the one condition required. In fact, a certain amount of short-term financing will be required to enable some function to pay before it receives its *DZ′* or its *DZ″* either in whole or in part; or else the superposed circuit will be a circuit in virtue of a lag; but such minor phenomena need not be discussed in the general inquiry.

17 The Balance of Foreign Trade

There is an evident analogy between the rate of new fixed investment and a favorable balance of foreign trade. In both cases the rates of current production exceed, within the given area, the sum of the rate of current consumption and of the rate of capital replacements and maintenance. In both cases there results accordingly a rate of pure surplus income which really is the new fixed investment or the excess export but has as well a monetary equivalent in the difference between total outlay, which is proportionate to total production, and total consumption and replacement income, which are proportionate to a fraction only of total production.

The interest of the free economies in a favorable balance of foreign trade has a very solid foundation. Prior to the full development of monetary techniques, an excess export of goods and services was balanced by an excess import of gold; this increased the quantity of money available in the economy; and this increase in the economy made possible an equal increase in the circuits. But the expansion of the circuits is, in large part, conditioned by the possibility of increasing the quantity of money available for the transactions of the circuits. Thus a favorable balance of trade, balanced by a favorable balance of gold imports, was a means of satisfying a principal condition for economic expansion.

However, this monetary interest in a favorable balance of trade is far from the sole interest in it. The favorable balance adds an equal amount to the rate of pure surplus income; with pure surplus income at the nerve center of economies based more and more on the ideal of the 'successful man,' this addition to the rate of pure surplus was, while it lasted, an unmitigated blessing. It augmented the rate of pure surplus in surplus expansions. It offset the rate of losses in depressions, and it did this in two distinct ways: first, it tended to cancel out any rate of losses that otherwise would appear; second, it tended to prevent such a hypothetical appearance. The first point is obvious. The second follows from the fact that the rate of losses results from the economy's inability to reduce sufficiently the rate of net aggregate savings; but the need of bringing about such a reduction rests on the fact that basic quantities are increasing more rapidly than surplus; evidently, in the measure in which the production of increasing basic quantities may be replaced by the production of increasing quantities of goods and services for an increasing favorable foreign balance, in that measure the turn of the process towards basic expansion is eliminated; and there follows the elimination of a tendency towards decreasing savings with the consequent rate of losses.

The theoretical significance of the foregoing is considerable. It provides an explanation both of nineteenth-century practice and of nineteenth-century theory. The nineteenth-century economy did not need, as we need, a rigorous adaptation to the pure cycle of the productive process, because then the phenomena of the pure cycle could be covered over by the favorable balance of foreign trade. Further, under such circumstances a theorist would not have his attention directed to cycles as matters of scientific moment, for the very good reason that, since their phenomena were covered over in part, they would be regarded naturally and spontaneously as incidental complexes of relatively arbitrary events. Accordingly, we turn to a more detailed consideration of the circuits involved in a favorable balance of foreign trade.

The assumption of the closed economy is now dropped. One supposes the existence of a number of economies, each with its redistributive function and its basic and surplus circuits. It will be convenient to assume that transactions between economies take place between their redistributive functions: thus goods and services leaving one economy for the benefit of another leave the one as redistributive goods or services and enter the other as redistributive goods or services; similarly, payments enter and leave by the redistributive function.

Consider, then, an economy that, over a series of intervals, has a favorable balance of foreign trade of $DZ' + DZ''$ per interval. Then in each interval it produces, over and above all domestic requirements, DZ' worth of basic goods and services and DZ'' worth of surplus goods and services. Exporters purchase these products by moving from the redistributive function to basic demand DZ', and to surplus demand DZ''; both sums are there spent to give $DE' + DZ'$ and $DE'' + DZ''$. The resultant receipts contain $DZ' + DZ''$ of surplus income, that is, of income that need be spent at neither final market; hence we have the movements $G'DO' + DZ'$ and $(1 - G'')DO'' + DZ''$ and then $DD'' - DZ' - DZ''$ as the surplus income is counted pure surplus and moved from surplus demand to the redistributive function. To close the circuit it is necessary to connect this movement of pure surplus income to the redistributive function with the movement by exporters of an equal sum from the redistributive function to the final markets.

Such a connection can be operated in a variety of ways. The exporters receive from abroad either a gold import or a foreign debt or the cancellation of a domestic debt abroad. For such payment to be acceptable to the exporters, it must be negotiable on the domestic redistributive market. The general condition of negotiability is that the exporters by their subsequent use of the money they receive do not drain the redistributive function of its funds. This general condition is satisfied by the movement of the pure surplus income into the redistributive function at the same rate as exporters move money out of the redistributive function. Provided then there exist markets in short-term bills and long-term securities or for gold, and provided the pure surplus is spent on these markets, the general condition will be satisfied.

The international monetary phenomena are quite simple. In a first period, payments are made in gold. The countries with the favorable balance are thus enabled to undertake expansions in virtue of their increased stocks of money. The countries with the unfavorable balance suffer equal contractions, until they discover the cause of the trouble. Then they practice the doctrine of mercantilism: foreign trade is controlled so that there is no unfavorable balance of trade. In the long run, the only countries that will balance an excess import by the export of gold are either gold-producing countries or else backward economies in which there exist stocks of gold which can be de-hoarded. In a second period, there develops the practice of foreign lending. Countries with unfavorable balances of trade have bills of exchange pile up against them in the exporting countries; these are liquidated by floating long-term foreign loans or, when an economy which previously enjoyed a favorable balance turns to an unfavorable balance, by selling domestically owned foreign securities.

Some of the domestic features of an economy enjoying a favorable balance have already been noted. The rate of excess export involves an equal rate of pure surplus income that augments the benefits of an expansion, provides a substitute for them when there is no expansion, counteracts the tendency for a rate of losses in a basic expansion, and tends to eliminate basic expansions by directing into an increasing excess export what otherwise would have been an increasing rate of domestic consumption with consequently contracting savings. Thus an economy operating with a favorable balance enjoys a cushioned domestic cycle. As far as the domestic cycle is concerned, it can proceed on the principles of increasing thrift and enterprise which are normative generally only in the surplus expansion. On the other hand, the favorable balance itself will be conditioned by the cycles in foreign economies. If the importing countries are sufficiently developed exchange economies to experience the cycle, and if the volume of international trade is sufficiently large to effect a general synchronism of cycles, then so far from mitigating domestic cycles the effect of foreign trade will be to reinforce them tremendously. On the other hand, when the synchronism is lacking, and still more when the importing countries are colonial economies with little domestic commerce or industry, such reinforcement does not occur. The existence of the cushioning effect would seem established by the fact that in England basic wage rates did not begin to rise until 1870; that would suggest that previous basic expansions had been avoided successfully by diverting increased potential into an increased excess export. And to some extent, at least, the same fact confirms the advantage of conducting foreign trade with colonies and primitive countries.

The inverse phenomena to the favorable balance result from the unfavorable balance of foreign trade. Then either or both the emergent standard of living and the increment of capital equipment of the economy are in excess of its basic and surplus rates of production. Insofar as the excess import does not enter domestic channels of industry and commerce, there is no superposed circuit: importers purchase and use or consume the excess import within the redistributive function. However, in that case they are not importers in the sense of a class of dealers; no large rate of import can be managed in that fashion, for large imports have to be sold on the regular final markets of the domestic economy. Let, then, the rate of the excess import sold on the domestic final markets be once more DZ' and DZ''. Then domestic entrepreneurs direct part of their gross receipts, as though they were pure surplus income, to surplus demand and thence to the redistributive function. This gives elements (3) and (4), namely, $G'DO' + DZ'$, $(1 - G'')DO'' + DZ''$, and $DD'' - DZ' - DZ''$. Thus domestic entrepreneurs purchase the excess import from the importers in the redistributive function and transfer it to the stocks of the domestic basic and surplus markets. There it is sold to the domestic public, to give $DE' + DZ'$ and $DE'' + DZ''$. It is true that the domestic public will pay more than DZ' and DZ''; however, the difference will be the wages, rents, and interest due to domestic production factors; it will circulate in the ordinary fashion; and so we need not be concerned with it. On the other hand, the DZ' and DZ'' ends up in the redistributive function where it pays the importers who pay the foreign sellers with gold, with the contraction of foreign debts, or with the sale of domestically owned foreign securities. The problem of the unfavorable balance is to close the circuit by moving to the domestic public the money the importers receive from domestic entrepreneurs and pay to domestic sellers of gold or securities. This involves the $DD' + DZ'$ and the $DD'' + DZ''$.

The $DD'' + DZ''$ is analogous to the rate of new fixed investment in the domestic expansion. Domestic surplus demand is borrowing from the redistributive function at the rate DZ'' per interval to purchase goods or services for the maintenance, replacement, or net increment of domestic capital equipment. But there is a grave difference. In the domestic expansion or in the purchase through borrowing (which may include borrowing from one's own holdings in the redistributive function) of domestically produced replacements, the rate of movement from the redistributive function to surplus demand is balanced by a rate of income moving from surplus demand to the redistributive function. But in the present case, the balancing movement is not a rate of income, for the goods sold were not produced domestically and so generate no income; the balancing rate is simply a rate of payment for the current supply of the goods and services of the excess import. The consequence is that, if the excess import is replacement goods, then domestic industry does not pay its own way but has to borrow, to the extent DZ'' per interval, to keep its capital equipment up to date. And if the excess import is an increment of existing capital yielding an acceleration of the process, then the economy conducts a long-term acceleration, at the rate DZ'' of new capital equipment per interval, without enjoying any pure surplus income such as is enjoyed when the increment of equipment is domestically produced. Hence, the greater DZ'' is relatively to DE'', the greater the difficulty of investors contemplating the maintenance, replacement, or increment of capital equipment; for evidently if capital notably fails to support itself and yields only a mediocre flow of pure surplus income, investment is unattractive. Hence, just as the favorable balance of trade intensifies the joy of expansion, so the unfavorable balance dims that joy. With foreign debts mounting or foreign holdings decreasing, the economy with an unfavorable balance reacts very sluggishly indeed to opportunities for expansion. And while brilliant prospects of great developments in the future may overcome this sluggishness in a young country, the matter is quite different in an old country that once was a creditor but since has become a rentier to the world.

Even more intractable is the other component of the movement from the redistributive function to demand, $DD' + DZ'$. The possibility of such a transference arises mainly in two cases; there is the case of oriental princes de-hoarding gold to purchase occidental trumperies; there is the case of the rentier class living on the interest or principal of foreign holdings. In either case money is moved at a rate, say DZ', from the redistributive function to basic demand. On the other hand, it is to be noted that rentier spending of interest, on domestic industrial bonds for instance, does not meet the requirements of the problem: such interest is a part of domestic income and must be spent interval by interval either in itself or equivalently by others spending more than they earn; hence it does not create the possibility of an additional movement from the redistributive function to basic demand.

Now evidently it may happen easily that the movement $DD' + DZ'$ fails to occur either in whole or in part. The consequences of such a failure vary with the country's balance of foreign payments and with the phase in which the economy is moving. Let us first suppose that the unfavorable balance of trade is necessary for the balance of payments; we deal then with an economy that once was a creditor but since has become a rentier; opportunities for foreign lending no longer keep pace with the interest and dividends due to former loans made abroad, and so if there is to be payment by foreign economies, the payment now must be in goods and services. In such a situation the failure of $DD' + DZ'$ may occur during a surplus expansion; then the required rate of savings tends to exceed the actual rate of savings, and so the failure is all to the good, for the excess import of basic products makes up for excessive monetary basic income. However, insofar as the excess import includes surplus goods and services, there are apt to be special difficulties in surplus expansion occurring, as was argued above; and so the problem of $DD'' + DZ''$ can make this happy solution of the failure of $DD' + DZ'$ somewhat rarer than might be anticipated.

Apart from the occurrence of a surplus expansion, the failure of $DD' + DZ'$ generates the phenomena of a depression. More goods and services are moving to the basic final market than there is monetary income to pay for them at current prices. The situation is repeated in each successive interval, and so prices fall continuously. Further, as they fall aggregate outlay and income shrink, both from the contraction of the price index and from the consequent reduction of scales of operation; hence the DZ' becomes relatively more and more important. Now, if prices are allowed to fall and the domestic economy to contract sufficiently, there comes a time when the excess import can no longer be sold on the domestic final market; it cannot compete with domestic prices, and it cannot be demanded by domestic rates of income. This, however, not only is a painful operation upon the domestic economy but also it will force foreign debtors to repudiate their debts since they no longer have any possibility of paying them in goods and services. The alternative to such a doubly unpleasant decision is to force the recipients of interest and dividends on foreign holdings to spend their income on the basic final market. Since such recipients will be relatively few in number, they cannot undertake personally so great a rate of consumer expenditure. However, the depression has notably augmented the numbers of the unemployed, and so the brilliant expedient of a steep income tax on the rich to provide a dole for the poor will effect the required $DD' + DZ'$; the upper leisure class of rentiers is recruited from a lower leisure class of unemployed. Obviously an economy that has worked itself into this impasse is not to be regarded as a model of enlightened legislation for other economies more fortunately placed; its 'social security' and other programs may or may not be defensible from the viewpoint of the difficulties they solve; but such a defense cannot be applied to mimic procedures in totally different situations.

So much for the unfavorable balance of trade that effects a balance of payments. When the unfavorable balance of trade means that a rate of foreign borrowing is needed to effect the balance of payments, phenomena are simpler inasmuch as the foreign borrowing can be ended by the introduction of sufficiently vigorous controls. The fact that Australia rationed the import of automobiles is suggestive. Modern ideas on 'managed money,' that is, of an expansion of credit in accordance with the needs of domestic industry and commerce, have to be complemented with the fear that the monetary expansion may stimulate the purchase of imported goods more than the industrial and commercial expansion stimulates the export trade. When such a fear proves grounded, there results an unfavorable balance; and the bold ideas on money, especially when put forward by confiscators of private property, do little to reassure foreign lenders. With foreign lenders not forthcoming, the unfavorable balance of trade has to end, and if the 'managed money' is to be maintained, it postulates a government control of imports and an orientation towards economic autarky. However, the issue before us is the movement from the redistributive function to the circuits that gives a $DD' + DZ'$ while the unfavorable balance of trade persists. In the situation of a bold monetary expansion stimulating the purchase of imports, the movement from the redistributive function is to the supply and not to the demand function; it is a $DS' + DZ'$ or a $DS'' + DZ''$ and not a $DD' + DZ'$. This movement initially finances an increment in entrepreneurial scales of operation, but instead of this increment being sold at the final markets, there is sold the excess import. The resultant contraction may be delayed, however, by a fuller boldness of monetary policy. As long as the increment in production is to be sold at surplus markets, it can be bought by borrowers, so that the problem of providing a $DD' + DZ'$ is being solved by providing both a $DS'' + DZ'$ and a $DD'' + DZ'$; the former DZ' expands turnover magnitudes, becomes basic income, is spent for the excess import, and so moves back to the redistributive function; the latter DZ' purchases the increment in the rate of production and then circulates normally to maintain that increment. This is a case of surplus expansion not yielding pure surplus income: the DZ' that moves to the redistributive function is not income but payment for the excess import; and it is accompanied by an increase in debts of $2DZ'$ per interval, apart from the increase due to DZ''. When, however, the domestic expansion puts goods on the basic final market, contraction results. The only escape is for these goods to be exported, and that will end the unfavorable balance of trade. Thus it should seem that a debtor country can meet the requirement for a $DD' + DZ'$ only during an expansion of the surplus stage of its productive process, and only by paying for the excess basic import by increasing its long-term capital debt by DZ' per interval.

18 Deficit Spending and Taxes

Deficit spending and the taxes which sustain it reproduce simultaneously the phenomena of both the favorable and the unfavorable balance of foreign trade. Let us suppose a public authority to borrow and spend DZ' per interval at the basic final market and DZ'' per interval at the surplus final market. Let us suppose that the taxation to meet interest and provide amortization against past and present borrowing is DY' per interval derived from the basic circuit and DY'' per interval derived from the surplus circuit. Then the superposed circuits will be

$$
\begin{array}{lllll}
(1) & DD' + DZ' + DY' & — & DD'' + DZ'' + DY'' \\
(2) & DE' + DZ' + DY' & — & DE'' + DZ'' + DY'' \\
(3) & G'DO' + DZ' + DY' & — & (1 - G'')DO'' + DZ'' + DY'' \\
(4) & DD'' - DZ' - DZ'' - DY' - DY'' & &
\end{array}
$$

We shall consider first the government spending, second the taxes, and third the ultimate alternative between bankruptcy and vigorous retrenchment, that is, the disappearance of DZ' and DZ'' and the intensification of DY' and DY''.

Government spending is simple. In each interval DZ' is spent at the basic final market for any type of goods or services that have no tendency to accelerate the productive process, while DZ'' is spent at the surplus final market for goods and services with that tendency. There results a corresponding increment in income which, as it has nothing to buy at either final market, is counted as surplus and is moved to the redistributive function where directly or indirectly it purchases government securities. Thus in each interval, labor, land, and capital are providing $DZ' + DZ''$ of goods and services. Those who do the required monetary saving are built into a solid and richly endowed rentier class at the rate $DZ' + DZ''$ per interval. The community possesses the goods and services but, unless it is going into business deliberately, their productive value will be slight. Finally, the public debt mounts by the same rate, $DZ' + DZ''$ per interval.

The rate of debt servicing, $DY' + DY''$, becomes more and more significant as the rate of deficit spending is maintained over a longer period. The movement from the circuits to the redistributive function causes no difficulty. Income is taxed, directly or indirectly, to give the third and fourth elements in this circuit. In the redistributive function, DY'' per interval is paid to amortization, and DY' per interval is paid as interest to the rentiers. However, if money is to be moved from the circuits to the redistributive function without causing a contracting, it is necessary that the inflow be balanced by an equal outflow.[1]

1 As Lonergan noted in the table of contents, this discussion is incomplete. The text reproduced in chapter 13 helps towards a more complete view, and the diagram at the conclusion of that chapter applies equally here. Useful also is Philip McShane, 'Government and Globe,' chapter 4 of *Economics for Everyone. Das Jus Kapital* (Halifax: Axial Press, 1998).

Appendix: The Date of 'For a New Political Economy'

FREDERICK E. CROWE

When 'For a New Political Economy' came to our attention some eleven years ago, it was known to be earlier than the 1944 work 'An Essay in Circulation Analysis,' and in a vague way we dated it around 1942. The present aim is not to overthrow that vague surmise but to provide it with a more solid basis in the evidence.

First, a word on the history of the manuscript itself, for as the proverb says, 'A book has its fortunes.'[1] Back in 1986, just a year after the Lonergan Research Institute opened, we had a visit from Eric Kierans, who brought with him for our Archives a precious typescript of whose existence we had been unaware. It was the work we publish now, as the first part of the present volume, under the title Lonergan gave it: 'For a New Political Economy.' Indeed, so succinctly does that phrase describe a major concern of Lonergan's in the early 1940s that we usurp it for the title of this whole volume of archival drafts and notes and fragments and scribbles on economics, here presented as volume 21 of the Collected Works.

Kierans had been taught by Lonergan at Loyola College, Montreal, 1931–33, and was regarded by him as one of the best pupils he had ever had. From 1933 to 1945, however, Kierans lived in Halifax, and lost contact with his teacher. In the fall of 1945, now back in Montreal, he was invited by Fr Eric O'Connor to be part of the newly opening Thomas More Insti-

1 Credited to Walter Pater in John Bartlett, *Familiar Quotations,* 11th ed. (Garden City, NY: Garden City Publishing, 1937).

tute where Lonergan also was active, so contact was renewed, and Lonergan became a frequent visitor to the Kierans home.

About 1948 Kierans, dissatisfied with the 'commercial' life and 'curious about the economic forces shaping the small manufacturer's world,' decided to go to McGill University and study economics. It turned out that 'he spent twenty-two years – fully half of his working life – as a student and a teacher at McGill.'[2] It is at this point that we pick up the story of 'For a New Political Economy.' Lonergan, now stationed in Toronto but still in close contact with his Montreal friends and associates, one day handed Kierans the manuscript of FNPE with the remark, 'I hear you are going to study economics. Well, here's a start. This is old stuff; I've written something new; this is easier to start on.'

One could write an interesting chapter here on the contacts Kierans mediated for Lonergan with McGill professors and other economists, but my present focus is the history of the FNPE manuscript, so I add simply that, in this context and some years later, when Kierans remarked on the possible interest of economists in Lonergan's work, the latter gave him a copy of his new work 'An Essay in Circulation Analysis,' and when asked whether he wanted the first one back, replied, 'No, this is much more up-to-date' – as if regretting that first effort. Indeed, later still by some years he seemed to have quite forgotten it for, when Kierans told him he thought the first thing was better, Lonergan replied, 'What first thing?'[3]

So we come to the present task and attempt to pinpoint the date of 'For a New Political Economy.' This is a matter of fixing on two sides the boundaries in time: necessarily after one date (*terminus ante quem non*) and necessarily before another (*terminus post quem non*). Further, we do this in a series of ever narrowing pincer movements that bring us to a period fixed with probability between the summer of 1942 and the summer of 1943.

Of no particular value for our detective story but of general interest is the way the 'early Lonergan' style shows up in this work, due no doubt to his eleven years in Europe, four of them in England. So we have 'lorries' (p. 16) instead of trucks, and 'It should seem' (passim) instead of the 'It would seem' more common on our side of the Atlantic.

But let us get to more precise boundaries. First of all, the essay is a war-

2 Jamie Swift, *Odd Man Out: The Life and Times of Eric Kierans* (Vancouver and Toronto: Douglas & McIntyre, 1988) 25.
3 Personal communication from Eric Kierans.

time work; references to 'wartorn Europe' (p. 31) and to the difficulties we will have to face 'after the war' (p. 4) make that clear enough. But there is a quotation from Churchill that gives us a very precise *terminus ante quem non*: 'Certainly we intend, as Mr. Churchill modestly remarked, to give a good account of ourselves' (p. 3). This is an exact quotation from an address broadcast by Churchill on 9 February 1941.[4] Further, it is not an insert into a previously completed manuscript; the typing and pagination show that it was integral to the final form of the work as Lonergan presented it in the manuscript we have. Allowing some months, then, for the final composition, we are safe in assigning a narrower boundary and fixing the date of the completed work as no earlier than the summer of 1941.

Now I believe it is possible to narrow down this boundary by one more year. It is highly probable, on the basis of an interview which Lonergan had with Richard Renshaw, that the *terminus ante quem non* can be fixed as the summer of 1942. For Renshaw brought up the topic of the reviews Lonergan wrote for a Montreal paper in the early 1940s and the interest they showed in a certain problematic, to which Lonergan replied: 'I did, and I was working on it for a while there. After I published [my] thesis, did the Gratia operans articles, I went back to economics; I had worked on that during the thirties before theology.'[5]

Lonergan goes on to speak of his professor of ethics in England, Lewis Watt, of *Quadragesimo anno* and its recommendation of a family wage, and so on. These are matters of considerable interest in the total history; my interest, however, focuses on the remark, 'After I published ... the *Gratia operans* articles, I went back to economics.' The final article in the *Gratia operans* series appeared in the December 1942 issue of *Theological Studies*, and in this article Lonergan refers over and over to the previous three articles, including the third, which had appeared in the September issue, in every case giving exact page references. Final tidying up of the fourth article (mainly inserting references) has therefore to be dated in the late summer of 1942 after the third article had appeared and, given Lonergan's care for accuracy in his published work and the need of a thorough

4 *Blood, Sweat, and Tears* (New York: Putnam's Sons, 1941) 460. There is a somewhat similar remark in a letter from Churchill to Roosevelt, 18 May 1940, but that was not public knowledge till after the war; see *Their Finest Hour* (Boston: Houghton Mifflin, 1949) 56.

5 Interview of 18 January 1973, p. 3 of the transcript kindly supplied by Fr Renshaw.

acquaintance with the earlier articles for accurate references in the fourth, I regard it as quite certain that he performed this final task himself.

Of course, an issue of *Theological Studies* does not appear overnight, but allowing for that factor and on the basis of the Renshaw interview I would suggest a scenario like this: Lonergan wrote the fourth *Gratia operans* article in the early summer of 1942, got the proofs back about September when the third article had now been published and come to hand, filled in the references to the third while correcting the proofs of the fourth, and some time around this period, perhaps in the early summer when the fourth *Gratia operans* article was on the way to the press, turned back to economics. In that case there is a fair probability that Lonergan did not begin work on FNPE till the summer of 1942. (There is a point to speaking of the 'summer,' of which more in a moment.)

The boundary on the other side, the *terminus post quem non,* could, by an excess of caution, be put forward to 1944, since that is the date of 'An Essay in Circulation Analysis,' and FNPE was prior to ECA, according to Lonergan's remark when he handed FNPE over to Kierans, 'This is old stuff; I've written something new.'

But, of course, we have again to allow time for the writing of ECA. How far back does that take us? One tends to think of 1943, for the great advances in ECA require time (see the Editor's Introduction above), and one last little piece of evidence supports the choice of 1943 as a *terminus post quem non* for FNPE. Our clue has to do with the famous 'baseball diamond' diagram. Neither FNPE nor ECA has the copyright sign on the top page of the manuscript, and neither of the two has it on the 'diagram.' But the 1978 version of ECA has 'Copyright © 1978' on the title page of the manuscript and, more important, the diagram, which is that of 1944 slightly altered, has 'Copyright © 1943, 1977' (p. 42). That '1943' is of some significance for our question. It suggests that Lonergan was working on the diagram of ECA in that year and so by this time had put FNPE aside.

If, then, at one end we allow some months, definitely after 9 February 1941, and probably after the early summer of 1942, for work on FNPE in its final form, and likewise at the other end allow a year for the writing of ECA, we can assign the date of FNPE with some probability as a point in time between mid-1942 and mid-1943. While this hardly changes our surmise of a decade ago, it does give us the academic satisfaction of collecting the clues and replacing a surmise with the available evidence.

Of course, we are talking about the final form of FNPE. What evidence is there of earlier drafts? I have to leave aside any evidence there may be in the archival papers but, given Lonergan's repeated statement that he had worked on the question from about 1930, and especially his remark[6] about his many tries at what finally became the 'baseball diamond' diagram, given also his 'old stuff' remark to Kierans, it is possible – I hesitate to say probable – that FNPE, or parts of it, had been drafted earlier in some form or other.

At this point it would be of interest to have a clear picture of Lonergan's general situation and work habits during those four years from 1940 to 1944. At least it would help us fit his concern with economics into the wider context of his theological career.

Lonergan had finished work for his doctorate, and was waiting in Rome to defend his thesis, when in May 1940 the war took a new turn and he was ordered home. He took ship at Genoa and arrived in New York on 24 May. For the next six and a half years he was to teach theology at the Collège de l'Immaculée-Conception in Montreal.

In these years he seems to have carried his full load of teaching, but found time to rewrite and publish his doctoral thesis in the four articles mentioned above (*Theological Studies* 1941–42), to contribute a major essay to the same journal ('Finality, Love, Marriage,' 1943), and to give a number of talks and write a number of short articles and reviews. For leisure during the long nights of one winter he read the first six volumes of Toynbee's *A Study of History*.[7]

His teaching, then, did not seem to involve his full capacity at this time. He would use some available textbook as the bread-and-butter basis of the course, and would sometimes provide a few pages of minor importance as a supplement. (The first major supplement was *De ente supernaturali*, written in 1946 and still the object of intense study by his students.) In any case we have his word for it that 'L'Immaculée' provided an environment of leisure for study and research, of protection from non-academic burdens, of high regard for the life of the mind.

On this basis one might ask whether he worked more or less continuously, or at least intermittently, on the economics, fitting that work into the free hours of his teaching schedule – a few hours here, a few days there. That is not impossible. Still, a work like FNPE seems to require somewhat

6 See *Caring about Meaning: Patterns in the Life of Bernard Lonergan*, ed. Pierrot Lambert, Charlotte Tansey, Cathleen Going (Montreal: Thomas More Institute, 1982) 85–86.
7 Ibid. 88.

longer periods of concentration, and in fact we have a good clue to what those periods may have been: his summer vacations. These he often spent at Regiopolis College, Kingston, Ontario, where his brother and fellow Jesuit, Gregory, was stationed during the relevant years. Many of the notes (now in the Archives) that Bernard made from his readings in economics are jotted down on Regiopolis College stationery, and presumably represent work done while he was visiting his brother Greg there. When, therefore, we hear him say, 'From 1930 to about 1944 I spent a great deal of my free time on economic theory,'[8] we may reasonably surmise that a good part of this 'free time,' at least in the early 1940s, consisted of his summer vacations.

That is as far as I can take the question of the date of 'For a New Political Economy.' Perhaps study of this volume and of materials still in the archives would throw further light on the matter – a possibility that is hinted at in Professor McShane's Introduction[9] – but that is a task I must leave to him and others as a follow-up to this volume.

8 *The Question as Commitment: A Symposium*, ed. Elaine Cahn and Cathleen Going (Montreal: Thomas More Institute, 1977) 110.

9 And see also his remark (pp. 213–14) on the relevance for the date of FNPE of a book by John Burnham that Lonergan refers to.

Index

Note. The general editors raised the question of functional specialization in the present task of editing, and the indexing raises that question more sharply. The index to follow reaches tentatively towards the genetic systematics mentioned in the Introduction.[1] It takes its stand on the most successful systematics of the field – that of Lonergan's 1944 essay – and hints at a beginning of genetic ordering.[2]

A peculiar difficulty of the indexing was the character of Part Two. First, while it belongs almost entirely in what I call the Einsteinian context of Part Three, in contrast to the Newtonian achievement of Part One, it is still somewhat transitional in system and expression. So, for example, to take the central character in the drama, pure surplus income is there named systematic profits. In Part One it is named net surplus or even surplus. There is a similar variation in symbolization: a glance at the index under the letters *F, G, H, K,* and *S* will give some sense of the problem. Second, Part Two is fragmentary, with unfinished sections. So, the question occurs regarding the non-survival in Part Three of some parts of its content. Were these parts found to be completely inadeqate? Or were they beyond the needs of a primary presentation? I incline to the latter view, and this is reflected in the index.

In keeping with the commitment of the Introduction I do not interfere with the usages in the three parts of the work, but the index draws attention occasionally to conflicts of usage, and is structured to carry the reader towards the systematics of Part Three. So, 'capitalist phase' is an entry for Part One: the relevant pages are

1 p. xxix.

2 I will elaborate on the stand and the hints, and deal with the problem of Lonergan's later confusing terminologies, in *Lonergan's Economics: Structures and Implementations* (Halifax: Axial Press, 2000).

given, but the pointers towards meaning are to be found under 'surplus.' I follow a somewhat similar strategy regarding symbols.

I have given the first occurrences of all significant symbols, but not of their differentials. So, acceleration factors *a* (Part Three) and *u* (Part One) are given, but not *da*, etc. The meaning of the symbols can be traced through their verbal counterparts. Some symbols are introduced more than once, because of Lonergan's separate treatments; that will be clear from the index. Further, as in the case noted of pure surplus income, the same symbol may be used in several contexts, or even conflictingly in the same context of meaning: again, this is noted.

I permitted myself two extravagances in preparing the index. One was mentioned earlier:[3] there are various references to Kalecki despite the fact that Lonergan was not familiar with his work at the time of writing. Might something similar be done eventually with others such as Friedman, indexed here only as mentioned in the title of a book? The question points to another specialist index. But I risk remarking that the sophistications pointed to in Part Two's turnover analysis of the quantities and velocities of layered money is quite beyond this century's theoretics.

My other extravagance is to bring into focus, by entries under 'Concomitance,' the total challenge of the new political economy. Are we to respect the heart-pulses of the productive machine, or are we to continue the 'absurdity' (*see* Index) of counterpulsing, locally and globally?

But the prior challenge of the work is to come to grips with the subtleties of the ideal pulsing, so that not only economists and leaders, but also general culture, might come to say with Wordsworth, 'And now I see with eye serene, the very pulse of the machine' ('She was a phantom of delight'). P.McS.

a: acceleration coefficients (factors), a', a'', 273, 302–6. *See also u*

A, angle between price and quantity vectors, 270–73

A_i, short-term acceleration rate, 244

Absurdity of eliminating cycles, 182, 281

Acceleration: abortive a., 144, 217 (*see also* Trade cycle); a. of accelerator, 14; airplane as a. analogue, 74; circuit a., 122–28, 259–68; coefficients of, 77–79, 270–73, 302–306; credit and a., *see* Credit; cycles of, 23–27, 51–53, 76–89, 128–48, 274–82, 285–307; foreign trade and a., 94–96, 199–200, 310–17; government and a., 96–97, 200–202, 318; increments required for, 136–51; limits to, 87, 242; long-term a., 241–45, 273–83, 296; money and a., 136–51, 163–74, 259–66; perpetual a. impossible, 97; potential for, 276, 294; reason to expect a., 277–81; short-term a., 241–45, 259–69, 276–77; sketched theory of, 217; structure of, 14–21, 132–48, 179–82, 244–45; superposed circuits and a., 94–97, 198–200, 310–18; uniform surplus a., 278

Accelerator(s): a. of levels, 14–17, 42, 70, 132–34, 241–42; *G* and *T* as a., 70; surplus as a., 132–34

Accountant's: meaning of costs and

3 p. 212, n. 9.

profits, 179, 301; unity, 236. *See* Bookkeeping
Adaptation: a. against economic frustration, 76; cultural a., 20; and enlightened self-interest, 231; a. to exigence of pure cycle, 276; a. of existing structure, 6; frame of reference for, 112, 211–12, 231–32; a. to harsh doctrine of decreasing profits, 81; a. to norms of price-spread, 78–81; a. to normative *G*s, 55, 208; over-adaptation, to surplus expansion, 276; a. of psychological attitude, 42; a. for survival, 43, 106
Adjustment: of inadequate analysis, 6; by forced savings, 287; to price variations, 293; of propensity to consume to cycles, 231; of rate of savings, 286–88
Advertising, 24, 36, 89
Africa, xvii
Airplane as acceleration analogue, 74
Algebra and economic variables, 13, 17, 238–40, 244–45
America, 21
Amortization, 95–97, 201–202, 317–18
Analysis, in economics: and description, 111; dynamic a., xxv, 52–53, 142–51, 211–12; equilibrium a., 113, 142–43; model a., xxv, 25–26, 133; need for, 3–10, 110–11; real a., xvi–xvii
Anatomy, 6
Anthropology of drivers and economics, 1C9
Anticipation: a. of dividends to self-love, 21; a. of entrepreneur, 142; a. of future, 125, 274; a. of future demand, 304; a. of market, 79; a. of price variation, 289–90, 304–306; a. of profits, 49, 53; a. and rational expectations, xxvi–xxvii nn. 14, 16; speculative a., 274
Anti-egalitarian, surplus expansion, 23–26, 55, 67–68, 124–26, 286–89, 296–98
Approximations in economics: control and a., 211–12; first and second a., 142–43; a. in measurements, 129–31, 178, 271–74, 286
Archival material, xi–xii, xvii–xxiv, 319, 321, 323–24
Aristotle, 6
Armaments, 25, 27, 31, 100
Aspiration of analysis, 203
Assumption of closed economy: as basis, 114, 246; dropped, 94, 196, 311
Astute investors, 79
Australia, 316
Autarky, 247, 316
Automatic progress, 111
Automobile tire as image of accelerations, 85

B_i, rate of replacement, 244–45
Babylon, 11
Backward economy, 199, 312–13
Balance(s): five types of, 58–59; b. of foreign trade, 94–96,197–200, 202, 310–16. *See also* Demand function
Bank(ing): b. credit as dummy, 40; emergence of, 20, 264 ; and gold, 41; and interest control, 290–92; b. liquidity, 58; b. as operative payment, 116, 252; b. as redistributive, 116, 252; b. reserves, 57; and money supply, 288; b. panic, 103. *See also* Credit
Bankruptcy: and bureaucrats, 35; and depression, 300; and government, 317; and traders, 89
Barratt Brown, Michael, xvii
Barter, 37–38
Baseball diamond, 118–19
Basic: b. acceleration, 305; b. advantage, 87–89, 122, 152, 156, 274–75; b. circuit, 252–58, 285–92, 301–306; b. con-

traction, 274–76; b. credit, 59–69, 71–73, 125, 265–66; b. demand, 58–59, 118, 121, 125, 134, 254–56; b. demand function, 58–59, 115, 254; b. equations, 43–45, 47, 119–20, 254–57; b. expansion, 122, 152, 156, 274–75, 278–80, 303; b. expenditure, *see* Expenditure; b. final payments, 43–45, 115–17, 249–50; function of b. activity, 16–17, 118, 233 (*see also* Standard of living); b. income, *see* Income; b. initial payments, 114, 166–74, 249–50; b. outlay, *see* Outlay; b. price spread, 76–81, 301–306; b. receipts, 115–17, 252–53; b. rhythm, 14–19, 28, 44, 53; b. transitional payments, 114–17, 166–74, 249–50, 267–68; b. supply function, 58–59, 115, 254

Bill(s): b.-broker, 20; b. of exchange, 37; short-term b., 312

Biology, 5, 111

Bond(s): b. and Consumer Dividend, 80; dealers in, 59, 80; b. and government spending, 96–97, 201; and invulnerable income, 299; and unfavorable balance of trade, 315

Bookkeeping: and economic laws, 51; of entrepeneurs, 149, 210; and gold, 104–105, 141–42; b. idea of costs 50–51, 301; as ledger-balancing, 141–42; public b., 103, 105

Boom(s): and anticipated market, 79; as artificial acceleration, 216; and increased surplus, 53, 72, 276, 290; and price rise, 282; and redistributive transfers, 265–66; speculative b., 301–307; and theorem of costs, 51

Borrowing, *see* Consumer, Credit, Finance, Investment, Trader

Bureaucracy, inadequacy of, 4–5, 21, 34–35, 41

Business ethos, 35

C: Consumer multipliers, *C′*, *C″*, 64, 70–73, 214

Calculus, 7

Cantillon, Richard, xxix

Capital: c. equipment, 181–82; increments of circulating c., 84–85, 100, 116, 139–40, 166–74; marginal efficiency of, 231; measurement of, xxvi n. 13, 237; and real analysis, xxviii–xxix. *See also* Monetary

Capitalist: idea, 279; phase, 23–26, 67, 70, 81–87, 91. *See also* Surplus

Carrying costs, 169

Casino, 61, 292

Cassirer, Ernst, 111

Centralization, 36–37. *See also* Control

Chemistry, 5, 20

China, 11

Churchill, Winston, 3, 32, 321

Circulation: c. analysis, 7–10, 109–14, 231–32, 246, 259; and angular velocity, 57, 259; broad definition of, 58–59, 114–21, 254–58; diagrams of, 64–65, 258, 318; and productive process, *see* Concomitance; c. trends, 152–62

Circuit(s): formulae for, 62–65, 114–21, 254–58; monetary c., *see* Monetary; possibility of c. acceleration, 121–62, 259–68; superposed c., 94–97, 196–202, 308–18; c. velocities, 163–74

Classes of payments, 59, 63, 114, 246–52

Closed economy. *See* Assumption

Colonial economies, 95, 199, 313

Commercial revolution, 83

Commodity market, 61

Comparative valuation, 189–90, 193

Competition: and fluid prices, 194–95, 215; c. for labor, 282; international c., 94–96, 198–99, 310–16; investment

market c., 78; markets and c., 32–35; and political interference, 34, 100, 190–92, 195, 200; trader c., 32
Concomitance(s) of money and product flows: and acceleration coefficients, 274; and basic income variations, 286–92; and capitalist phase, 86; and circuit acceleration, 263–66; and control, 211–12, 269–74; and crossover, *see* Crossover; and equilibrium theory, xxv, 51–53, 113, 142–51, 211–12; and essential problem of finance, 100; and flows, 39, 60–62, 113, 231; frame of reference for, 58–65, 114–21, 128, 153–55, 253–58; fundamental types of, 27, 155–57, 274–77; general theory of c. needed, xvi–xvii, xxv–xxviii, 7–9; and monetary phases, 60–62; and normative proportion, 53–54; and price oscillations, *see* Price; and profit motive, 54, 56, 80–81, 94; and theorems of continuity, 56, 73–75, 125–28, 133–34; and transition payments, 157–62, 165–74; and variations of pure surplus income, 49–50, 179–81, 276–81, 292–301; and verifiability, 124, 138–39, 181, 211–12, 269–74
Confiscation, 45, 97, 200
Constancy of money, 37–38, 40–41
Consumer: c. balances, 58–59; c. borrowing, 68, 71–72, 89, 145–51, 199, 265–66, 314–15; C. Dividends, 80–81; c. multipliers, 70–73; and producer goods, 14–21, 117–18, 233–37; c. response, 71–73; c. satisfaction, 70–71; surplus level as c., 240, 246
Continuity: c. of consumer spending, 84; theorems of, 47, 56, 66, 73–75, 154
Contrafactual history, xxvi–xxvii
Control, in economics: of acceleration, 121; character of normative c., 211–12; democratic c., xxvii, 3–5, 109–10, 231; determinate c., xxvii, 237; external c., 109 (*see also* Bureaucracy, Planning); factual c., 10 (*see also* Concomitance, verifiability); market c., 34
Copernican revolution in economics, 42
Copernicus, 6, 42
Corporation(s): breakup of, 140; emergence of, 195; large c., 182. *See also* Liquidation
Cost(s): non-ordinary sense of, 49, 76, 301; theorem of, 50–51
Cost price(s), 76–81, 301–303
Crash: financial, 103–105; stockmarket, 306–307. *See also* Liquidation
Creative imagination, 20–23, 37. *See also* Ideas
Credit: c. balances, 58–59; circular movement of, 57; consumer c., 68, 71–72, 89, 145–51, 199, 265–66, 314–15; creation of, 59–61, 63, 67–68, 282–84; curtailment of, 282, 288; c. as dummy, 37, 40; c. and gold, 100–105; government c., 96–97, 200–202, 317–18; and inflation, 90; international c., 197–201, 264, 310–17; and installment buying, 68; investment c., 59–61, 68; long-term c. problem, 100, 104, 160; over-expansion of, 283 (*see also* Speculative); short-term c., 58, 103–104, 116, 127, 160, 309 (*see also* Short-term credit); and transitional payments, 136–51
Creditor nation, 94–96, 197–99, 311–17
Crisis: c. of amortization, 97; c. of finance, 103–105; c. of financial lull, 98; c. of mounting debt, 95; rhythms of, 78–81, 304–307; c. and stockmarket, 307; violence of depression c., 301

Criticism in economics, 3–10, 109–10, 237
Crossover difference: and condition of continuity, 42–48, 54, 74, 295; and disequilibrium, 148–50, 206, 209, 218; and economic control, 211; and equilibrium, 48, 70, 119–20, 153–54, 182–83, 263, 265–66; and income groups, 182–83; c.d. introduced, 46–48, 119–20, 160, 163, 254–58. *See DG, G*
Crowe, F.E., xv
Cultural phase, 23–27, 70, 106
Culture and economics, 12, 17, 21–27
Curvature of exchange equations, 51–53
Cushioned: c. domestic cycle, 94–95, 197–98, 310–13; c. profits, 198
Cycle(s): c. of basic income, 285–92; c. of basic price spread, 301–307; c. of economy, 23–27, 51–53, 76–89, 128–48, 274–82; c. of long-term advance, 11–12, 18–21, 81, 242, 306; phase structure of, 243; c. of production process, 242–45, 274–81; c. of profit, 68–70, 83–87, 91–93, 154, 179–82, 292–301; pure c., 133, 242–45, 277–81, 292–301; c. of surplus income, 292–301; as theoretic construct, 133; trade c., *see* Trade
Cytology, 6

D, symbol of rate, 252–53
DA: fundamental rhythms, *DA*, 12–13; *DA′*, *DA″*, 16–17; *DA**, redistributional activity, 45; <u>*DA*</u> (lagged *DA*), 47
Dashes, for basic and surplus, 16–17, 166, 253
Date, for FNPE, xiv–xv, 319–24; for sketch, xiv
DC: redistributional flow to consumer balances, *DC′*, *DC″*, 60. *See DD*
DD: redistributional flow to basic demand, *DD′*, *DD″*, 259. *See DC*
DE: flow of expenditure 43, 115, 252; *DE′*, *DE″*, 45, 118, 252; <u>*DE*</u> (lagged *DE*), 47
Debt: domestic d., 96–97, 198, 318; foreign d., 95–96, 198, 312–17; d. servicing, 200–201, 318
Decisions to exchange, 31–34
Decreasing returns, xvi, 21–23, 27
Deepening: and capitalist phase, 52; and economic transformation, 26–27; and crossover, 46; and increasing returns, 23–26; and net surplus income, 89
Deficit government spending: and circuit acceleration, 266; and debt servicing, 200–201, 318; and effective zero, 181; and Major Douglas, 80; and price pattern, 99; and public bookkeeping, 103–105; and social security, 199; superposed circuits and d.g.s., 96–97, 196, 200–202, 308, 317–18; and systematic profits, 231; and taxes, 96–97, 199, 201–202, 317; treatment of d.g.s. in chapters 13 and 19, xxii
Deflation: avoidance of d., 41; and consistency of prices, 176–77; and constant dummy value, 38; and price spread, 88, 304–307; and primary consumer income, 176–77; systematic d., 101
De-hoarding gold, 199, 314
Demand: basic d., 58–59, 118, 121, 125, 134, 254–57; estimate of, 262, 304; d. for credit, 60, 104–105, 148; d. for gold, 61, 95, 102–103, 145; d. for increased wages, 146; d. for money, 145–50, 160–62, 165–74, 177, 208–11; effective d., *see* Effective demand; export d., 94–96; d. functions 118–21, 254–56; and planning, *see* Planning; potential d., *see* Effective demand; d. schedule, 187–88; and supply, 8,

32–35, 58–59, 70–73, 187–89; surplus d., 58–59, 118, 254–57; variations of, 55, 67–68, 70–73, 77–81, 90–91, 195, 275–81, 286–90, 294–307
Democratic economics, 3–5, 26, 37, 110
Deportation, 45
Depreciation: and bookkeeping, 51; and crossover, 46, 119; d. as fund for maintenance, 46, 50, 63, 66, 71; d. as initial payment, 97, 246, 253; d. in static phase, 52, 97
Depression: d. offset, 310, 315–16; pure surplus income and d., 297–301, 305–307
Description and economics, 7–10, 25, 111–12
DG: crossover difference, 119, 255
DH: relative change in crossover fractions, 122, 207–208
DI: income flow, 43, 115; *DI′*, *DI″*, 45, 118, 252; <u>*DI*</u> (lagged), 47
Diagram(s): copyright date of, 322–33; d. of circulation, 64, 65, 118, 196, 202; and control, 211–12; d. of monetary functions of closed economy, 258; d. of superposed circuits, xxii, 202. *See also* Tables
Differential rent: and lack of price consistency, 177, 185–86; legitimation of, 185, 192, 251; and uniform prices, 34
Discontinuity: of markets, 130–31; of prices, 129–30
Discounting houses, 61, 264
Disequilibrium: basic and surplus d., 122–23, 133, 150, 156; dynamic d., 132–34, 303–307; d. of prices, 76–81, 129–30, 302–307; d. of supply and demand, 32–33. *See also* Equilibrium
Distribution of income: basic, 47–48, 55, 70–75, 285–92; normative, *see* Concomitance; pure surplus, 49–50, 54, 68–70, 292–301; surplus, 47–48 (*see also* Maintenance)
Distributor multiplier(s), 66–68
Dividends: and basic demand, 124; concentrated d. as capital, 71; as initial payment, 63, 66, 114, 116, 249, 252, 253; and ownership, 29, 46; and pure surplus, 72, 87, 298; shrinking d., 63
Divisibility of money, 37
Division(s): d. of payments into operative and redistributive, 115, 247–48, 251–52; d. of payments into basic and surplus, 117, 248; d. of payments into initial, transitional, final, 116–18, 249–52; proprietary d., 236–37; d. of specializations in economics, xvi, xxviii–xxxi
DM: redistributional increment of money, 60; *DM′*, 145, 148, 255–56; *DM″*, 148, 256
DO: outlay flow, 115; *DO′*, *DO″*, 118, 252
Dole, 18, 195, 199
Douglas, Major Clifford, 80–81
DP: average increment of price, 129; increment in vector price index, 270
Dq′, rate of primary production, 76
Dq″, rate of secondary production, 76
DQ: flow of final product, 43, 239; *DQ′*, *DQ″*, 45, 240; <u>*DQ′*</u>, <u>*DQ″*</u> (lagged), 47; *DQ** (redistributional), 45 ; tables of *DQ′*, *DQ″*, 274–75; average increment of quantity, 129
DQ′/*DQ″*: ratio of primary (basic) and secondary (surplus) final production, 53
DQ/*Q*: proportionate variation of production, *DQ′*/*Q′*, *DQ″*/*Q″*, 274
DR: flow of receipts, 115; *DR′*, *DR″*, 118, 252
Dresses and point-to-point flexibility, 236
DS: redistributive flow to supply func-

tion, 116; *DS'*, *DS"*, 118, 256. *See also* *DT*

DT: redistributive flow to trader balances, *DT'*, *DT"*, 59. *See also DS*

Dummy of money, 37–41, 57–58, 61

DY: flow of export gold, 94; net surplus income from government spending, 96; *DY'*, *DY"*, taxation, 317

Dynamic system, xxv, xxix–xxxi, 109–11

DZ: aggregate payments per interval, 269; *DZ'*, *DZ"*, superposed flows, 308; *DZ'*, *DZ"*, foreign trade flows, 311; *DZ'*, *DZ"*, flows of government borrowing/spending, 317; *DZ*, rate of payment, 177

Economic: dynamics, xxv; praxis, xv; science, xxiv–xxxi, 3–10, 30, 109–11; statics, xxv; surges, xxvi, 11–12, 24, 242; synthesis, 36. *See also* Analysis

Economics: approximations in e., *see* Approximations; models in e., 25–26; e. of nineteenth century, xxix, 3–4; normative e., xxvi (*see also* Concomitance); e. not a department of politics, 194; object of, 12

Economy: advanced e., 94–96; backward e., 199, 312–13; exchange e., 28–41; heritage of, 12; old political e., 4–5, 7, 37, 41, 110–11

Education needed, 37–38, 89, 98, 100. *See also* Adaptation, Adjustment

Effective demand: balance of actual and potential e.d., 55, 72–73, 77, 208, 301–307; and crossover, 55, 208; and cumulative action of multipliers, 72; potential e.d., 64, 72, 73, 77; primary and secondary e.d., 72; and price spread, 77, 301–307

Effective zero of surplus production, 18, 22–23, 69, 98

Efficiency: e. of economic science, xxix–xxxi; finance's lack of, 83; increased e. with new ideas, 279; more e. of capital equipment, 276; and velocity of money, 62

Egalitarian, 36, 287–89, 298

Egypt, 11

Einstein, Albert, 6–7, 261

Elasticity, 41, 91, 195

Emigrants, 285

England, 3, 21, 24

Enterprise(s), sound and unsound, 91–93

Entrepreneur(s): and acceleration, 125–26, 293–301; bookkeeping and e., 149, 210; and contracting price spread, 78–79, 303–306; e. as figurehead, 141; e. getting what they spend, 71–72, 154, 161, 179–80, 212 n. 9; and imports, 198, 314; e. and initiative, 41; losses of, 299; and pure surplus income, 292–301; and short-term loans, 116, 160; successful e., 180–81, 194, 294, 298; and turnover, 135–48, 164–74, 261–63; and windfalls, 265

Entrepreneurial unit(s): during expansion, 296–97, 299; invulnerable e.u., 91–92, 169, 182, 299; e.u. level-indifferent, 16, 237, 249, 251, 278, 282; new e.u., 52, 98, 161, 179; transitional e.u., 166–74, 267–68; and turnover, 261–63; unsheltered e.u., 35, 91–92, 140, 180, 182, 299–300; wholesale, retail e.u., 44, 169–70, 249

Equilibrium: e. analysis, 113, 142–43; crossover e., 120–25; dynamic e., 51–53, 142–51, 211–12; idea of, 57–59, 76; market e., 32–35. *See also* Concomitance

Errors: in economics, 4–5, 8; in Lonergan's text, xxiii, 65, 270, 271, 278

Essay in Circulation Analysis: ECA of 1944,

xi, xv, xvi, xx–xxii, 320, 322; ECA of Volume 15, xxiv, xxvii, 286
Estimate(s): indeterminate, 237; of frequency, 262
Ethos: of business, 35; of capital deepening, xxvii; of neglect of real analysis, xvi, xxv, xxviii–xxix, xxxi
Euclid, 6–7, 113
Euphrates, 11
Evolution, 6
Exchange economy: function of, 29, 34, 246; introduced, 28, 184; relation to sales, 246–48
Exchange value, 31–32, 38–39
Exchanges: division into basic and surplus, 117, 248; division into operative and redistributive, 115, 247–48, 251–52
Executives: intelligent e., 24; and pure surplus, 298
Expansion(s): geometric, 304; speculative, 301. *See also* Basic, Surplus
Expectation(s): criticism of analysis of, xxvi, 132, 237; rational e., xxvi; subordination of, 110
Expenditure: and continuity, 142–44, 166–72, 282–84, 287–90; distinction between basic and surplus e., 43, 45–51, 115–21, 252–57; and Keynes, 214, 231; investment e., 89; measurement of, 268–74, 282–84; and normative proportion, 53–56, 67–68, 87; and price level, 83, 282–84, 303–307
Exploitation of ideas, 23, 74, 81
Export(s) and superposed circuits, 94–96, 197–99, 264, 266, 310–17. *See also* Favorable balance of trade
External control of economy, 109. *See also* Bureaucracy, Planning

F: ratio of pure surplus to total income, 294. *See also H*
Factors, of production, 239
Factory: F. Act, 195; and levels of production, 14, 16, 233–35; sale of, 251
Family wage, 321
Fascism, 3–4
Favorable balance of trade: and analogy with new fixed investment, 310, 314; and net (surplus) income, 95, 99, 199; and superposed circuits, 94–96, 196–99, 308–13
Final: markets, 43–47; payments, 43–45, 249–50; products, 17, 114, 247–50
Finance: absence of function for, 98; basis of, 37; essential problem of, 100, 104–105, 160; future possibilities and f., 20–21; gap in f., 59; inefficiency of, 83; long-term f., 103–104, 145–51, 264–65; operations of, 116, 251–52; power of, 294–98; problems of, 100–106; real analysis and f., xvi–xvii; redistributive home of, 120; responsibility of, 82, 88; short-term f., 58, 103–104, 116, 127, 309 (*see also* Short-term credit); techniques of, 59–63, 90–91, 115–16
Finland, 7
Five-point system of analysis, 58, 117–21, 249–51
Five-year plan, 4, 24, 89–90, 132, 241
Flaw: in classical theory of prices, 99; in contemporary view of interest, 290–92; in ethos of profit-making, 53–54, 80–81, 88, 92
For a New Political Economy: date of, xi, xv–xvi, 207–208, 213–14, 319–24; duplication of FNPE's table of p. 55, 207–208
Forced savings: and costs analysis, 179, 302; and price spirals, 78; and surplus expansion, 287–88
Foreign: holdings, 315–16; payments, 246; securities, 197; trade, 246

Frame of reference of new economics, 58–65, 111–12; 114–21, 128, 153–55, 253–58
Freedom, 4, 8, 20, 105, 109, 193
Freedom of exchange, 193, 231, 276
Frequency. *See* Turnover
Friedman, M., xxx n. 26
Führer, 36
Function(s): monetary f., 121, 254; f. of levels, 13–27; f. of prices, 231; f. of transition payments, 44, 168–69; f. of velocity of money, 172
Functional: f. division of productive process, 14–18, 114–18, 234–42; f. relations, 111; f. specialties, xii, xvi, xxvii–xxxi

g: income fraction of basic demand, g_i, 285
G: distributive multipliers, *G′*, *G″*, 47; *G′*, fraction of basic income to surplus demand, 47, 119, 254; *G″*, fraction of surplus income to basic demand, 48, 119, 254; *G*, rate of savings (= *G′*), 283
G″/*G′*, normative proportion, 54, 119; table of, 55, 208
Galilei, Galileo, 6–7, 11
Gambling on stocks, 61, 72, 292, 305
Gardening: future, 20; primitive, 11, 19–20, 184, 232, 234
General: g. breakdown, 75, 301; g. long-term acceleration, 305; g. services, 237, 278, 282; *G. Theory* of Keynes, 3, 9, 231
Generalization: g. of acceleration, 241–42, 281; g. as cultural challenge, 20–21, 26, 41, 112, 297–98; g. of expansion, 282; frame of reference for, 58–59, 109–12, 128, 117–18, 253–58; g. of meaning of costs, 50, 301; g. as normative model, 25–26, 126, 142–43, 172, 211–12; g. as shift in idea, 6–10, 36, 41, 109–12, 297–98; g. of shipbuilding analysis, 165–74; g. in statistics, 112
Geometry, 5–6, 113
Germany, 3–4
Global dividend, xxvii
Gold: g. as basis of money, 40–41, 101–104, 198, 216; and credit, 61, 145, 264; de-hoarding of, 199, 314; fundamental problem of, 100–106; import of, 94–95, 197–99, 310–13; reserves of, 102; g. standard, 102–104, 264
Goods (and services): consumer g., 119–20, 124, 131; distinct levels of, 14–16, 58, 115–18, 180, 233–41; leisure as g., 18–20, 22, 25, 189; g. and markets, 40; measurement of, 177–79, 185–95, 268–74; and money-velocity, 61–62; g. in process, 232; redistributive g., 61, 93–96, 115, 197–99, 250–52; surplus g., 131; types of, 129–32 (*see also* Differential rent); turnover of, 135–51, 164–74; unfinished g. and transitional payments, 135–51, 164–74; and variation of *DA*, 43. *See also* Standard of living
Good will and redistributive area, 84
Gordon, Robert: critique of, xxxi n. 28; and propensity to consume, xxvi n. 14
Government operations, 96–97, 200–202, 301, 317–18
Graham, Nicholas, xix
Greek, 11

H: acceleration fraction, 276; *H′*, *H″*, 276; ratio of systematic profits to total income, 181 (*see also F*)
Hawtrey, R.G., and trade cycle, 102 and n. 7
Herrenvolk, 36
Higher synthesis, 36
Historical synthesis, 9–10

History of systems, xxix, xxxi, 9–10
Homeric hides, 175
Homogeneity of money, 37

Idea(s): absence of i. of pure surplus income, 297–98; capitalist i., 279; emergence of, 20–27, 74, 90–91; i. of equilibrium, 57–59; exploitation of, 23, 74, 81
Idealism, 36
Immigrants, 285
Import(s), and superposed circuits, 94–96, 197–99, 264, 266, 310–17. *See also* Unfavorable balance of trade
Impulses in the economy, xxvi, 11–27, 242–45, 276, 294. *See also* Industrial revolution
Incentive to save, 290–91
Income: basic and surplus i., 43–51, 118, 252; capitalist phase and i., 83–86; causes of surplus i., 179–80; crossover and i., 48, 54–55, 125, 182, 254–55, 284; cycle of basic i., 286–92; cycle of surplus i., 292–301; i. groups, 285–90; materialist phase and i., 87–89; normative proportion and i., 53–55; pure surplus i., 179–80; and price spread, 76–77, 301–307; rate of absorption and i., 157; turnover and i., 164–72; i. velocities, 148, 209
Increasing returns, 21–23, 27
Indeterminacy: of acceleration ratios, 281; of capital-output ratio, xxvi n. 13, 132, 234–37; of control, 211–12; of cost price, 302; of depression dynamics, 300–301; and inconsistency of price, 34, 132–33, 176–77, 185–86, 192, 251; of price and quantity indices, 129–31, 271–74; and price spread, 78–81, 302–307; of velocity of money, 126–28, 134–51, 163–74, 261–65
Index of prosperity, 248
India, 11
Indices. *See* Price, Quantity
Industrial revolution: colonialism and i., 312–13; conspicuous expansion of, 67, 132; direction of, 4; and investment, 83; pioneering advance of, 83, 181–82, 241; and price pattern, 83; straitjacketing of, 156
Inequality, human, 36
Inertia of process to finance, 83, 134
Inevitable cycle, xiv, 204–205
Inflation: and consistency of prices, 176–77; i. of consumer income, 78, 86, 89–90; and economic phases, 87–89, 287–88, 296; of labor income, 201; and Major Douglas, 80; and money-value, 38, 41; and price-spread, 78, 296, 304–307
Initial payments, 117, 249–52
Installment buying, 67, 89
Insurance, 58, 85, 93, 116, 252
Interest: Barton's view of, xxviii; i.-bearing bonds, 299; i. bill, 169; and government debt, 96–97, 200; and imports, 313; i. as initial payment, 114, 249, 252, 253; i. as pure surplus, 298; Schumpeter's theory of, xxx n. 26; and standard of living, 97, 201; i. as topic in economics, 8; traditional theory of, 285, 290–92
International monetary phenomena, 94–96, 197–200, 312–17
Investment: i. absent in static phase, 97–99; and expansion, 83–86, 122–24, 145–46, 152–53, 156–57, 265–66, 292–94; i. expenditure, 42–53, 55; fixed and liquid i., 293; i., 'got when spent,' 71–72, 146, 154, 161, 179–80, 212 n. 9; i. halt, 73; and industrial revolution, 67–68; i. market, 78; new fixed i., 294–99; i. not equal to savings, 84, 87, 91, 125, 263; i. oscilla-

tions, 292–301; i. receipts, 298; i. saturation, 78; and savings, 89–91; and transition payments, 136–44, 166–74
Invulnerable rate of savings, 299–300
Iron, on each level, 14–16
Italian: Fascism, 3–4; Renaissance, 264

J, basic price spread ratio, 302
Juglar, Clément, 306
Juridical, 2, 12

K: expansive fraction of surplus outlay, 180 (*see also F*); gold-reserve multiplier, 101
Kaiser, Henry, 260
Kalecki, Michael: and Kaleckians, 212–13; and Lonergan, 212; and paradigm shift to functional specialization, xxv; and sectorized taxes, xxvi; K.'s slogan (*see* 212 n. 9), 71–72, 146, 154, 161, 179–80, 212; as twentieth-century economist, 213 n. 9
Kepler, Johannes, 6–7, 11
Keynes, John Maynard: xxv, 3, 9–10, 212–13, 231; K.'s *General Theory*, 3, 10
Kierans, Eric, xv, 319–24
Kitchin, Joseph, 306

Labor: competitive demand for, 282; l.'s consumption income, 119, 303; demand for l. in industrial revolution, 24; l.'s demand for wage increase, 146; division of l. in economics, xxviii–xxxi; and government spending, 96; hiring of, 70; l. leaders, 82; level-determination of, 235; l. market, 82–83; migration of, 25, 241; l. as negative leisure, 189; organized l., 100, 195; and price spread, 303; and social security, 195, 199, 316; and varying wages, 55, 68, 78–81, 313, 321; and widening/deepening, 18–21, 241–42
Lack of adaptation: l.a.a burden on taxpayer, 99; l.a. of invulnerable income, 299; and liquidation, *see* Liquidation; multiple l.a., 297–98, 301; l.a. to relative and absolute price differences, 289; l.a. results in trade cycle, 245
Lag(s): acceleration l., 276; l. analysis, 47 n. 1, 64–66, 77 n. 1, 154, 157, 239–40; l. diagrammed, 64, 65; effect l. of finance, 83; effect l. from levels, 244; l. disregarded, 154; expansion l., 280, 296; l. between income and expenditure, 121–26, 207; l. of interest change effect, 291–92; and monetary-velocity variation, 127–28; outlay l., 268; price-spread response l., 77–81, 303–306; production l., 146–48, 239–40; replacement l., 276; l. in sales, 138–40, 147–48, 157, 261–65; l. and superposed circuits, 197
Laissez faire, 4, 110
Land: clearing of, 16; cultivation of, 20–22; ownership of, 29, 44; purchase of l. redistributional, 44, 59, 86; rental of, 29
Law(s): absence of surplus l., 51; l. of diminishing and increasing return, 21–23; l. of economics, 42, 110; l. of falling bodies, 25–26
Ledger: bank l. as medium of exchange, 176; l.-balancing as topic, 141
Leisure, 18–20, 22, 25, 189
Level floor, principle of, 93
Liberty. *See* Freedom
Limitations: l. on behavior, 76; l. of *DD'* effect, 206; l. of economic structure, 27, 74, 76, 234, 242; l. of exchange economy, 35–37; l. of old guard, 36–37; point-to-point l., 234; l. of potentiality, 27; l. of present economics, xvi–xvii, xxv–xxxi, 3–5, 109–11;

l. of widening, 27; l. of world production, 97
Limited liability, 35
Lion's share of profits, 92
Liquidation(s): l. of debts, 116; and depression, 299–301, 305–307; and mergers, 140; and monopolies, 91–92; and need for level floor, 93; and price oscillations, 99, 305–307; and redistribution, 44; and Schumpeter, 213; and traders, 63
Loans. *See* Consumer, Credit, Finance, Investment, Trader
London, 29
Lonergan, Bernard: and archival material, xii, xiv–xxiii, 322–24; and date of Part One, xvi–xvii, 319–324; and functional specialization, xi–xii, xxviii–xxxi; and lag theory, 93 n. 4; and methodological concerns, xi–xii, xxiv, xxvii; and primer, xxiv; and real analysis, xvi, xxviii–ix; and search for generalization, 275. Works referred to: CWL 15 xxiv, xxvii, 286; *De ente supernaturali*, 323; 'Finality, Love, Marriage,' 323; *Gratia operans*, 207, 321–22; *Insight*, xvi; *Method in Theology*, xvi
Lonergan, Gregory, 324
Long-term: acceleration, 81, 180–81, 292–95; credit, *see* Credit, Finance; foreign loans, 95, 199, 314–15; planning, 243

Machine tools: different levels of, 14–16, 26–27, 117–18, 234–37, 244–45; and effective zero, 18–19; and point-to-line relations, 132, 234–37
Magnitude. *See* Turnover
Maintenance: absence of, 51; ambiguity of, 236; and costs, 46, 301; m. as effect of surplus activity, 26–27, 46, 49–50, 117, 119, 132, 240, 276, 293; and effective zero, 18–19, 27, 52, 87, 98, 242, 245; and foreign trade, 310–14; m. limiting expansion, 242; measure of, B_n, 244–45
Maldistribution and crossover, 55
Management: m. as part of process, 232–33, 247; universal m., 27
Marginal: m. analysis, xxviii; m. comparative evaluation, 189–93; m. efficiency of capital, xxvi n. 13, 231; m. firms, 92
Market(s): commodity m., 61; m. continuity, 129–30, 177–79, 269–74; m. control of prices, 34; m. discontinuity, 130–31; m. equilibrium, 35; initial, final, and transitional m., 43–45; m. structure of supply and demand, 32–35, 187–89
Marxist, 9, 78
Mass(es): and advertising, 24, 36; m. production, 19; psychological condition of m., 200; psychology of m., 20–21
Materialist phase, 23–27, 67–69, 70, 81–82, 87–89. *See also* Basic
Mathematical errors in Part Three, xxiii, 270, 271, 278
McShane, Philip: *Economics for Everyone*, xxviii, xxxi, 202, 242; *The Redress of Poise*, xxxi
Measurement: m. of aggregate production, 239, 267–78; approximations in m., *see* Approximations; m. of capital, xxvi, 237; m. of exchange value, 31–32, 240; indeterminacy of, 129–31, 178, 235–37, 239–40, 272–73; limits to m., 9, 13–14; money as m., 37–41; possibility of, 13–14, 17, 45, 112, 129–31, 205, 268–74; m. in science, 5; m. in statistics, 112; table of normative m., 55, 208
Mechanical structure of process: outlined, 42–56, 114–21, 232–37,

252–58; equilibria of, 57–75, 123–28, 274–82
Medieval exchange process, 28
Mercantilism, 28, 45, 60, 100–101, 264
Mergers and transitional payments, 140
Method in economics, xi–xii, xvi, xxvii, 3–10, 109–12
Middlemen: consumers not m., 117; and transitional payments, 62, 146, 168–70
Mixed phase, 274
Models in economics, xxv, 133, 142–43
Monetary: m. accelerations, 122–62, 259–68; m. accelerators, 74–75; m. circuits, 175, 179; m. circulation, 34–35, 59–75, 114–21, 140, 252–58; m. continuity, 60, 62; m. correlatives of production, 43–48, 115–21, 246–52; m. contraction, 60; m. expansion, 60; m. functions, 120–21, 254; m. phases, 59–62, 122–29
Money: m. of account, 101–102; m. available in circuits, 264; banking and m., *see* Banking, Credit; commodity m., 104; constant value of, 37–38, 41; creation of, 59–62, 90; efficiency of, 101; excess release of, 74; function of, 40; and gold, 38, 40–41, 61, 95, 100–106, 198–99; increments of, 145, 170–74, 209, 256–57; idle m., 115, 254; international m., 94–95, 197–99, 312–17; 'm.' introduced, 37, 186, 192; and liquid investments, 293–94; m. as medium of exchange, 37–41, 175, 186; 'more' m., 216; and prices, *see* Prices, indices of; properties of, 37–41; quantity of, *see* Quantity; m. in reserve, 254, 308; redistributive operations and m., 45–46, 100–102, 115–16, 248, 250–52; and rate of investment, 290–92; rigid m., 215; saving of, 81, 84; m. as store of wealth, 40; superposed m., 94, 196–97, 266, 308–309; velocity of, *see* Velocity
Moneybags, 68, 88
Moneylenders, 98, 103
Monopolist: m. advantage, 168–69, 193; and age of corporations, 195; and interlocking directorates, 92; and marginal comparative valuation, 193; Robinson Crusoe as m., 247
Monopsonist buyer, 193, 195, 247
Motorcars: and critique of present economics, 109; and middlemen, 62
Multipliers: consumer m., 70–73; cumulative effect of, 72, 85, 127; distributor m., 66–68; six m., 74; trader m., 68–70

National debt, 96, 196, 200–202, 318
Natural resources, 11–12, 57, 205, 232–33, 252
Nerve center of economy, pure surplus income, 294, 310
New: n. capital equipment, 182, 195, 199, 280; n. companies, 52, 98, 161, 179, 195, 213; n. fixed investment, 293–94, 297–98, 310, 314; n. ideas, 18–21, 23, 90, 195, 262; n. inventions, 34; n. men, 181–82, 195; n. political economy, 3, 5, 7; n. perspective, 9, 42; n. static phase, 81, 183
New York, 29
Newton, Isaac, 6–7, 11
Niagara of sentiment, 36
Nile, 11
Nineteenth century: and industrial revolution, 24; and real analysis, xxix; 19th-c. theory and practice, 3–4, 28, 37
Nonoperative exchanges. *See* Redistributional
Normative: n. analysis, xxvi, 3–5, 109–11, 231 (*see also* Concomitance); n. phases, 121–34; n. proportion,

53–55, 67–68, 84, 87; n. trends, 152–55

O'Donovan, Conn, xii, xix
Ogpu, 7
Old country, creditor becomes rentier, 314
Old political economists, 4–5, 7, 37, 41, 110–11
Operative payments, division into initial, transitional, final, 14–19, 114–18, 248–52
Ordinary final products, 17, 22, 24
Organized labor: and claim to higher wages, 24, 288; and fluctuating employment, 82–83; o.l. in modern period, 195; and trade unions, 24; transformation of, 36
Oriental princes de-hoarding, 199, 314
Outlay (basic, surplus): and expansions, 152–53, 156–57; fundamental character and equations of o., 115–28, 207–208, 252–57; and net transfer, 134–44, 154–62; and turnover, 134–44, 154–62
Overhead: cultural o., 12, 17, 22, 24; o. final product, 17, 22, 24, 46
Overproduction and crossover, 55
Ownership: exclusion of, 195; o. of foreign securities, 313, 316; o. as ground of exchange, 29–32, 44, 46, 248; and hope of profit, 117; o. of industrial power, 294; and redistributional activity, 44–45, 58, 115, 248, 250–52; o. standard of living, 77, 88, 98, 293

p: average price, p_i, 269; cost-price indices, p′, p″, 77, 302; price indices, p_{ij}, 175, 184
P: price level, 43; *P′*, primary (basic) price level, 45; *P**, redistributional price level, 45; *P″*, secondary (surplus) price level, 45; *P*, vectorial price measure, 269; *P′*, *P″*, vectorial basic and surplus price measures, 272–73; *P*, weighted averages, 272
Pattern of prices and quantities, 129–30, 177–79, 187–94, 269–78
Payment(s): and accelerations, 49–54, 59–75, 128, 248, 263–68; classes of p., 44, 114, 246–52; rates of p., 43–48, 115–21, 252–57; and velocity of money, 163–70, 260–63
Phase(s): capitalist p., 23–27, 52, 83–87; circuit acceleration p., 282–84; cultural p., 23, 106; four types of, 23–26; four types of p. and trader multipliers, 69–70; p. freshly defined., 121, 274 (*see also* Trends); materialist p., 23–27, 52, 87–89; normative p., 121–28; static p., 23–27, 52; table of, 122; p. within cycles, 128–34, 274–75
Philanthropy, 34–35, 50, 54, 77, 88, 91
Plan(ning): p. authority, 190; bureaucratic p., 4–5, 21, 34–35, 41; p. board, 110, 191–92; central p., 4–5, 37; credit p., 104; five-year p., 4, 24, 89–90, 132, 241; p. to level rhythms, 182, 281; long-term p., 278; socialist p., 105, 190–91, 194–95, 277; p. vs enlightenment, 4, 110, 194, 231
Point-to-point, etc.: defined, 14–16, 132, 181, 235–37, 240; flexibility of, 232, 236; and standard of living, 238, 249, 250
Political economy: difficulty and need of new p.e., 3–10; nineteenth-century p.e., 111; old and new p.e., 3–7
Population: culture of, 232; variations of, 25
Post-Keynesians, xxviii
Postulate of continuity, 125–28
Potential effective demand. *See* Effective
Potentialities of nature, 11–12, 57, 205, 232–33

Precepts to mankind, 5, 7–8, 110–11
Preferences; p. an economic factor, 114, 231; and objective effect of exchange, 193; strategic p., 231 (*see also* Concomitance, Rational expectations)
Price(s): absolute change in p., 289–90; actual, hypothetical p., 32, 103, 215; averages of p., 43, 45; basic p. and *C'*, 73; changes in p., 269–78; competition and p., 32–33, 187–89, 215; consistency of p., 176–78, 215; continuity of p., 47, 53–54, 57; cyclic variations in p., 81–83; dialectic of p., 194–95; effects of changing p., 31–35; and exchange value, 31–35; falling p., 82, 126, 216, 299; flawed theory of p., 99; p. increments,178, 269–74; indices of, 129–31, 175–79, 184–93, 269–74, 315; and international trade, 94–95, 198–99, 315; p. levels, 43, 45–46, 69, 266; measure of, *see* Price, indices; monetary and real p., 186–87; money and p., 37–41; nature of, 31–35, 189–92; p. oscillations, 92, 94–95, 126, 301–307; redistributional p., 46; relative change of, 289–90; rigidity of, 215; rising p., 39, 88, 95, 126, 287; spirals of, 78, 82–83, 87, 288–89; p.-spread, 76–81, 301–307; uniformity of, 33–34 (*see also* Differential rent); variations of, 181–83
Primary circuit, 16–19, 21, 23–27, 44–56, 58–59. *See also* Basic
Primer in economics, xxiv, xxxi
Primitive gardening, etc., 11, 19–20, 184, 232, 234
Principle of level floor, 93
Process: p. indices, 177–79; pure p., 11–27. *See also* Productive
Production factors: estimated, 190; layered, 14–19, 26–27, 117–18, 234–37, 244–45
Production management, 190. *See also* Planning
Productive process: p.p. as current, 232; p.p. defined, 235–45; divisions of, 233–37; possibility of controlling p.p., 211–12; possibility of measuring p.p., 268–74; p.p.'s relation to monetary process, *see* Concomitance; p.p. wrecked by stupidity, 70
Profit(s): absence of, 82; anticipation of, 53, 142; biased criterion of, 92, 124; costs limiting p., 301–302; cushioned p., 198; decreasing return of p. motive, 54, 56, 80–81, 94; level floor of, 92–93; limitations of p. motive, 49, 54, 56, 80, 88; net p., 46; p. as operative payment, 251; and pure surplus, 49–50, 72–73, 84–86, 89–91, 179–82, 293–301; significance of, 290–92; speculative p., 287, 305–306; systematic p., 179–80, 231; superposed circuits and p., 196, 198; turnover and p., 135, 169–70; undistributed p., *see* Undistributed; variations in p., 52–53, 91–92, 78–79, 287–88; windfall p., 179
Propensity to consume, xxvi and n. 14, 231
Property: broad category of, 115; and government spending, 96; idea of, 99; and right, 29–30; and redistributive function, 115–16; p. rewarded, 191
Proportionate: contraction, 274–75; expansion, 274–76, 296
Proprietary: p. barriers and mergers, 140; p. division of productive process, 236–37; p. locus of payments, 30, 248; p. network, 247
Psychology: p. of business personality, 35–36; p. of masses, 20–21, 200; p. of motivation, 7; normative p. of self-interest, *see* Concomitance; p. problem of static phase, 98; p. of propensi-

ties, xxvi n. 14, 231; p. of property, 11; and rational expectations, xxvii–xxviii; p. of success, 180; and vague self-interest, 42

Ptolemy, 6

Pure: p. analysis and approximations, 25–26, 83, 85, 133–34, 142–43, 211–12; p. analytic case, 25–26, 85, 133; p. cycle, 82, 105, 133, 242–45, 275–81, 285, 296; p. cultural superstructure, 22; p. desire, xxvii n. 29; p. formulation, xxvii n. 20; p. frequency acceleration, 143–44, 268; general character of p. process, 11–12, 26–29; p. indeterminacy of velocity of money, 138; logic of p. case, 29, 105, 133, 150, 242–45; p. quantity acceleration, 143–44; p. surplus income, xxvii, 50, 53, 179–82, 292–301, 310; p. theory of *DA*, 43; p. theory and payment increments, 171–72; p. theory of social economics, 205

Purges, 45

q: quantity index, q_i, 129, 175, 184, 269

Q: basic quantity index, Q', 129; redistributional quantity, Q^*, 45; surplus quantity index, Q'', 131; ultimate products, Q_i, 239; vectorial quantity measure, Q, 269–73; vectorial basic and surplus quantity measures, Q', Q'', 273; Q, weighted average, 272

Quadragesimo anno, 321

Qualitative distinctions of variables, 13

Quality of life, xxvii n. 17

Quantity: contraction, 269–74; increase, 269–74; pattern, 269–74

Quantity of money: q. of m. acceleration, 146–48 (*see also* Money, increments of, Interest, Velocity); fixed q. of m. and expansion possibility, 84, 101, 259–68; increased q. of m. and acceleration, 147, 256–66; increased q. of m. and trends, 156–57; increased q. of m. and turnover, 134–51, 172–74; q. of m. and rates of payment, 163–74, 256–57; q. of m. and transition payments, 136–51, 166–71

Quesnay, F., xxix

r: aggregate of initial basic payments, r_{ij} (*sic*), 137, 166; aggregate of inital surplus payments, r''_{ij}, 166; average value of initial basic payments, r_i, 137

R: ratio of surplus to basic activity ($= p''Q''/p'Q'$), 302; sum in redistribution function, 120

Rate(s): r. of absorption, *DA'*, *DA''*, 137; r. of payment, 43–48, 115–21, 252–57; r. of production, 239–42; r. of saving, *G*, 283–87; superposed circuits and r., 93–97, 196–202, 308–17

Rational expectations, xxvi

Redistributional: r. balances, 58; division of r. area, 93–94

Redistributive: r. control of acceleration, 121; r. exchanges, 44, 116, 248, 250–52; r. function 44, 93–97, 116, 196–202, 254, 308–17; r. markets, 43–46; r. payments, 43–45, 115–16, 250–52; r. transfers, 134–51, 264–66

Reference system for exchange, 58–59. *See also* Frame of Reference

Regiopolis College, Ontario, 324

Renaissance, 24, 264

Renshaw, Richard, 321

Rent: as added to import costs, 313; as initial payment, 114, 249, 252, 253; as pure surplus, 298

Rentier: r. class, 97, 201; r. middle class, 54; r. nation, 95, 314; recruits to r. class, 316

Repair, Replacement. *See* Maintenance

Reserve: r. funds, 265; money held in r., 58–59, 118, 254
Retailer(s), 44, 169–70, 249
Returns: decreasing r. and capitalist idea, 279; decreasing r. of profit motive, 54, 56, 80–81, 94; decreasing r. of widening, 22–23, 27; generalized law of decreasing and increasing r., 21–23; increasing returns of capitalist idea, 279; increasing r. of deepening, 22–23, 27
Rhythms, in economy (Part One): basic r., 11–13, 16–17, 21, 23–28; surplus r., 16–19, 21–28; universal r., 11–16, 26
Robinson Crusoe: R.C. excluded from exchange economy, 12, 247; R.C. as illustrating production process, 23–24, 44, 151; and key problem of monetary economy, 151; and marginal comparative valuation, 190
Robinson, Joan: and measurement of capital, xxvi; critique of, xxxi n. 28.
Roman, 11
Royalties: as basic demand, 124; as initial payments, 114, 249, 253; as pure surplus, 298
Rules to guide democratically, 3–5, 110–11. *See also* Adaptation, Bureaucracy, Education, Planning
Russians, 4, 24, 90

s: aggregate transition basic payments, s_{ij} (*sic*),137, 166; aggregate transition surplus payments, s''_{ij}, 166; average transition basic payments, s_{ij}, 137
S: aggregate basic demand, *S'*, 120; aggregate surplus demand, *S''*, 120; the (pure) surplus ratio, 49
Salary: as basic demand, 124; as initial payment, 114, 116, 249, 252, 298; as pure surplus, 298, 301
Sales: anticipation of, 142, 274; s. changing turnover period, 159, 164–65, 261–63; s. as economic data, 32, 211–12, 273–74; export, import s., 94–95, 197–99, 311–17; future s., 304; s. included in production, 114, 136, 247, 249; lagging s., 138–40, 157, 261–65; s. management, 232, 247; mergers and transitional s., 140; redistributive s., 115–16, 248; secondhand s., 84, 251–52
Samuelson, Paul, and textbooks, xxxi
Saving(s): adjustment of rate of, 290–92; forced s., 78, 179, 287–88, 302; and foreign trade, 31–32; s. incentive, 290–91; s. not equal to investments, 84, 87, 91, 125, 263; and redistributive function, 209; and surplus income, 89–91
Scarcity, 31, 113, 282
Schumpeter, Joseph: and dynamic economics, xxv; and Hawtrey, 102 n. 7; and Lonergan, xxv n. 10, 212–13, 306; and real analysis, xvii n. 4, xxviii–xxx; and theory of interest, xxx n. 26. Works referred to: *Business Cycles*, 306; *History of Economic Analysis*, xxv, 102; *Theory of Economic Development*, xxv
Science: generalization in s., 7–10, 26; nature of, 4–10
Secondary circuit (Part One), 16–19, 21–27, 44–56, 58–59. *See also* Surplus
Secondhand trade as redistributive, 44, 59, 84, 86, 116, 196, 248, 250, 252
Securities: foreign s., 197–98, 312–13; long-term s., 312
Self-interest: enlightened, xvi; insufficiently enlightened, 194, 231; vague but intelligent, 4, 42
Selling- and cost-price indices, 77, 302
Services. *See* Goods
Sheltered firms, 91–93, 299
Ship(s): indeterminacy and s., 234; turnover and s., 135–37, 164–65,

260–61; s. under construction, *see* Shipbuilding; use of s., 132, 135–37, 233
Shipbuilding: and levels of production, 15–16; and problem of turnover, 135–37, 164–65, 233–35, 260–61; turnover analysis of s. generalized, 165–74
Shoe industry as layered, 132, 247–48
Short-term: s.-t. acceleration, 241, 276–77, 280–81, 305; contraction and expansion of s.-t. loans, 127; s.-t. credit, *see* Short-term credit; s.-t. decreasing returns of capitalism and business, xvi; s.-t. enterprises and interest rate, 292; s.-t. financing, 58, 309; s.-t. loans and current practice, 104–105, 160
Short-term credit: and briskness of business, 127; and change of quantity of money, 160; and long-term problem, 100, 104–105; s.-t.c. renewal problem in slump, 103; strategic s.-t.c., 57–58, 116, 309
Sinking funds: and government spending, 201; as initial payments, 249, 253; and pure surplus, 301
Slump(s): and basic expansion, 276–77, 289; and contracting price-spread, 79; and prices, 282; and propensity to consume, 216; and pure surplus income, 297–98, 300–301, 306–307; and theorem of costs, 51; and trade cycle, 82, 91, 276; and trader multiplier, 69; and war effort, 183
Smith, Adam: *Wealth of Nations*, xxx
Smoothing out of cycle, absurd, 182, 281
Social dividend, 286
Social security, 195, 199, 201, 316
So much every so often: and concomitance of money and product, 61; and economic activity as velocity, 15, 205–206, 238; s. under higher law of transformation, 23; s. as measured in exchange units, 43; and money velocity, 101; s. in surplus as accelerator, 85
Soviets, 4, 24, 42
Speculation: on commodity market, 61; as reach for perspective, 20; in stock market, 86–87, 93
Speculative: activities of cycles, 301–306; anticipation, 274; producers, 160
Spiralling of prices. *See* Prices
Squeeze, 216, 298–300
Stages of productive process, 238–42, 246, 248–50, 278
Stalin, Joseph, 89
Standard of living: and ability, 36; and aggregate primary costs, 50; and balance of trade, 312–16; and culture, 23–27; future s. of l., 20; and government bonds, 200–201; higher s. of l., 67, 88, 195, 293; and higher levels, 249; s. of l. of moneylenders, 98; nonimprovement of, 132; s. of l. as ordinary final product, 20, 23, 205–206, 232–35, 238–40, 253 (*see also* Leisure); ownership s. of l., 77, 88, 98, 293; and price spread, 79–81; and profit-grabbing, 92–93; rentier's s. of l., 97, 201, 315; and static phase, 98–99; s. of l. unimproved in surplus expansion, 132–33, 242; and widening/deepening, 17–19
Static phase: and effective zero, 23, 52, 69; idea of s.p., 23–27; new s.p., 133, 183; possibility of, 25, 97–100; s.p. term of basic expansion, 81–82
Statistics, xxvi, 7, 112, 158–59
Stock market: s.m. crash, 73, 103, 105, 306–307; s.m. as gambling, 61, 72, 88, 292; s.-m. quotations, 88; s.m. as redistributive, 44
Stocks, 58–59, 93, 241
Strikes, 100

Successful man: entrepreneur's view of, 298; and pure surplus income, 180, 293–94, 310
Superchemistry, 20
Superposed circuits, xx, xxii, 93–97, 196–202, 265–66, 308–18
Superstructure of culture, 12
Supply and demand: distinct levels of, 58–59; and markets, 32–35; and prices, 187–89; s. and d. as subject of economics, 8; variations of, 70–73
Surges in economy, xxvi, 11–27, 242–45, 276, 294
Surplus: s. advantage, 83–87, 122, 274–75; causes of, 89–91; s. circuit, 218, 252–58; s. contraction, 274–75; s. credit, *see* Investment; s. demand, *see* Demand; s. demand function, 58–59, 115, 254; s. equations, 43–45, 47, 119–20, 254–57; s. expansion, 83–87, 276–78, 303; s. expenditure, *see* Expenditure; s. final payments, 43–45, 115–17, 249–50; and foreign trade, 198, 200–201, 312–15; s. income, *see* Income; s. initial payments, 249–50; s. outlay, *see* Outlay; pure s. income, xxvii, 50, 53, 179–82, 292–301, 310; s. receipts, 115–17, 252–53; s. rhythms; 16–19, 28, 44; s. supply function, 58–59, 115, 254; theorem of s., 49–50; s. transitional payments, 114–17, 136–51, 166–74, 248–50
Synchronized: s. international cycles, 313; s. turnovers, 158–59
System of reference: s. of r. applied, 93–94, 211–12; s. of r. for exchange, 58. *See also* Frame of reference
Systematic: s. costs, 179–82; s. deflation, 101; s. guidance missing, 109; s. profits, 179–82, 231
Systematics: s. as functional specialty, xxvii; genetic s., xxix–xxx
t: transitional basic payments, t_{ij} (*sic*), 267
T: trader multipliers, T', T'', 63; turnover differences, T', T'', 158
Table(s): t. of G''/G', 55, 208; t. of phases, 152–53, 274–75; t. of trends, 152–53, 156
Taxes: and crossover, 46; and deficit spending, 95–97, 201–202, 317–18; and Kalecki, xxvi; t. incompletely treated, xxii; and overhead product, 46, 50; and primary costs, 50; and profits, 88; t. sectorized, xxvi, 95–97, 201–202, 317–18
Tennyson, Lord, 31
Terrorism, 35
Theological Studies, 321–22
Theorem(s): abstract t. of modern economics, 3; t. of 'basic' equation, 43; t. of continuity, 47, 56, 66, 73–75, 154; t. of costs, 50–51; t. of money velocity, 164; t. of the (pure) surplus, 49–50; t. of trends, 157–62
Theory. *See* Economics, History, Pure, Science
Thomas More Institute, 319, 324
Thrift (and enterprise), 4, 24, 88, 90, 95, 110, 125, 312
Titanothore, 20–21
Tories, 24
Totalitarian economics, 3–5, 7, 19, 105, 110
Toynbee, Arnold, 323
Trade, balance of. *See* Favorable, Unfavorable
Trade cycle: t.c. cuts off basic, 82, 91; conditions of excluding t.c., 203; t.c. grounded in inadaptation, 243; and negative acceleration, 242, 245, 275; and Hawtrey, 102; and Juglar, Kitchin, 304–306; and misinterpretation of pure surplus, 297–301

Trade unions: and fluctuating employment, 82–83; higher synthesis and t.u. , 36; and increase of wages, 24. *See also* Organized labor
Trader(s): t. balances, 58–60; and capitalist phase, 84–87; t. equations, 64–66; t. multipliers, 68–70, 74–75; t. operations, 63, 67–68; primary and secondary t., 50, and (pure) surplus income, 49–50; and static phase, 98–100
Trains and point-to-point flexibility, 232
Transformation of economy, 12–21, 36, 242–43
Transfer(s): net t., 143–51; rates of, 152, 252–57; and trends, 152, 155
Transitional: function of t. payments, 44, 168–69; t. markets, 43–45, 63, 78; t. payments, 43–44, 115, 117, 136–51, 166–74, 248–49, 267–68
Trends: circulation t., 152–62; classes of t., 152–53, 155–56; normative t., 121–28, 274–76; process t., 155–56
Turgot, Anne Robert Jacques, xxix
Turnover(s): t. difference, 159–61; effect of interest on t., 291–92; and efficiency, 262–63; fractional t., 216; t. frequency, 135–51, 157–62, 260–68; t. magnitude (size), 135–51, 157–62, 260–68; measure of, 136; t. period, 135–51, 260–61; variations in t., 87, 91, 140; wholesale and retail t., 170
Twentieth century: challenged by nineteenth, 37; and Kalecki's economics, 213 n. 9; and real analysis, xvi–xvii, xxviii–xxix

u: acceleration multiplier, 77 (*see also a*); u_i, multiplier for increments of circulating capital, 170
Un(der)employed, 18, 89, 92, 98, 285
Underproduction, 89
Underwriter: and functional distinctions, 116; u. idle in static phase, 98; and redistributive balances, 93
Undistributed profit: as initial payment, 114, 117, 249, 253; as pure surplus, 298
Unfavorable balance of trade: and reversed cushioning, 198–99; as superposed, 95, 196, 198–99, 308, 312–17
Unfinished product. *See* Transitional payment
Union of Soviet Socialist Republics, 44
United States, 13
Universal acceptability of money, 38
Unsheltered/unsound business, 91–93
Use, as part of process, 14–16, 117, 233–35, 240
Usury, 264

v: transitional payment multiplier, v_i, 138, 169; *v*, a velocity of money, 135
V: average velocity of money, 101
Value: absolute v., 30–31; actual, normative, probable v., 32; v. added to pure type, 8; economic v., 30–32; exchange v., 30–35; production a process of, 114; relative v., 31; v. theory, 113
Variations: v. in basic income, 301–306; v. in economic phases, 71–72; v. in prices (and quantities), 129–31; v. in expenditure and income, 70–73; v. in production, *see* Accelerations, Cycles, Phases; v. in supply and demand, 71; v. in surplus income, 292–301; v. in velocity of money, 103–105
Vast: v. enterprises, 56; v. mechanism of credit, 145; v. task of transformation, 37, 112 (*see also* Adaptation, Education)
Vectorial measures for *P*, *Q*, 269–73
Velocity, of money: notion of v., 163–64;

possibility of changed v., 62, 259–68; and postulate of continuity, 126–28; and rates of payment, 256; and transition payments, 136–51, 166–71; and turnover problems, 134–51, 163–65, 172–74, 260–63
Viewpoint of this work, 3–10, 109–11, 231. *See also* Concomitance

Wage(s): and costs, 301–303; and crossover, 46, 124, 255; demand for higher w., 78; depressed w., 55; and imports, 313; w. as initial payments, 114, 116, 117, 249, 252, 253; rising w., 67, 81, 146; and savings, 295–96; subsistence w., 80, 85; surplus w., 46; and trade unions, 24, 36, 146; w. variations and price-spread, 78–81, 301–304
Walras, Léon: and markets, 51; and neutral money, xxviii. *See also* Equilibrium analysis
War: after the w., 4; and date of FNPE, 321; economics of, 12, 25; the present w., 3, 131; and the price system, 100; slump to w. effort, 183
Watt, Lewis, 321
Weaker firms, 300
Wealth: and gold, 40–41; increase of, 23; w. in process as object of economics, 8, 23, 233; static w. beyond process, 233
Weighted: w. averages for *P*, *Q*, 272; w. average production period, 126; price-w. quantities, 179; w. quantities, 156
Whigs, 24
Wholesaler(s), 44, 178, 249
Widening: and capitalist phase, 52; and crossover, 46; and decreasing returns, 22–23, 26–27; and economic transformation, 17–19; and net surplus income, 89
Will: good w. and redistributive function, 84; weak w. of finance, 88
Windfall losses, 264–65
Windfall profits: and entrepreneurs' preferences, 265; w. p. not systematic, 179, 231
World Bank, xvii n. 2

X: debt service per interval, *X′*, *X″*, 200

Y: rates of sinking-fund accumulation, *Y′*, *Y″*, 200

Z: Superposed flow, *Z′*, *Z″*, 196. *See also* *DZ*
Zero: z. acceleration, 217–18, 305; effective z., 18–19, 22, 24, 69, 87, 98; z.-income group, 285–86; z. profits, 231; z. surplus, 53